Making sense of Buddhist art & architecture

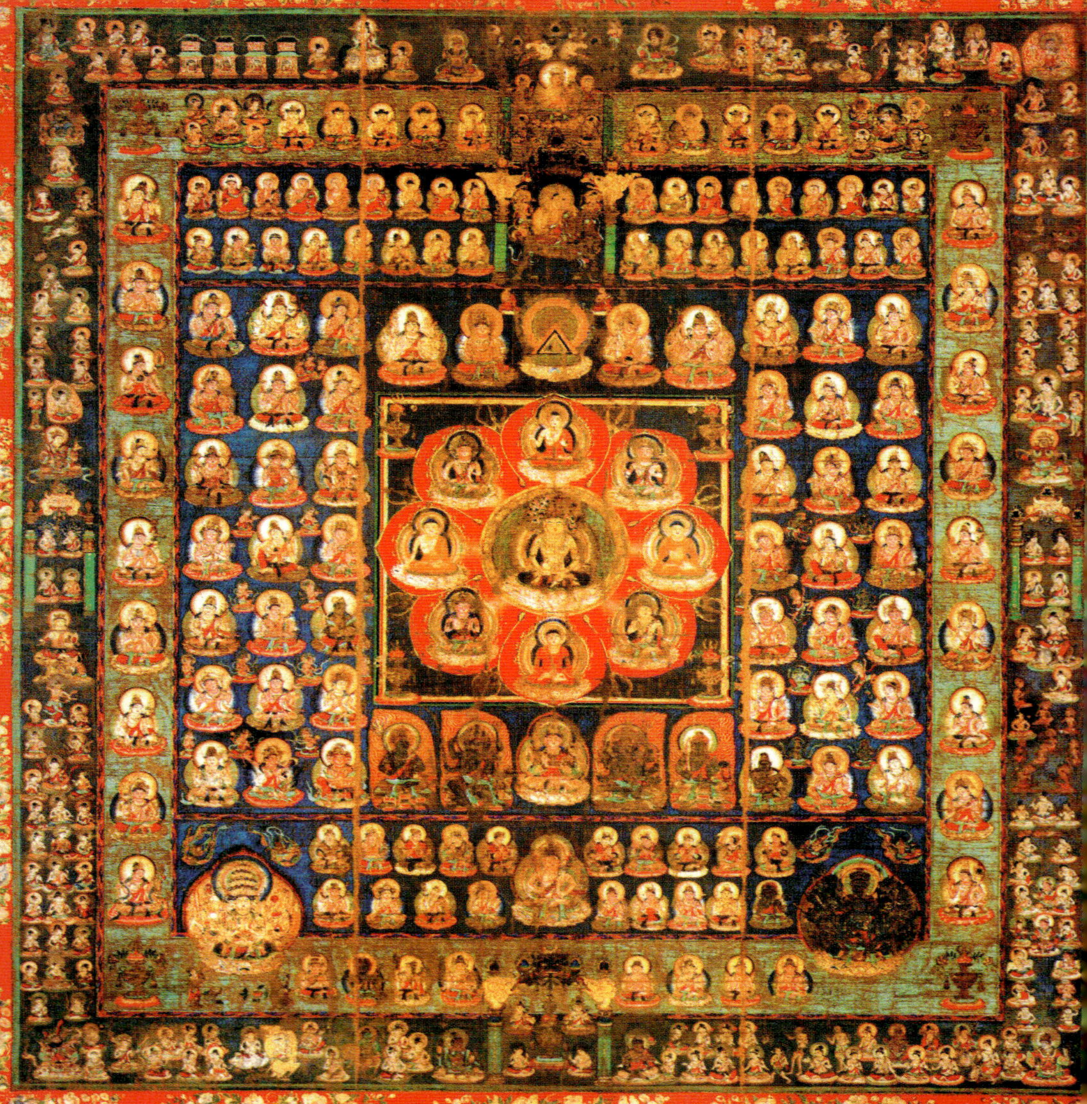

Making sense of Buddhist art & architecture

Patricia Eichenbaum Karetzky

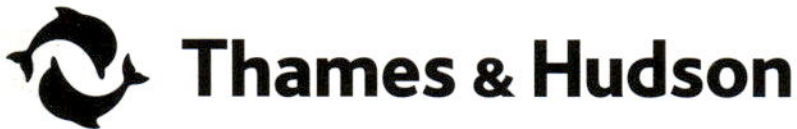

Thames & Hudson

First published in the United Kingdom in 2015 by

Thames & Hudson Ltd,
181A High Holborn,
London WC1V 7QX

© 2015 Quintessence Editions Ltd.

This book was designed and produced by
Quintessence Editions Ltd.
The Old Brewery,
6 Blundell Street,
London, N7 9BH

Project Editor	Juliet Lough
Editor	Francis Ritter
Designer	Josse Pickard
Production Manager	Anna Pauletti
Editorial Director	Jane Laing
Publisher	Mark Fletcher

British Library Cataloguing-in-Publication Data
A catalogue record for this book is available from
the British Library

ISBN 978-0-500-29169-6

Printed in China

To find out about all our publications, please visit
www.thamesandhudson.com.

There you can subscribe to our e-newsletter, browse or download
our current catalogue, and buy any titles that are in print.

Contents

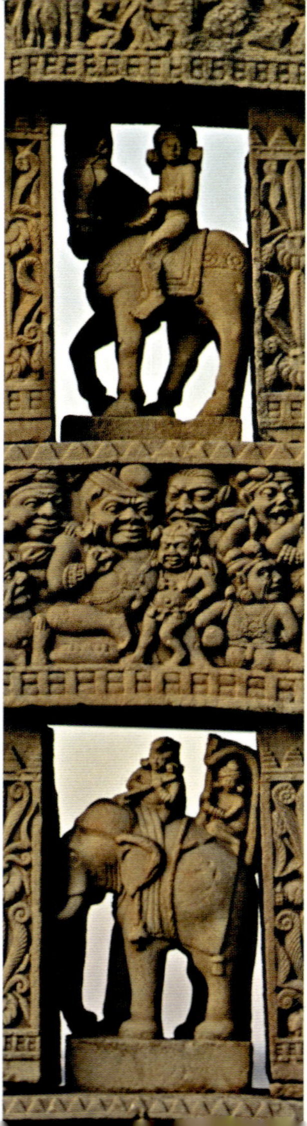

Introduction

To understand Buddhism, it is important to know that it is not a monolith of beliefs, and that in the 2,500 years since the birth of the Buddha it has undergone continuous changes. Yet certain traditions have remained constant. When Buddhism travelled from India, it brought its own architecture, including the stupa (a monumental reliquary for the remains of the body of the Buddha), monastic buildings, image halls and libraries. There were also Buddhist sculptural, painting and literary traditions, and new technologies for the production of art and architecture.

Buddhism assumes a belief in karma, or infinite rebirths determined by moral conduct. Buddha, observing that lives are filled with the pains of old age, sickness and death, saw that the prospect of perpetual rebirths promised infinite pain. It became his goal to end karma and escape the wheel of causation. He devised Four Truths, as follows: all life is suffering; the cause of suffering is attachment; to end suffering one must destroy attachments, even to life itself; and one must follow a moral and meditative code known as the Eight-fold Path. This Path of the Dharma, or doctrine, is the second of the Jewels of Buddhism: first is the Buddha; third is his group of disciples.

In Buddhism's earliest stage, Theravada, earthen mounds or stupas were located in the places made sacred by the presence of the Buddha or his remains, and ritually circumambulated. In time Buddhists used more permanent materials, bricks at first and later stone, and excavated cave temples and stupas from the living rock of mountains. Located high above the everyday world, these caves were the spiritual destination of devotees, who ascended the mountain to engage with the resident monks and worship.

Around the 1st century CE, Buddhism changed dramatically. Perhaps due to contact with other religious traditions, there developed a new belief in a number of saviour gods. Rather than being solely responsible for his or her spiritual progress, an individual could appeal to these divine beings for help. Primary among them were the bodhisattvas, who postponed their own enlightenment for the sake of others. The new movement, known as Mahayana, brought its own pantheon, scriptures and ritual practices. There arose a belief in the Buddha of the Future, whose cyclical appearances are separated by aeons; before his arrival, the world falls into decay, degeneration and immoral behaviour, but his birth heralds a golden age. Also important is the Buddha of Infinite Life, or Light, to whom the faithful could appeal for rebirth in paradise, a place of everlasting life. Through such ritual practices as visualization of the paradise and the repetition of the Buddha's name, the devotee could gain entry. In time, Manjusri, Bodhisattva of Wisdom, and Avalokiteshvara, Bodhisattva of Compassion, individually became independent foci of worship.

The third development of Buddhism, esoteric or Vajrayana, began around the 6th century with the introduction of new texts. These proposed that enlightenment was possible in this life but was extremely difficult to attain. The help of a teacher was required, with special kinds of art, sacred words, hand gestures and rituals along with a new pantheon of gods.

The three schools of Buddhism were widely adopted by the cultures of South-east and East Asia. During the process of selection, those peoples decided which form was the most appealing to follow, while often clinging to aspects of their old religions. The Buddhist proselytizers did not oppose this, simply maintaining that the alien deities were of no value in attaining enlightenment, being themselves subject to karma. And, just as it posed no threat to the new cultural environments, Buddhism was able to adapt to local practices. Thus, despite certain regional changes in its art and architecture, the basic vocabulary of Buddhist forms remained relatively consistent and recognizable.

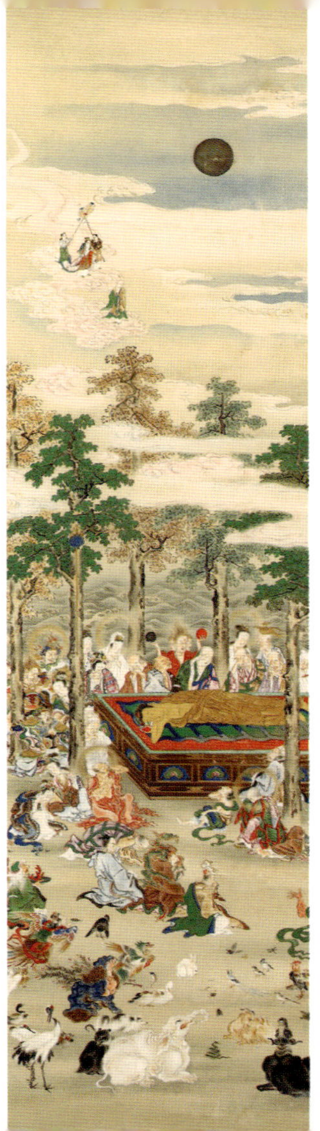

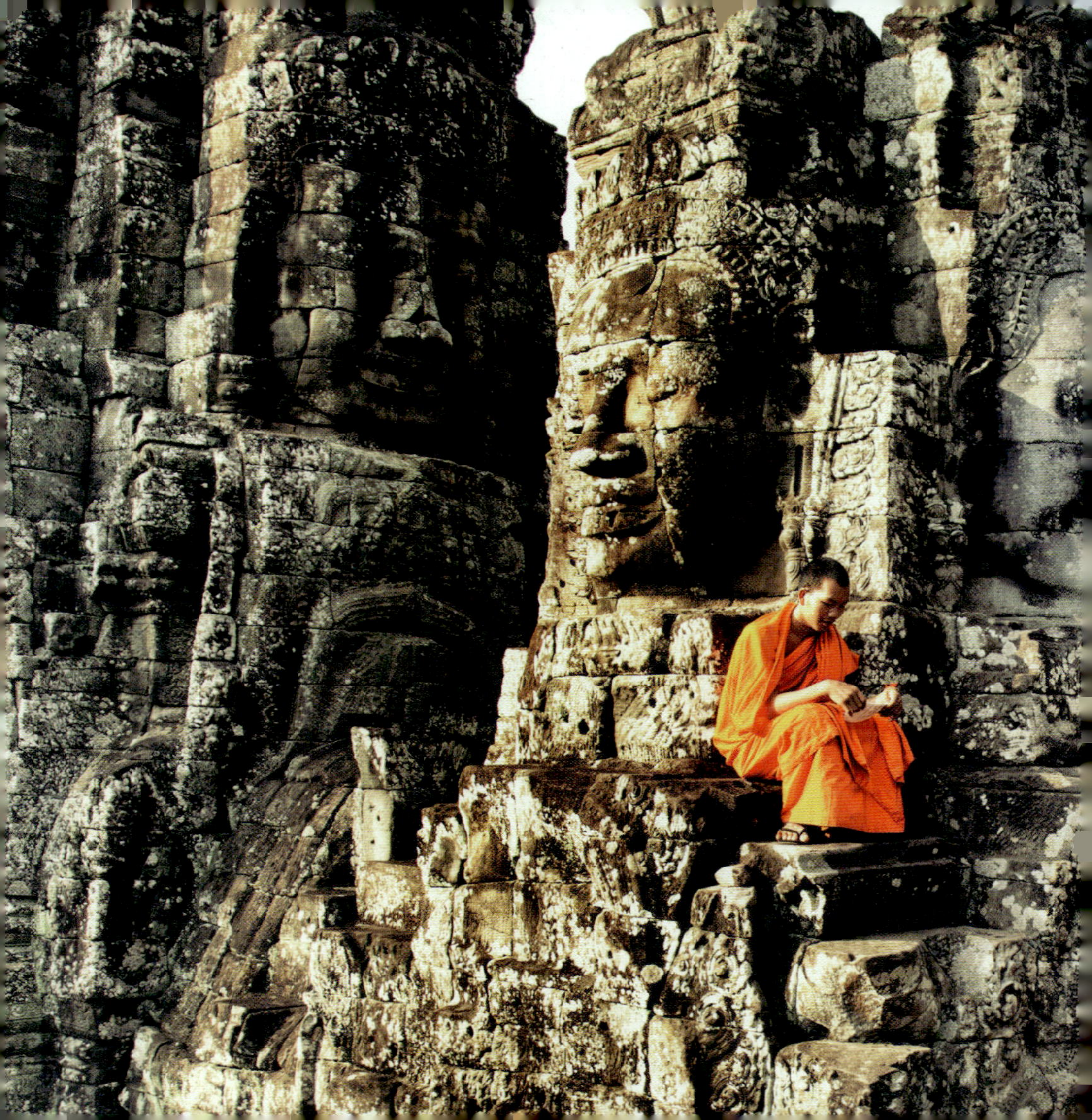

Sacred Precincts
I

Lumbini Garden

c. 6th century BCE **Rupandehi District, Nepal**

PREVIOUS NAME Rummindei   **TOTAL AREA** 768 hectares/1898 ac.
LOCATION 3.2 km/2 miles north of Bhagavanpura

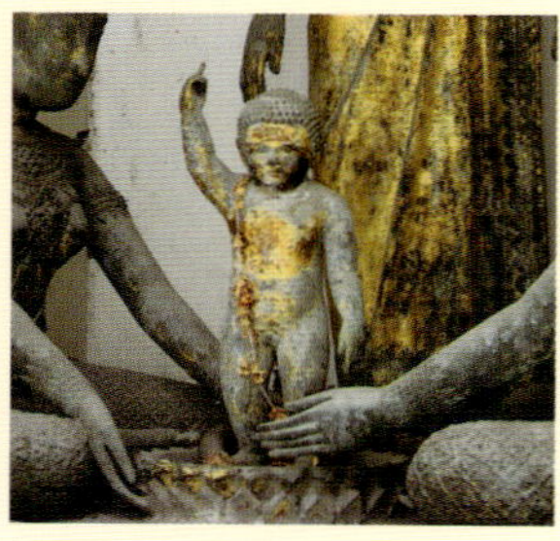

The Buddha's First Bath

Small bronze sculptures of a child standing in a basin with his hand raised are found in Thailand, Korea and Japan, and painted portrayals can be found throughout the Buddhist world. In this Thai example, at Wat Arun, Bangkok (*c.* 1656), royal ladies wash the child, but often that task falls to the officiating priest.

'Among all divine beings, only I am lord, most holy and victorious. The three realms are all sorrowful. I have come here through immeasurable births and deaths for the benefit of men and gods.'

BUDDHA, ACCORDING TO
XIUXING BENQI JING

Lumbini Garden is where Siddartha Gautama was born, but the date of the birth is highly contested; many hold that it was around the 6th century BCE. Visiting this holy site in the 3rd century BCE, the famed imperial patron Emperor Ashoka commemorated the area with the construction of four stupa mounds (memorial shrines) and a stone pillar with a figure of a horse, on top of which is inscribed, 'King Piyadasi [Ashoka], beloved of devas, in the 20th year of the coronation, himself made a royal visit, Buddha Shakyamuni having been born here; a stone railing was built and a stone pillar erected to the Bhagavan having been born here, Lumbini village was taxed, reduced and entitled to the eighth part (only).' Today the archaeological area is under the protection of UNESCO. It includes a 3rd-century BCE brick temple, dedicated to the Buddha's mother, Maya, that marks the place of the birth, and the *Puskarini* or Holy Pond in which she took a bath before giving birth, and where the newborn had his First Bath. There are also a number of ancient *viharas* (monasteries), stupas and a Bodhi, or sacred fig tree. After the birth the baby was bathed, though the texts disagree about who helped, whether *nagas* (snakes), elephants or goddesses with ewers. He then took seven steps marking out his dominion of the four directions, plus nadir, earth and zenith, and declared his lordship (see left). In this way he demonstrated that he was not an ordinary child but, like Jesus, born with full knowledge. At Lumbini and many other Buddhist sites, annual ceremonies are held to celebrate the birth of the Buddha and ritually reenact the First Bath.

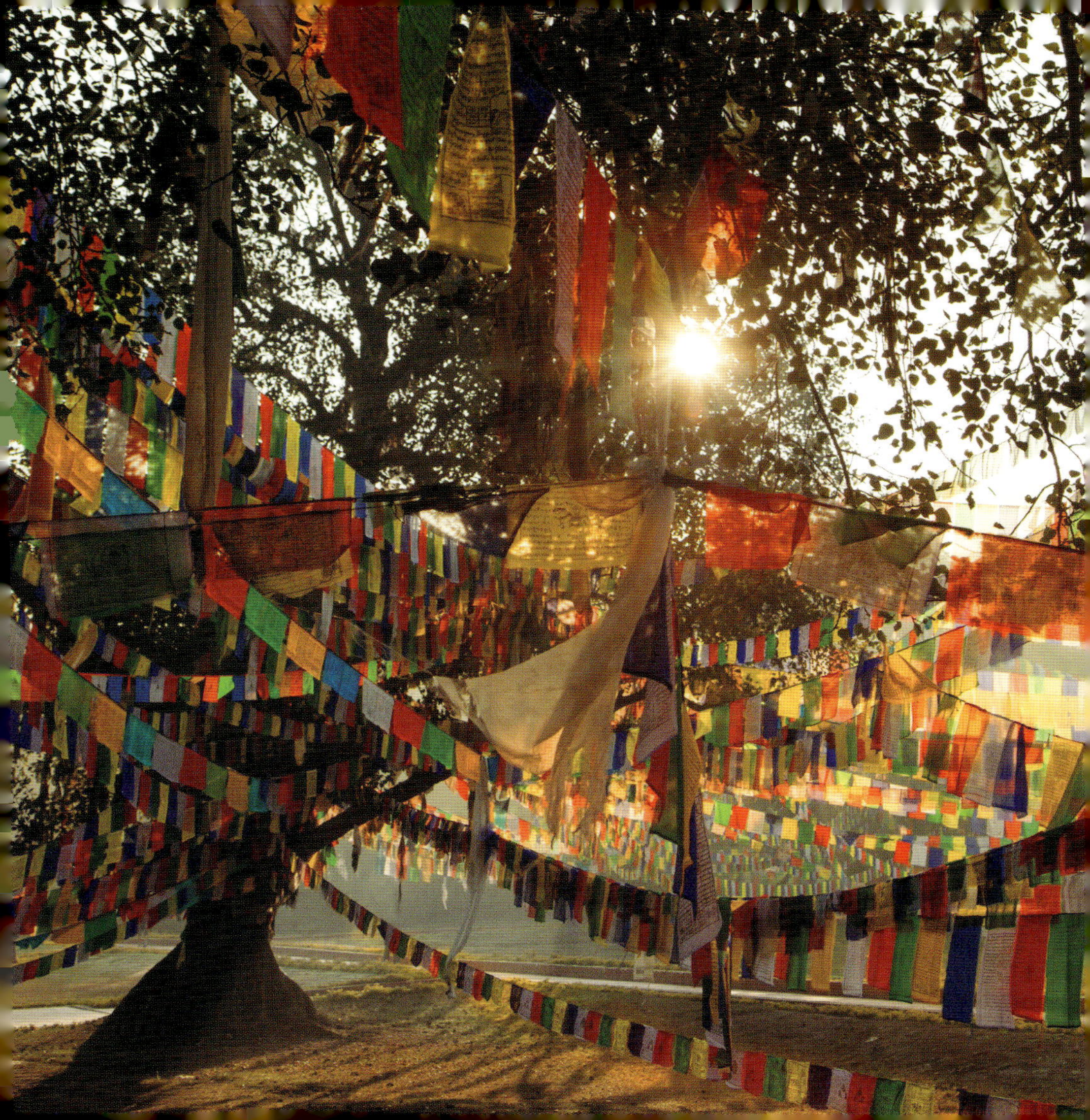

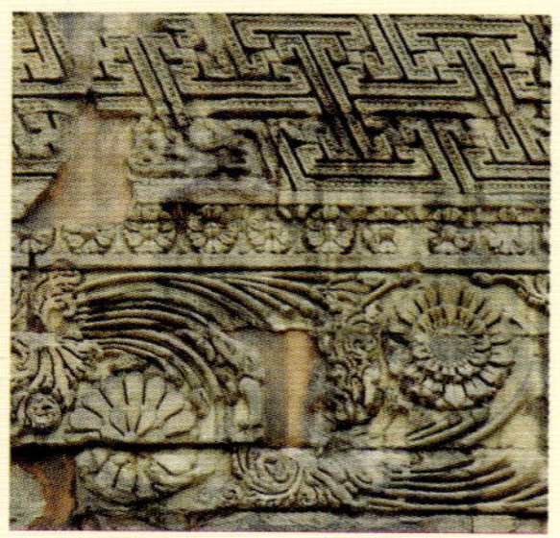

Stupa Decoration

The stone facing of the lower trunk of Dhamekh Stupa is decorated with two bands of delicate floral carvings of Gupta period. Between the vegetal bands is a broad band of swastikas (*fylfot*), carved as different geometrical patterns, which to Buddhists signified God and eternity. The swastikas are bordered by fine lotus wreaths.

'The Middle Way of the Tathagata is enlightened, it brings clear vision, it makes for wisdom, and leads to peace, insight, enlightenment and Nirvana.'

DE BARY, *THE BUDDHIST TRADITION* (1972)

Sarnath Stupa

c. 6th century BCE **Varanasi, Uttar Pradesh, India**

COMMISSIONED BY Emperor Ashoka **DATE** 3rd century BCE
MATERIALS Stone, brick **DIAMETER** 28.3 x 30 m / 93 x 98 ft

After Enlightenment, the Buddha remained in meditation until he thought that he might share his hard-won knowledge. He returned to the deer park, or Mrigadava, a sanctuary for deer and sages, to speak to the five men with whom he had practised austerities. This event, known as Turning the Wheel of the Law or *Dharmachakra*, was the beginning of the Buddha's teachings. The men became the first members of the monastic community, the Sangha, and one of the Three Jewels, or *Triratna* (the Buddha and his Dharma, or teachings, were the other two). In the early 19th century a British archaeologist, Colonel Alexander Cunningham, discovered an inscribed stone tablet on which was written the word *Dhamekha*, or 'the place Buddha where delivered his first sermon', and the Dhamekh Stupa at Sarnath is built where the First Sermon took place. The base of the Dhamek Stupa may date to the 3rd century BCE and the patronage of Emperor Ashoka, but the brick and stone stupa above it was built in the 7th century CE. The stupa, seated on a series of tall cylindrical drums, once had a crowning dome. Carved into the base are eight niches that once held Buddhist icons, and the stupa's rich, deeply sculpted decorations of lush vegetal forms and geometrical designs were copied throughout the Buddhist world. Sarnath is one of Buddhism's four primary pilgrimage sites and contains other monuments that celebrate the First Sermon: these include the Dharmarajika Stupa; a 5.24-metre (17-ft) column with four lions on its capital; the monastery where the Buddha spent the rainy season; a number of later monasteries; an apsidal temple; and many smaller votive stupas.

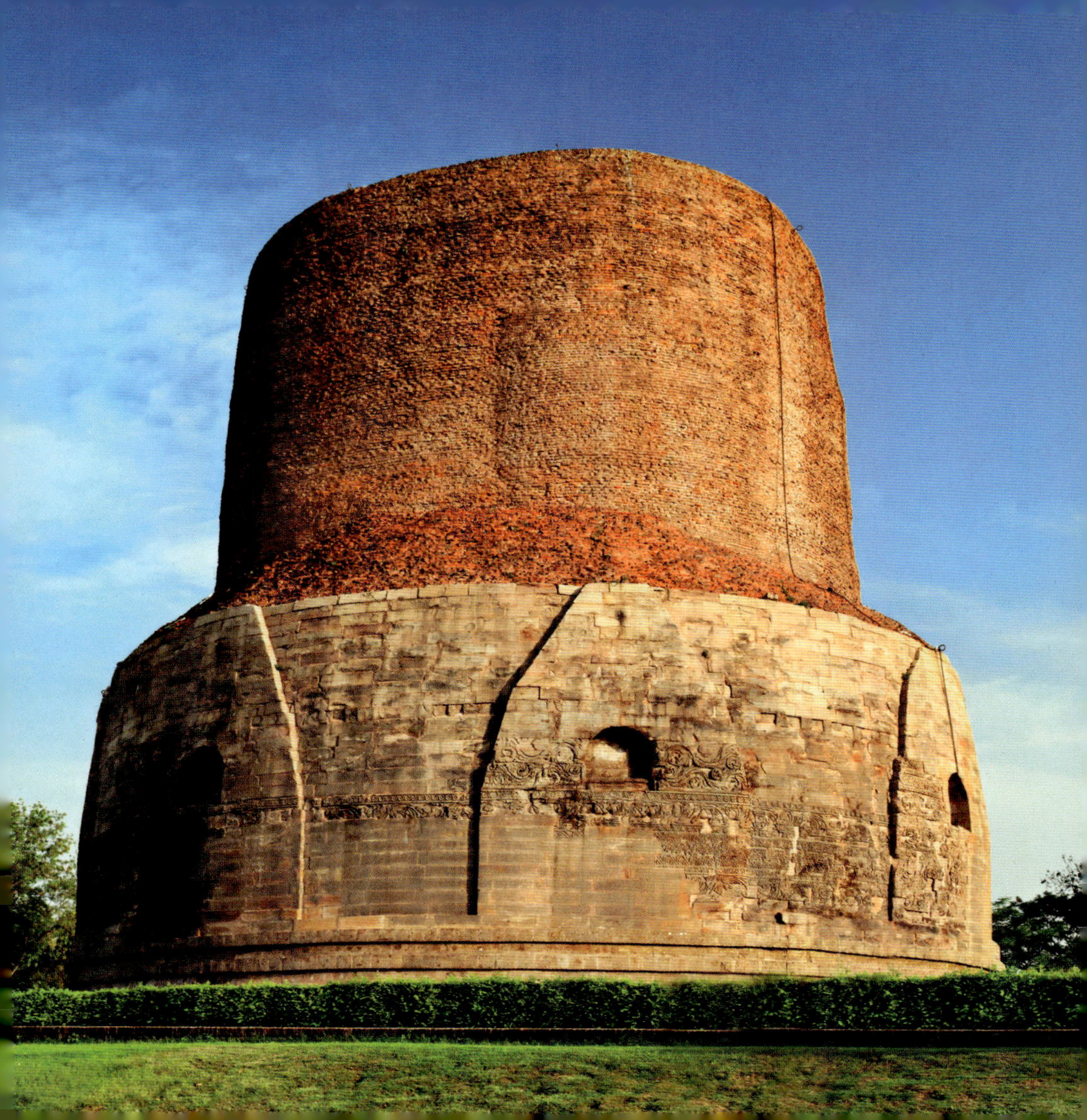

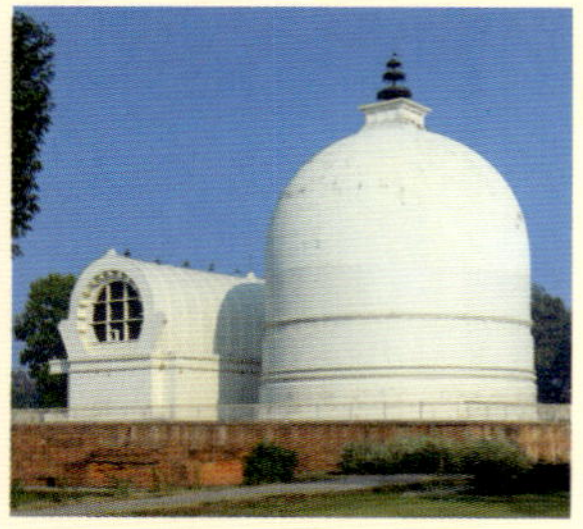

Modern Shrine

The temple that now stands over the stupa at Kushinagar was built by the Indian Government in 1956 as part of the commemoration of the 2,500th year of the Mahaparinirvana, or death of the Buddha. The shrine is located among the ruins of various monasteries that have occupied the site over the centuries.

'On his deathbed, the Buddha turned to his Disciples, and said to them: "Everything comes to an end, though it may last for an aeon ... The time for my entry into Nirvana has now arrived. These are my last words!"'

ASVAGHOSA, *BUDDHACARITA*

Kushinagar Stupa

c. 4th century BCE   **Kushinagar, Uttar Pradesh, India**

COMMISSIONED BY Malla tribe   **HEIGHT** 12 m/40 ft
RECLINING BUDDHA PARINIRVANA 7.3 x 1.7 m/24 x 5½ ft

In his eightieth year, the Buddha grew ill from a gastrointestinal illness. He called for his personal attendant, the monk Ananda, to take him to Kushinagar and place him on a bed between the twin trees of the Sala grove, that he might say farewell to his disciples. They gathered around him and he bid them to do their best. After he passed away, his lay followers cremated the body and gathered the post-crematory remains. A fight to secure these broke out among them, until a wise brahmin distributed the relics equally and each of the eight tribes returned home. The tribes each encased their share in a special container, buried it deep in the ground and erected a mound of earth, a stupa, to mark the presence of a great man, as was traditional in ancient India. The Malla tribe buried their eighth of the ashes at Kushinagar, and at the site today are the ruins of a brick stupa and a shrine; these have undergone many stages of reconstruction. In 1897, the archaeologist A. C. Carlleyle excavated the stupa and discovered a copper vessel; it bore a Brahmi inscription proving that the Buddha's ashes were buried there. Today, a large hall houses an oversized sculpture of the Buddha reclining – the standard way of depicting his *parinirvana*, or extinction. Before the creation of this icon, the architectural monument of the stupa was the representation of the passing away of his physical form. Smaller votive stupas surround the large one. Kushinagar is one of Buddhism's four most important pilgrimage sites, and at the height of its prosperity four monasteries and stupas awaited the monks and laity who made the pilgrimage there to worship and study.

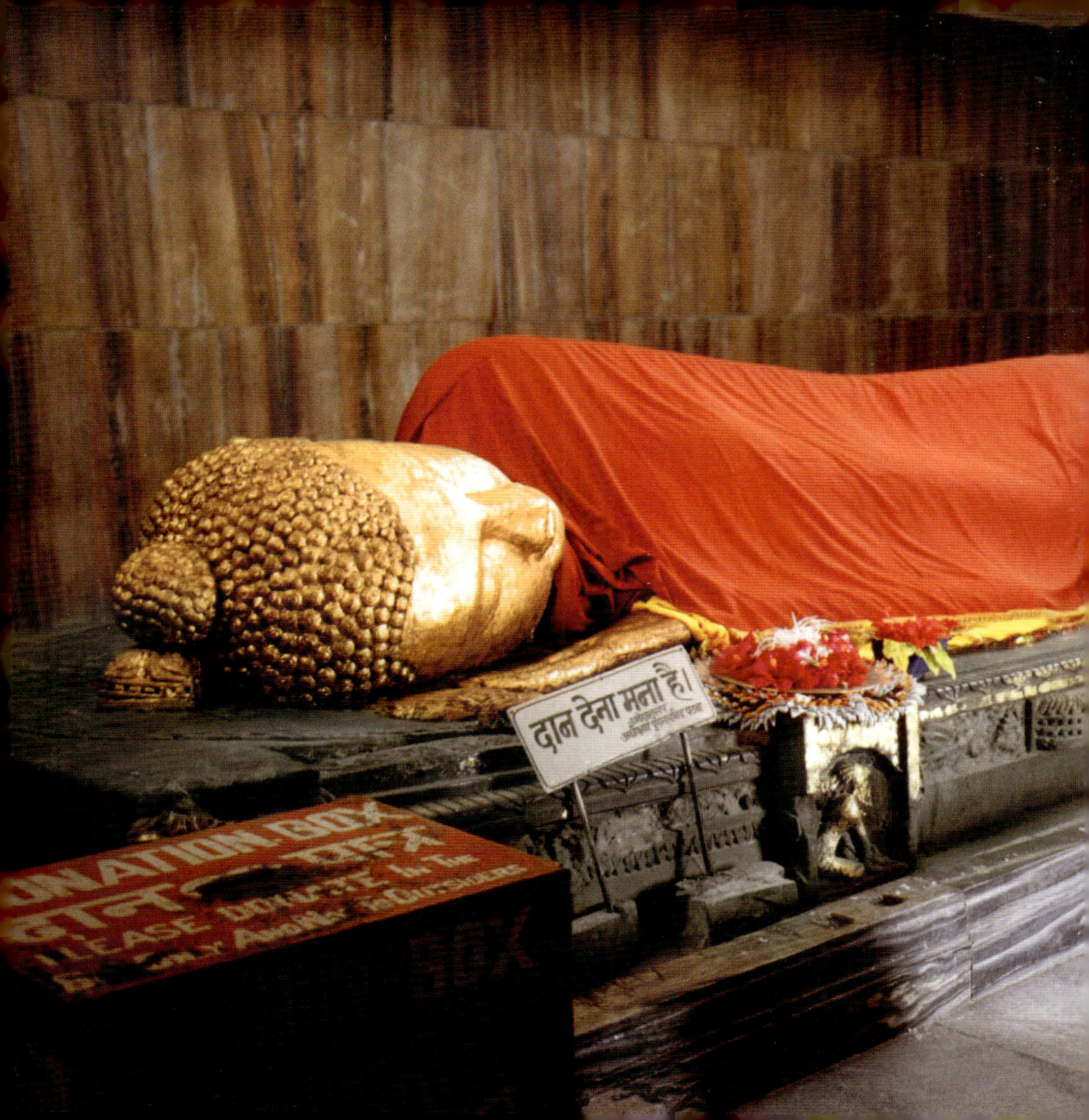
दान देना मना है।
DONATION BOX
PLEASE DONATE IN The
ONLY AT DONATION BOXES

Great Stupa at Sanchi

c. 3rd century BCE **Sanchi, Madhya Pradesh, India**

COMMISSIONED BY Emperor Ashoka   **MATERIALS** Earth, brick, limestone
DIMENSIONS 36 x 16 m / 118 x 52½ ft

The Great Stupa at Sanchi, founded by Emperor Ashoka in the 3rd century BCE but rebuilt over the centuries, is ascribed to the 1st century CE. Like all Buddhist stupas, it is a commemorative monument built over deeply buried relics. A wooden mast, acting like a cosmic axis, emerges from the top of the stupa's dome, and the superstructure includes a balustrade and umbrella that signify the heavens. The stupa encases the Buddha's sacred remains and is thus a symbol of his physical body; its representation in narrative art is intended as an indication of his passing. Around the stupa is a protective railing, based on wooden prototypes of post and lintel construction; this is pierced by four ornamental gateways oriented to the four directions. The railing marks out the ritual pathway for *pradaksina*, or clockwise circumambulation, of the stupa. Tradition holds that Ashoka dug up seven of the original eight stupas built to house the Buddha's remains, redistributing their relics among the 84,000 stupas that he had newly built. Although the parts of the Great Stupa are standard, their decoration reflects regional preferences and local artistic traditions. The earthen body encased by brick (a sacred building material in India) is undecorated, but the gateways have all manner of deeply incised decorative themes and bas-reliefs. There are illustrations of scenes from the life of the Buddha in which his presence is suggested by the use of symbols, *jataka* stories that tell of events in the Buddha's previous lives and scenes of worship of symbols that represent the Buddha. In Indian tradition, some of the gateway pillars feature courtly guardians armed with spears, standing to protect the sacred precinct.

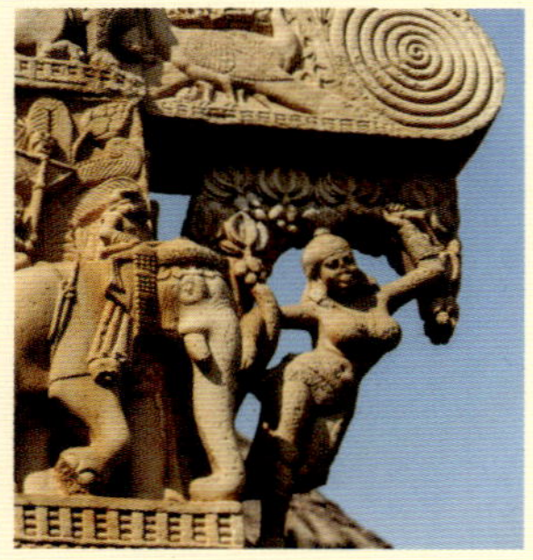

Mythical Beings

Emblems of fecundity and auspiciousness adorn the four gateways at Sanchi. They include native deities of the earth, such as yakshas, shown as a pot-bellied dwarves supporting the Western Gate's lintel, and a yakshi or tree spirit, a beautiful, nude, bejewelled woman who poses beneath a tree, the ensemble acting as a decorative bracket on the Eastern Gate. In Buddhist tradition, a woman desiring pregnancy would kick the tree to stimulate the flow of its sap.

'All religions should reside everywhere, for all of them desire self-control and purity of heart.'

EDICT OF ASHOKA, C. 257 BCE

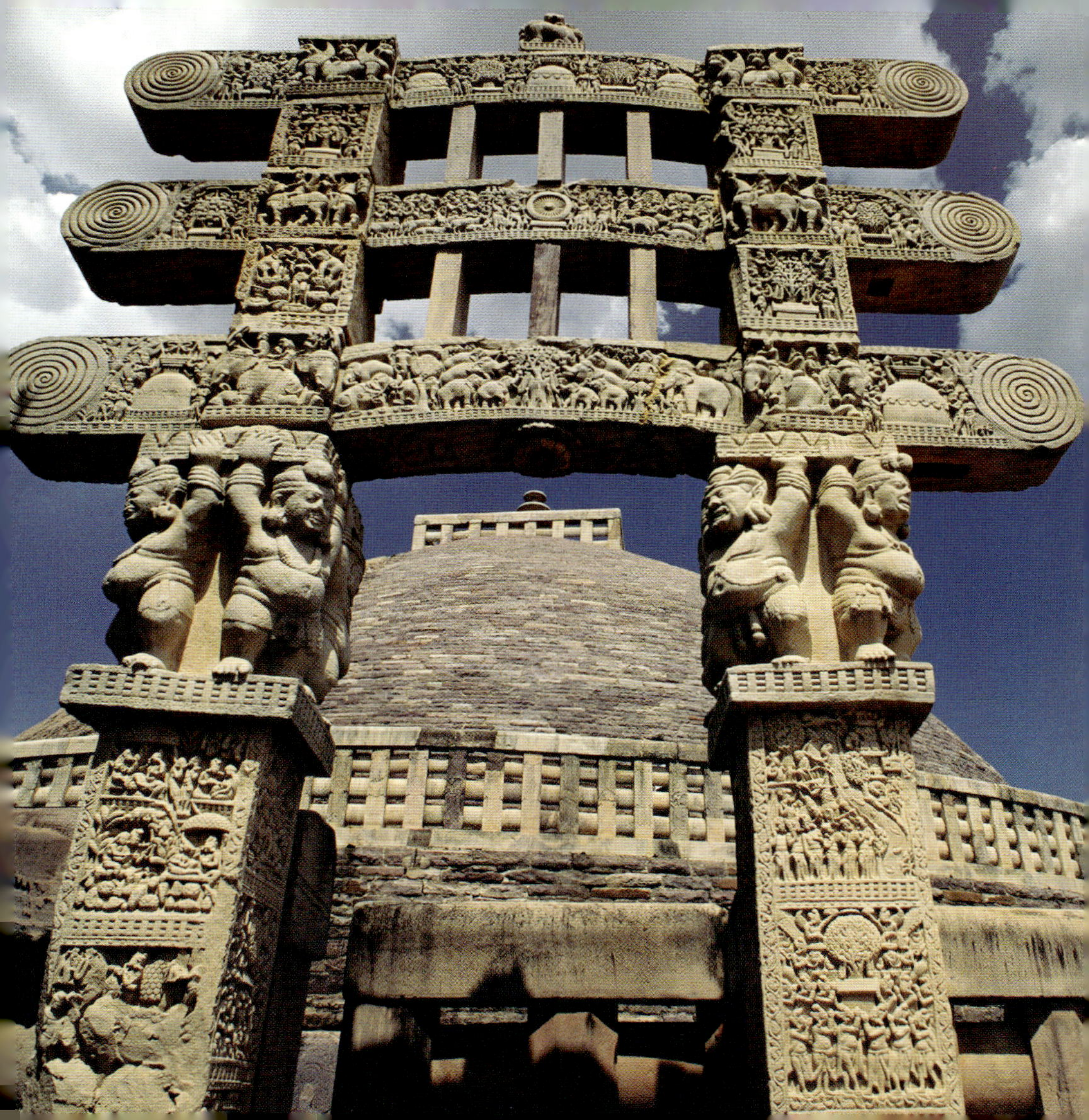

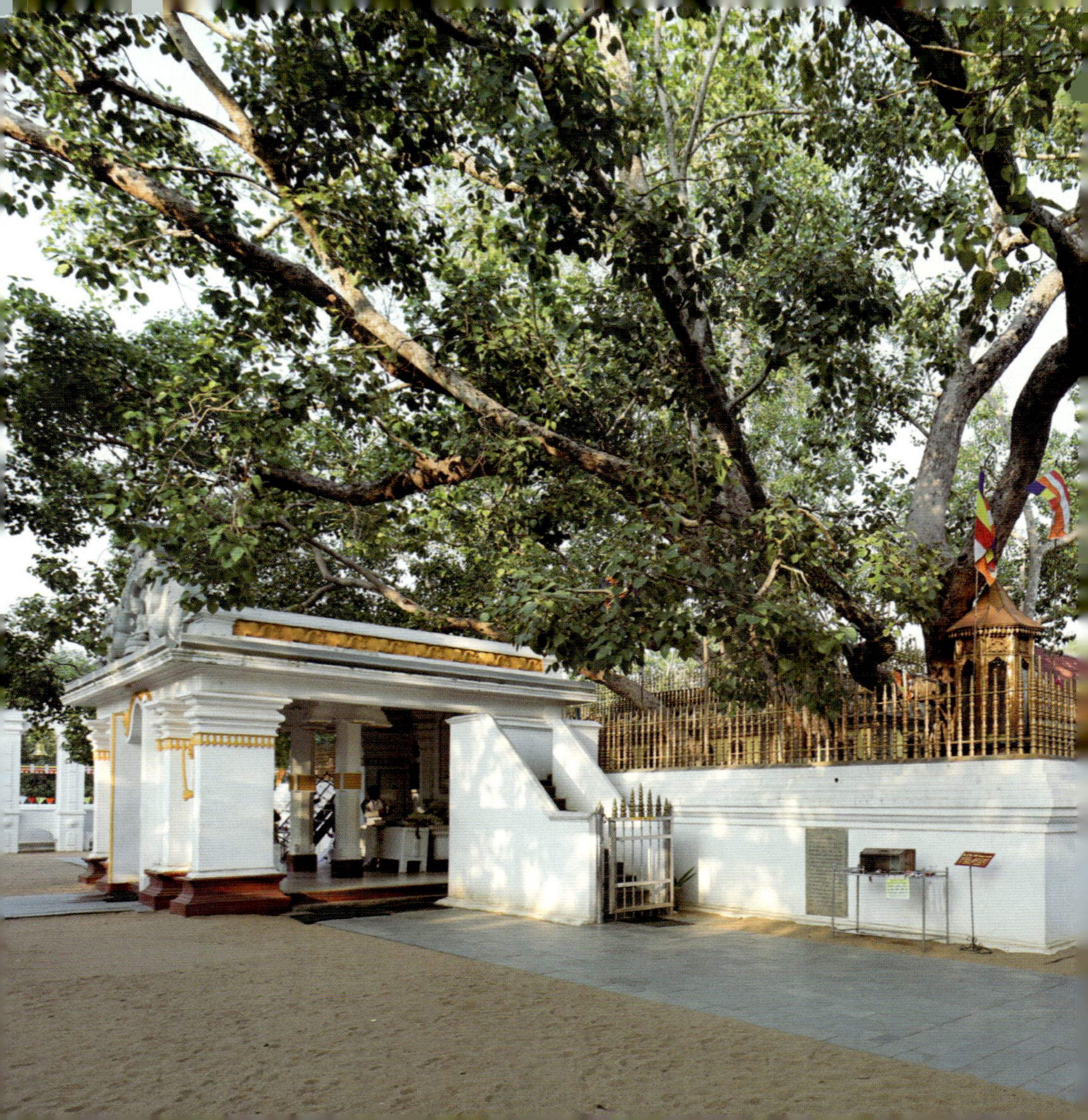

Mahabodhi Temple

288 BCE Bodh Gaya, Bihar, India

COMMISSIONED BY Emperor Ashoka **REBUILT** 2nd century CE
LATEST REBUILD 1889 **HEIGHT OF REBUILD** 55m/180ft

After six years of meditation and extreme self-mortification in the forest, Siddhartha realized that the pleasure he experienced in the palace and the pain of an ascetic life were one and the same, both of them results of stimulation of the senses. So he bathed, found new cloths to wind round his body, ate a meal offered by a passing milkmaid and sat in meditation under a shady tree in the forest. He sat in meditation through the night and with the rising sun he had Four Realizations and became a Buddha. Subsequently, his followers were to seek traces of his presence and come to honour the tree and remember his accomplishments. Among his most famous devotees was Emperor Ashoka (3rd century BCE), who had a stupa and temple built, a stele erected and perhaps a stone carved to mark the exact spot of enlightenment, known as the Diamond Throne – this is still extant (see right). Ashoka also sent his daughter with a cutting of the tree to Sri Lanka, where it and Buddhism thrived. When the original tree at Bodh Gaya died, it was replaced with a cutting of its descendant in Sri Lanka, which survives today. Visitors would worship in front of the tree at Ashoka's Mahabodhi Temple, which was rebuilt around the 6th century CE. The rebuilt temple had a brick pyramidal tower, topped by a stupa. In a modern restoration, four smaller towers were added at the four corners of the tower base. At one time, replicas of this building were constructed all over Asia, and the one at Bagan, Myanmar (Burma) is still in use. The Bodh Gaya site contains traces of many other ancient stupas and shrines built to honour the Buddha's moment of enlightenment.

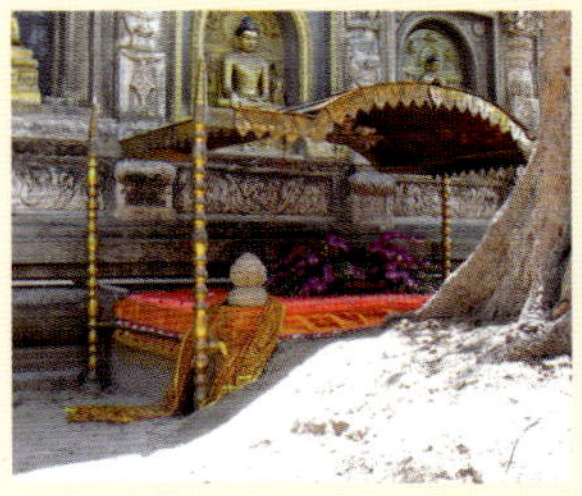

Diamond Throne

Seated in meditation under the Bodhi tree, where the Diamond Throne stands now, Siddhartha realized four things: that all life is suffering; suffering is caused by attachment (ultimately to life itself); to end suffering, one must destroy attachments; and detachment may be achieved through right livelihood, words, deeds, views, intention, effort, mindfulness and concentration. Accordingly, Siddhartha was enlightened and freed from karma and rebirth.

'The Lord of the World [Buddha] worshipped you, O Mahabodhi Tree. I too worship you. All honour to you, O King of Enlightenment!'

ANCIENT BUDDHIST CHANT

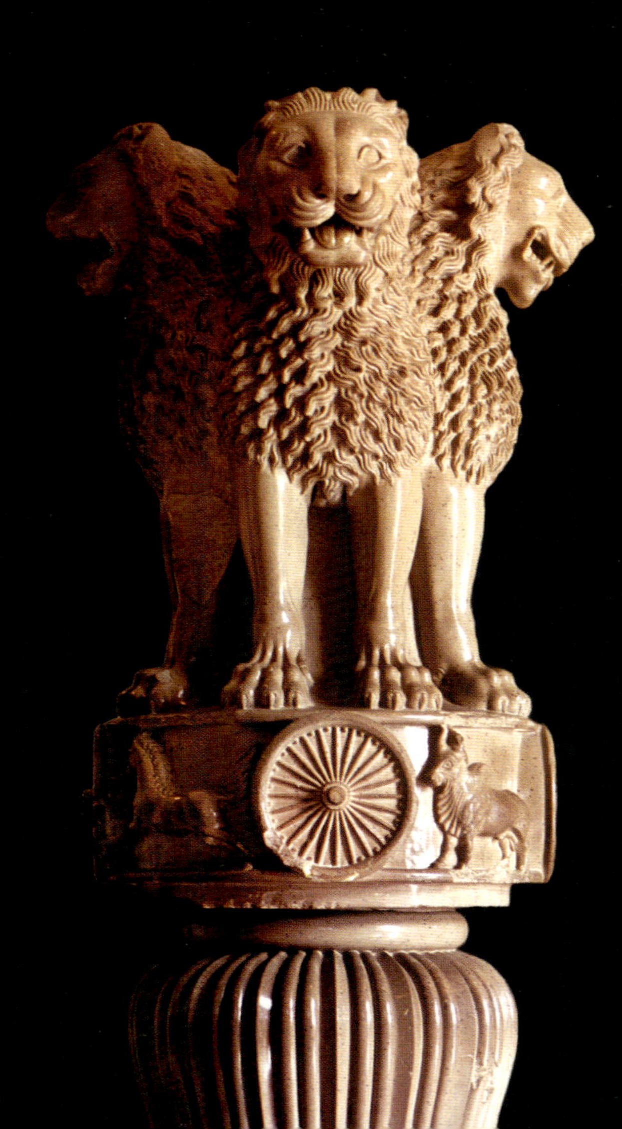

Lion Capital

C. 250 BCE **Archaeological Museum, Sarnath, Uttar Pradesh, India**

STYLE Indian and Achaemenid Persian   **MATERIAL** Polished sandstone
DATE OF REDISCOVERY 1904   **HEIGHT** 2.15 m/7 ft, including base

One of the important antiquities at Sarnath, the place where the Buddha preached his First Sermon, is a tall column erected by Emperor Ashoka in the 3rd century BCE. Throughout his empire, Ashoka established many columns surmounted by capitals decorated with animals. They were representations of the *axis mundi* or the axis that connected heaven and earth, and were erected throughout the Buddhist world by Ashoka to proclaim his belief in the Buddha. They also attested to the geographical extent of his political power in India. Today, only a few remain: the pillars of polished chunar sandstone, some of which reach a height of 12 metres (40 ft); the capitals have been placed in the protection of museums. The Sarnath capital is exemplary for its complexity and symbolic meanings. Four lions, seated back to back, look out in four directions; they stand on a plinth decorated with four wheels alternating with four animals: a horse, elephant, lion and bull, placed on top of an inverted lotus. A large wheel representing the law formerly rested on top of the lions, and the column has an inscription by Ashoka urging unity among the Buddha's disciples. In this early stage of Buddhist art, symbols and styles of neighbouring civilizations were appropriated. In this animal capital, the lions' hieratic poses and the stylized treatment of their heads and manes are carved in the Persian style, which contrasts with the naturalistic depiction of the animals on the plinth. The lion was chosen as the national emblem to be engraved on the rupee issued after Indian independence in 1947; it remained there until the currency was redesigned in 2010.

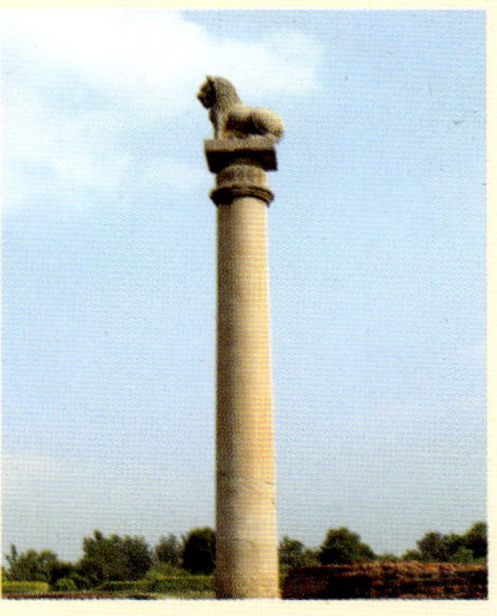

Pillar at Vaishali
Emperor Ashoka was converted to Buddhism by remorse over war. An exemplar of royal patronage, Ashoka built a legendary 84,000 stupas and commemorated the sites with stele and tall columns topped by animal capitals, such as the lion at Vaishali, Bihar, India (above), where Gautama Buddha preached his Last Sermon.

'All those who pray fervently before it, see, from time to time, according to their petitions, figures with good or bad signs.'
XUANZANG, *SI YU KI, BUDDHIST RECORDS*

Thuparamaya Dagoba

3rd century BCE **Anuradhapura, Sri Lanka**

COMMISSIONED BY King Devanampiyatissa **LAST REBUILT** 1862
MATERIAL Coral stone **DIMENSIONS** 18 x 3.45 m / 59 x 11¼ ft ft

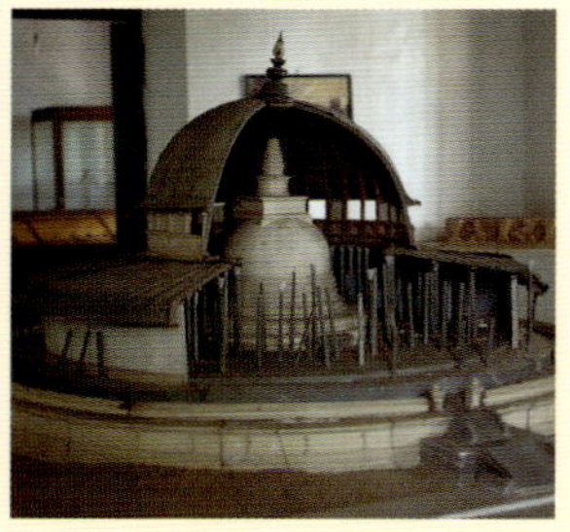

Wooden Housing

Recreated here in a model held in a local museum, the stupa of the Thuparamaya Dagoba was originally enclosed by a protective wooden building. A high dome covered the stupa, while the path of circumambulation was sheltered by a lower, sloping roof. The stone pillars that helped to support the ambulatory roof are the only part of the protective structure to have survived into the present day.

'First the Great Monastery; second the lovely Cetiya (monastery); the Sanctuary monastery was third ...'

LISTING OF BUDDHIST PROJECTS, *MAHAVAMSA*

Sri Lanka was one of the first countries to convert to Buddhism. The religion was first brought to Sri Lanka by Mahindra, son of Emperor Ashoka, who converted King Devanampiyatissa (c. 306–266 BCE). The king, whose many Buddhist projects were listed in the *Mahavamsa* (c. 3rd century BCE), built a *dagoba* (Buddhist sacred place of veneration) at the Thuparamaya. It is the oldest in Sri Lanka. Sanghamitta, daughter of Ashoka, then brought a cutting of the Bodhi tree under which the Buddha attained enlightenment, and also founded an order of Buddhist nuns. Sri Lanka is a centre of Theravad (Way of the Elders), the early school of Buddhism whose Pali scriptures form the basic canon. Located in Anuradhapura, the political and religious capital of the Buddhist kings, the Thuparamaya Dagoba was one of the first Buddhist monuments to be built. The stupa, which houses a collar bone of the Buddha, has been destroyed and remodelled many times over the centuries. The most recent reconstruction, in 1862, has a dome raised by a base of five concentric, circular tiers, one set upon the next. The dome is topped by a tall finial consisting of a series of fused discs, in the local style. Outside the stupa, four sets of steps, oriented to the cardinal directions, lead up to the ritual path of circumambulation that circles around the stupa's exterior. The path is paved with granite and studded by two circles of stone pillars (see also above left). Like all such Buddhist monuments in Sri Lanka, the buildings are painted white. Anuradhapura was the site of several royal building campaigns that raised many large-scale stupas. The capital was abandoned around the year 998 CE.

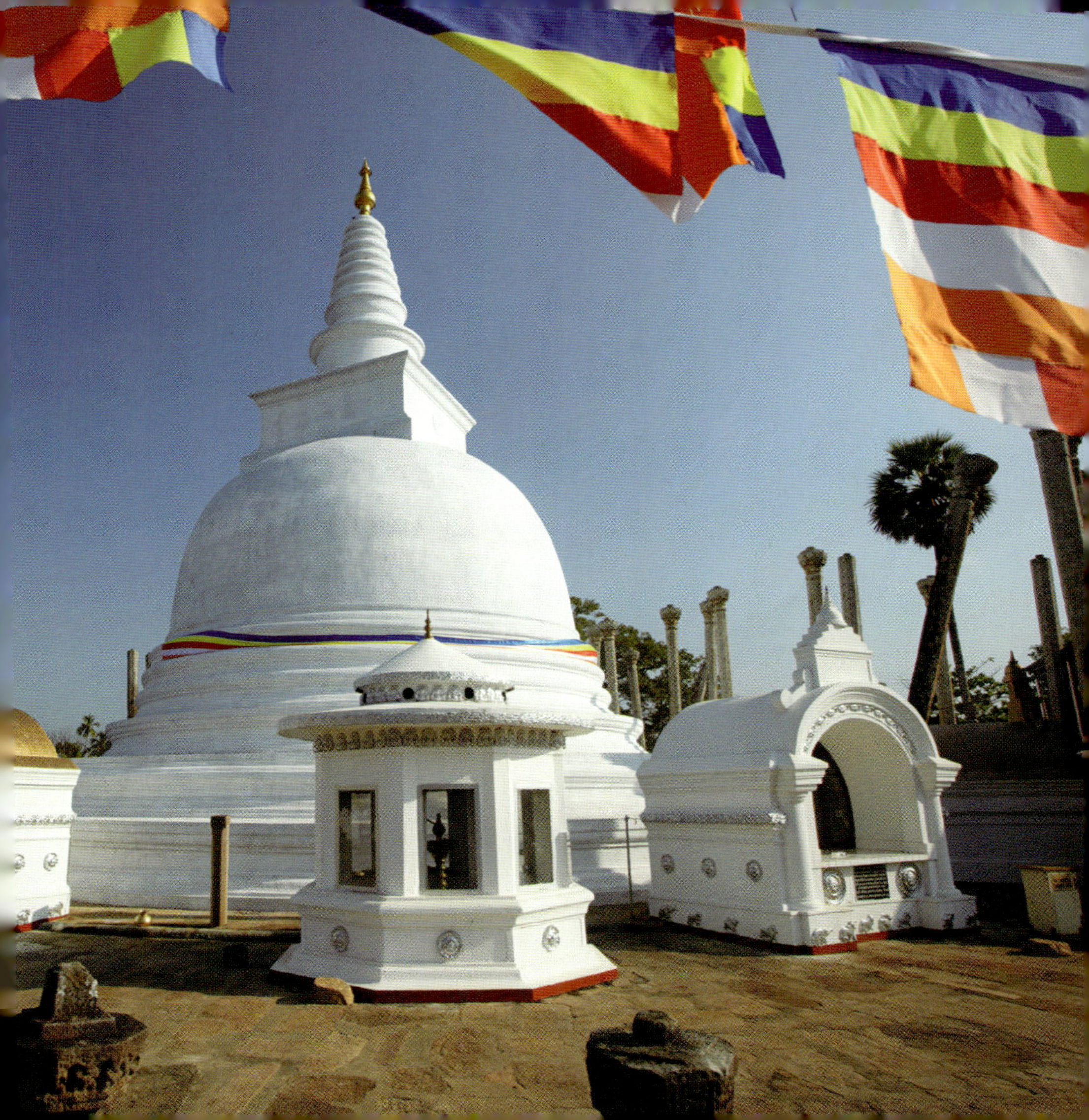

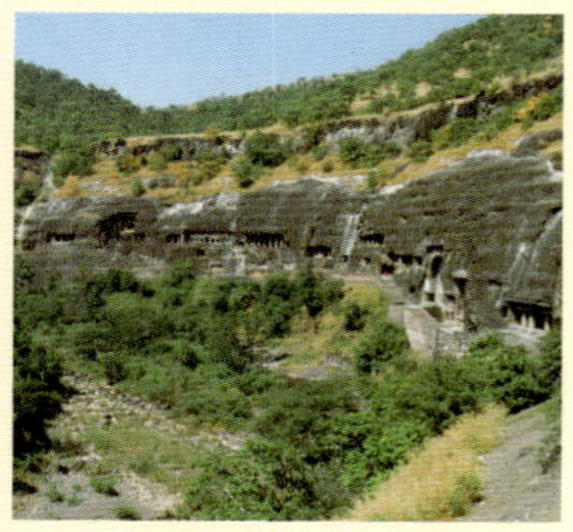

The Ajanta Caves

The caves were rediscovered in 1819 by a British army officer out on a hunting expedition. He and his fellow soldiers cut away the centuries of overgrowth, revealing the cave complex carved from the living rock, which had been abandoned for over 1,000 years. In 1844, the Royal Asiatic Society appointed Major Robert Gill to make copies of the frescoes on the cave walls, a task to which he dedicated the next three decades of his life.

'The paintings and sculptures of Ajanta, considered masterpieces of Buddhist religious art, have had a considerable artistic influence.'

UNESCO WEBSITE

Ajanta Cave 26

c. 460–480 CE **Jalgaon, Aurangabad District, Maharashtra, India**

COMMISSIONED BY Asmaka kings   **ABANDONED** *c.* 480 CE
STYLE Vakataka   **FLOOR AREA** 25.5 x 11.5 m / 83 x 38 ft

Located in the Western Ghats mountain range of north-western India, the Ajanta Caves are carved from a horseshoe-shaped bluff overlooking a ravine. The site was populated from the 2nd century BCE until the 6th century CE, and its cave art provides an illustrated summary of Buddhist architecture, sculpture and painting during that period. Five of the caves served as apsidal cave-chapels and twenty-four as rectangular monasteries, and at its peak the complex may have had some two hundred monks and artisans in residence. The earliest caves are *chaitya-grihas*, or stupa halls. Each is apsidal in ground plan, with a plain stupa at the rear and an aisle of columns flanking the nave to mark out the path for *pradaksina* or ritual circumambulation. Later caves, hewn in the 5th century CE, feature a more complex ground plan and monumental sculptures of preaching Buddhas. The stupa of Cave 26, to single out one in particular, has been made taller than most by the addition of a series of drums at the base and elongation of the dome, the terminal balustrade and umbrellas. Deeply carved jewels and floral subjects adorn the stupa's base, with the motifs echoed by bands of ornamentation on the columns marking out the ritual path. A row of seated Buddhas appears in the frieze above the columns and at the clerestory level. A Buddha with pendant legs, carved out of the front of the stupa, exemplifies the merging of ancient architectural images of the Buddha with later anthropomorphic icons. A sculptural bas-relief on one side-wall depicts the Buddha's Enlightenment; a sculpted reclining figure on the other represents the Death of the Buddha.

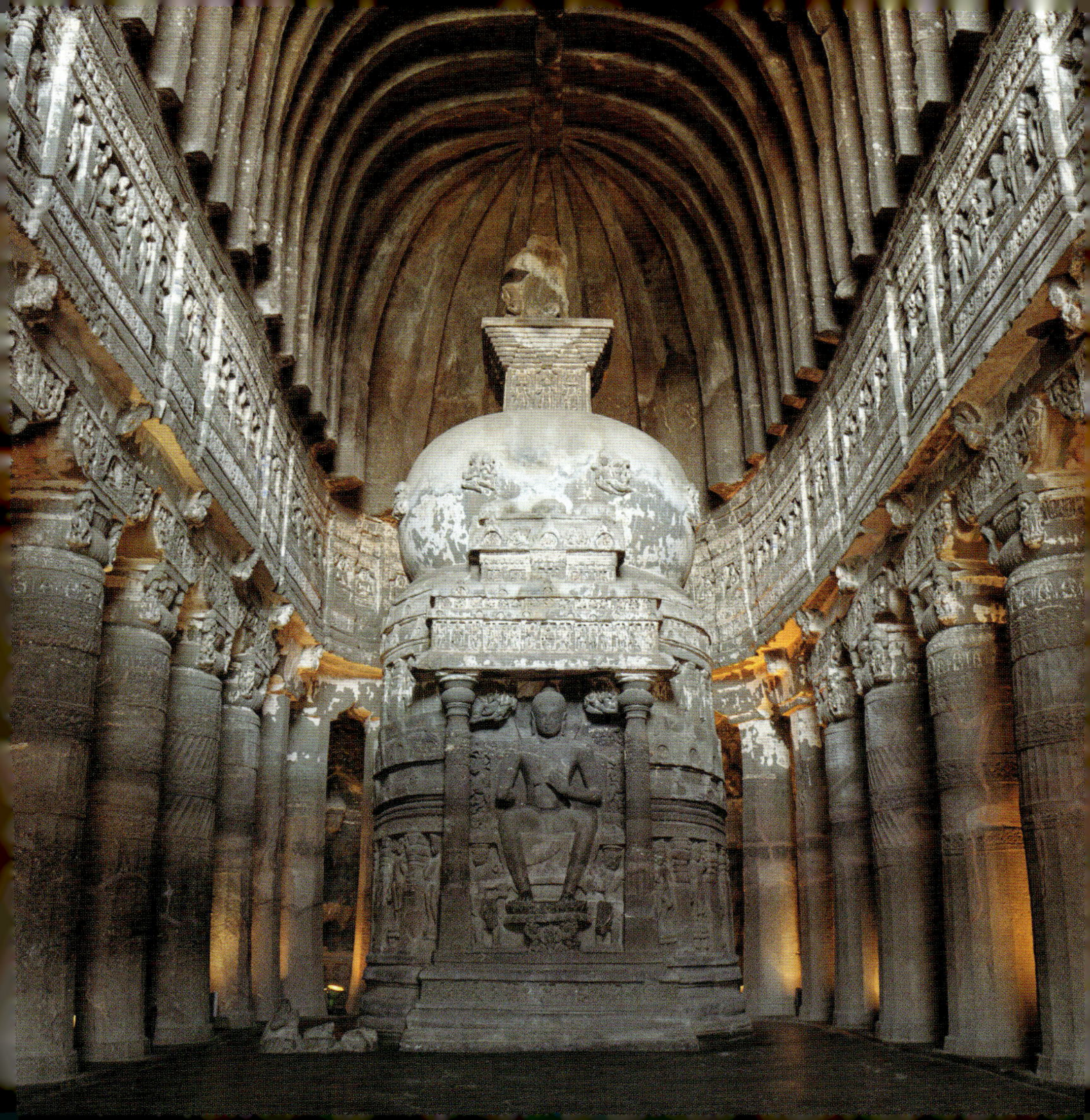

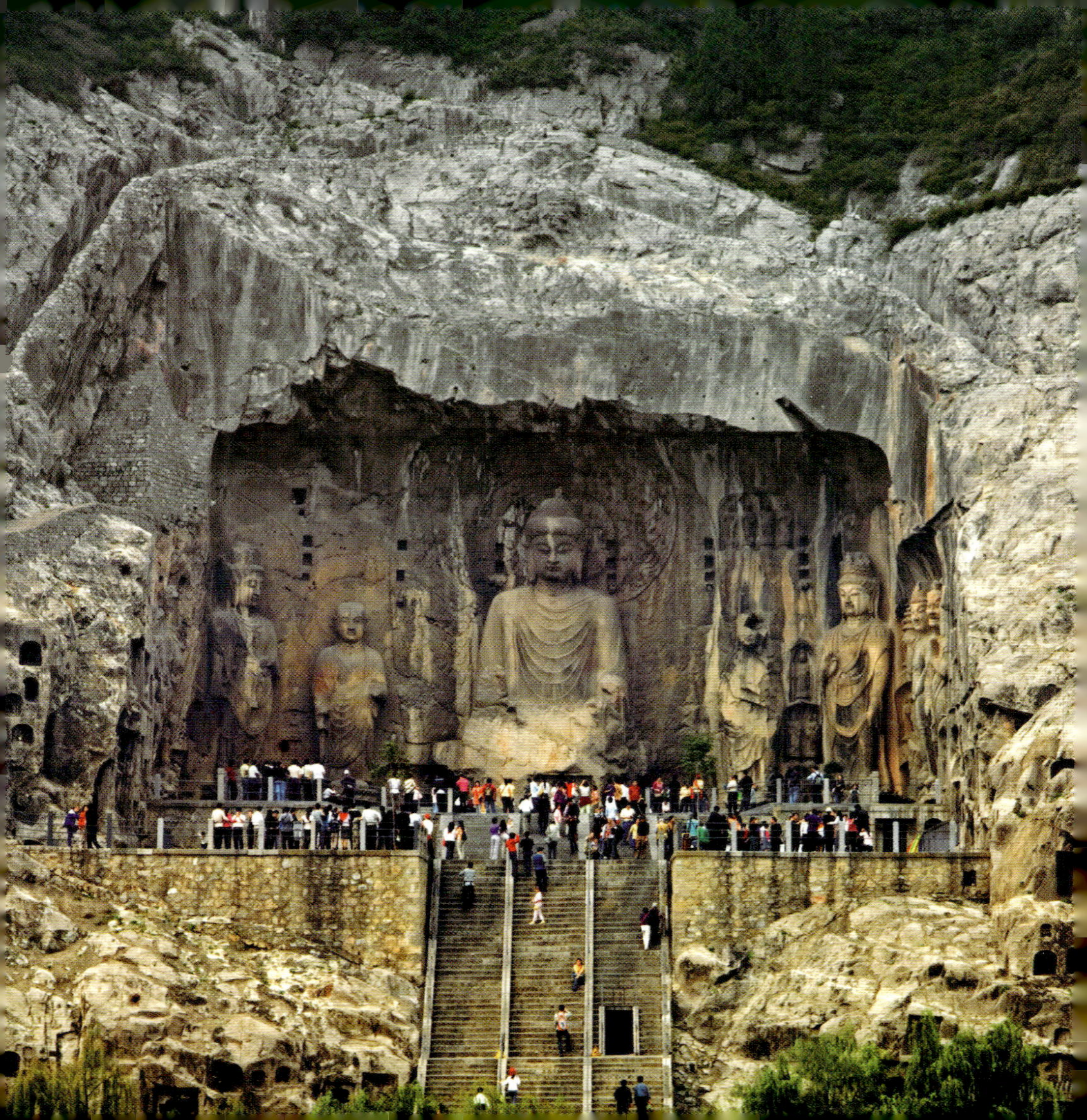

Longmen Grottoes

493–1127 CE **near Luoyang, Henan, China**

COMMISSIONED BY Emperor Xiaowen **HEIGHT OF BUDDHA** 17.1 m / 56 ft
AREA OF FENGXIANSI CAVE 39 x 35 m / 128 x 115 ft

Soon after Buddhism entered China, local kings erected cave-chapels for worship, based on Indian prototypes recreated in central Asia. When the Northern Wei rulers of northern China moved their capital south to central China in around 500 CE they opened the caves at Longmen with imperial excavations on a grand scale. Later, in 672–75, Empress Wu Zetian, renowned as a great supporter of Buddhism, a builder of lavish monuments and the only woman to rule in her own name, oversaw the opening of the Fengxiansi cave, a huge project. Her personal knowledge of Buddhism made her a most informed patron and she sponsored many different schools of teaching. The cave, monumental in scale, contains a group of nine figures whose presence suggests a new, more robust kind of doctrine. Flanking the central seated Buddha — carved to resemble the empress — are two monks, two bodhisattvas and four divine guardians. Originally a large wooden façade protected the figures, with diffused light from a large rose window emphasizing their mystery. In support of their empress's espousal of Buddhism, many of her court excavated smaller caves in the vicinity of the great one, and groups of laymen, monks and nuns also gathered together to sponsor small ones carved on the periphery of the bluff. Donors were assured that any effort to propagate Buddhism would earn them spiritual credit and make their endeavours worthwhile. The active poses of the guardians, and growing naturalism in the depiction of the figures, their clothing and jewels, attest to increased contact with the West and the increasingly cosmopolitan culture of the Tang court.

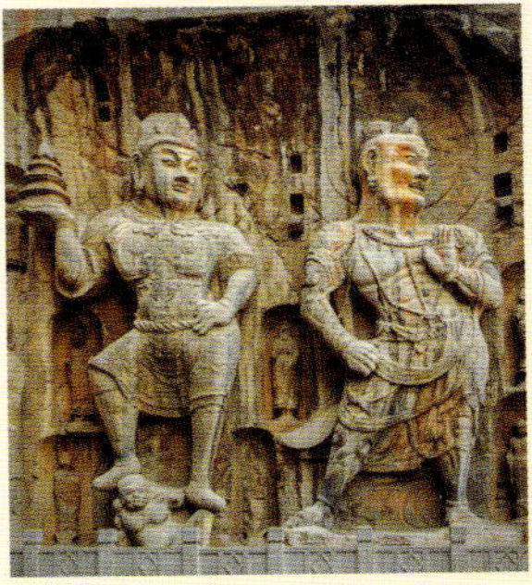

Guardian Figures

An appealing aspect of Buddhism was the sense of security that it offered believers. At Longmen, sculptures of military figures in defensive postures, set on either side of the Buddhist icons, promise that protection. Here, a heavenly guardian king (left) is dressed in armour and bedecked with jewels; with him is a muscular defender of the faith.

'The True Doctrine has flown over the East for over 700 years, yet this large Buddha niche is the greatest meritorious deed ever offered.'

INSCRIPTION AT LONGMEN GROTTOES

Nalanda University

c. 5th century CE **Nalanda, Bihar, India**

COMMISSIONED BY Kumaragupta I **ABANDONED** 13th century
AREA 488 x 244 m/1,600 x 800 ft **HEIGHT** At least 31 m/100 ft

Archaeological evidence has established that this monastic complex was a centre of learning from the 5th century CE to 1197. It is estimated that at the height of its prosperity there may have been as many as ten thousand students and two thousand teachers here. The main stupa is huge, even in its incomplete state. Exterior steps lead to the top of a square base that once supported a large drum and dome, both of which are now missing. Of the four smaller stupa towers that stood at the corners of the base, two still exist. Large and small votive stupas, some retaining their images of the seated Buddha, fill the surrounding area. Further afield, set among lakes and parks, four large temples face eight monasteries, with two more monasteries adjacent. The overall ground plan has a vertical axis. Each monastery consists of a square central court surrounded by small monastic cells equipped with a shelf for an oil lamp, water jar or scriptures. At the centre is a platform for effigies or lecturers. Nearby, small buildings with fire pits functioned as kitchens and dining areas. Nalanda University was famous for its extensive library, located in a tripartite nine-storied building. The curriculum was not strictly religious; in addition to theology it offered grammar, logic, astronomy, metaphysics, medicine and philosophy. Students came from many Buddhist countries – Korea, Japan, China, Tibet and Indonesia – and several of them kept a record of their experiences. Students and pilgrims took scriptures and icons with them on their travels, and in this way they made the art styles and schools of Buddhism practised at Nalanda familiar to Buddhists in South-east and East Asia.

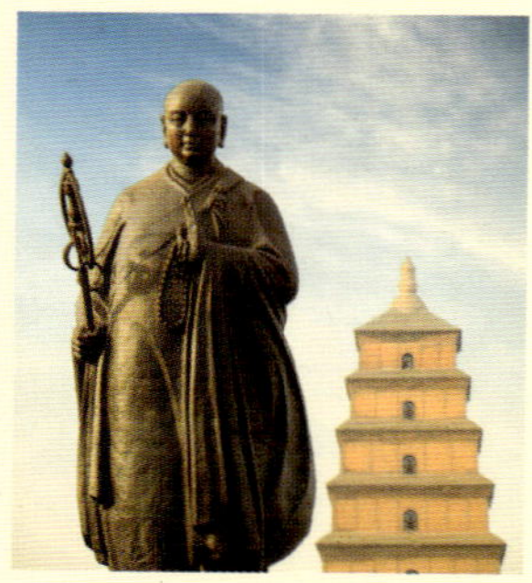

Xuanzang

In the 7th century CE, the Chinese monk Xuanzang set off on an epic journey to India. Among the places he visited was the famous seat of learning at Nalanda. When he returned to China eighteen years later, he brought with him over 600 Sanskrit texts.

'The lives of all these virtuous men were naturally governed by habits of the most solemn and strictest kind. Thus, in 700 years of the existence [of Nalanda], no man has ever defied the rules of discipline.'

XUANZANG

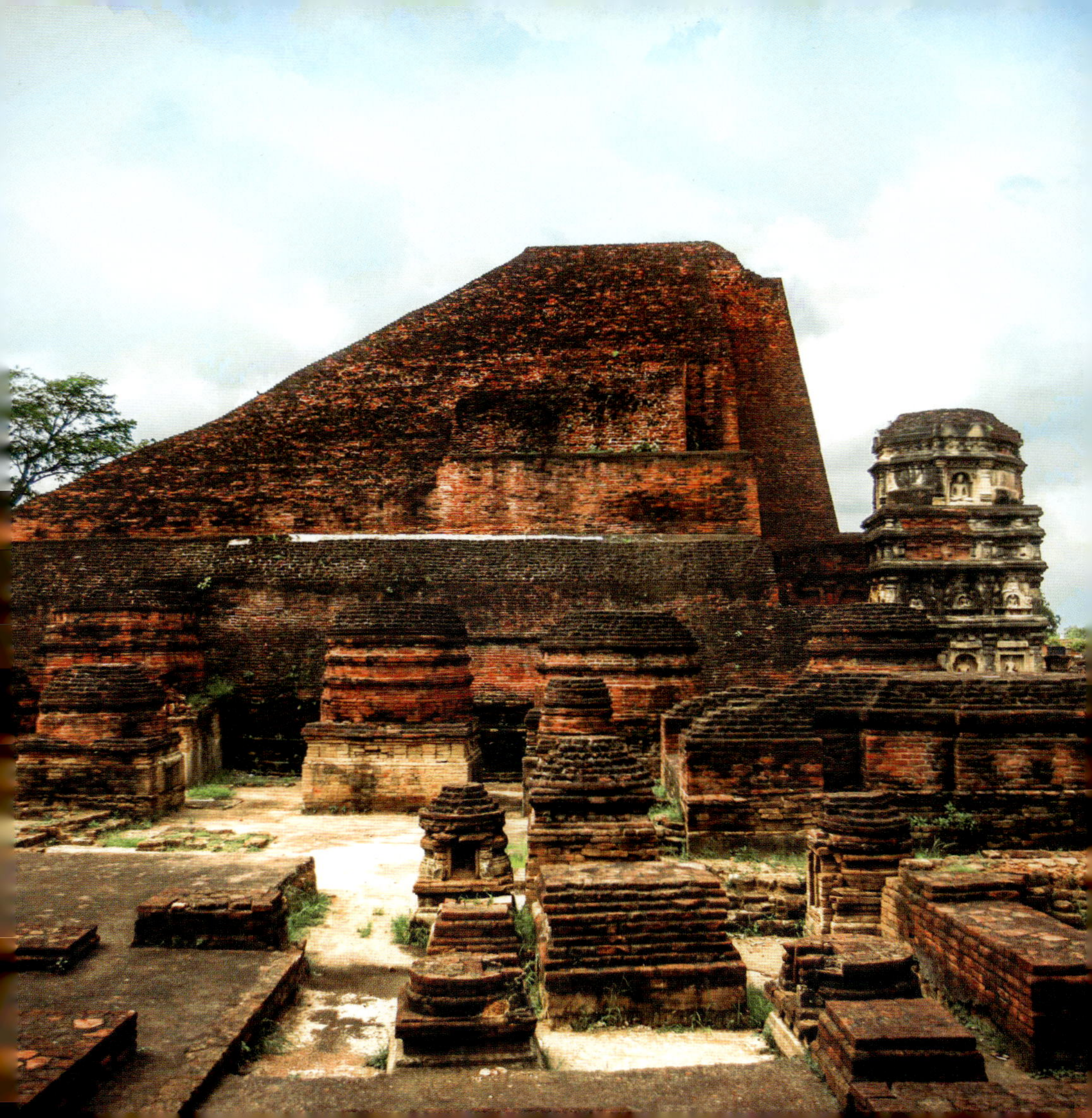

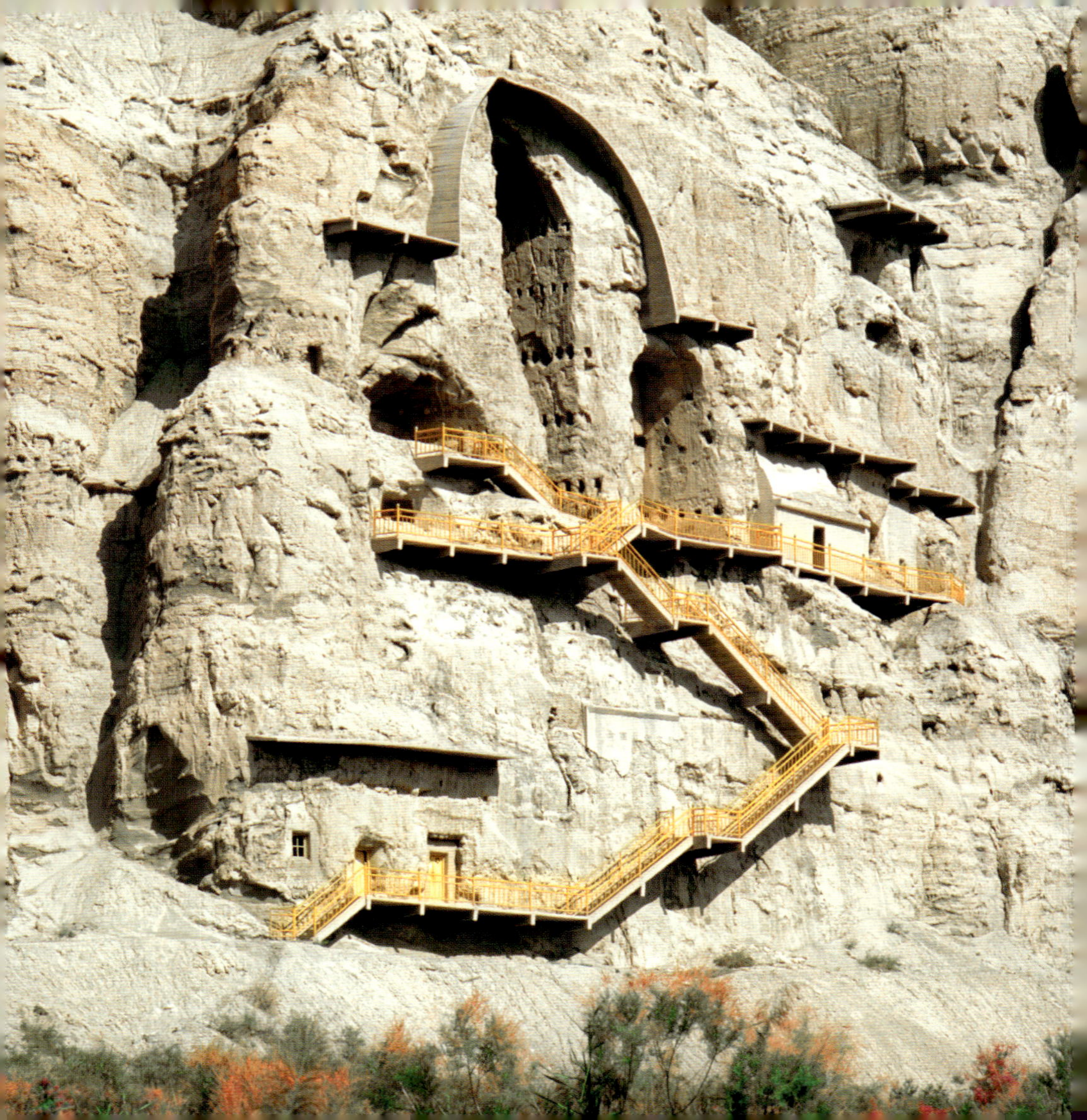

Kizil Caves

6th century CE **Kizil, Xinjiang, China**

COMMISSIONED BY Tocharian kingdom of Kucha **TOTAL OF CAVE-CHAPELS** 236, over a 2-km/1¼-mile site **ABANDONED** 8th century

The caves at Kizil are cut into the northern bank of the Muzat River near Kizil Township (Qizil). They are among the best preserved of several cave sites located on the Silk Route linking India to China, including Kumtura and Bezeklik. Similar to Indian prototypes, typical cave-chapels at Kizil comprise a fore hall and a main chamber, but here, instead of a stupa, most have a central square pillar for ritual circumambulation. The main icons appear on the front face of the pillar – for example, a large sculpture of a seated Buddha, and an upper area with a lunette-shaped arch containing a painting of the Buddha of the Future. In addition, a niche in the rear wall behind the pillar typically bears a representation of the dying Buddha. Paintings of seated Buddhas appear in every part of the cave, sometimes with scenes of the life of the Buddha. This accords with the practices of the resident Sarvastivadin sect, who focused their worship on the historic Buddha. Ceilings typically bear complex lozenge designs of the Buddha's life and previous, historical existences, while the central zone has sky imagery, suggesting the vault of heaven. In contrast to the lavish decor of the cave-chapels, the monastic caves (*viharas*) are unadorned. In the earlier caves the style of painting is naturalistic and resembles Indian prototypes; later artists express local traditions and the figures are stiffer, more rigidly drawn and in harsher colours. The caves, visited by monks, missionaries and merchants on the Silk Road, were an important model for cave-chapel complexes in northern China, such as Yungang. Kizil was a centre of Buddhist studies, and the teacher and translator Kumarajiva (4th century CE) studied there.

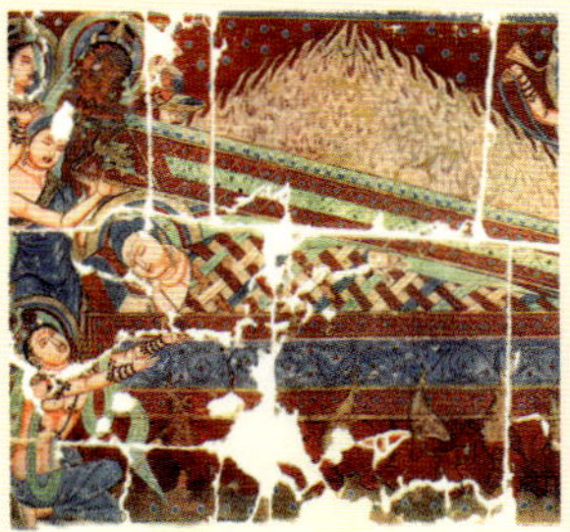

Parinirvana Mural

This mural at the Kizil Caves is a representation of the Buddha having attained *parinirvana*, or nirvana-after-death, which implies release from karma or rebirth. The flames above his coffin indicate that his attendants are in the process of cremating his corpse.

'There is a statue of the Buddha richly adorned and carved with skill surpassing that of men…. Outside the western gate of the chief city, on the right and left side of the road, there are two erect figures of Buddha about 90 feet high.'

XUANZANG AT KIZIL

Horyu-ji Pagoda

607 CE Ikaruga, Nara, Kansai, Japan

STOREYS Five   **MATERIAL** Wood
TEMPLE AREA 14.6 ha/36 ac.   **HEIGHT** 32.45 m/106 ft

According to the *Nihon Shoki*, or Japanese *Records of History*, the Korean King Seong of Baekje introduced Buddhism to Japan in 522 CE by sending Buddhist monks, nuns, images of Buddha and a number of scriptures. After a period of resistance and accommodation, the court, guided by Prince Shotoku (572–622), accepted Buddhism. Prince Shotoku built temples like Shitenno-ji and Horyu-ji to spread Buddhist culture and protect his empire. Like the monastic complexes of China, Horyu-ji, set out on a vast, flat tract of land, is surrounded by a wall and monumental entrance gates. There are twenty-one buildings in addition to the pagoda, among them an image hall, treasure hall, lecture hall, refectory, library, monastic quarters and other buildings. The pagoda itself is the oldest wooden structure in the world. It is in the Chinese style, set on a tall, stepped, stone base, with four identical faces but only one functional door. The tower, a hollow structure, is supported by massive wooden beams, and the spire rising from the core beam is encirled by a series of round disks, like the 'umbrellas' of the Indian prototype. A Chinese bracketing system supports the heavily tiled, upturned roofs, and small bells hang from the roof corners. Horyu-ji is said to contain a fragment of a bone of the Buddha, buried in the ground beneath the central mast. The pagoda is further distinguished by its unique interior altar with four sculptural tableaux, created in 711. The small-scale scenes of sculpted clay represent the death of the Buddha, division of the relics, a debate between a Chinese sage and the Bodhisattva of Wisdom and the Paradise of the Buddha of the Future.

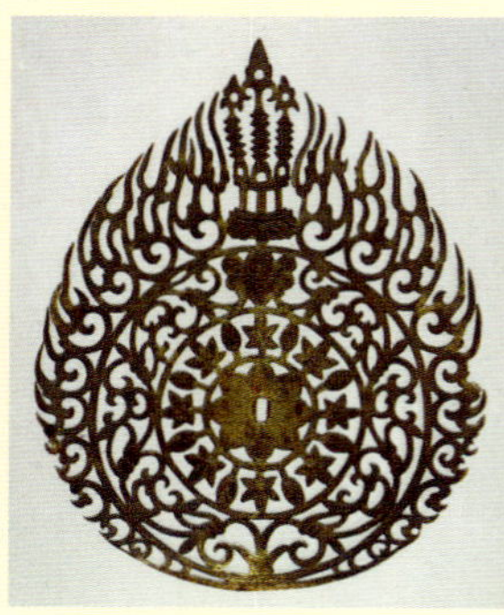

Gilt-bronze Halo

Among the treasures of Horyu-ji is a collection of *kouhai*, or gilt-bronze haloes, from the 7th century CE (see example above). Originally they were made for specific statues but over time haloes and statues have become mismatched, so now the haloes are displayed separately. Most are made from bronze plate.

'[Relics at Horyu-ji were] first placed in a small glass bottle, then in gold, silver and bronze containers, and finally in a large jar.'

SEIICHI MIZUNO, *ASUKA BUDDHIST ART* (1974)

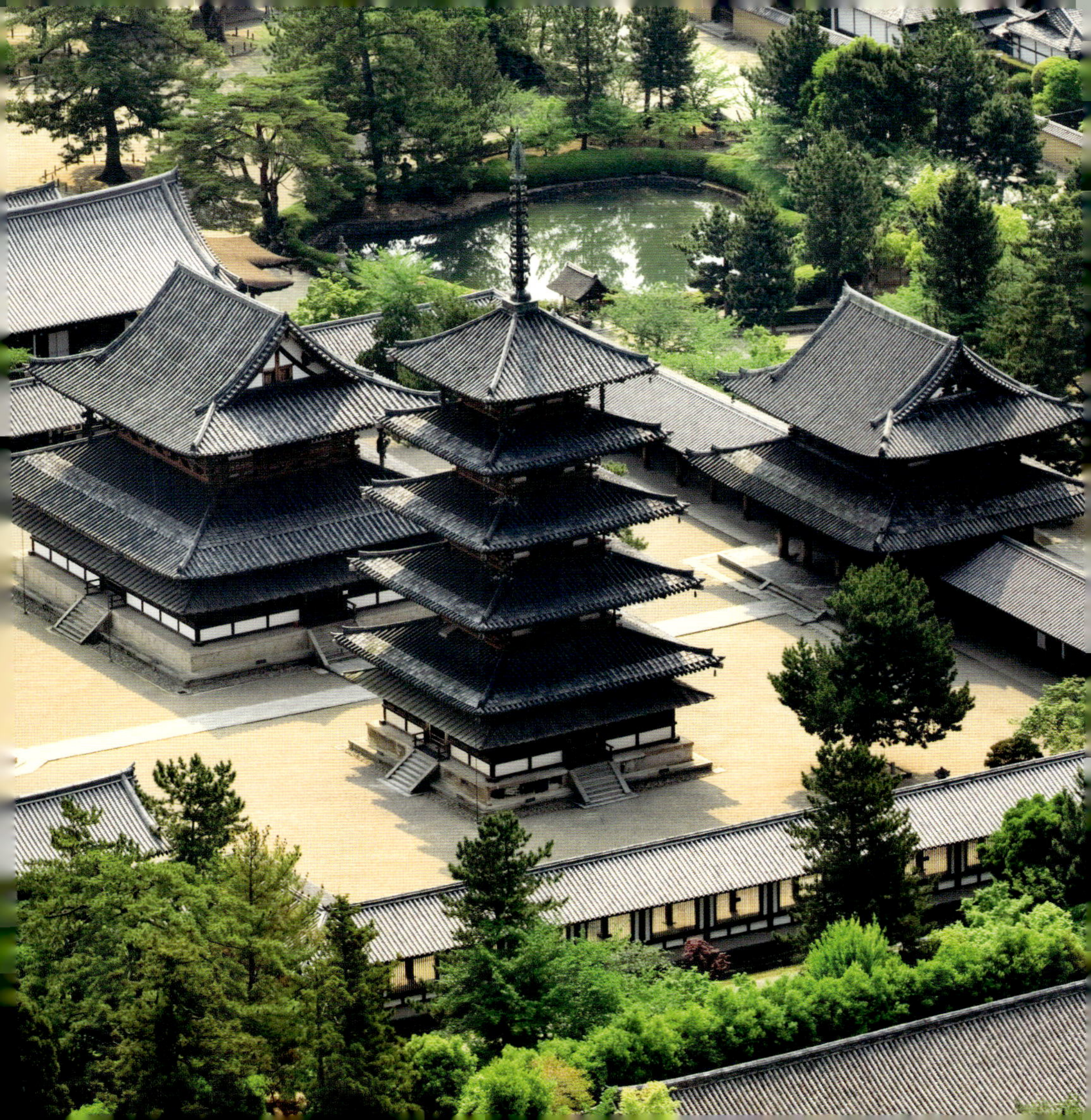

Giant Wild Goose Pagoda

652 CE **Southern Xi'an, Shaanxi, China**

COMMISSIONED BY Emperor Gaozong   **CHINESE NAME** Dayan Pagoda
MATERIALS Wood and brick   **CURRENT HEIGHT** 64 m/210 ft

The pagoda structure, present at most Buddhist temple compounds regardless of the sectarian affiliation, is a Chinese interpretation of the stupa. The tower-like form evolved from the later, more developed stupas of northern Pakistan, where the addition of numerous, tiered square bases increased the height of buildings that at times resembled stepped wedding cakes. For example, a tower associated with the Kushan King Kaniska (*c.* 2nd century CE) in Peshawar, Pakistan, is said to have been 180–210 metres (590–689 ft) tall, but all that remains of the wooden structure is the reliquary that was once embedded within its base. The pagoda's architectural form also relates to towers built in the native Chinese style at intervals along the Great Wall in north China, and to the square pillars located at the center of Buddhist cave-chapels, such as Cave 6 at Yungang, in Shanxi Province, China. Pagodas are tall, multiple-storied constructs with vertically diminishing levels; an upturned tile roof tops each register. Pagodas may be circular, but most, like the Giant Wild Goose Pagoda at Xi'an, are square in plan. Later pagodas have eight to sixteen sides, such as the octagonal Tianning Pagoda at Changzhou, Jiangsu Province. Pagodas are usually empty, and traditionally worshippers do not enter the building; as with the stupa, ritual worship comprises circumambulating the outer perimeter. Like its Indian prototype, the pagoda is a marker of the Buddha's presence and often holds a relic in a special container buried beneath it. The Giant Wild Goose Pagoda was commissioned to enshrine Buddhist materials brought from India by the monk Xuanzang (602–64).

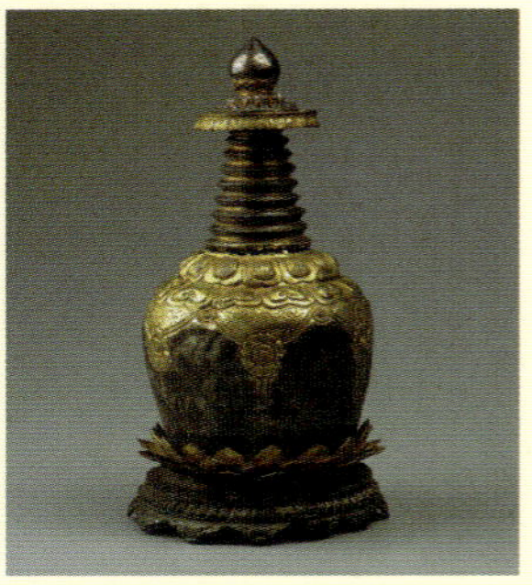

Korean Reliquary

Buddhist reliquaries often take the architectural shape of a stupa. They contain a sacred relic of the Buddha or special Buddhist teachers, and coins and small precious objects made of pearl, crystal and copper. This gilt silver, 14th-century Korean reliquary is stupa-shaped with an elongated, egg-shaped body and tall umbrellas that indicate the heavenly realm. Inside were bronze and glass fragments.

'The emperor thought that brick [not stone] would be a more prudent compromise.'

SICKMAN ET AL, *ART AND ARCHITECTURE OF CHINA* (1974)

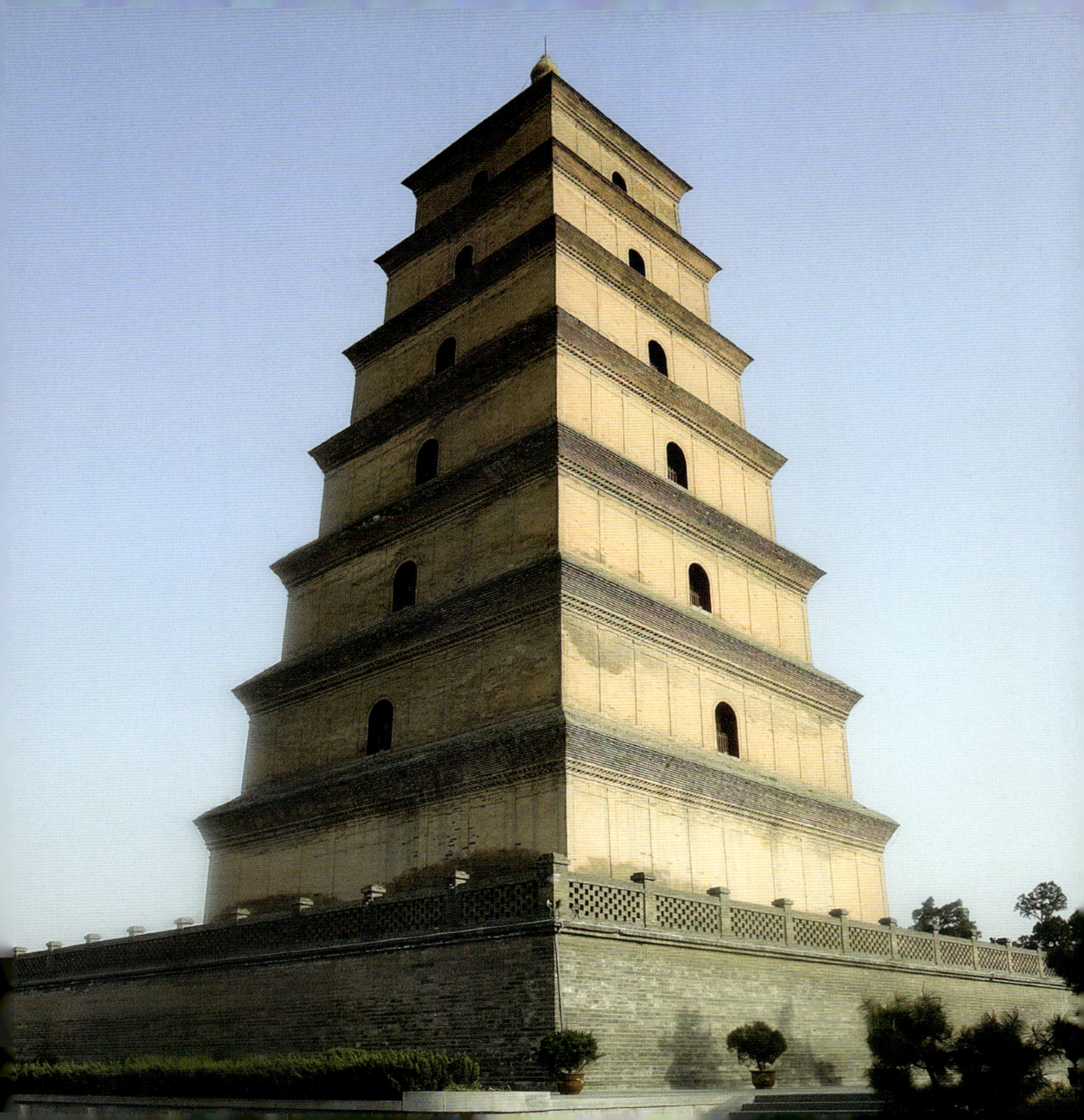

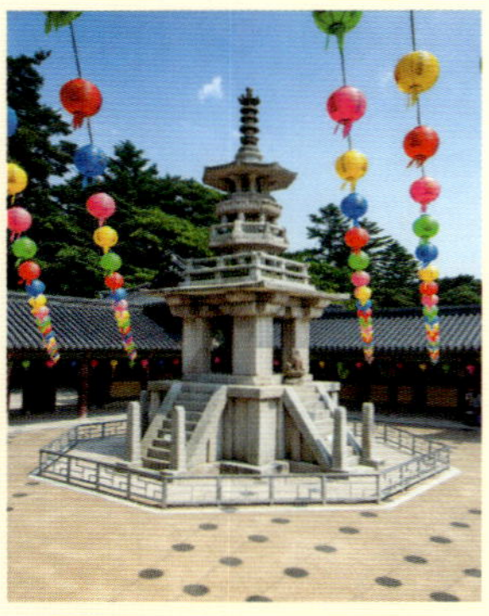

Paired Pagodas

The stone Dabotap Pagoda (above) at Bulguksa resembles a Chinese pagoda in that it is octagonal but stands on a cruciform base with stone staircases on all four sides. Its companion, the three-storey Seokgatap Pagoda, is in Korean style with a stone foundation.

'And in this world system, Ananda, there are no hells, no animals, no ghosts, no Asuras and none of the inauspicious places of rebirth.'

DESCRIPTIONS OF A HAPPY LAND, BUDDHIST SCRIPTURE

Bulguksa Temple

751 CE **Gyeongju, North Gyeongsang, South Korea**

COMMISSIONED BY King Beop-Heung **LAST RENOVATED** 1973
HEIGHTS OF PAGODAS Dabotap: 10.2 m/33½ ft; Seokgatap: 8.4 m/27½ ft

Bulguksa Temple, possibly the oldest in Korea, was founded in 528 CE by the Silla Kingdom. King Beop-Heung (514–540) commissioned the building for his wife and to assure the peace and prosperity of the state. Two hundred years later it was rebuilt and greatly expanded by Kim Dae-Seong (700–774). The main temple rests on raised stone terraces and has heavily tiled roofs supported by complex bracketing in the Chinese style. The temples are dedicated to three different Buddhas: Birojeon (the Vairochana Buddha Hall), Daeungjeon (the Hall of Great Enlightenment of Shakyamuni) and Geungnakjeon (the Hall of Supreme Bliss of the Buddha of the Western Paradise). Located on a mountainside, the temple is reached via a staircase leading to a bridge, with further stairs and bridges connecting the Shakyamuni Hall and the Hall of Supreme Bliss. Some see these typically Korean joined stairways and bridges as symbolically connecting the earthly realm with the world of Buddha above; others say that they symbolize mankind's journey from youth to old age. Also distinctive are two pagodas that stand on an east–west axis in the temple's main courtyard; the pagodas are not identical. The practice of erecting a pair of pagodas in the central area before a main temple may be traced to a twin-stupa miracle described in the *Lotus Sutra*. While Shakyamuni was giving a sermon on Vulture Peak, a stupa appeared in the sky with Prabhutaratna Buddha inside. Shakyamuni rose to sit beside him and have a discussion. The story attests to the Mahayanist belief in the supernatural powers of the Buddha, and in the existence of a multitude of Buddhas.

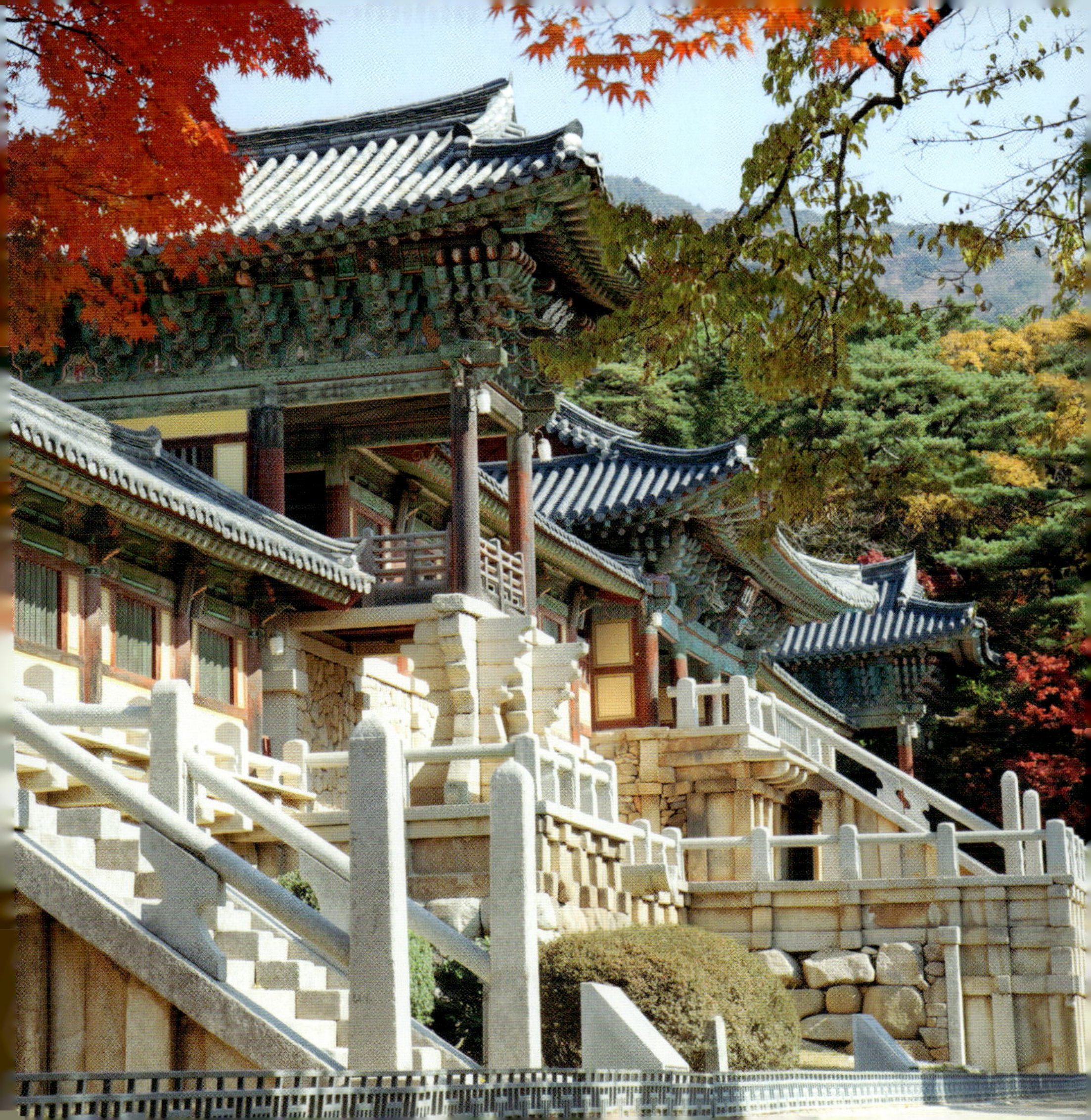

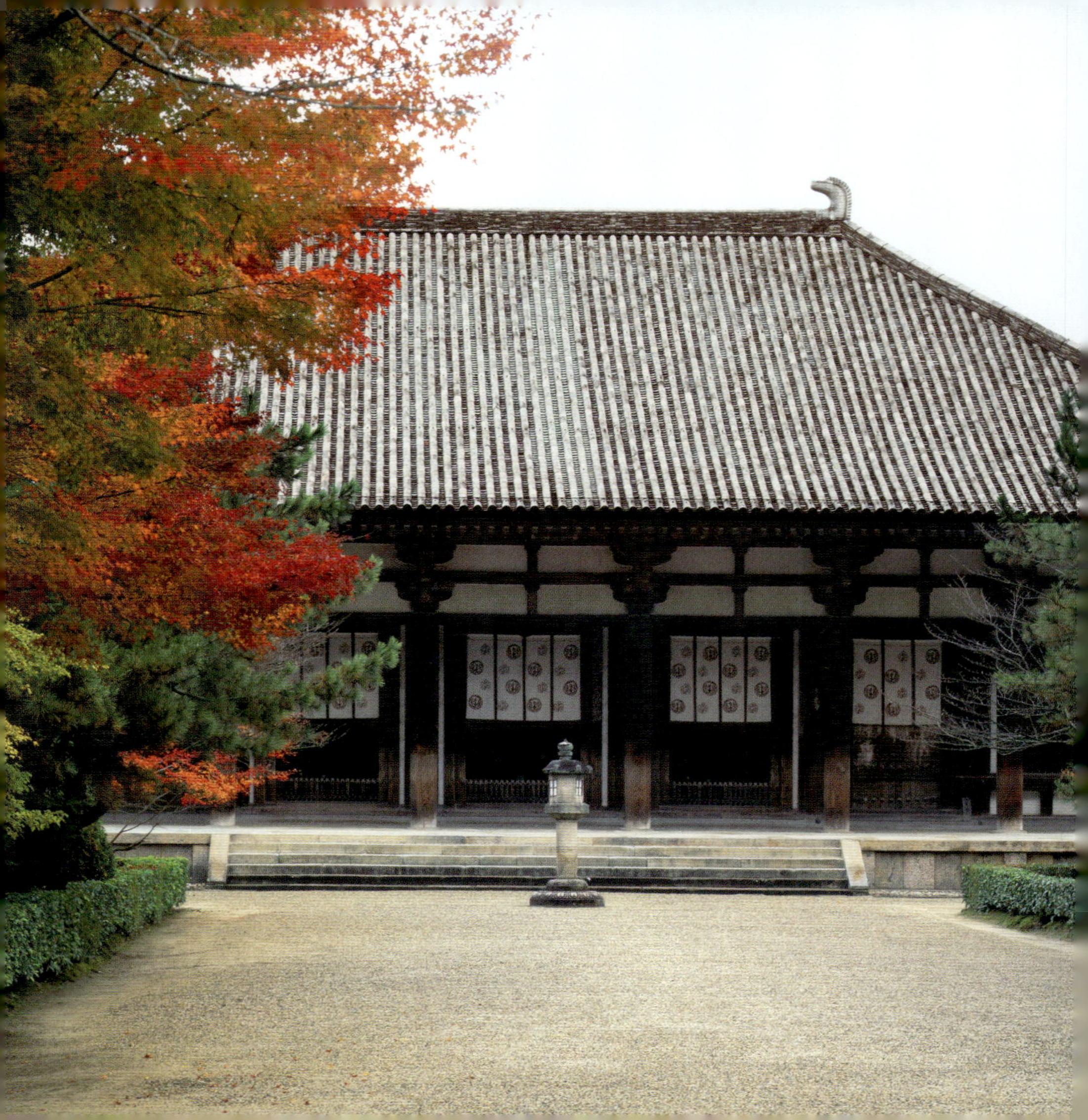

Toshodai-ji Kondo

759 CE Nara, Kansai, Japan

COMMISSIONED BY Emperor Shomu   **LAST REBUILT** 2009
MATERIALS Wood, ceramic tiles

The Golden Hall (kondo) of this Nara Era temple is one of the greatest exemplars of classical Chinese-inspired architecture in Japan. It was founded by Ganjin (688–763), a Chinese monk who came to Japan because the Emperor Shomu (r. 724–48) had requested a priest to regulate practices. In preparation for his mission, Ganjin spent years gathering scriptures, icons and ritual objects, but his attempts to arrive by sea met with several disastrous shipwrecks, each one followed by another period of years preparing the necessary materials. When, after six attempts, he finally arrived in 754, he was blind, perhaps the result of his tragedies at sea. The Japanese, impressed by his determination and devotion, constructed the buildings of Toshodai-ji according to his specifications. Among his important accomplishments were regulation of the ordination of monks and establishment of rules of conduct, the ancient Indian vinaya. The name 'Toshodai' is Japanese for 'invited from Tang China', a reference to Ganjin. The large image hall, or kondo, is part of a great temple compound that includes several important buildings, including a pagoda, lecture hall, treasure house and sutra storehouse, all of which are listed as national treasures. The great altar at the centre of the kondo bears images of a new school of teaching introduced into Japan: the Cosmic Buddha, whose large-lobed halo carries 1,000 small Buddhas; a 1,000-armed, 11-headed standing Kannon; the Bodhisattva of Compassion; and the Healing Buddha. Clay images of the personification of the moon and sun flank the platform, along with the Heavenly Guards of the Four Directions.

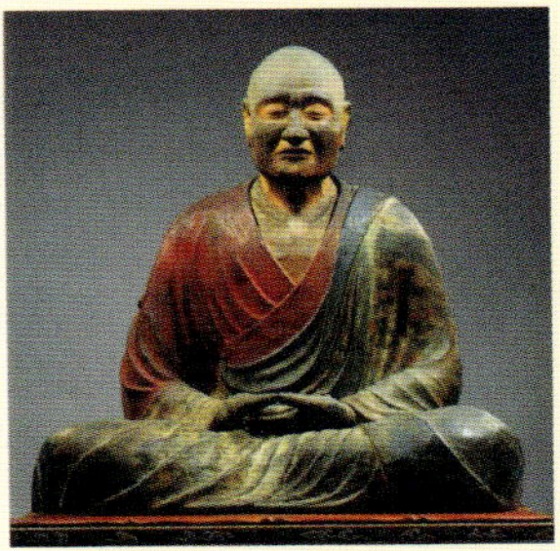

Portrait of Ganjin

Soon after Ganjin's death, disciples commissioned a portrait of him. Made of dry lacquer, the sculpture depicts him as bald and wearing monastic robes, his eyes closed in meditation. The artists, working in the Chinese naturalistic style of the era, skillfully rendered his frail body, his hands in meditative posture and his deeply concentrated facial expression. The artists were restricted by their dry-lacquer technique, which did not allow the sculptural definition of the figure to be any deeper.

With this wealth ...
We have resolved to create this venerable object of worship.'

EMPEROR SHOMU (743 CE)

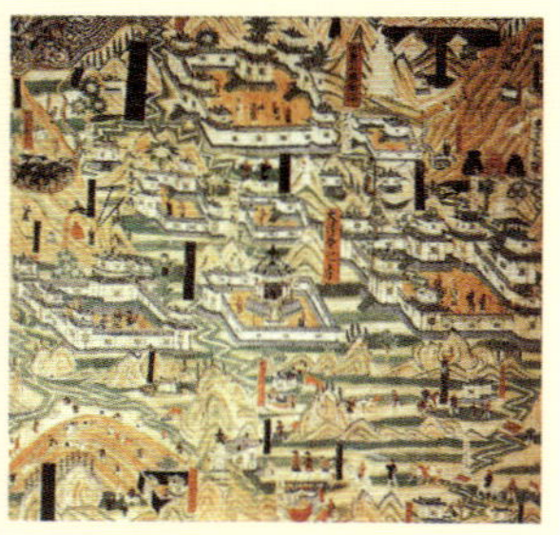

Cave 61, Dunhuang

Wutaishan was such a popular pilgrimage place, and so vast a complex, that 10th-century artists at the Dunhuang Buddhist caves in Gansu province painted a mural to map out all of its details. Not only did they recreate the many temples located among the peaks of the mountain – the number rose to 360 – and carefully label all of the buildings with small panels of writing, but they also depicted the mountain roads that led to it, recorded mystical apparitions that had occurred, and showed many of the area's visitors and local residents.

'Once he alone suddenly saw five beams of light shining ... into the hall.'

EDWIN REISCHAUER, *ENNIN'S TRAVELS IN T'ANG CHINA* (1955)

Wutaishan

c. 8th–9th century CE   Mt. Wutai, Shanxi, China

AREA OF MOUNTAIN 2,837 sq km/1,095 sq miles   HIGHEST PEAK 3,061 m/10,043 ft   AVERAGE PEAK HEIGHT 1,000 m/3,280 ft

Mountains are sacred sites in China; elevated and closer to heaven, they are used for worship. According to legend, Wutaishan, the tallest mountain in northern China, has been a Buddhist sanctuary since the 1st century CE, when a foreign monk identified the site as the home of the Bodhisattva Manjusri, Buddhist god of wisdom, who is believed to be the only god to have been born in China. Places of worship have been established there since the medieval period. Despite the ravages of history and anti-Buddhist campaigns, a brick pagoda dating to the Northern Wei Dynasty (386-534 CE) is still intact. There are also two wooden image halls with murals, and large-sized altars with polychrome sculptural icons constructed during the Tang dynasty (618–906). The arrangement of icons on one, the altar of Foguansi (857), replicates the mountain's unique geomorphology of five peaks. Wutaishan became the focus of worship of Manjusri. The *Mahavaipulya Buddhavatamsaka Sutra*, compiled in the 3rd and 4th century CE, states: 'To the north-east there is the Mountain Coolness, where Bodhisattvas often take up residence. The current occupant is a Bodhisattva by the name of Manjusri who lives there with 10,000 members.' Manjusri is identifiable by his lion mount, sword (representing sharp mindedness) and five coils of hair (signifying wisdom). At the height of the Wutaishan complex's importance, during the Tang era, hundreds of monks travelled from India, Nepal, Sri Lanka, Myanmar (Burma), Vietnam, Korea and Japan to study there. Wutaishan has been home to Tibetan Buddhism since the Yuan dynasty (1271–1368).

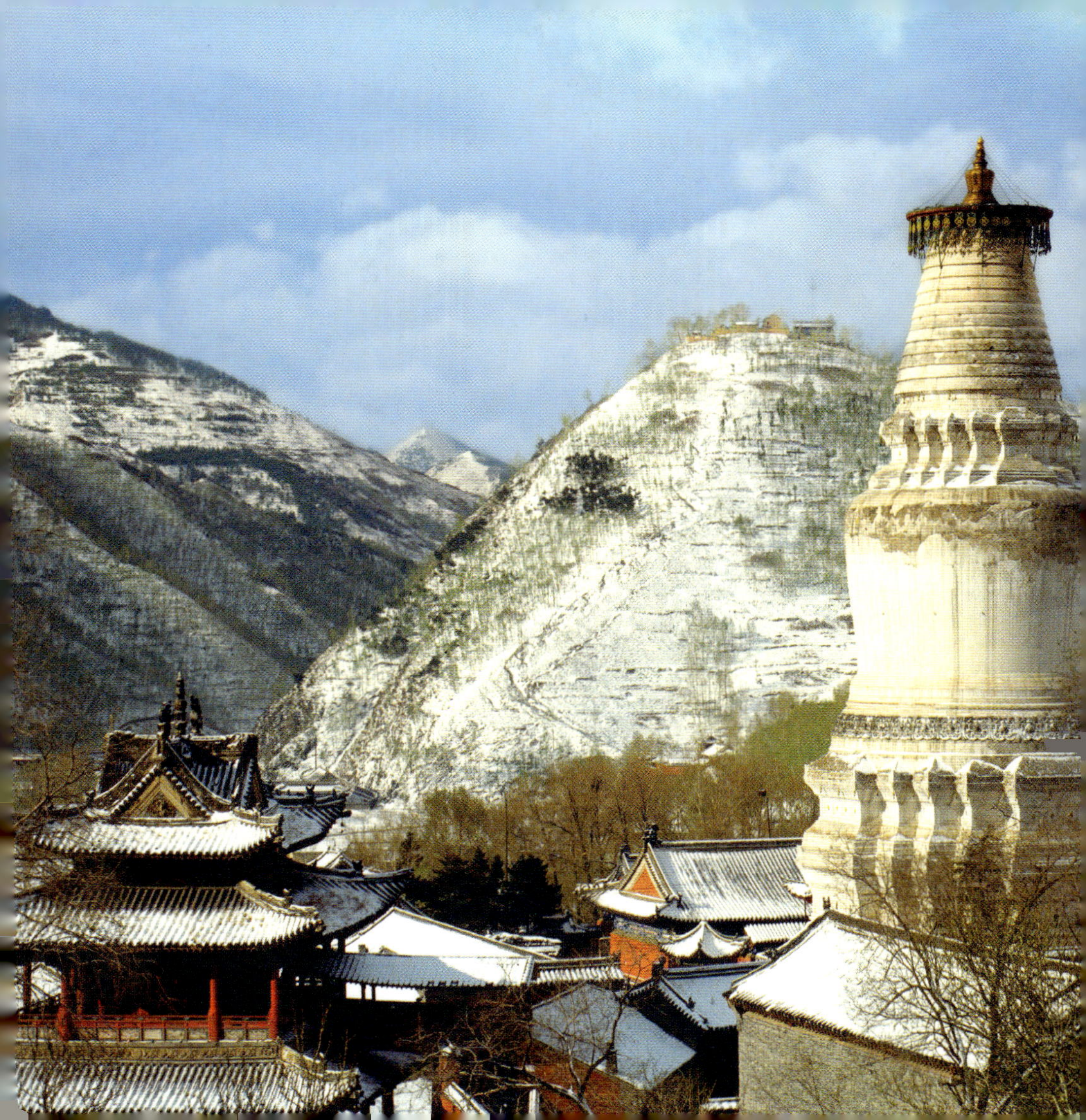

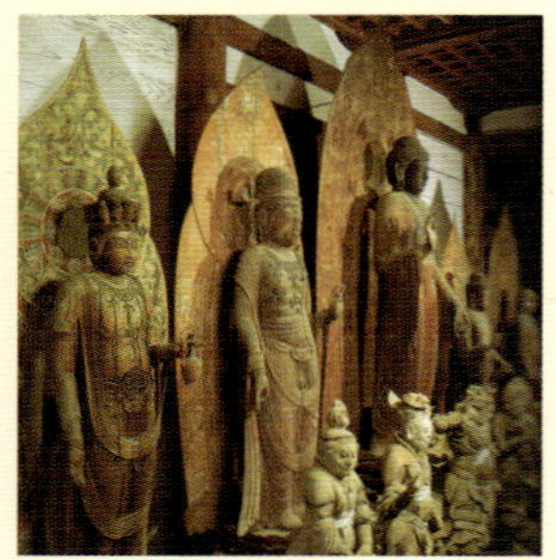

Esoteric Icons

In addition to traditional icons of the Buddha, the altar of the *kondo* at Muryo-ji features representations of the deities of esoteric Buddhism, which flourished in Japan during the Heian period (794–1185). Including the Eleven-headed Kannon (Bodhisattva of Compassion) and fierce warrior guardians, these often had an extraordinary appearance. The deities are sculpted from wood, sometimes from a single tree trunk, and are moderate in size.

'A rather literary, poetic mood ... dominates the whole scene.'

TAKAAKI SAWA, *ART IN JAPANESE ESOTERIC BUDDHISM* (1976)

Muro-ji Kondo

c. 9th century CE **Uda, Nara, Kansai, Japan**

COMMISSIONED BY Emperor Temmu   **STYLE** Esoteric (Shingon) Buddhist
MATERIALS Wood, thatch and stone

In the mid-9th century CE, turmoil in China ended in xenophobic rage and the expulsion of foreigners. In its isolation, Japan developed its own aesthetic. When the Japanese capital moved to Heian (modern-day Kyoto), the aristocracy sponsored the construction of new temples. The absence of foreign influences, combined with the new doctrine of esoteric Buddhism popular at the time, led to a new type of temple architecture. In particular, esoteric Buddhism held that everything, from the smallest mote of dust to the entire cosmos, is the Cosmic Buddha; thus, native Shinto deities and teachings came to be seen as parallel to Buddhist ones. Chinese temples had been built to grand, symmetrical plans requiring large tracts of flat land, but the Kyoto architects began to invent ingenious techniques to situate their temples in the mountains encircling Kyoto. At Muro-ji, all the buildings rest on the slope of a low mountain that overlooks a minor river. Near the top of the mountain is the pagoda, and midway up is the *kondo*, or image hall. The latter building adopts Japanese rural architecture, materials and building techniques. It is of a large farmhouse construction, topped by a thatched roof (still supported by Chinese bracketing) rather than tiles, and raised on piles to eliminate contact with ground moisture. Large stones support the front of the building, and wooden pillars prop up the rear. The main hall has a later portico. The native Japanese religious appreciation of man's harmonious relationship with nature is evident in how the manmade structure is fitted unobtrusively into the divine mountains.

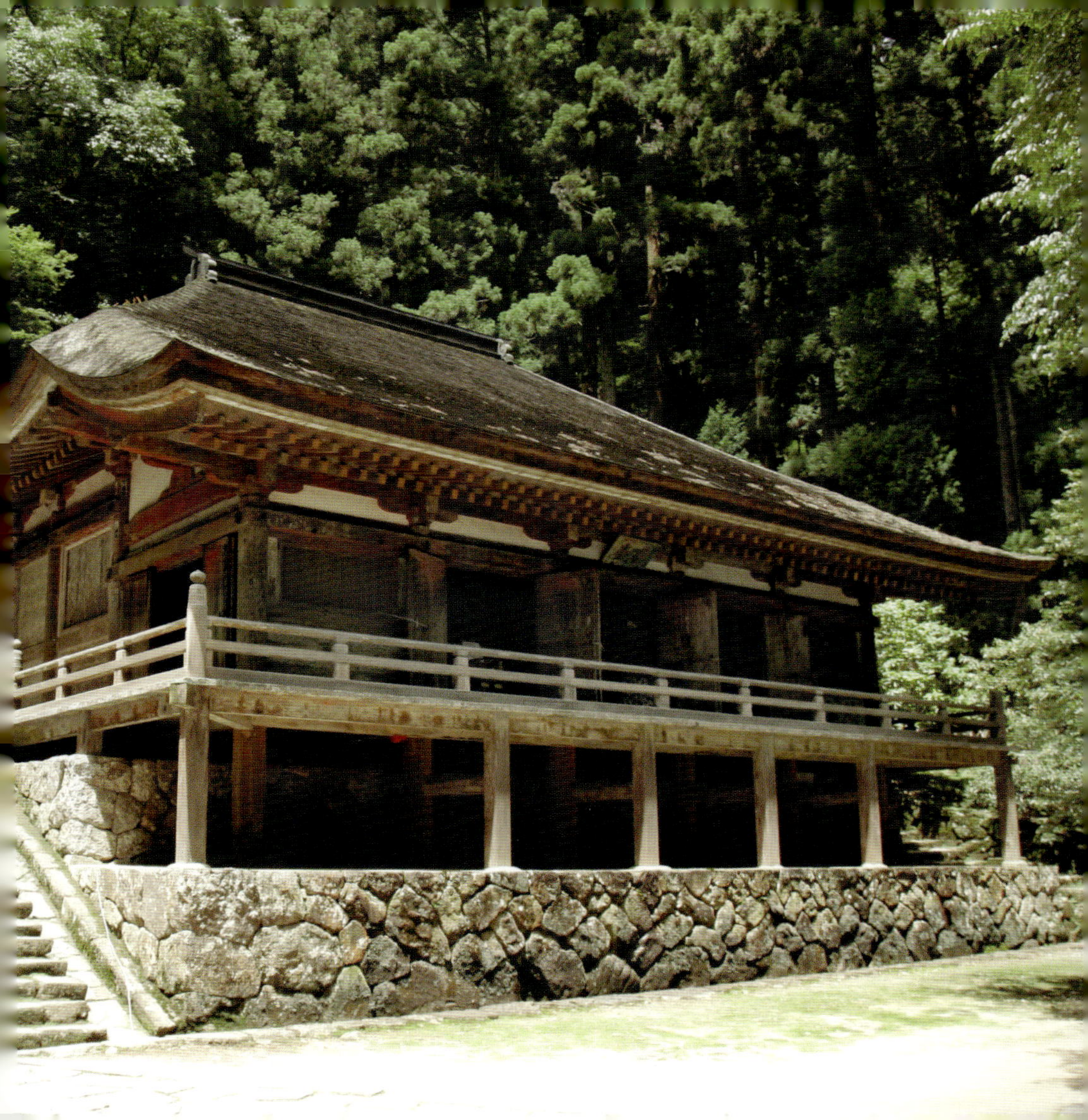

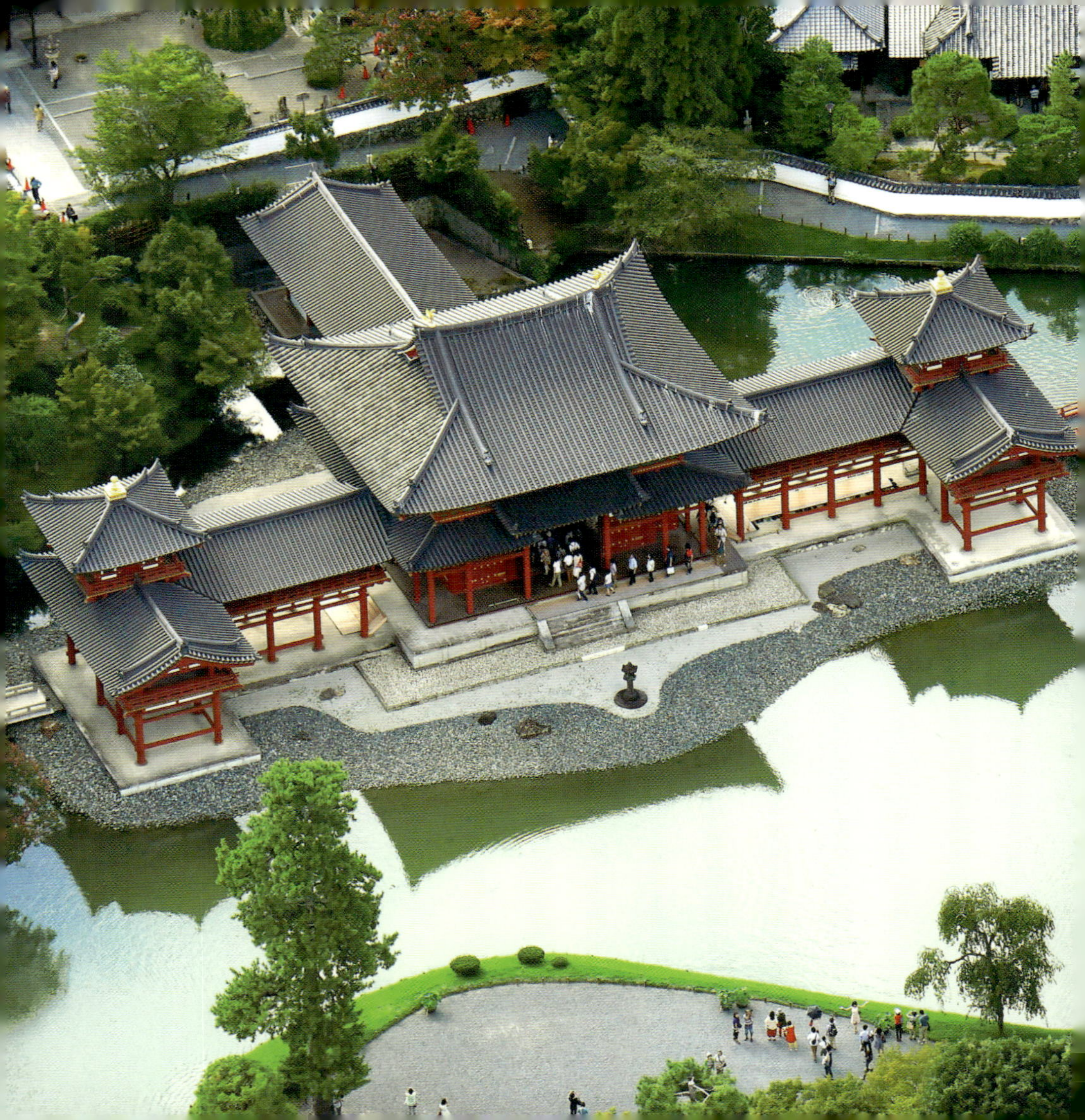

Byodo-in Phoenix Hall

1052 CE Uji, Kyoto, Japan

COMMISSIONED BY Minister Fujiwara no Yorimichi **MATERIALS** Wood and tiles **AREA OF PONDS AND ISLANDS** 0.8 ha/2 ac.

Buddhist theology holds that the world evolves continuously in cycles of birth and destruction. In times of the absence of the Buddha the world gradually degenerates, until its imminent total annihilation, or *mappo*, which is heralded by the Buddha's death. The birth of a new Buddha initiates another cycle. Buddhists anticipate the era of destruction when they witness growing moral corruption, and they use mathematical formulations to predict when destruction will occur after the death of the Buddha. Because the threat of *mappo* was predicted for the early 11th century, Fujiwara no Yorimichi (922–1074), a nobleman in Kyoto, in the hope of salvation in a degenerate world, turned his luxurious villa into a temple to worship Amida. Yorimichi had the landscaping remapped as a large pond partly filled by islands that appear to float. The villa, reconfigured into a central Buddha hall, is an adaptation of traditional Japanese one-storey structures that are raised above the ground. Twin pavilions are connected to the hall by covered aisles, and a long corridor extends from the rear. All are covered by uniform tiled roofing. The ensemble resembles a descending immortal phoenix with outspread wings perched at the water's edge. This and the paradisiacal setting of lush gardens help to create a vision of the Western Paradise of the Buddha of the West. When Emperor Goreizei (r. 1045–68) visited in 1067, there was music and a recitation of Buddhist texts. Belief in the Western Paradise was strong; one noble devotee had his priest and monks dress up as Amida and his twenty-five bodhisattvas and assemble around his deathbed.

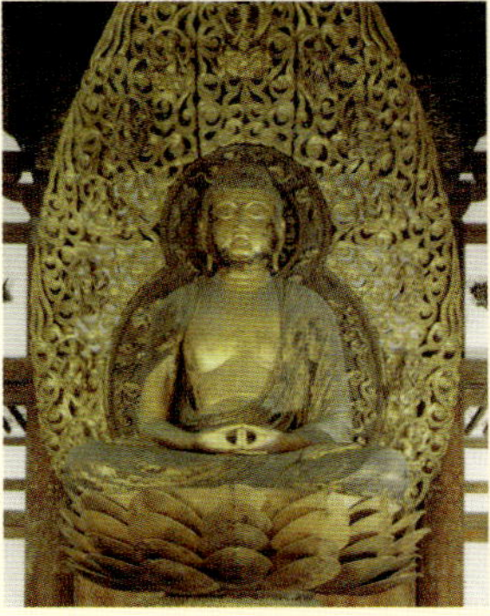

Seated Amida Buddha of Western Paradise

Inside the Phoenix Hall, the image hall of Byodo-in Temple, a gilded wooden Buddha of the Western Paradise, 3 metres (10 ft) high, sits in meditation; the surrounding walls are adorned by fifty-two small wooden angels playing music, with murals representing Amida's descent to earth.

'Regent Michinaga (966–1028) sought in his final moments to facilitate Amida's descent to lead him to the pure land...'

PAUL VARLEY, *JAPANESE CULTURE* (2000)

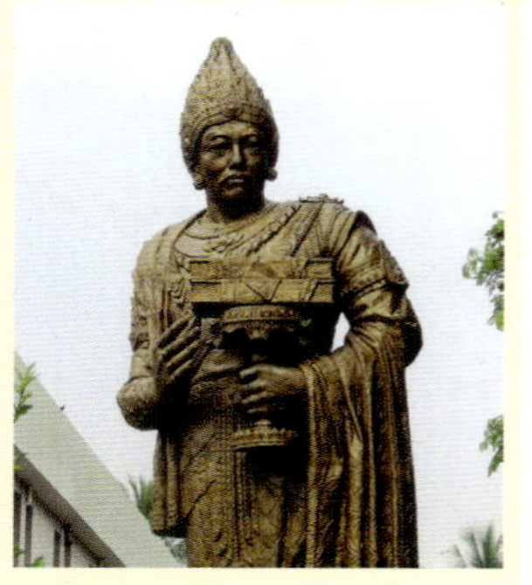

Royal Patron

When, in 1057, the Buddhist King Anawrahta (above) requested a copy of the *Tripitaka*, the Buddhist teachings, from Manuha, King of the Mon Kingdom of Thaton, he was refused. He then invaded Thaton, took relics of the Buddha's hair and built Shwesandaw to enshrine them.

'The Buddha hath the causes told/Of all things springing from causes/ And also how things cease to be/ 'Tis this the Mighty Monk proclaims.'

VOTIVE TABLET BY KING ANAWRAHTA

Shwesandaw Pagoda

1057 CE **Bagan, Myanmar (Burma)**

COMMISSIONED BY King Anawrahta **MATERIALS** Stone and brick
DECORATION Terracotta plaques (now missing) **HEIGHT** 100 m/328 ft

Tradition asserts that Emperor Ashoka (3rd century BCE) sent two Buddhist monks from India to Myanmar (Burma), where the religion thrives until the present day. In the capital of Bagan (9th–13th century) royal patrons built over 2,000 brick Buddhist monuments: there is evidence of 900 temples, 500 stupas, 400 monasteries, and 30 libraries and ordination halls. Shwesandaw Pagoda, sponsored by King Anawrahta (1044–77) and built in the early Bagan style, has a dome of elongated, ovoid shape, supported by drums resting on five square terraces of diminishing size, with a staircase at the centre of each side. The stupa, originally unpainted, is topped with a golden multi-tiered *hti*, or spire, in the shape of a series of ceremonial umbrellas fused together. Here, some elements of the Indian stupa prototype have been altered; most notably, the five terraces have been added. However, the decorations, hundreds of terracotta plaques with depictions from *jatakas* (tales of the previous lives of the Buddha) that formerly encircled the terraces, reflect the bas-reliefs of north Indian prototypes. In native Burmese style, replicas of the stupa finials adorn the corners of each of the terraces, and sculptures of local gods protect the four sides of the terraces. Worshippers climb the stairs before circumambulating the stupa. Deep within the temple is a chamber that contains sacred hairs of the Buddha, with small images made of sandalwood, glass, gold or ivory, scriptures and votive plaques. In this early period, one of the beneficial attributes of a Buddhist stupa was its spiritual protective function, and such massive temples brought a sense of peace to the inhabitants.

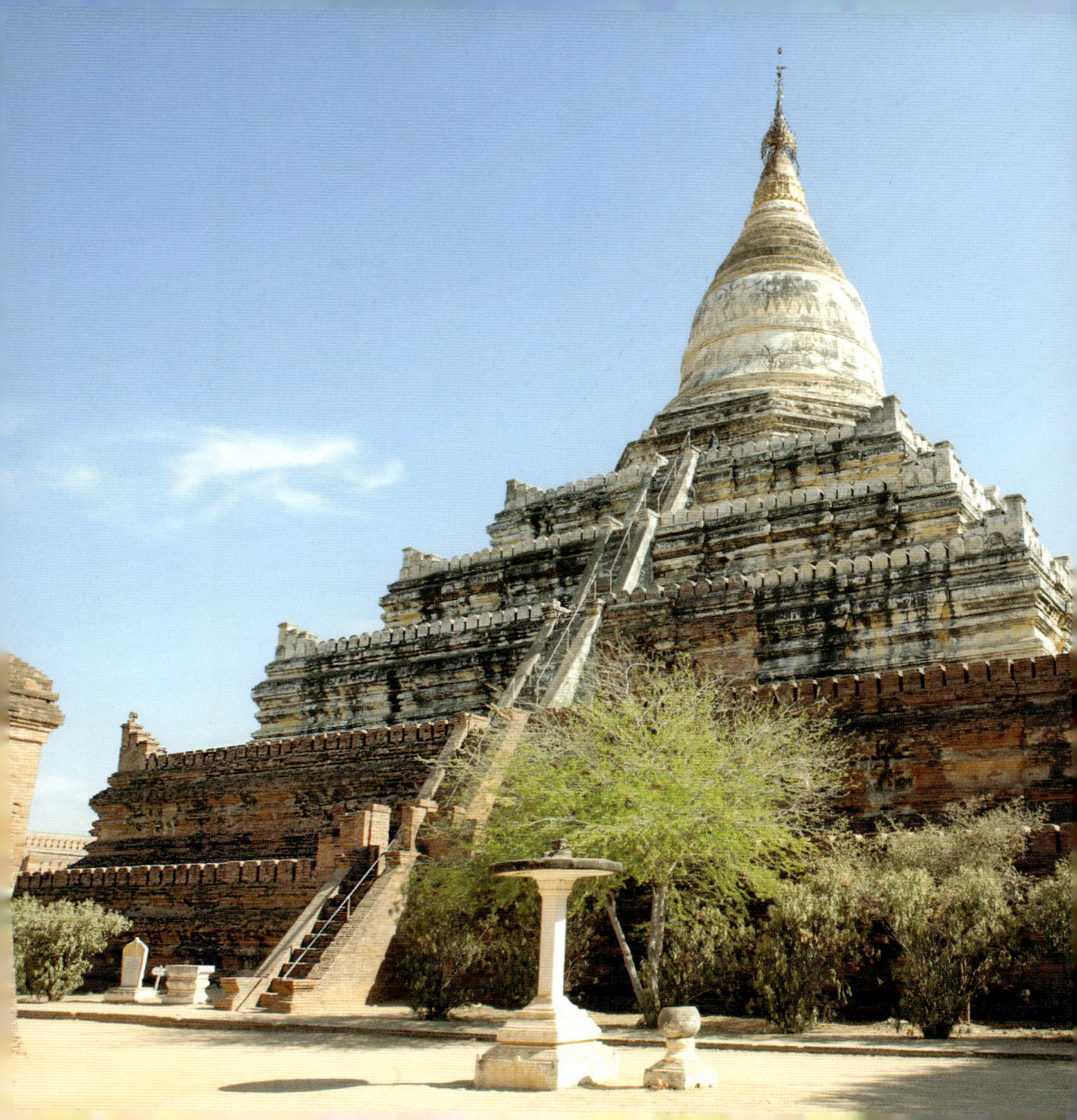

Tianning Temple Pagoda

c. 1100–19 CE **Changzhou, Jiangsu, China**

COMMISSIONED BY Buddhist Association of China   **MATERIAL** Stone, wood
AREA OF SITE 57,000 sq m/613,500 sq ft   **HEIGHT** 153.79 m/505 ft

After the period of the Cultural Revolution (1966–76), when the practice of religions was suppressed, the Chinese government relaxed its policies and began to allow the restoration of Buddhist and Daoist temples for public use. Fundraising on a local, national and international level enabled the rebuilding of monuments that were destroyed in the past. Although the Tianning Pagoda at Changzhou is new, it is part of a temple compound that was established in the Tang dynasty period (618–906 CE). Tianning Temple, one of the four largest Zen Buddhist temples in China, was destroyed and rebuilt five times over a period of 1,350 years. Thanks to the determined fundraising efforts of Songchun, abbot of Tianning Temple, in 2007 the Buddhist Association of China, together with other Buddhist groups, raised enough money to begin construction of the Tianning Temple Pagoda or Heavenly Tranquility Pagoda; it took five years to finish. The massive octagonal tower, built in the Chinese style, sits on a three-tiered white marble base. The structure has thirteen storeys of uniform depth, each topped by an upturned tile roof supported by traditional bracketing. At the top of the pagoda is a golden spire and a large bronze bell weighing 30,000 kilogrammes (66,000 lb), which can be heard from a distance of 5 kilometres (3 miles). The restoration of the ancient monument attests to the financial success of this small city, located near Shanghai, while the efforts that are being expended in rebuilding and refurbishing destroyed or damaged Buddhist temples all over China demonstrates a growing renewal of faith in Buddhism in the country.

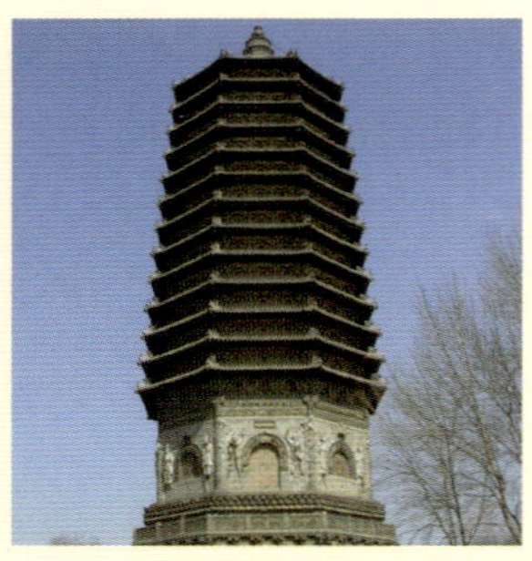

Tianning Pagoda, Beijing

Tianning Pagoda in Beijing was erected during the Liao dynasty period (916–1125 CE) on the site of a wooden pagoda constructed in 602 CE by the Sui dynasty. For this pagoda, the architects used stone to imitate the original wooden structure. The thirteen-storey tower, 57.8 metres (190 ft) tall, is a multipartite design: the tower rests on a series of six-sided stone courses, and a restricted upper section creates an hourglass-shape.

'Sit in meditation, the boundless universe is before you; Visit here by boat, the most magnificent temple is built here.'

INSCRIPTION AT CHANGZHOU

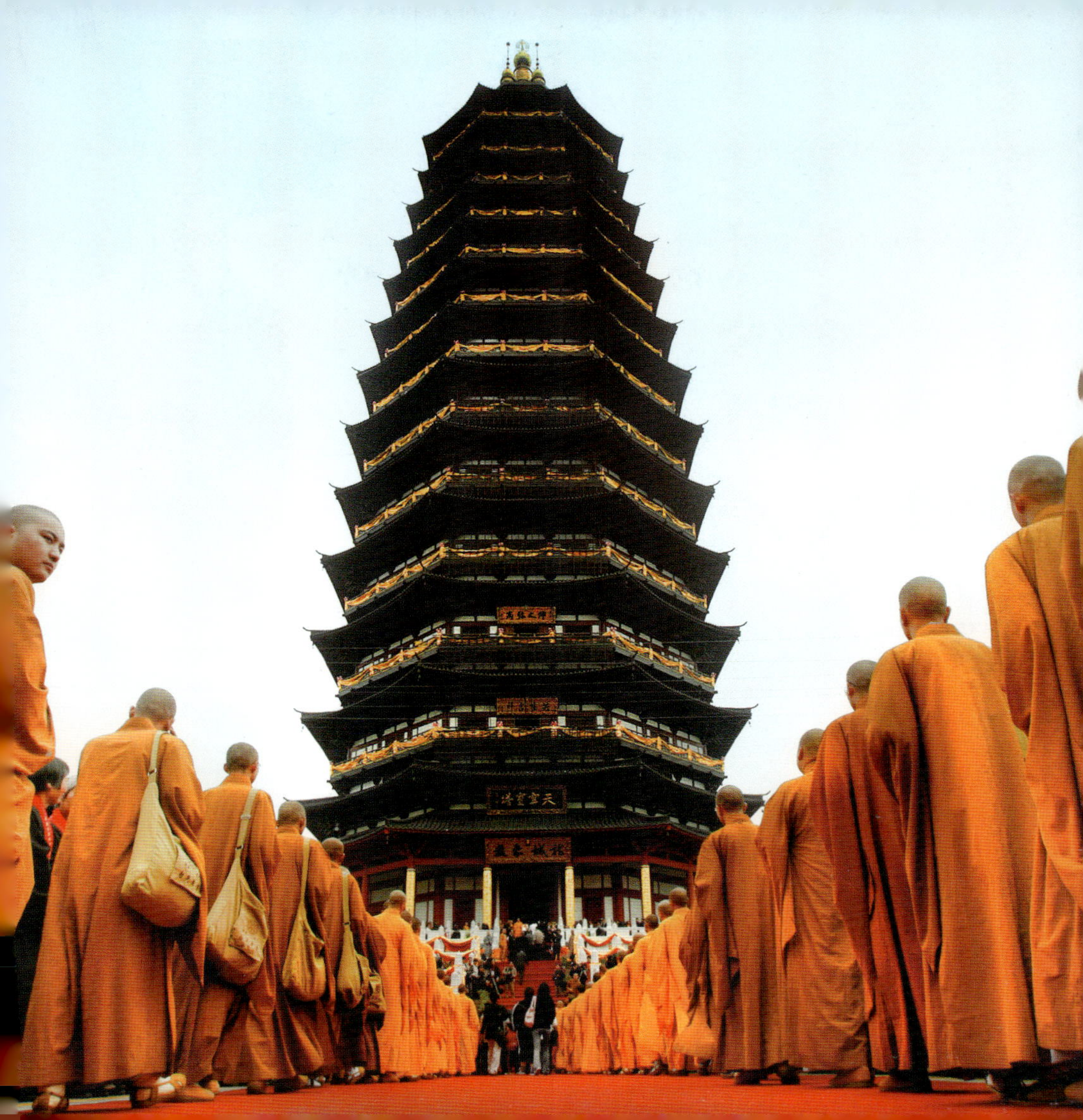

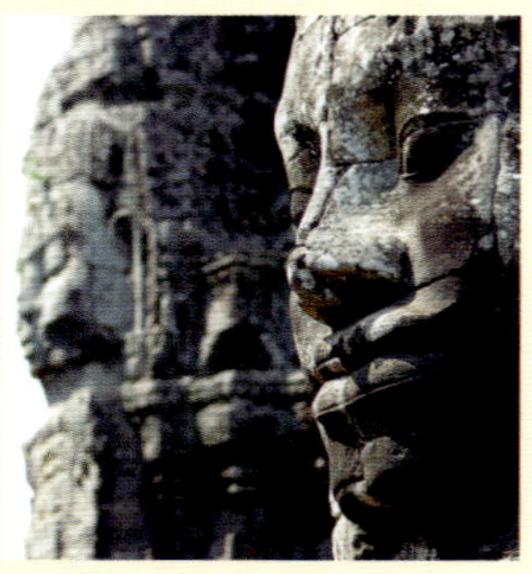

Colossal Heads

The 200 heads that look out from the four sides of the fifty towers at Bayon are said to resemble King Jayavarman VII, whose likeness was also sculpted in a number of portraits.

Angkor Bayon Temple

c. 12th century CE **Angkor Thom, Cambodia**

COMMISSIONED BY King Jayavarman VII **ABANDONED** 15th century CE **STYLE** Khmer **SURFACE AREA** 9 sq km/3.5 sq miles

King Jayavarman VII (1125–1220), who reigned over the Khmer Empire between 1181 and 1218, remains a symbolic figure of national pride for Cambodians. After his accession to the throne, he established his capital city at Angkor Thom. Like other important Buddhist kings in Asia, he inaugurated his reign with the construction of a national temple to consolidate his political and spiritual power, in the manner of Ashoka, India's first emperor. At the centre of his capital he built the state temple, the complex of Bayon. The massive structure basically comprises three receding stepped terraces; the uppermost has a central tower that rises 43 metres (141 ft) above the ground. The surrounding terraces once carried fifty towers, of which only thirty-seven survive. On each of the four sides of the towers are large-scale portraits of a beatifically smiling, bejewelled Bodhisattva Avalokiteshvara (Lokeshvara); there are 200 of these colossal heads in all. The towers and terraces are linked by covered aisles; two outer galleries enclose the temple. Mythical and historical narrative bas-relief carvings cover the walls of the galleries. The principal icon at the heart of the temple is a statue of the Buddha seated on the coils of the cobra Muchalinda; the snake's nine-headed hood protects the meditating Buddha's head. The temple's stepped terraces with their multiple towers resemble the cosmic Mount Sumeru, and the complex geometry of the ground plan may be seen as a mandala, with the power at the centre radiating outwards. Thus Bayon, being situated at the political centre of the capital city, may be seen as a cosmic model of spiritual power.

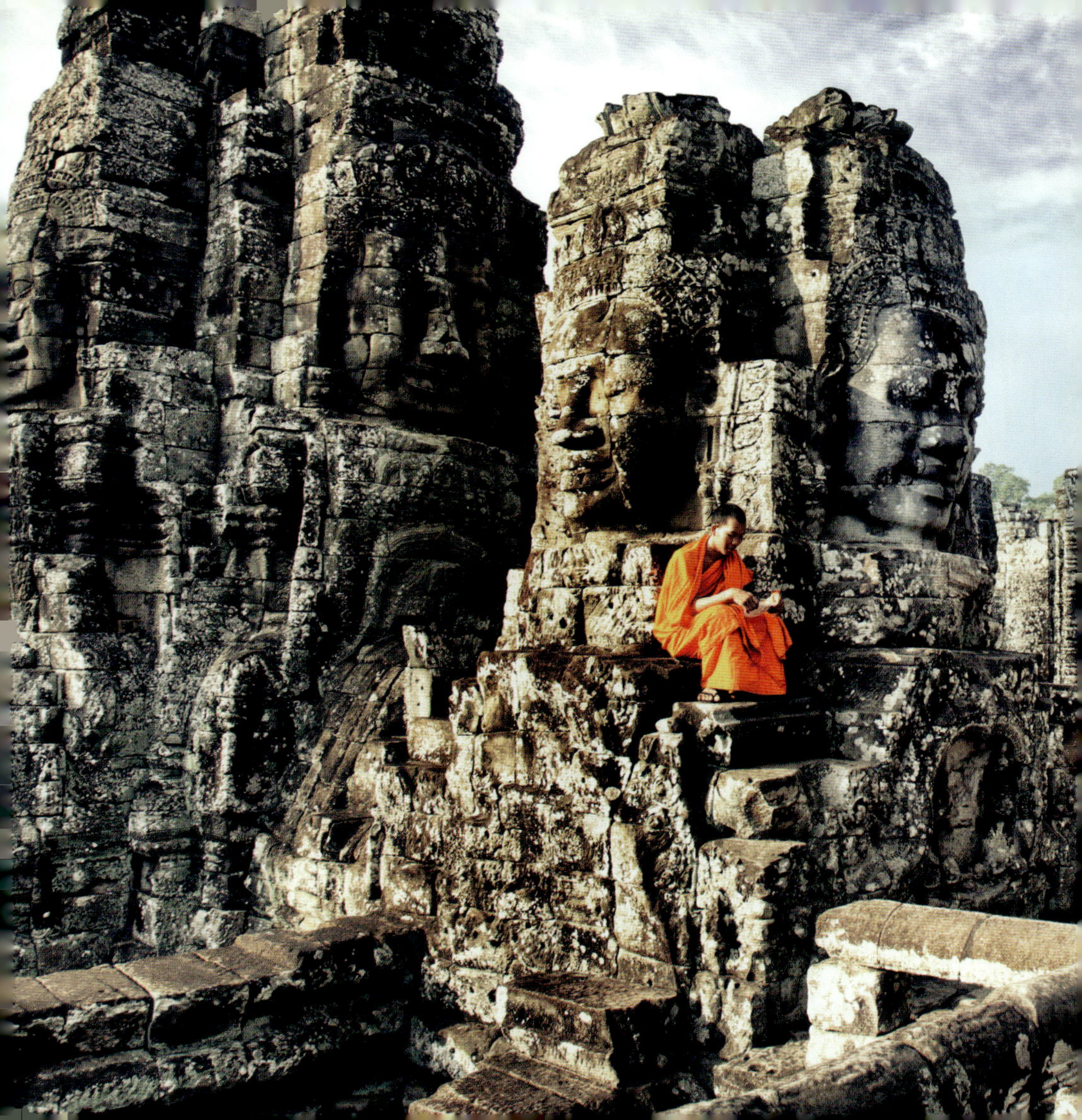

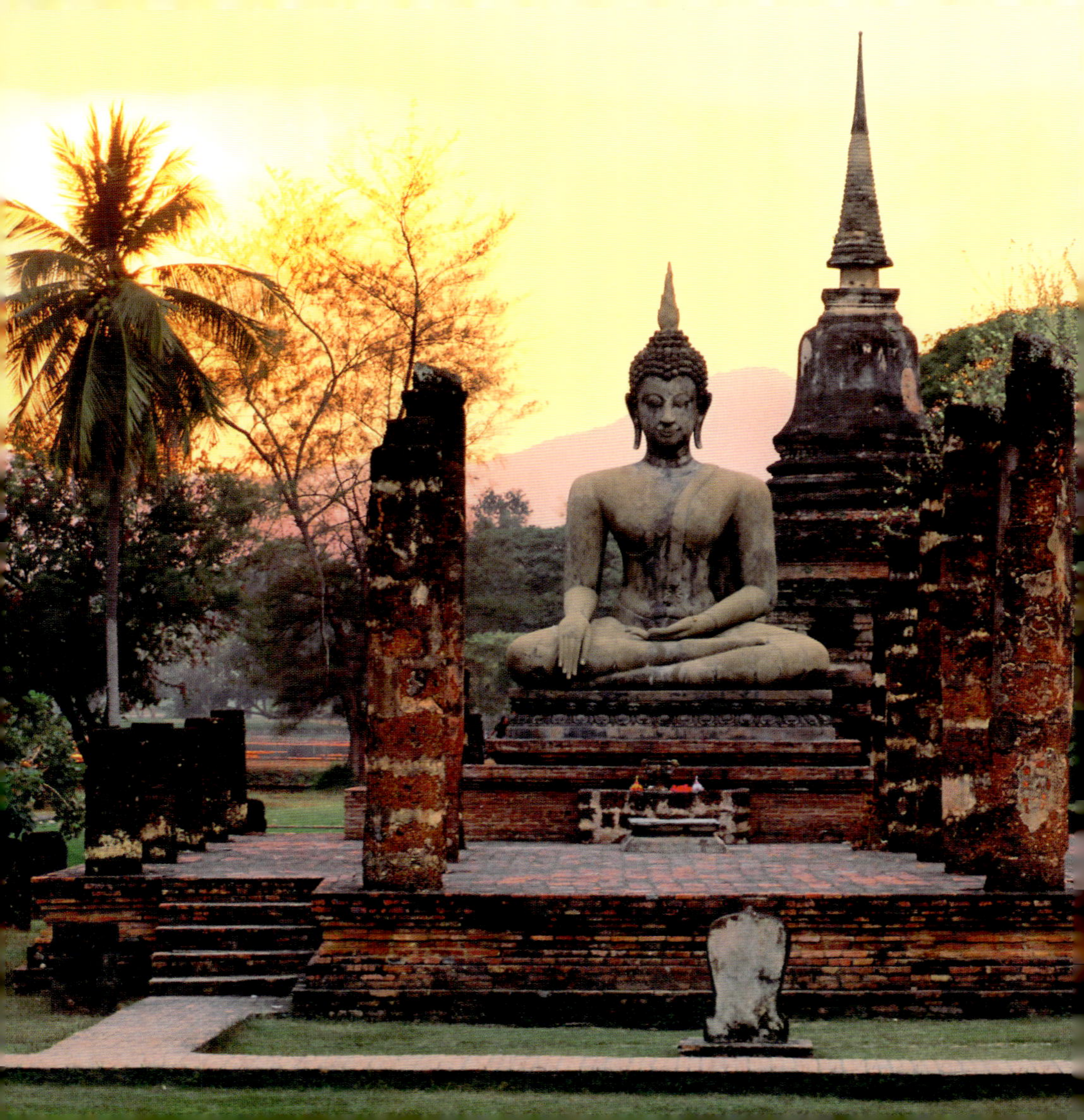

Wat Mahathat

13th–14th century CE **Sukhothai, Thailand**

COMMISSIONED BY Sri Indraditya **MATERIALS** Stone, brick
STUPAS Nine major, 200 minor **AREA** 200 sq m/2,150 sq ft

Before the formation of the Thai national state there existed independent realms that followed all three schools of Buddhism. One example is the Dvaravati kingdom of the Mon people in the south, which lasted from the 6th to the 11th century. All that changed with the rise of the Thai of Sukhodaya, who are considered the first native dynasty. They established their capital in 1238 CE and began building Buddhist temples and making sculptures. According to traditional history, in the mid-13th century King Rocaraja requested a famous image of the Buddha from the king of Sri Lanka. As a result of their subsequent relationship, Theravad, or the Way of the Elders, became the dominant school of Buddhism. The school focuses on Shakyamuni Buddha, and the monks play an important role in Thai society. Lay people support them and pray to be born as monks in the next life so that they may begin their path to enlightenment. The temple known as Wat Mahathat (the name means 'temple of the great relic') features Buddhas that are fleshy but slender, abstract in treatment with elongated limbs; a tall, flame-like finial emerges from the top of the head. The temple's stupas have bell-shaped domes supported by several round drums, with a series of umbrellas fused into a finial that rises from the dome. The image halls have pillared interiors, with an oversized Buddha seated on tall altars to the rear. Worshippers perform circumambulation, chant, pray and offer flowers, incense and candles. The court abandoned Sukhothai and moved to Ayutthaya in the south in 1350, but people still wind golden silk around the images today.

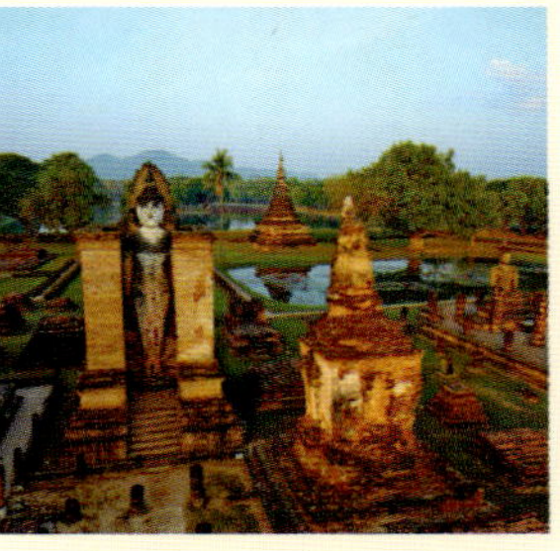

Temple Complex

Lying at the centre of the ancient city of Sukhothai, Wat Mahathat is a vast temple complex that is separated from the surrounding city by a wall. The gardens within the sanctuary are flourishing and there are several large ponds with lotus flowers. The sacred precincts contain the architectural remains of 200 *chedis* or stupas and ten *viharas* or monastic buildings. In ancient times, additional canals and ponds demarcated the area.

'He saw a Great Holy Relic of the Lord Buddha performing a miracle. He had stakes brought … to mark the spot.'

ROYAL CHRONICLES OF AYUTTHAYA

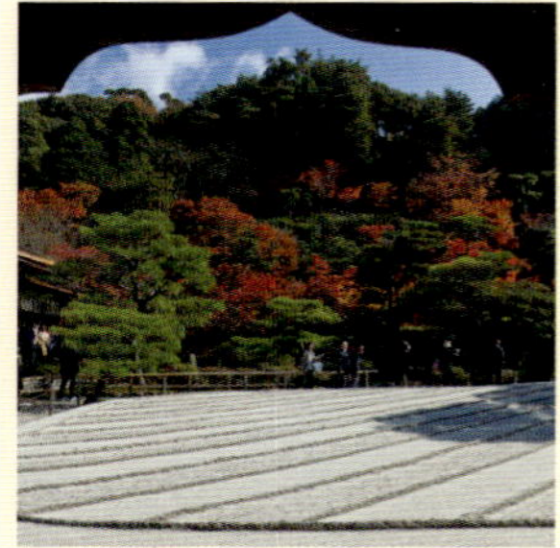

Sea of Silver

In Japan the practice of Zen Buddhism inspired the creation of a variety of types of garden. Some were composed of different mosses, or a combination of ponds and greenery; others were rock gardens or so-called dry gardens of sand. Here at Ginkaku-ji is a dry garden that represents the unchanging, eternal aspect of the universe. It is best seen from a stationary position in the moonlight. Each day monks meticulously rake its pebbles and sand into abstract configurations that suggest aspects of natural mountain forms.

'How can I show you Zen unless you first empty your cup?'

MUJU, ZEN EPIGRAM

Ginkaku-ji Temple

1490 CE **Kyoto, Japan**

COMMISSIONED BY Shogun Ashikaga Yoshimasa **MEANING** 'Temple of the Silver Pavilion' **GARDEN DESIGNER** Soami (*d.* 1525)

A retired military ruler of medieval Japan, Shogun Ashikaga Yoshimasa (1436–90) built this elegant but rustic retreat for aesthetic pleasure and as a distraction from the disastrous state of his country. Influenced by Zen practice, which found spiritual energy in all types of creative activities, the shogun personally designed this two-storey building surrounded by gardens. The architecture is a harmonious blend of temple hall and rural residency. The first floor, for the reception and entertainment of guests, follows native architectural prototypes, albeit with fine materials executed with expert craftsmanship. The upper floor, with its ogee-shaped, Indian-style windows, is for meditation. The building was never covered in silver as intended. In front of the pavilion is a pond surrounded by a large collection of oddly shaped, highly prized rocks, plants and trees. Paths lead to small bridges and islets in the ponds, from which the house can be viewed to good effect, and to ornamental miniature waterfalls in the hills. The garden changes with the passage of the four seasons, and a walk through the garden with its incidental scenes was intended to be a pleasurable journey, a respite from worldly cares. Zen philosophy, which holds that everything can be interpreted as the Buddha, informs all activities and turns them into a form of meditation. The courtiers at Ginkaku-ji practised calligraphy, poetry, music–making, the tea ceremony, incense smelling contests, and Noh dramatic plays. Through the creation and contemplation of a spare and refined aesthetic, as exemplified by Ginkaku-ji, they sought the realization of Zen principles.

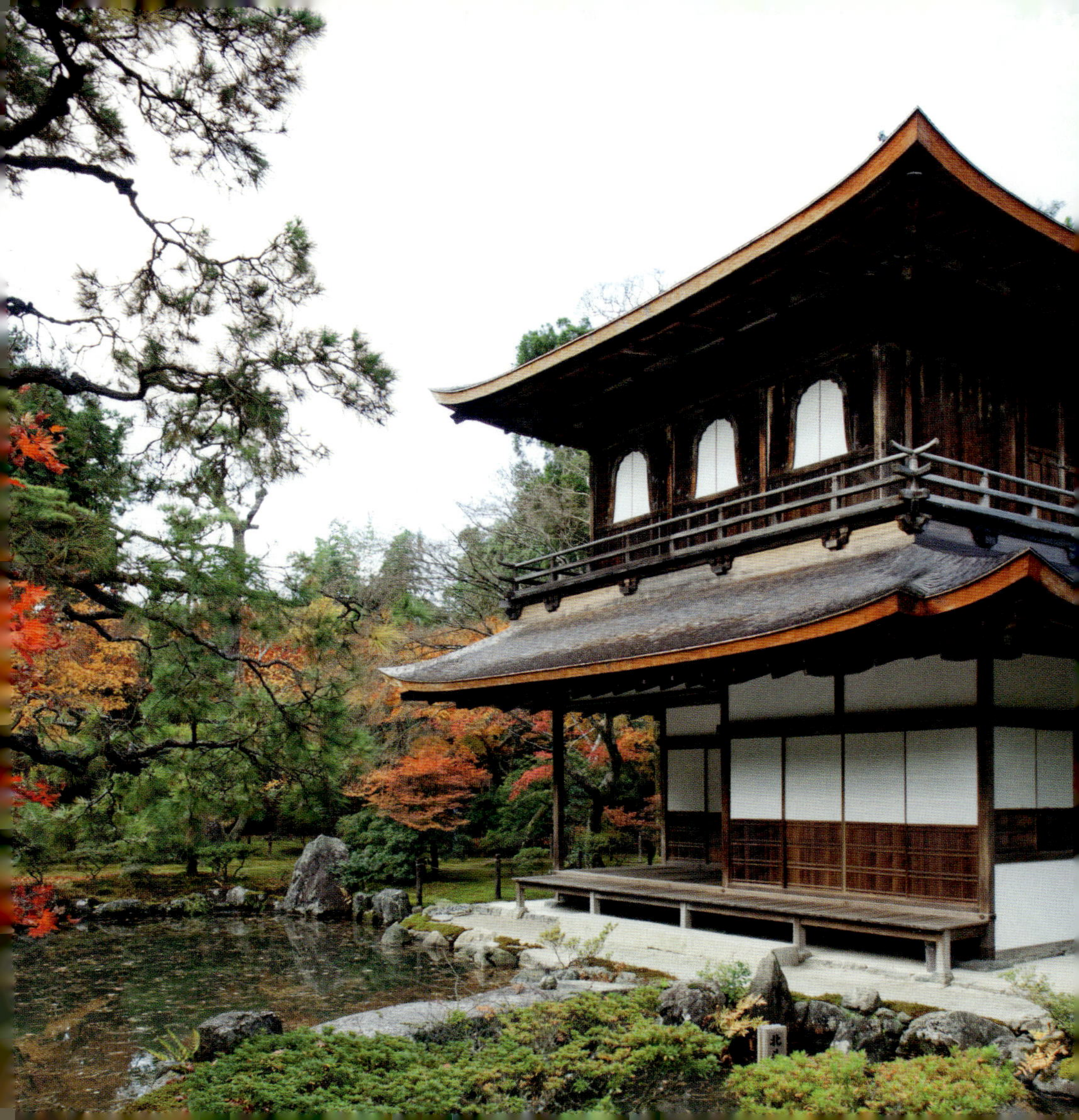

Pha That Luang Stupa

1566 CE **Vientiane, Laos**

COMMISSIONED BY King Setthathirat   **RESTORED** 1930s
AREA 4,556 sq m/49,000 sq ft   **HEIGHT** 45 m/148 ft

Throughout the Buddhist world the stupa or pagoda is not only a place for worship of the Buddha, it is also a political monument attesting to the power, influence and spiritual commitment of the donor, as well as a force to protect the local people. The stupa at Pha That Luang has undergone several major rebuilding campaigns, and the temple's history reflects the complex political events of Laos. Legend asserts that emissaries of Emperor Ashoka of India established the temple as early as the 3rd century BCE, interring a sacred breastbone relic of the Buddha beneath the structure. In the 13th century the Khmers conquered the kingdom and rebuilt the temple. King Setthathirat of Lanna, Thailand moved his capital to Vientiane in the 16th century and restored the temple after centuries of disuse. Subsequently the Burmese, Thai and Chinese attacked the temple. The French colonists tried to restore the building in 1900 but this version was unsuccessful and the temple was reconstructed to a modified design in the 1930s. Throughout Asia, the stupa has been submitted to local style variations. Here, the basic construction of the temple consists of a pyramidal shape seated on a square base, with a tall spire that looks like a simplified version of the upper railing and umbrellas of Indian design. Pra That Luang's tripartite construction symbolically represents Indian Buddhist cosmology, comprising the lower realms, earth, and heaven. On the wide base surrounding the building are thirty small, similarly shaped stupas. Covered by 500 kilogrammes (1,100 lb) of gold leaf, the Pha That Luang stupa is the national symbol of modern Laos.

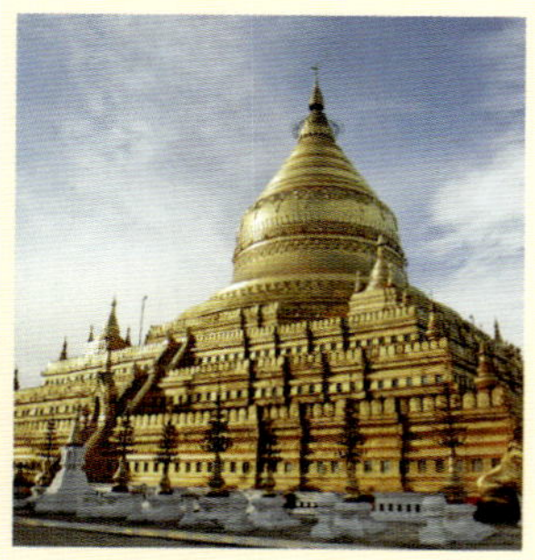

Shwedagon Pagoda

The Buddhist stupa has the same basic composition everywhere: a terraced foundation, a central mound and a superstructure in the shape of a multi-tiered umbrella. However, local influences affect the choice of building materials, shapes and proportions. The stupa at the Shwedagon Pagoda (above) in Yangon, Myanmar (Rangoon, Burma) is in the form of a delicate bell, while Pra That Luang's stupa is pyramidal in shape.

'People line the streets and give the passing monks food, earning merit in return.'

ANNE KISLENKO, *CUSTOMS AND CULTURE OF LAOS* (2009)

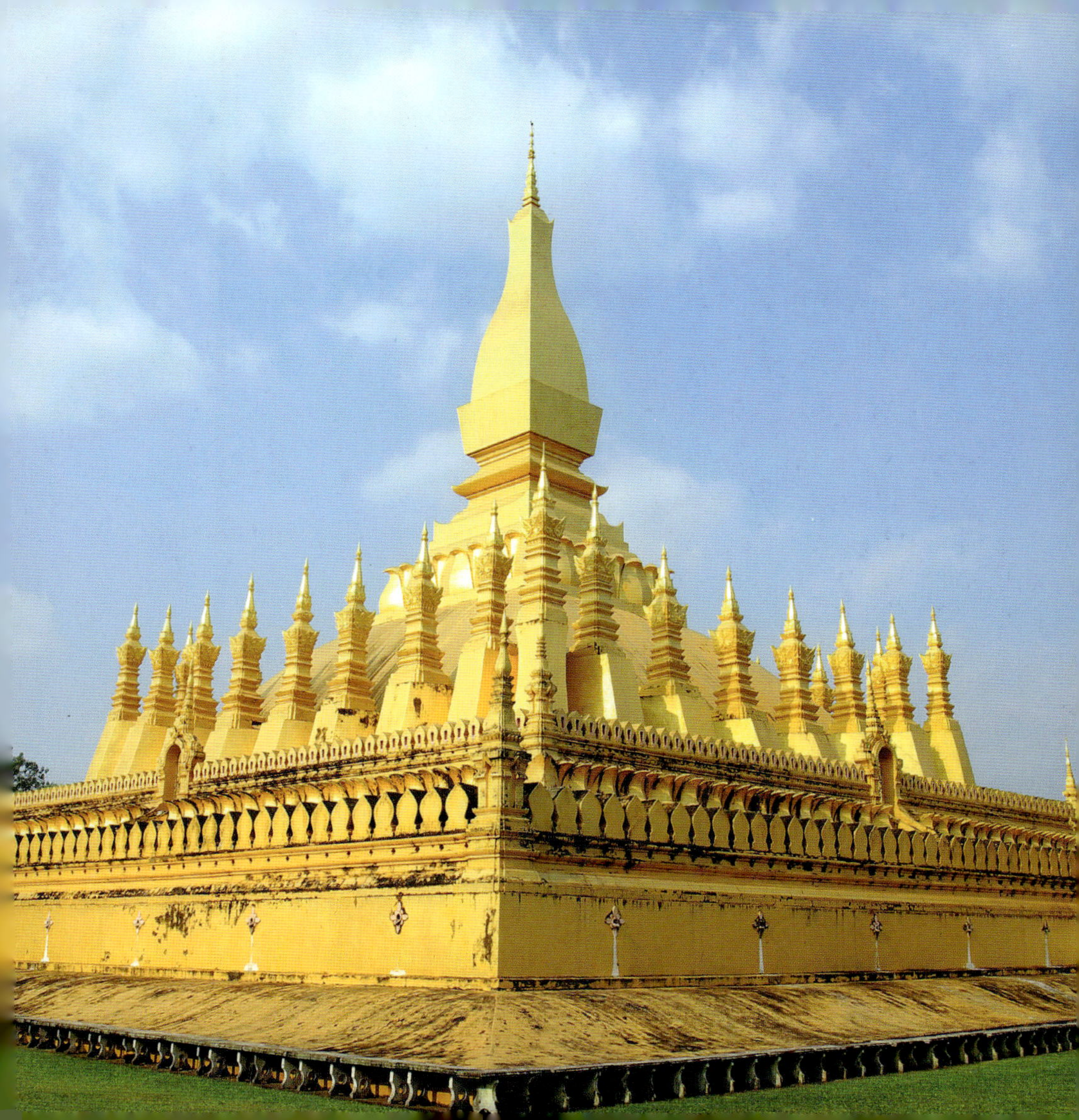

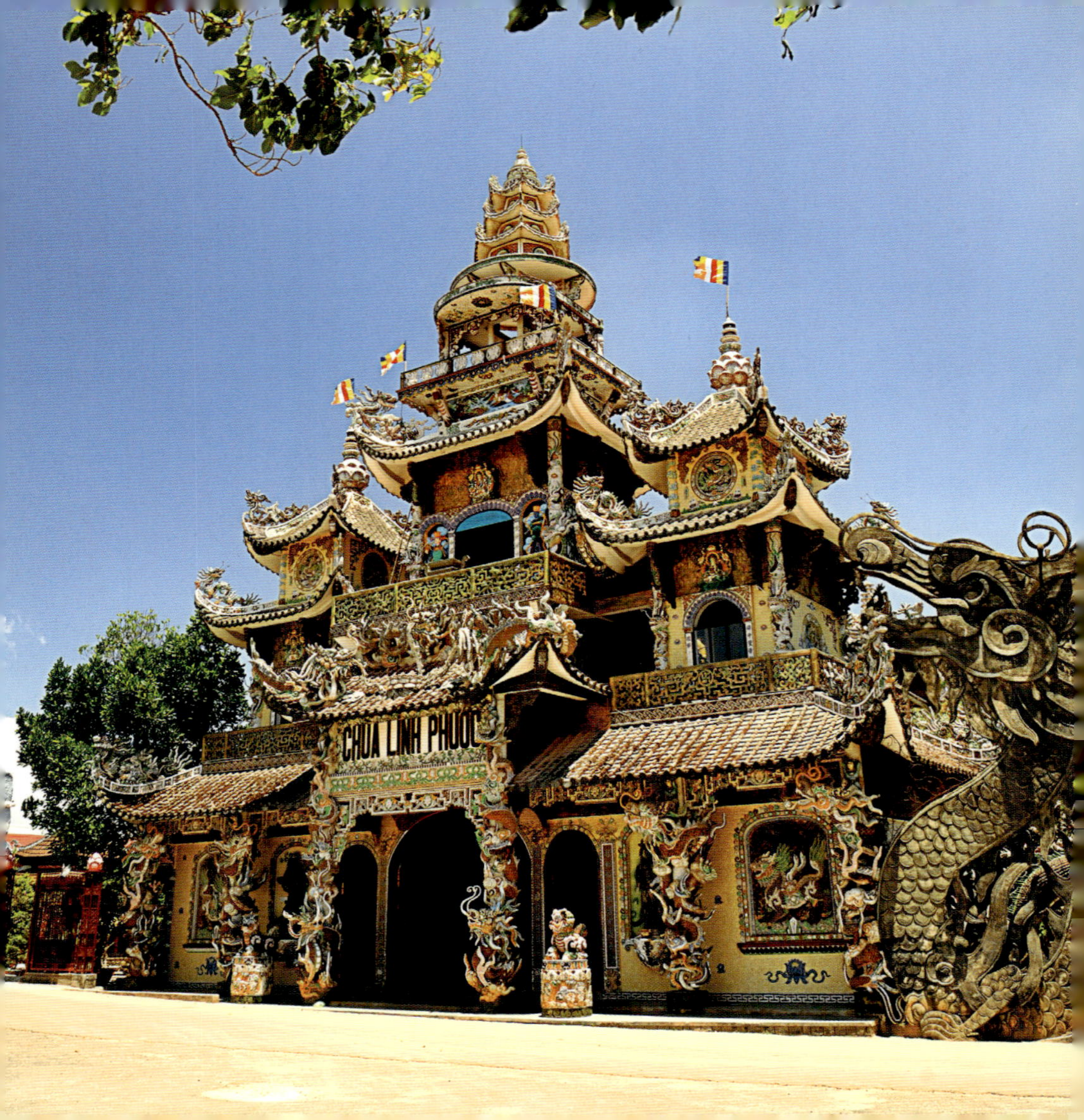

CHÙA LINH PHƯỚC

Linh Phuoc Pagoda

1952 CE **Dalat, Vietnam**

COMMISSIONED BY Mahayana Buddist monks and nuns   **RESTORED** 1990
STYLE Southern Chinese   **FLOOR AREA** 33 x 22 m / 108 x 72 ft

Open to influences from South-east Asia's sea routes and from China, with which it shares a border, Vietnam has espoused Buddhism since the 3rd century BCE. Around 1000 CE, Vietnam won independence from China, and Buddhism became the state religion. In the following centuries, Buddhism suffered in Vietnam due to uncertain conditions, foreign invasions, colonialism and, in the modern era, the rise of communist ideology in the north. Even so, a preponderance of pagodas, often the largest structures in an area, is testimony to the importance of Buddhism in Vietnam. For the most part these adopt Chinese-style construction and decoration in the shape and articulation of their receding courses, tiled, upturned roofs, bracketing and geometric profile; one example is the seven-storey, octagonal Chùa Thiên Mu pagoda near Hue, built in 1601. In contrast to these austere monuments is the Linh Phuoc Pagoda. Located near Dalat in the Vietnamese Highlands, it was built between 1949 and 1952, and restored in 1990. The builders took their inspiration from theatrical architectural designs of the Chinese opera, and from the ornate temple styles of southern China, such as those at Xiamen in Fujian province. The intricate and baroque building is also known as the Ve Chai ('pieces of broken glass bottles') Pagoda because it was created from broken porcelain and glass shards – a unique statement of faith and available materials. Near the pagoda are a bell tower, places for monks to stay, flowering gardens, many large-scale images of Buddhist deities and a 49-metre (160-ft) dragon made from 12,000 empty beer bottles.

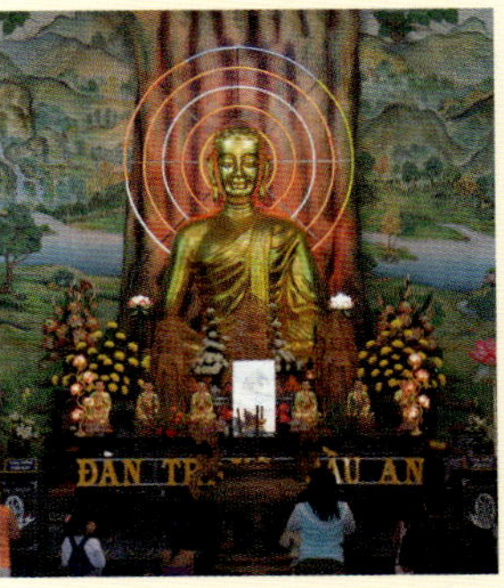

Interior Altar

At the back of the image hall is a seated meditating Buddha Shakyamuni made of concrete and gilded with gold; behind it is a painted backdrop of the local landscape. The hall also contains two rows of columns inlaid with broken glass and terracotta.

'When the envelopment of consciousness has been annihilated [a man who has approached the *Prajnaparamita* (wisdom) of the Bodhisattva] becomes free of all fear ... enjoying final nirvana.'

E.B. COWELL, *BUDDHIST MAHAYANA TEXTS* (1968)

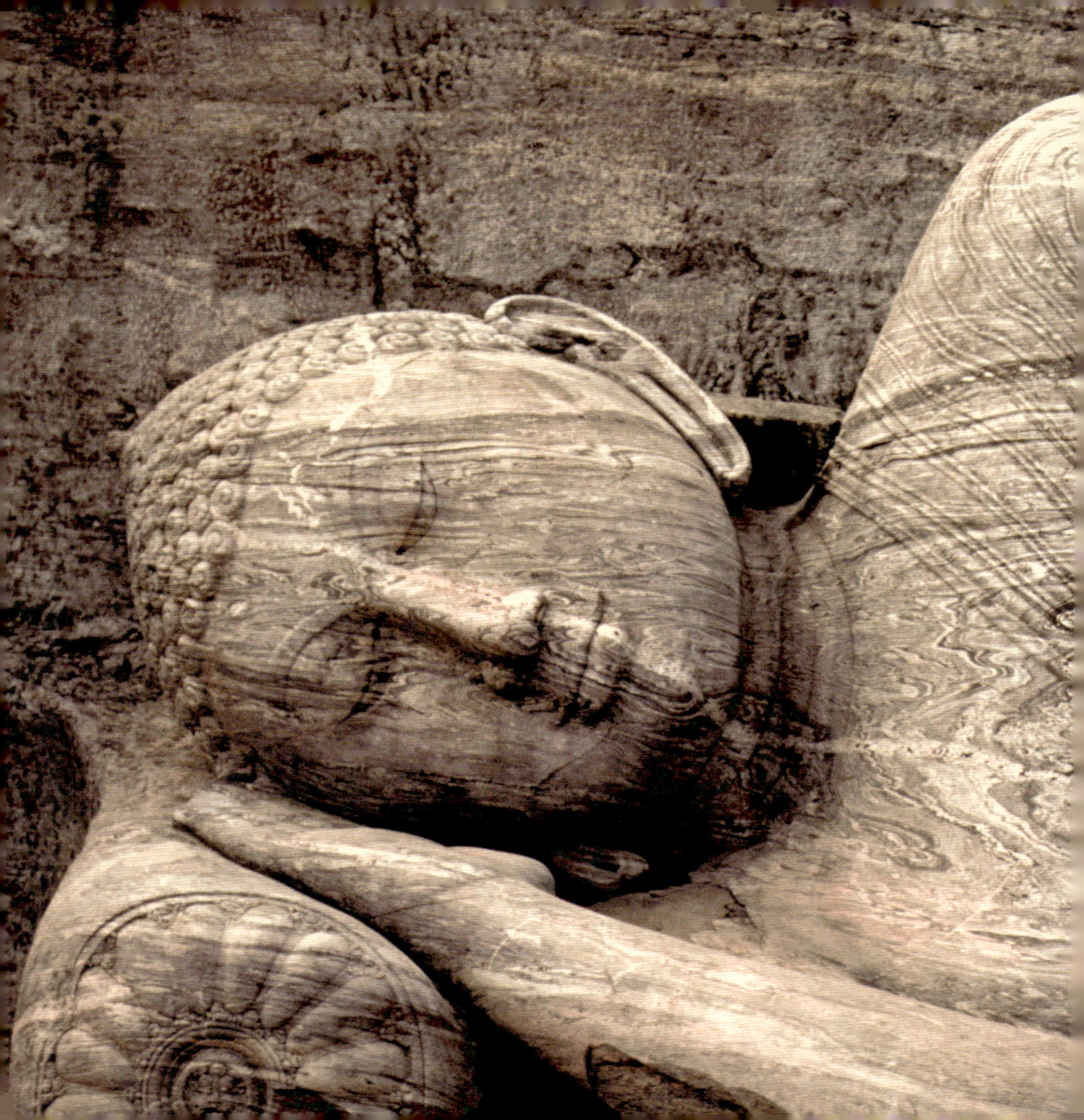

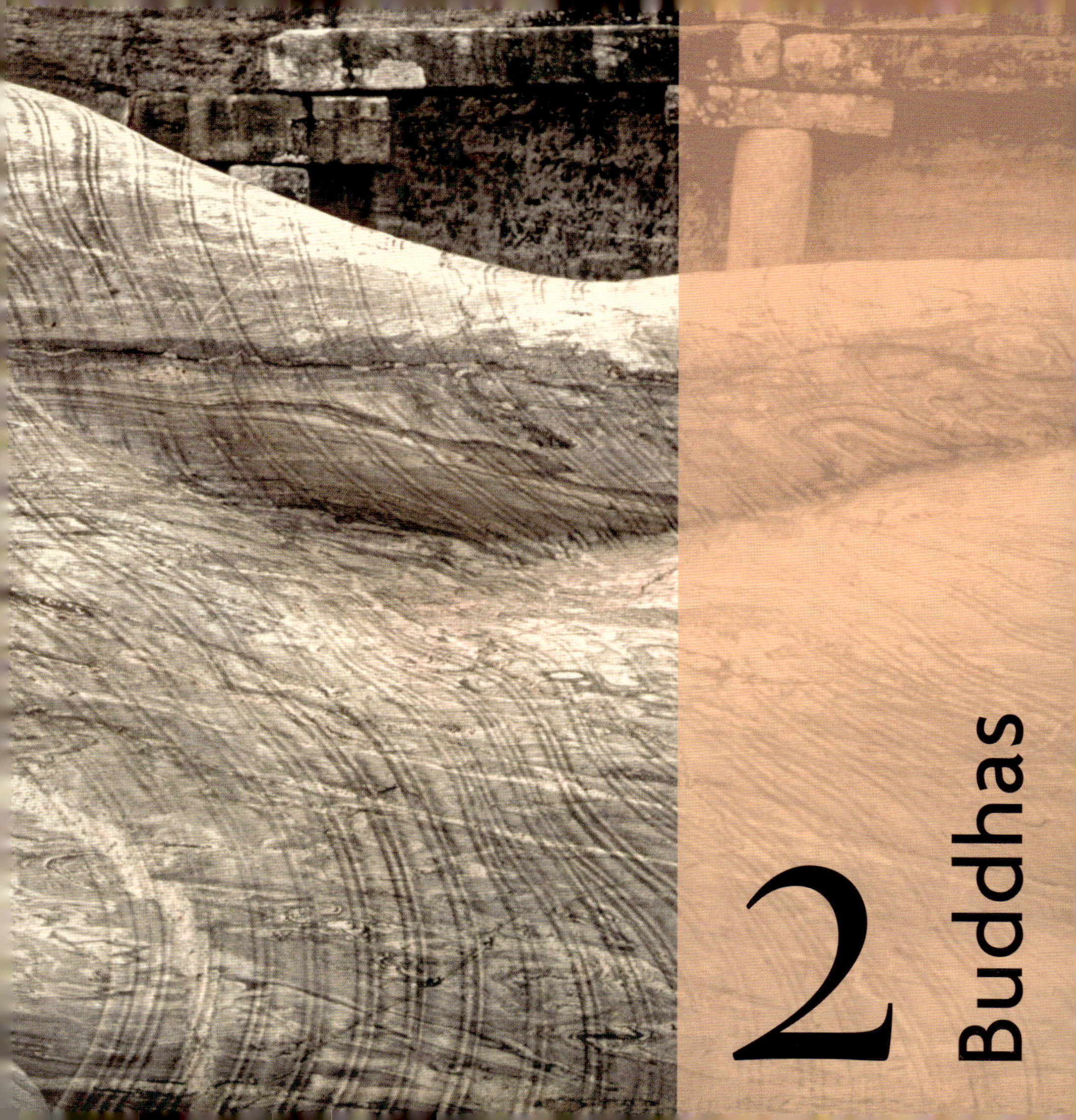
2
Buddhas

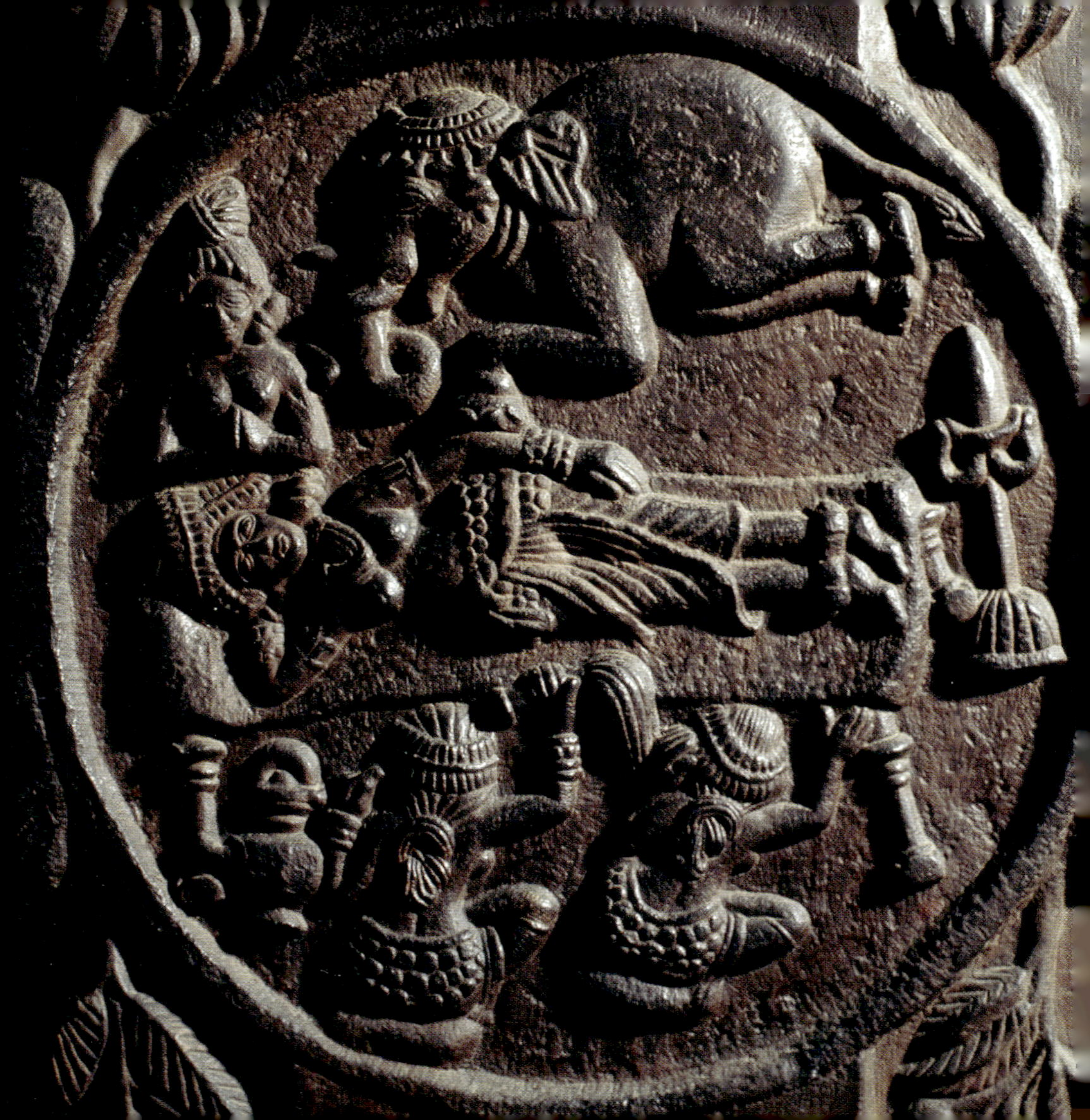

Bas-relief from Bharhut

2nd century BCE **Indian Museum, Kolkata, West Bengal, India**

COMMISSIONED BY Sampaka **STYLE** Shunga
MATERIAL Red sandstone **DIAMETER** 45 cm/18 in.

These fragments of a stone gate, post and lintel railing from Bharhut, Madhya Pradesh, India, are the oldest ones extant. They are part of a structure that once encircled a stupa mound at Bharhut, but British Commander Alexander Cunningham, finding all in disrepair, brought them to a safe place in 1874; later they entered the Indian Museum. They include decorative roundels with illustrations of *jataka* stories, lintels adorned with portraits of patrons and floral motifs and terminal posts bearing carved images of kings and male and female native gods. The roundel shown opposite is the earliest extant depiction of the Conception of the Buddha. The story goes that one night the Buddha's mother, Maya, dreamt that a white elephant entered her belly; she saw a great light, and when she woke she felt a heaviness. A brahmin was called, and he interpreted the dream as auspicious and heralding the birth of a great person. Here, Maya, heavily adorned with armlets, belts, ankle bracelets and jewels in her braided hair, reclines on her bed asleep. A flaming lamp on the right indicates that it is night time. In front of her bed two women, seen from the rear, are harem attendants who have fallen asleep; behind the bed, a divinity clasps his hands in acknowledgment of the momentous event. At the very top is a white elephant; this is the Bodhisattva, identified by his crown and large size. Flanking the roundel are lotus flowers on tall stalks, an allusion to the purity of the Buddha. The inscription above the roundel identifies the event. This is one of the most important scenes in the nativity cycle and is much represented in Buddhist institutions throughout Asia.

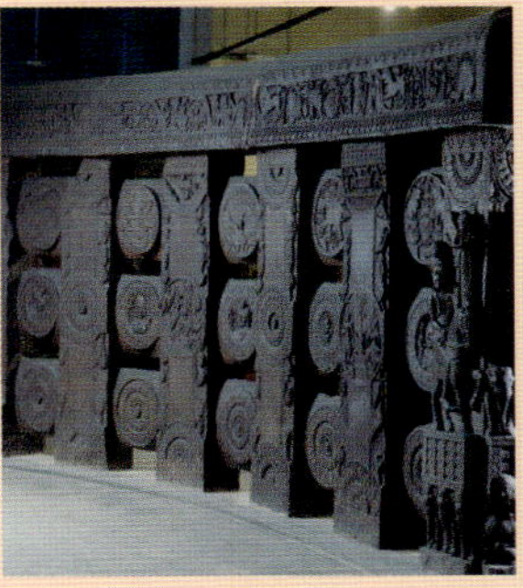

Bharhut Stupa

A railing and four monumental gateways encircled the stupa, a domed monument that contained relics of the Buddha. Orientated to the four directions, the gateway and railing marked the area within – used for circumambulation – as sacred. At this very early stage of Buddhist art, native emblems of prosperity and fecundity are adopted for symbolic portrayals of the previous and historical lives of the Buddha.

'A brilliant light filled the earth and [Maya] heard the sound of musical instruments and singing.'
XIUXING BENQI JING

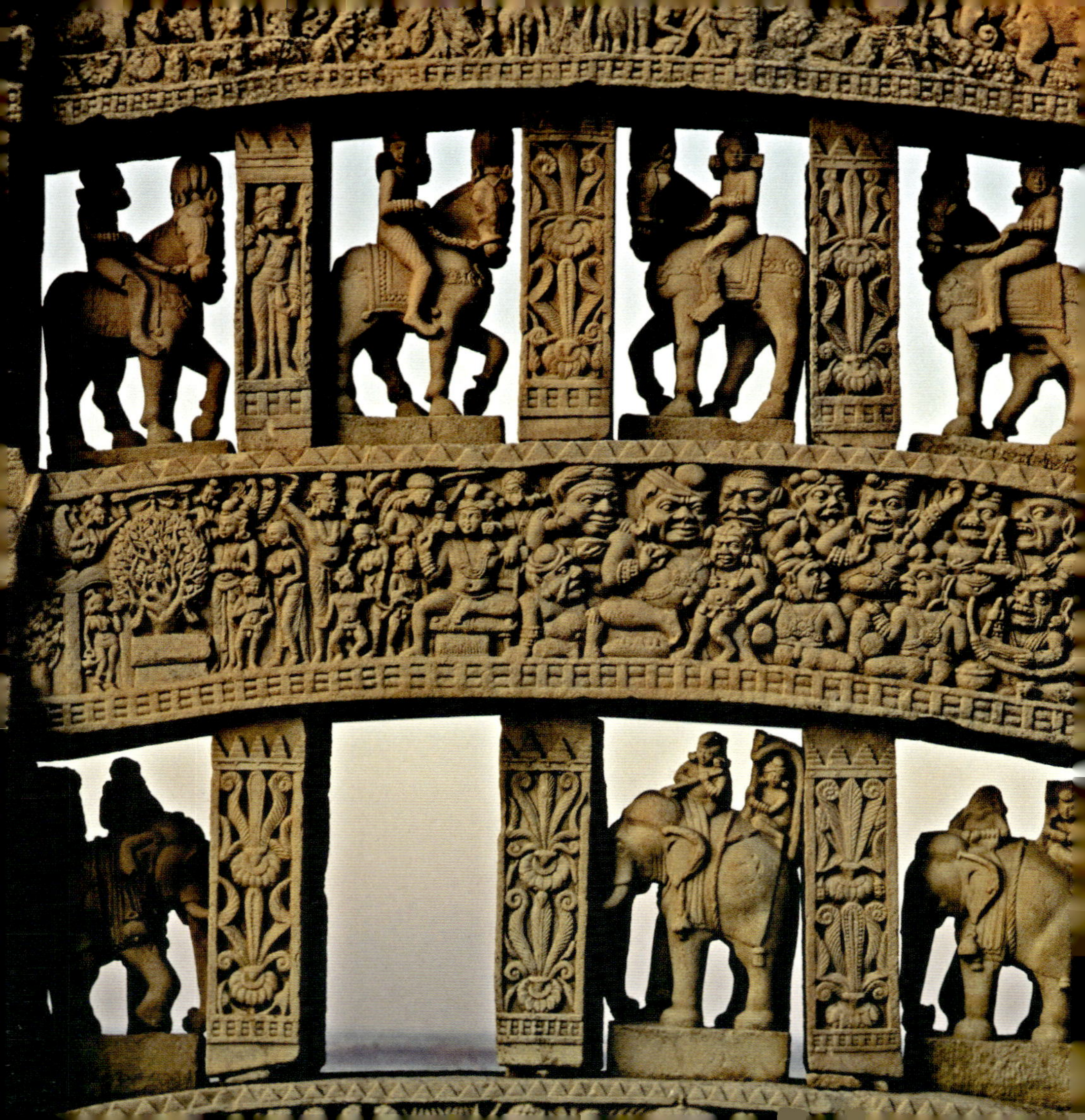

Temptation of Mara

1st century CE **Sanchi, Madhya Pradesh, India**

COMMISSIONED BY Shunga dynasty   **MATERIAL** Granite
LENGTH 813 m/2,667 ft   **HEIGHT** 28 m/92 ft

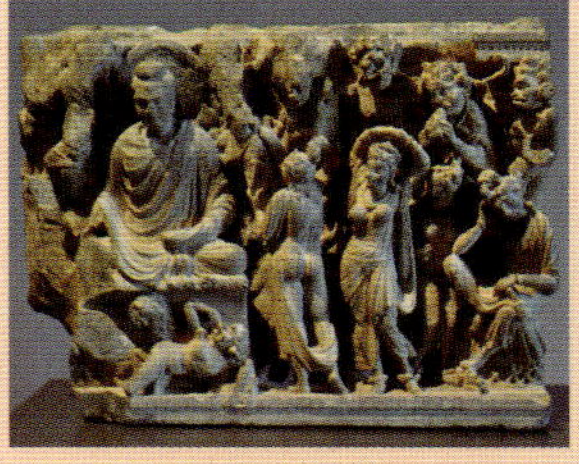

Buddhist texts relate that, as Siddhartha sat in deep meditation under the Bodhi tree, the god of Karma, Mara, grew fearful that, should the sage succeed, everyone would seek release from the cycle of life and death and his kingdom would empty. His three lovely daughters, noticing his distress, sought to remedy the problem by seducing Siddhartha. When their efforts failed, Mara tried to tempt him with sweet words, offering him the highest station in the heavens, his own. When that failed, his awesome army descended, darkening the skies and throwing boulders and uprooted trees. The earliest surviving depiction of this assault was installed in the middle lintel of the northern gateway of Sanchi stupa, in Bhopal, India. At the centre is Mara, the handsome prince of desire, seated on a low throne; to the right are a dozen of his warriors – misshapen, dwarf-like creatures with oversized heads, in poses of anger with their mouths shrieking and agape. To the far left is Siddhartha, here represented by the tree under which he sits in meditation, because at this time the anthropomorphic image of the Buddha was not yet in use. Instead, aniconic images associated with his life – such as the tree, stupa, wheel and footprints – indicated his presence. Resisting Mara's tri-pronged attack, the sage points his right hand to the earth, calling those on earth to witness the many rebirths and evolutions that have led to his elevated spiritual state, and the enlightenment that he has attained. The earth shakes and Mara's troops scatter with the rising sun. A milkmaid on the left, near the tree, indicates that victory is won, and afterwards he accepts her offering of food.

Roman Influences

This 2nd–4th-century slate bas-relief from Pakistan (now in the Museum Rietberg, Zurich) has figural representations influenced by Roman prototypes. Beneath the seated Buddha are two of Mara's fallen warriors; their postures echo those of soldiers carved on the column of Marcus Aurelius in Rome (2nd century CE). The rear view of the figure of one of Mara's nearly nude daughters is also based on Roman prototypes. The Buddha's right hand (now missing) once pointed to the earth, calling it to witness that he had solved the problem of suffering.

'Lust thy first army is called, discontent the second, the third is called hunger and thirst, the fourth is desire.'

BUDDHA'S WORDS TO MARA

Standing Buddha

1st–2nd century CE **Museum of Indian Art, Berlin, Germany**

STYLE Greco-Buddhist **MATERIAL** Grey schist and marble
ORIGIN Gandhara, Pakistan **HEIGHT** 160 cm/63 in.

For over five hundred years, representation of the Buddha relied on symbols associated with his life – the tree, the wheel, the stupa or his footprints. The anthropomorphic image of the Buddha was first created in the 1st century CE after the invasion of northern India by the Kushans (central Asian nomads and Buddhist patrons who were involved in trade along the Silk Route). Artists articulated some of the Buddha's thirty-two marks of beauty or *laksana* as described in the scriptures: a tall cranial protrusion, a wart symmetrically placed between the eyebrows and golden skin. Buddhas were given elongated ear lobes, the result of wearing princely ear ornaments. In this example, he is dressed as a monk with three pieces of untailored cloth wound around the body, a style still common in South-east Asia. Scholars see similarities between such Kushan art and Western icons, in particular Apollo, god of the sun, including the contrapposto, heroic muscular anatomy and the naturalistic treatment of the hair and seemingly wet drapery. In the Indian tradition, the Buddha stands not on the ground but on a simple base. His solar disc halo, indicating illumination, was adopted from Persian iconography. The Kushan patrons also wrote down the scriptures, which ended the five-hundred-year-old oral tradition. They commissioned illustrations of the scenes of the life of the Buddha as described by the scriptures, arranging them in linear chronological order, in contrast to native traditions that use a vertical hierarchy to render the progression of time. Monks, missionaries and merchants brought art created for the Kushan kings east along the Silk Road.

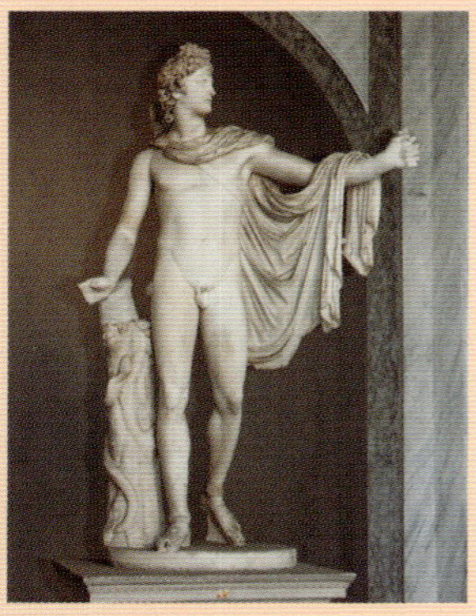

Apollo Belvedere

This marble sculpture of Apollo, now standing in the Vatican Museum, is a Roman copy, made *c*. 120–140 CE, of a Greek sculpture of the sun god, *c*. 350–325 BCE, depicted as a beautiful young man. Images of Apollo inspired the artists of Gandhara to create the first anthropomorphic images of the standing Buddha.

'The Hellenistic free-standing Buddhas are the most beautiful, and probably the most ancient, of the Buddhas.'

ALFRED A. FOUCHER,
GANDHARA

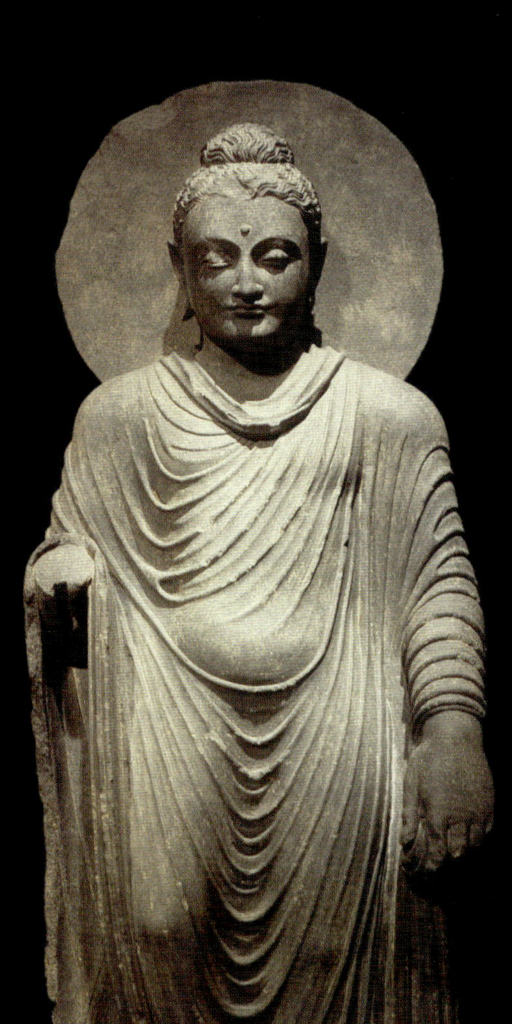

Death of the Buddha

2nd–3rd century CE **Victoria & Albert Museum, London, UK**

STYLE Kushan, Gandhara school, possibly Loriyan Tangai **MATERIAL** Schist
ORIGIN Pakistan **DIMENSIONS** 53 x 48 cm/21 x 19 in.

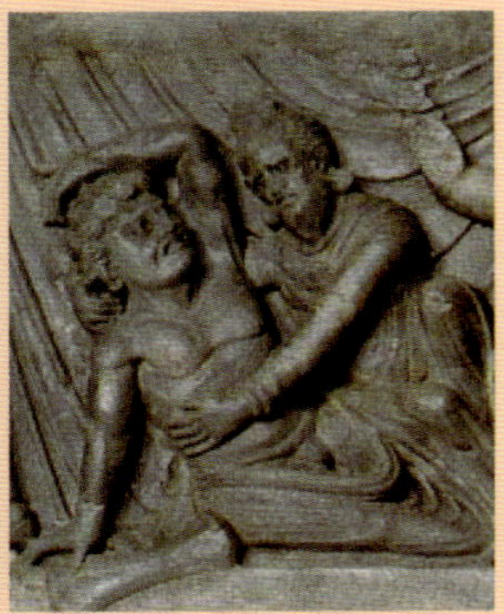

Grieving Disciples

In another Gandhara *parinirvana* bas-relief, also held at the Victoria & Albert Museum, five disciples are seen lamenting in front of the drapery of the Buddha's deathbed. In this detail, the stricken figure of Vajrapani is being comforted by a bearded man with a top-knot and earrings.

'All that Malla host wept piteously and lamented; whilst some concealed their grief nor spoke a word, others sank forth prostrate on the earth …'

ASVAGHOSHA,
LIFE OF THE BUDDHA

At the age of eighty the Buddha contracted an illness. He was nursed by his youngest disciple, Ananda, but, knowing his death to be imminent, he instructed Ananda to take him to Kushinagar and to gather the monks that he might bid them farewell. As he was on his deathbed an ascetic named Sumadhi spoke with the Buddha and then sat in meditation by his bed. After the Buddha died, petty kings attended to his cremation, but the fire would not start. One of the wisest of the Buddha's disciples, the monk Kasyapa, was away travelling, but he made his way to Kushinagar, and when he arrived he touched the Buddha's foot in farewell. Only then did the fire alight. In Buddhist art, the monks Ananda and Kasyapa form a pair; respectively, they represent the path of personal devotion through the heart, and the path of knowledge through the intellect. This bas-relief representation shows the Buddha as described in the *Mahaparinivana* texts, lying on his right side, his head supported by his right hand, his feet resting one on top of the other. He has a halo, and his monastic clothes maintain their U-fold configuration, as if this were a standing figure laid on its side – the laws of gravity do not apply to the Buddha. On the right, by his feet, the monk Kasyapa holds a walking staff, and Sumadhi meditates in front of the couch. One figure, Vajrapani, whose identity has yet to be determined, throws down his *vajra*, or thunderbolt as he faints from grief. No doubt Ananda would have been in his traditional place at the head of the bed, but this part of the stone is missing. Behind the bed, weeping inconsolably, are the lay followers responsible for the funeral preparations.

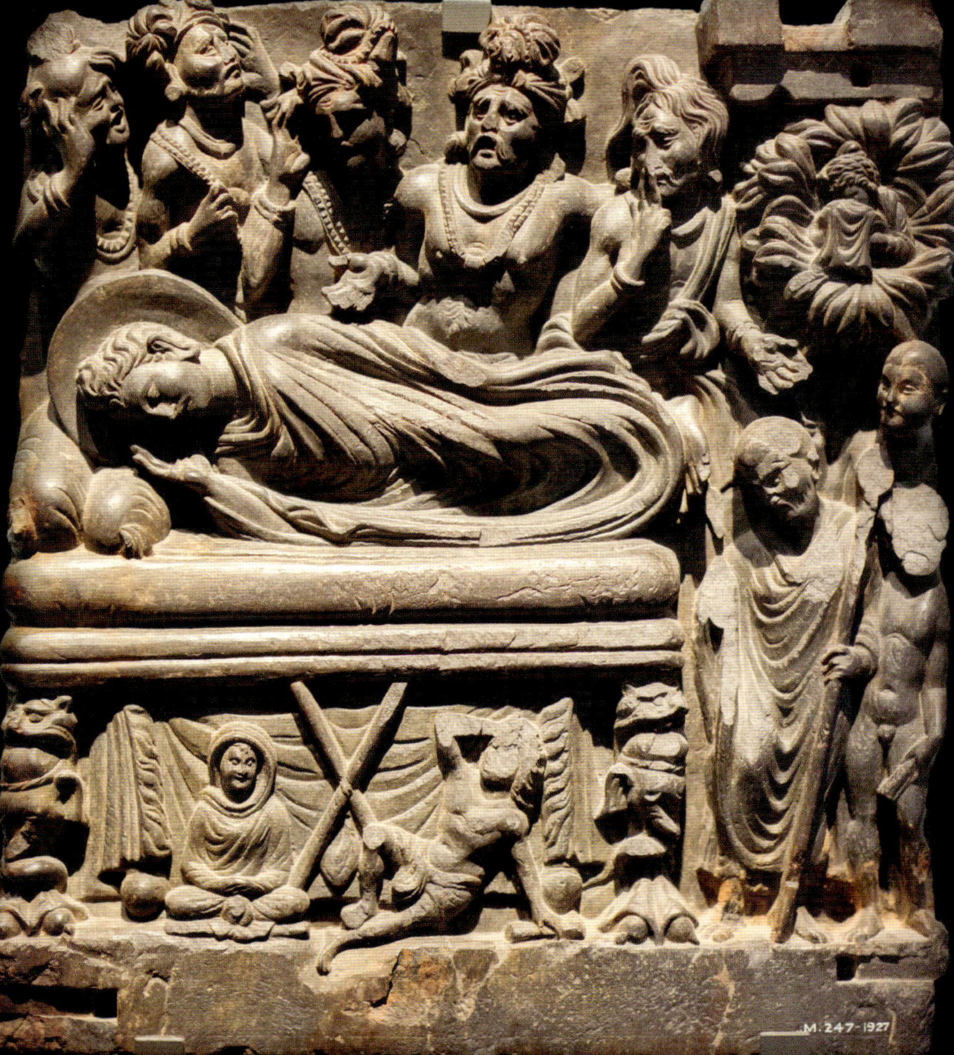

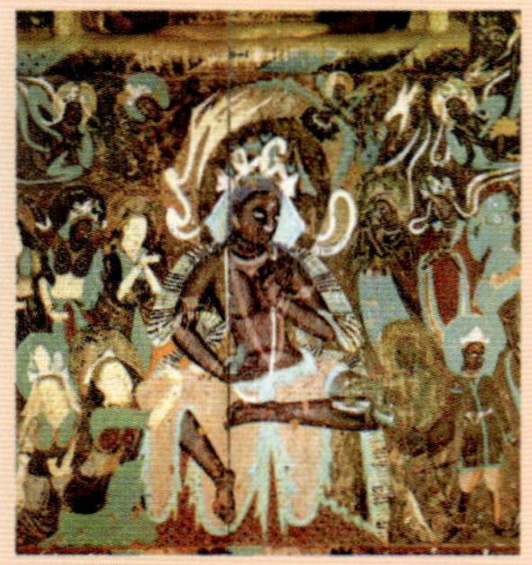

King Sibi Jataka

The story of King Sibi was rarely illustrated in East Asia, but in the early period artists at the caves at Dunhuang, China, depicted the *jataka*. To the left of the king his attendants call out in anguish for him to stop; to the right the surgeon slices off the flesh. Western prototypes may be seen in the highlights, shadows and modelling of the king's skin.

'This creature has fled to me for protection, and I cannot abandon it, therefore I will give you an equal weight of some other kind of flesh.'

SIBI, *KATHASARITSAGARA SOMADEVI* (1070 CE)

Bas-relief of King Sibi

2nd–3rd century CE **British Museum, London, UK**

STYLE Kushan, Gandhara school   **MATERIAL** Schist
DIMENSIONS 23.3 x 32.4 x 5.5 cm / 9 x 12 ¾ x 2 in.

Tales of the previous lives of the Buddha, *jatakas*, were popular as decorative themes on early Buddhist monuments. In each, the Bodhisattva demonstrates extreme compassion and lack of attachment, and thus his spiritual progress is presented as a model for the faithful. This stone bas-relief from Gandhara, modern Pakistan, refers to the story of King Sibi, who was relaxing in his palace when a dove entered his hall, soon to be followed by a hawk intent on eating the dove. The king protected the dove, and the hawk assailed him for interfering with the natural order. The king then ordered the court surgeon to cut from his flesh a portion equal to the weight of the dove. But the dove, the god Indra in disguise, grew heavier and heavier until large portions of the king's flesh were sliced off. In the bas-relief, the king slumps on a chair as his flesh is removed. Two female servants attend him, a central standing figure holds the balance scale, and the crowned and haloed figure to the right is Indra, who in the end reveals himself and congratulates the king on his compassion; to the far right is the native god Brahma. This style of art is a hybrid one that combines indigenous artistic traditions with Western ones imported from Rome by way of the Silk Route. This is most apparent in the athletic bodies of the participants, some in hip-slung poses; in the variety of postures – profile, three-quarter profile and frontal view; and in the meticulous rendering of the intricate details of the figures' clothes, jewels and furniture. Such bas-reliefs commonly adorned the bases of stupas and were viewed by the faithful during circumambulation.

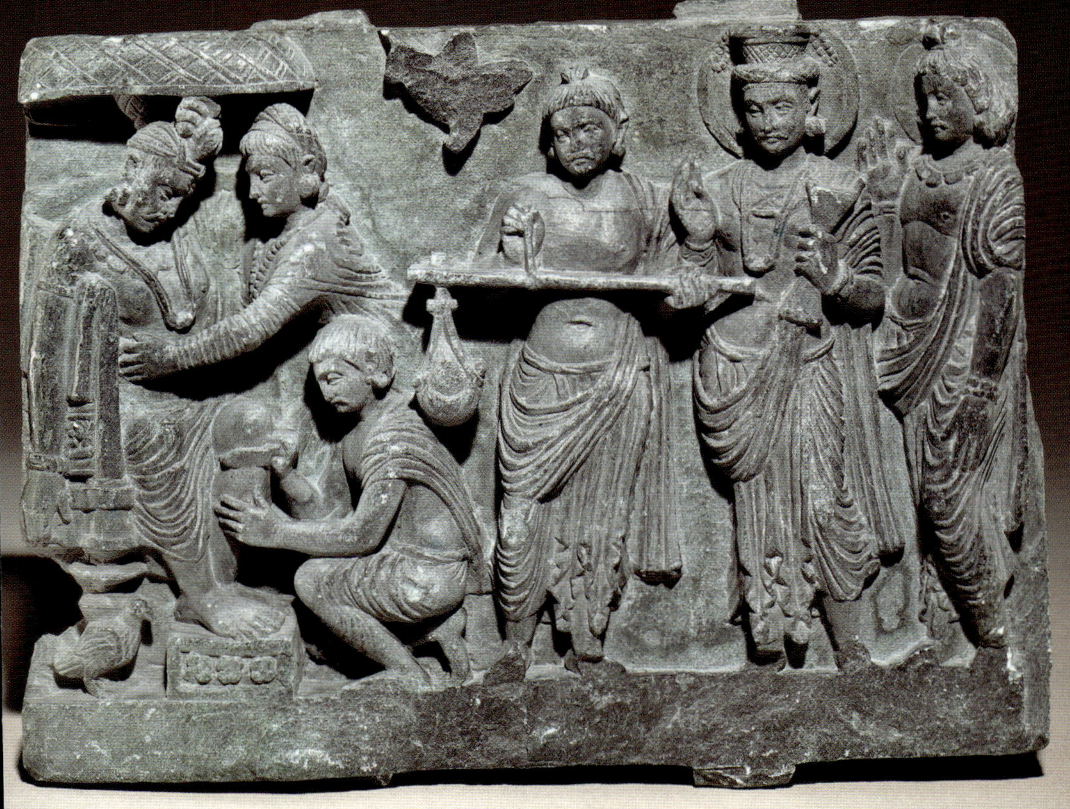

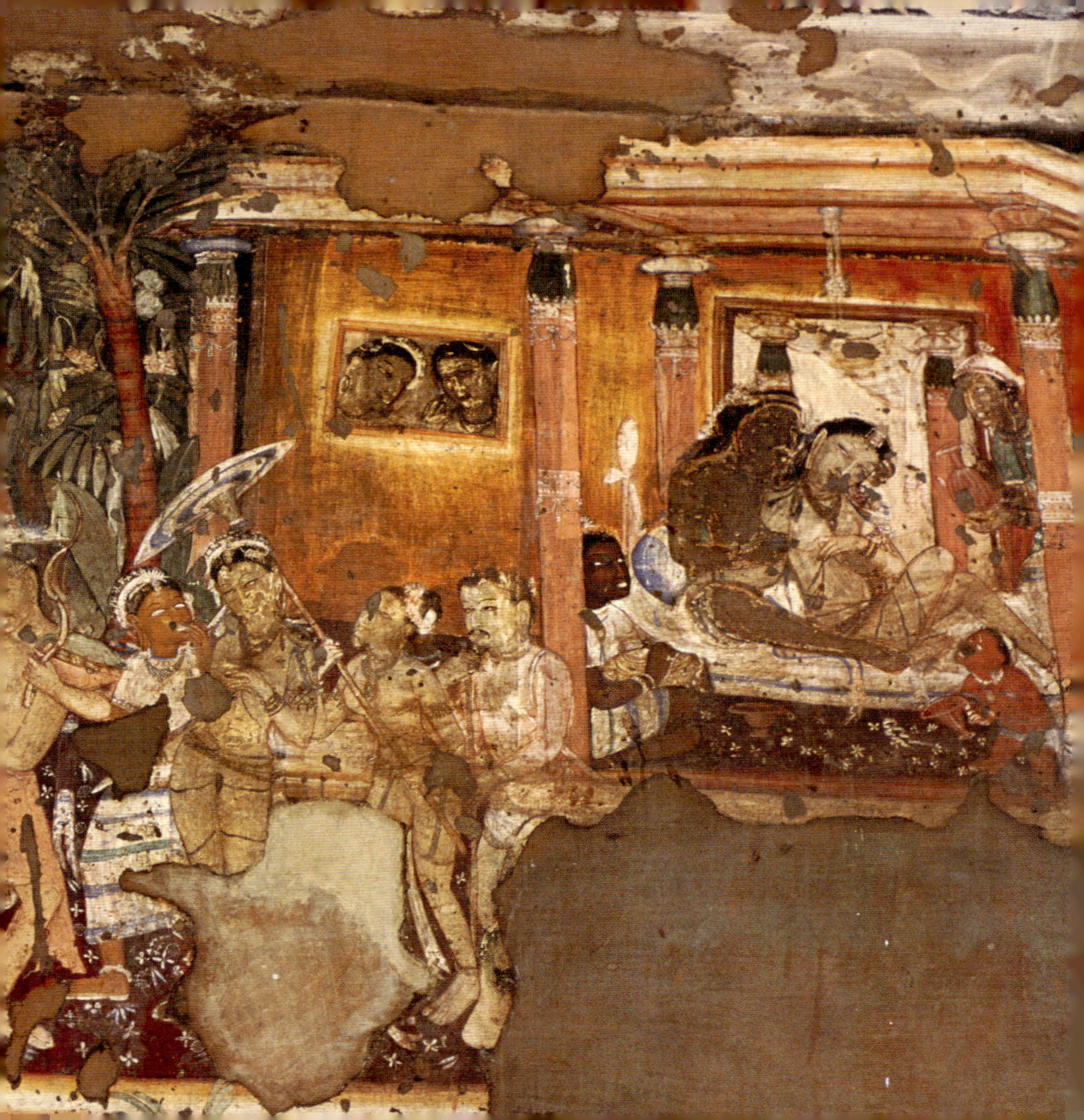

Vessantara Cave Painting

*c.*460–480 CE **Jalgaon, Aurangabad, Maharashtra, India**

COMMISSIONED BY Asmaka kings **ABANDONED** *c.*480 CE
STYLE Vakataka **MATERIALS** Pigments, glue, lime-washed surface

The Ajanta caves contain many paintings illustrating the *jatakas*, or stories of the previous lives of the Buddha. The Vessantara *jataka*, represented in Cave 17, concerns a selfless and generous Bodhisattva who sacrifices all of his possessions to the disguised god Indra, who is testing him. The dark-skinned prince is seen happily seated, embracing his beautiful wife in a portico of his palace. They are attended by servants, two of whom observe the royal couple from an upper window. The god Indra asks for the realm's lucky white elephant, which brings great bounty by ensuring that sufficient rain falls. To the left of this scene, the *jataka* is taken to its conclusion; here, the prince is identifiable by his large size, dark skin and the umbrella held over his head. The suppleness of all the figures in the painting exemplifies the Indian yogic ideal of the body, and the delicate clothes, jewels, ornate architectual embellishments and serving utensils express the luxury of palatial life. The increasing ability of the artists of Ajanta to portray the narratives realistically made their works even more compelling for the believers who travelled great distances to see them. In India at this time, sensuality, clearly evident in the embracing couple, was inseparable from spiritual expression. Even so, the painting shows a distinct Western influence in the convincing modelling of the bodies, the perspectival angle of the roof of the pavilion and the procession of figures along a diagonal. The artists at Ajanta did not lay out the narratives in an ordered fashion, however. Instead, they filled every available surface; the scenes shown here were painted above the jamb of a door.

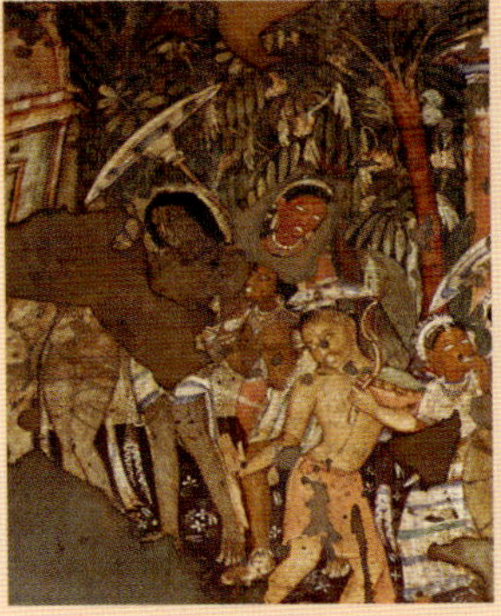

Outcome of the Jataka

To the left of the same painting, the Bodhisattva, having granted the elephant, is exiled by his father for endangering the well-being of the state. Wandering in the forest with his wife and two children, he is then asked to give up his horse and chariot, wife, children and clothes. These he willingly offers, and he emerges alone and naked from the forest.

'So when Vessantara the prince his generous gifts had given; He died at last, and fully wise, he passed away to heaven.'

VESSANTARA JATAKA 547

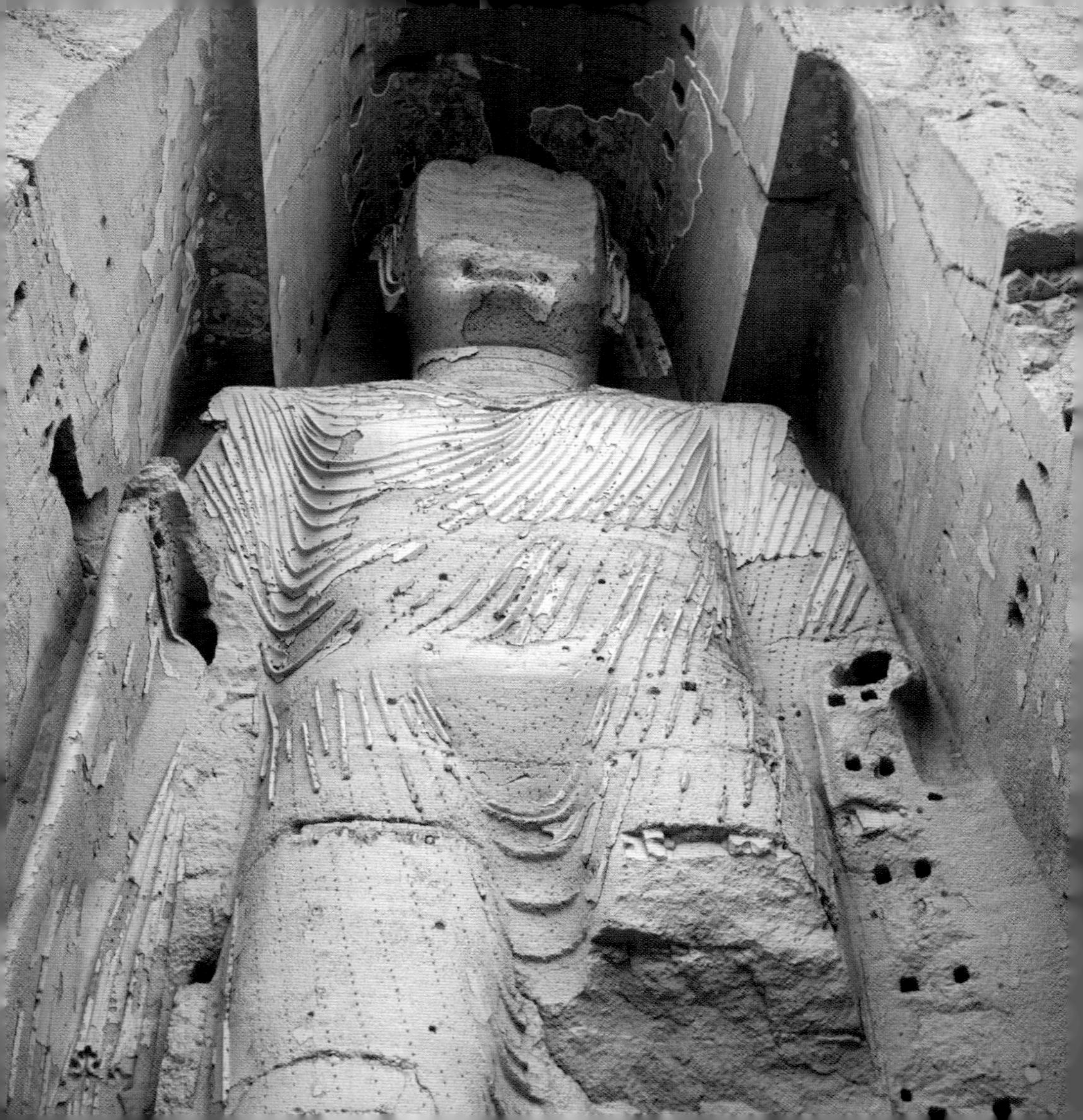

Buddhas of Bamiyan

c. 5th century CE   **Bamiyan Caves, Bamiyan, Afghanistan**

STYLE Kushan   **ALTITUDE OF SITE** 2,500 m/8,200 ft
HEIGHTS OF THE TWO BUDDHAS 53 m/174 ft and 38 m/125 ft

The Kushan Empire (1st–4th centuries) was justly famous for two of the largest Buddhas in existence. Excavated from a mountain of the Hindu Kush near the Bamiyan River, 264 kilometres (164 miles) from Kabul, the colossal Buddhas of Bamiyan stood in caves at either end of a bluff, carved from the living rock. Drapery clung to the bodies of the giant figures, but little more can be said about the style of the images due to damage inflicted over many centuries. The Buddhas were of great significance in the transmission of Buddhism east to China, as travellers on the Silk Road were highly impressed by their size and grandeur. The side walls of the caves, and cupolas over the heads of the colossi, bore paintings, one of which was a representation of the sun god Apollo in his quadriga. Neighbouring caves were also decorated with Buddhist sculptures and paintings. Excavations nearby have revealed the remains of a fortified citadel that accommodated travellers on the Silk Road. In the Kakrak Valley, also in the vicinity, fragments of a 10-metre (33-ft) tall standing Buddha were found, along with a hundred caves dating from the 6th to the 13th centuries. Being situated directly on the trade routes linking east and west, Afghanistan was repeatedly invaded in antiquity. Alexander the Great arrived in 326 BCE, followed by the Hellenic Seleucid dynasty (4th–3rd centuries BCE); the Maurya dynasty of northern India (3rd–2nd centuries BCE); the Central Asian Kushans (2nd century BCE–2nd century CE); and the Persian Sasanians (3rd–5th centuries CE). All this movement resulted in Afghanistan becoming a multi-cultural station on the Silk Road.

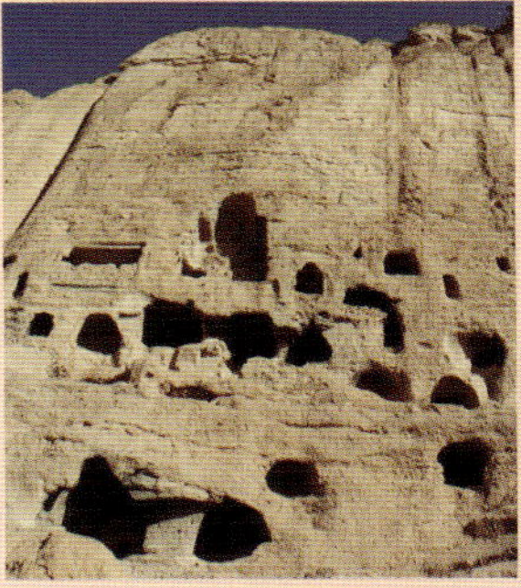

The Bamiyan Caves

The Buddhist monasteries and cave-chapels at Bamiyan suffered several destructive attacks, beginning with looting by the early 13th-century army of Genghis Khan. The Mughal emperor Aurangzeb and the Persian king Nader Afshar both had cannon fired at them. Most recently, the Taliban blew them up in 2001, calling them an affront to Islam, which eschews the depiction of humans and animals.

'[The statue's] golden hues sparkle on every side and its precious ornaments dazzle the eyes by their brightness.'

XUANZANG, 7TH CENTURY

Buddha of Sarnath

Late 5th century CE Archaeological Museum, Sarnath, India

STYLE Guptan **MATERIAL** Sandstone
HEIGHT 0.7 m/2 ft 3 ½ in.

One of the four most important events in the life of the Buddha was his First Sermon at Sarnath. This statue, recovered from the sacred site, depicts the Buddha seated in full lotus posture. The sage's yogic body is articulated in the local relatively soft chunar standstone. Large areas of smooth flesh are interrupted only by slight suggestions of his monastic robes, at the ends of the sleeves and by the ankles. His hands assume the *dharmachakra mudra*, a gesture signifying the turning of the wheel of the law, or Dharma. His fingers count off the Four Noble Truths of the First Sermon. On the base, two deer shown in profile identify the location of the First Sermon, the deer park at Sarnath. The central wheel symbolically represents the event and the Buddha himself; it is one of several ancient and important emblematic representations that continued to be used long after the invention of the Buddha image. On either side of the wheel are five monks, the audience of the First Sermon, and a sixth figure, a woman, who may be a patron. Indicating the universal significance of the event is the grand throne on which the Buddha sits; at its periphery are richly carved rampant mythological terrestrial and aquatic figures. Rising behind the head of the Buddha is an ornate halo; this has a circular zone with a rich floral pattern bordered by rows of pearls. At the top, two flying angels celebrate the event. The face features eyes that are all but closed, rounded cheeks, highly arched eyebrows, full lips and elongated ears that recall the heavy earrings the Buddha wore in his former life as a prince. Snail-shell curls cover his head, a consistent feature of the Buddha thereafter.

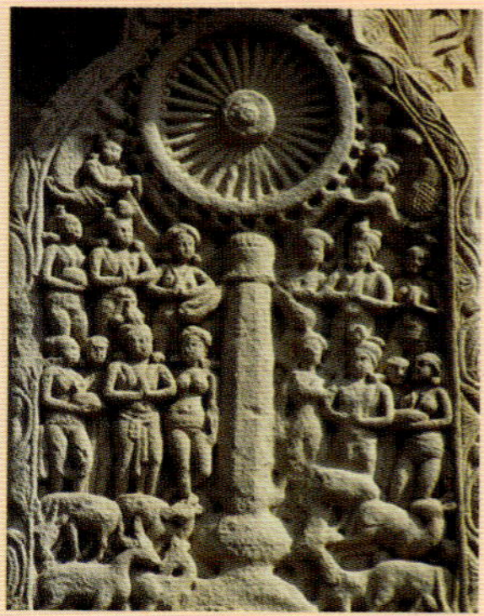

Buddha as a Pillar

Perhaps the earliest preserved illustration of the First Sermon appears at the 1st-century CE Sanchi Stupa in Madhya Pradesh, India, on the northern pillar of its southern gate. Here, a pillar supporting a wheel represents the Buddha. Such symbols persisted after figurative images of the Buddha were introduced. At the base of the pillar, a herd of deer identifies the location as the deer park at Sarnath. Worshippers flank the upper area.

'Following the Middle Path I have obtained complete Samadhi.'

SUTRA OF CAUSE AND EFFECT

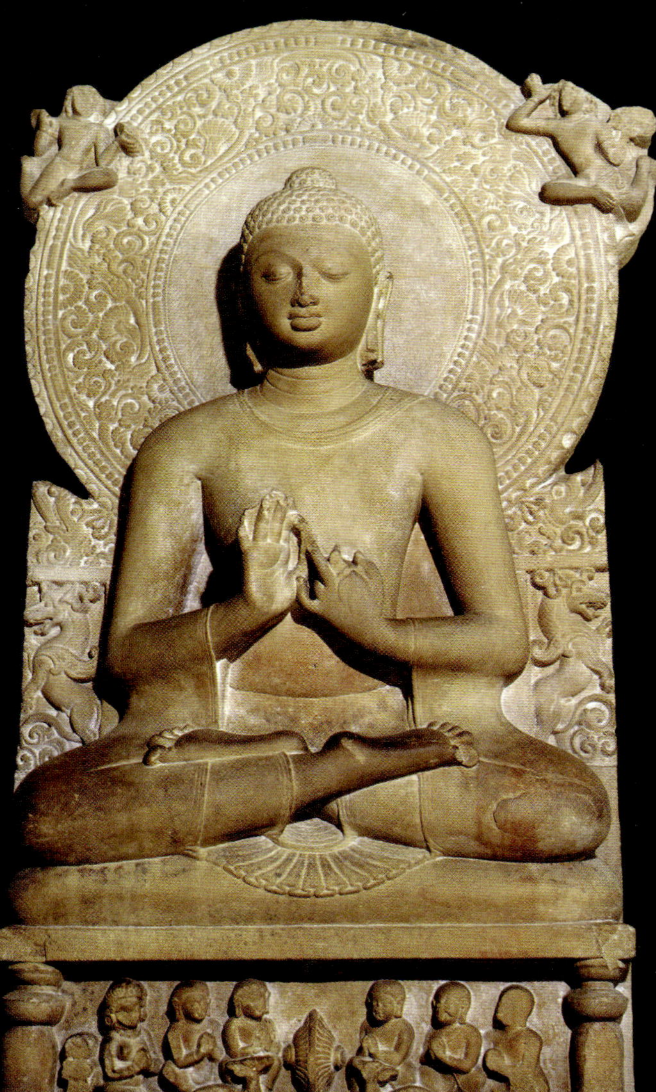

Yungang Buddha

Late 5th century CE **Datong, Shanxi, China**

COMMISSIONED BY Northern Wei Emperor Xiaowen
LOCATION Cave 5, also known as the Big Buddha's Cave

The cave site of Yungang, located in the far north in Shanxi province and one of the earliest Buddhist sites in northern China, was established with imperial support in the mid-5th century CE. The caves, carved into a sandstone bluff, are distinguished by five exterior niches each filled with a colossal sculpture of the Buddha. Narratives were not a primary concern of the artists of Yungang; rather, every available niche of the caves was filled with seated Buddhas, bodhisattvas, flying angels and worshippers. Located in Cave 5, this portrayal of the Buddha has him seated with his right hand raised in the fear-not gesture. The event is identifiable as his First Sermon by the two deer that flank a triangle of three wheels – these stand for the Three Jewels of Buddhism: the Buddha, the Dharma (teaching) and the Sangha (monks). On the left, in diminished scale, are five standing haloed monks in monastic garb with shaven heads; these represent the audience of the First Sermon. Haloed worshippers, perhaps donors, appear on the right. Carved polychrome figures crowd the upper ranges of the wall, including a host of celestials carrying a garland and angels in postures of adoration. At the top is a pillared arcade housing worshipping and music-making angels. Every available surface presents reverential figures and no area is left undecorated. This *horror vacui*, or fear of empty spaces, characterizes the early phase of Buddhist art in China. Also typical are the flames defining the Buddha's mandorla, and the dragons on either side of the arch. Enough of the original colouring survives to demonstrate the dazzling effect of the carvings.

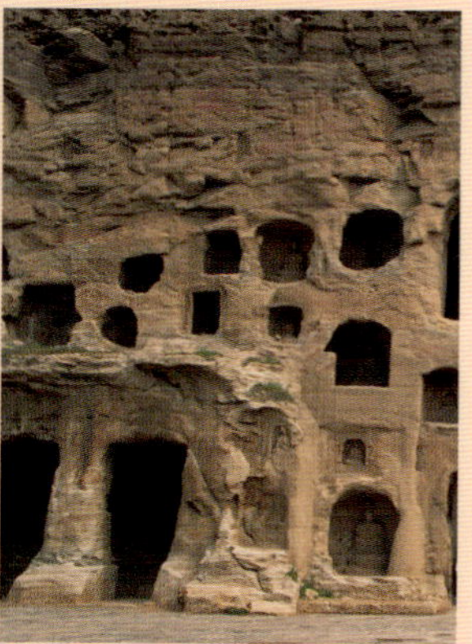

Yungang Caves

In all, at Yungang in Datong there are fifty-three caves of various sizes with more than 51,000 Buddha statues and statuettes. Imperial sponsorship of the site ended after 500 CE when the Northern Wei moved their capital south to central China. Once there, they established caves at the site of Longmen in Henan.

'By meditation, those that enter upon this Path win release from the bondage of Mara.'

ASVAGHOSA, *BUDDHACARITA* (*c.* 1ST CENTURY CE)

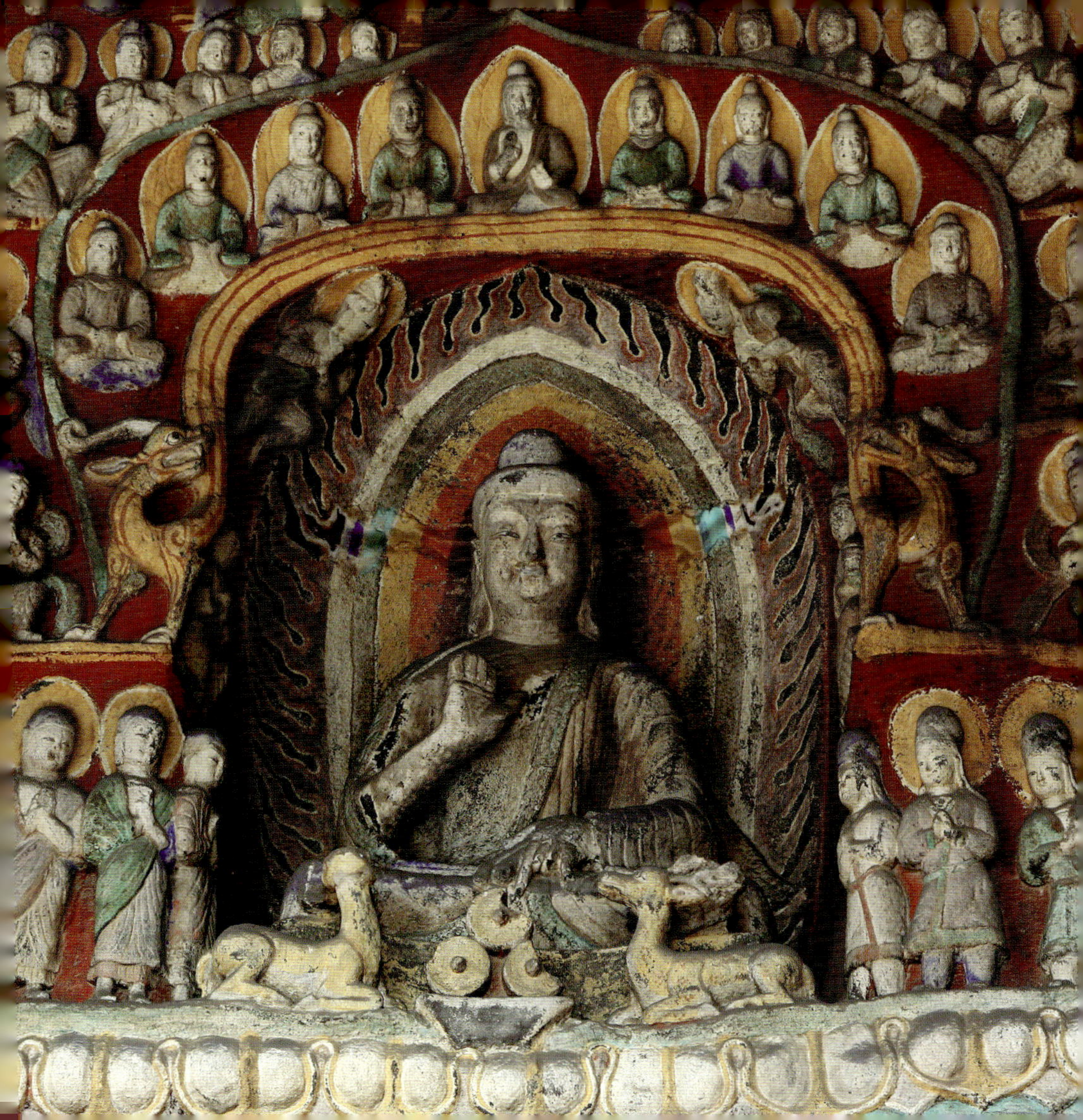

Yungang Colossal Buddha

Late 5th century CE **Datong, Shanxi, China**

COMMISSIONED BY Northern Wei Emperor Taiwu　**MATERIAL** Sandstone
HEIGHT OF SEATED COLOSSUS WITHIN CAVE 20 17 m/55¾ ft

The largest monuments at the cave site of Yungang in northern China are five colossal Buddhas, commissioned by Emperor Taiwu of the Northern Wei dynasty (385–535 CE). Buddhist practices, especially the rejection of filial piety implied by a monk leaving his family and giving up his personal identity, often offended native sensibilities. Buddhists believed that spiritual merit earned from supporting the religion could be transferred to parents and others, assuring their spiritual progress. Taiwu's father, Emperor Mingyuan, had prohibited Buddhism, and Taiwu, fearful of the consequences, had the Buddhas carved, attributing the spiritual merit of one to his father and dedicating the remaining four to prior generations of his family's patriarchs. For Buddhists, producing children to continue the ancestral line was meritorious, but the transfer of spiritual credit was preferable. In Cave 20 at Yungang there are two icons, representing the seated and standing Buddha. In this early period, such northern Chinese Buddhas resemble Gandharan examples brought east along the Silk Road. The colossal Buddha, seated in meditative posture, wears monastic garb revealing a massive chest, and has Western facial features. His large ears, extended by earrings worn in his earlier princely life, are associated in China with longevity because ears grow with increased age. To his left, the smaller standing Buddha wears another style of monastic dress, with drapery covering both shoulders and falling in U-shaped folds down the median of the body. Wooden facades, admitting only dappled light, once shielded the caves and protected their images, but they are gone.

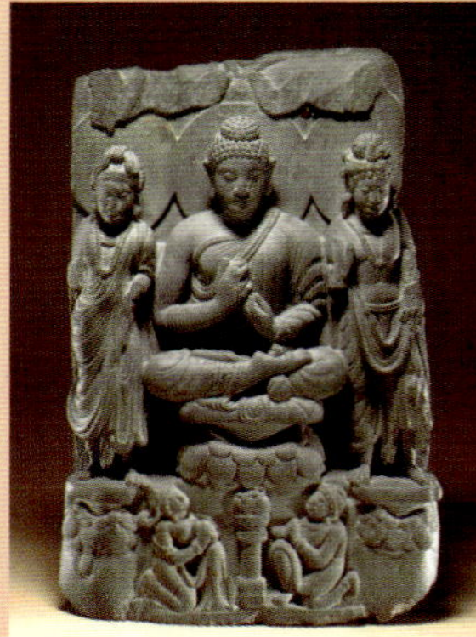

Seated Stone Buddha

This Buddha from Gandhara in India, ascribed to the Kushan era (2nd–4th centuries CE), is the kind of image on which Yungang artists based their colossal sculptures. After this, Buddhas tended to have a more slender body hidden by thick robes, and a narrower head with Chinese facial features.

'Caves were constructed by monks and lay people to ... receive the protection of the Buddhas.'

LAGERWEY AND PENGZHI,
EARLY CHINESE RELIGION

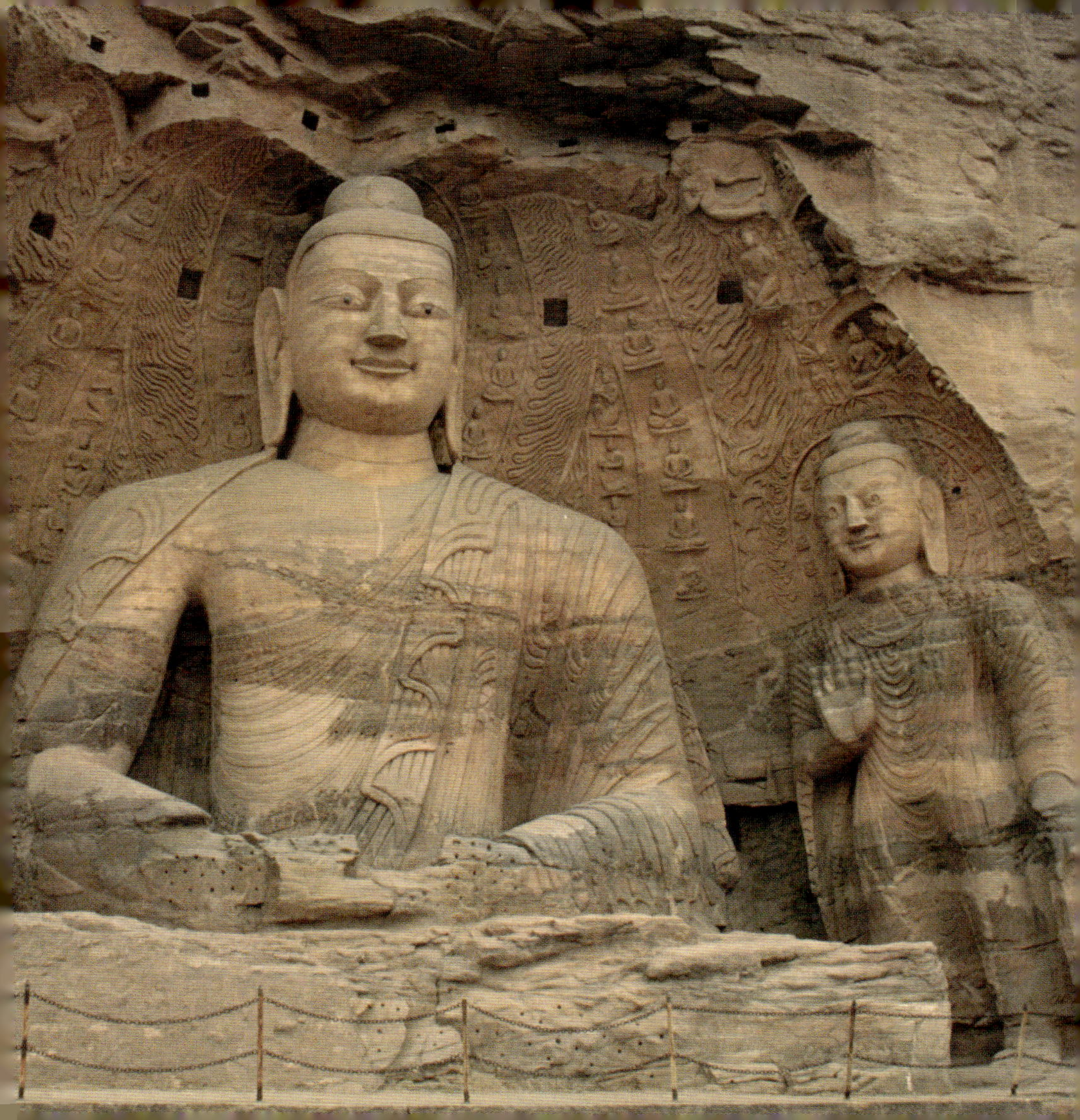

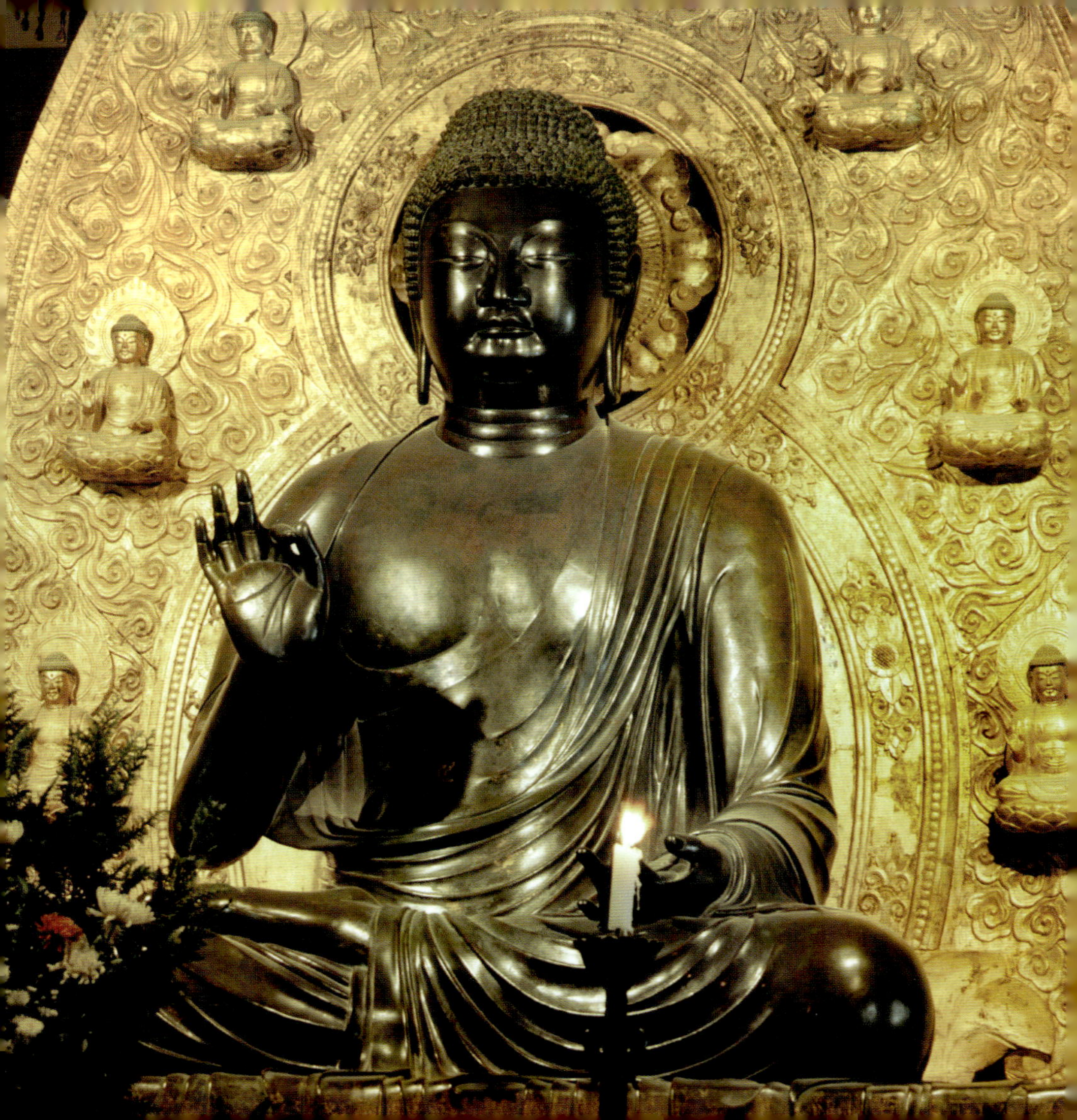

Yakushi-ji Healing Buddha

698 CE **Nara, Kansai, Japan**

COMMISSIONED BY Emperor Tenmu   **MATERIAL** Bronze, formerly gilded   **HEIGHT** Buddha: 2.55 m/8½ ft; pedestal: 1.5 m/5 ft

Yakushi, the Healing Buddha of the Eastern Paradise (Bhaisajyaguru in Sanskrit), was introduced early into Japan; for example, he is one of a trinity of figures on the altar of Horyu-ji temple (early 7th century CE). The Healing Buddha at Yakushi-ji is celebrated as among the first in the country to exhibit the international style favoured by the Chinese Tang court of the late 7th century CE. Monks and merchants travelling the Silk Route brought Indian art of the Guptan period (5th century CE) together with new forms of iconography to China, where it had a great impact. The style was subsequently adopted in both Korea and Japan. The Yakushi-ji Healing Buddha demonstrates a new appreciation of the flesh of the body, greater definition of anatomical details such as the nipple and navel, and a more relaxed and natural treatment of fabric. The bronze alloy used for the sculpture was oxidized by a fire that ravaged the temple and seems particularly dark in contrast to the gilt of the halo, which was replaced after the fire. Japanese tradition asserts that the Yakushi-ji temple and its image of the Healing Buddha were commissioned by Emperor Tenmu (c. 631–686), who made a vow, promising the Buddha both the temple and its image if his consort recovered from a serious illness. She did recover, and succeeded him as Empress Jito after his death. At Yakushi-ji, the Healing Buddha is attended by his two bodhisattvas, the Sun and Moon (Nikko and Gakko, or Suryaprabha and Candraprabha in Sanskrit). The Yakushi statue once held a medicine jar in his left hand. It is easy to appreciate the appeal that the Healing Buddha would have for the faithful.

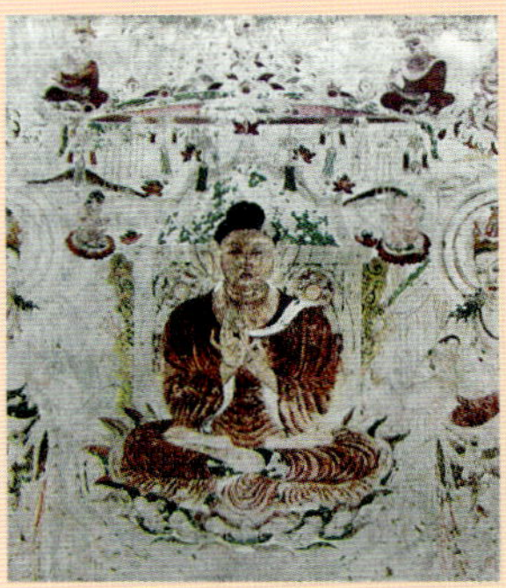

Amida Paradise

Murals at Horyu-ji (early 8th century CE) depict four Buddhas in their paradises. These are Bhaisajyaguru, the Healing Buddha in the east; Shakyamuni in the north, Maitreya to the south and Amitahba in the west. The paintings reveal Indian origins in the naturalism and sensuality of the delineated figures.

'Once a Bodhisattva made twelve great vows, many of them dedicated to helping the sick and infirm; he ... became Bhaisajyaguru, the ... Medicine Buddha.'

MEDICINE BUDDHA SUTRA

Sokkuram Great Buddha

8th century CE **Sokkuram, Mt. T'oham, South Korea**

COMMISSIONED BY Prime Minister Kim Dae-seong
STYLE Guptan Indian **MATERIAL** Granite **HEIGHT** 3.5m/11ft 6in.

Korea's relation with China goes back at least to the Han dynasty, (206 BCE–220 CE), when Chinese writing, literary forms, architecture and decorative arts were assimilated. Later the Koreans adopted the icons, scriptures and temples of Chinese Buddhism. Rock-cut caves were not feasible on the crest of Mount T'oham, so the architects created a cave-like structure comprising a domed main cella (inner chamber) and forehall covered by piles of rock. Construction of the grotto itself, begun in 751 and completed in 774 CE, was supervised by Prime Minister Kim Dae-seong; he commissioned it in the name of his parents, both in his present life and from a previous life. The Prime Minister also undertook the construction of Bulguksa Temple at Gyeongju. The experience of entering a dark cave, replicated at Sokkuram, begins at a door guarded by eight bas-relief carvings of athletic celestial protectors in dynamic martial postures. Two Indian-style columns mark the doorway of the main room. Near the back of the cella is the large, centrally situated Buddha, made of a single piece of granite. Once there was a marble stupa in the rear of the chamber, but the Japanese removed it early in the 20th century. Now the faithful circumambulate the Buddha, who sits in lotus position with his right hand touching the earth, a gesture that is associated with attaining enlightenment. His body is exposed to view and naturalistically articulated. The complex drapery is simplified, and rather than obscuring, clings to the form beneath. By replicating the Indian Guptan model adopted by Tang China, the sculptors were deliberately rejecting more recent sinification of the image.

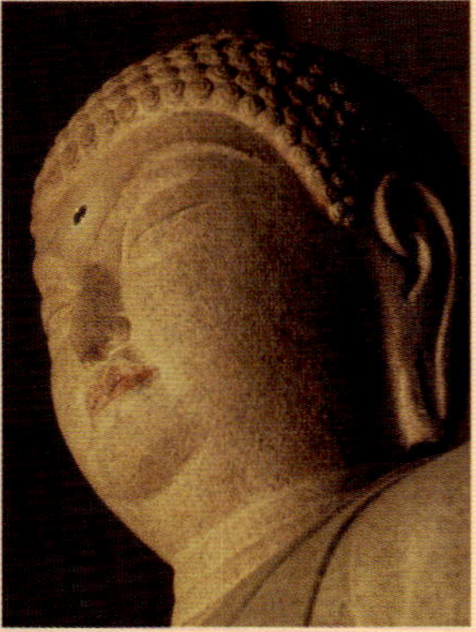

Guptan Influence

The Korean sculptors of the Great Buddha sought to replicate authentic Indian Buddhist art. The fleshy face has highly arched brows, pursed lips and three rings of flesh at the neck, and the hair is treated as snail-shell curls, hallmarks of the Guptan style.

'I fear life and death being here ... For the day we meet in the land of Amitabha I wait while following the path.'

MONK WOLMYEONG
(8TH CENTURY CE),
FOR HIS SISTER

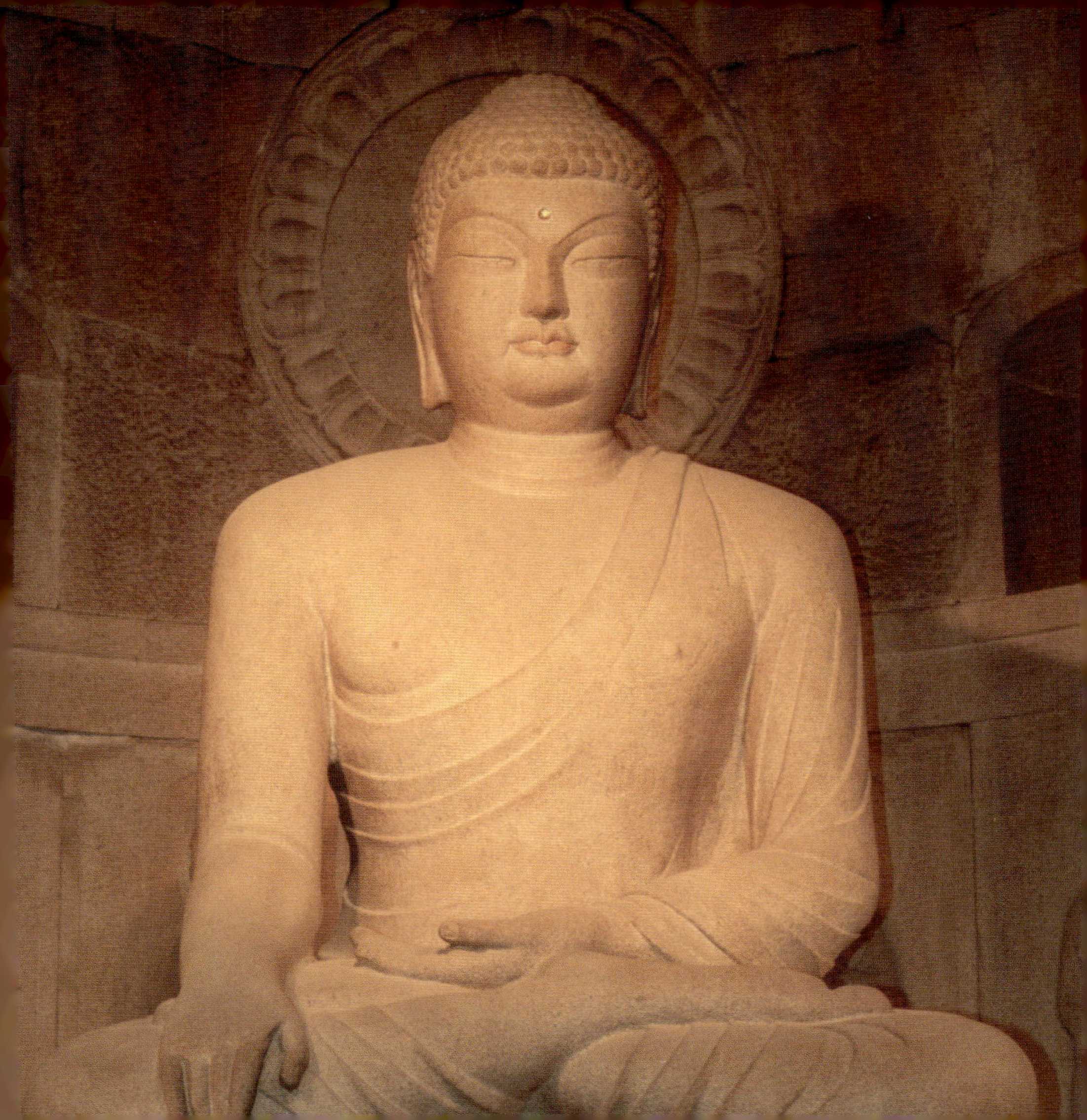

Temptation of Mara

8th century CE **Jobon Rendai-ji Temple, Kyoto, Japan**

COMMISSIONED BY Emperor Shomu   **MATERIALS** Ink and colours on paper   **HEIGHT** 27 cm/10½ in.   **LENGTH** Scroll copies vary

In this context, the Temptation of Mara is a scene from a long scroll from an illustrated life of the Buddha. The work is based on a Chinese scripture, the *Sutra of Cause and Effect*, or *E inga kyo* in Japanese, first translated into Chinese by Gunabhadra in the mid-5th century CE. The scroll is thought to be a near approximation of others executed in China, though no Chinese version has survived. Emperor Shomu (701–56), a devout Japanese Buddhist patron, set up a scripture-copying office staffed by dozens of skilled draughtsman and calligraphers. The scrolls, featuring passages of text with corresponding illustrations above, were each signed by a member of the office and his rank. The text is written in Chinese, the language of early Buddhist texts in Japan. This is the section that illustrates the temptation of Siddhartha by Mara, god of karma. Tall mountains with trees frame the composition and set the scene in the wilderness. Siddhartha, dressed in red, meditates in a cross-legged posture, one hand clasped over the other in his lap. The text explains that he is crossing the sea of causality, or enlightenment, and indeed a body of water is shown below him. He is flanked by Mara, in Chinese court robes, and his sisters holding skulls. Above, Mara's monstrous army gathers in menacing postures. Some are dressed in battle gear, others are disembodied animal heads; some menacingly threaten him with snakes – artists delighted in the depiction of the deformed martial creatures. But despite their assault, Siddhartha did not move and not a strand of his hair stirred. With the coming of dawn, the Buddha was enlightened, and Mara and his troops departed.

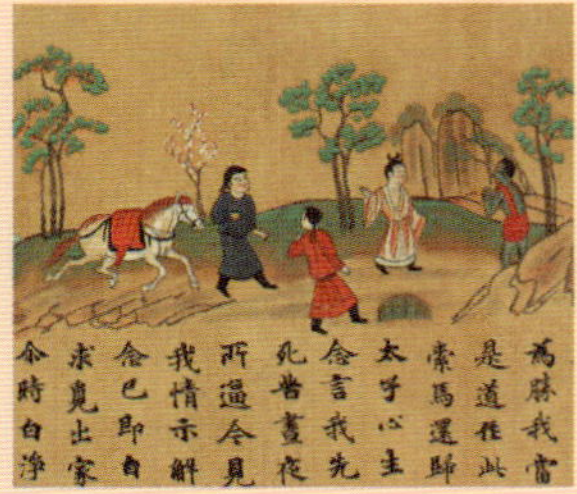

Life of Buddha

Hand scrolls are unrolled bit by bit, and the text is read from right to left, top to bottom. The scene above is from another 8th-century version of the *E inga kyo*. In addition to illustrating scriptures, hand scrolls were used to present temple histories, historical events, biographies of eminent monks, novels and other literary forms. In some, text 'pages' alternate with pictures.

'As [Mara] was thinking this, his soldiers came forward filling the sky. Each had a different kind of body and head. Some of them held scabbards or swords or carried large trees above their heads.'

SUTRA OF CAUSE AND EFFECT

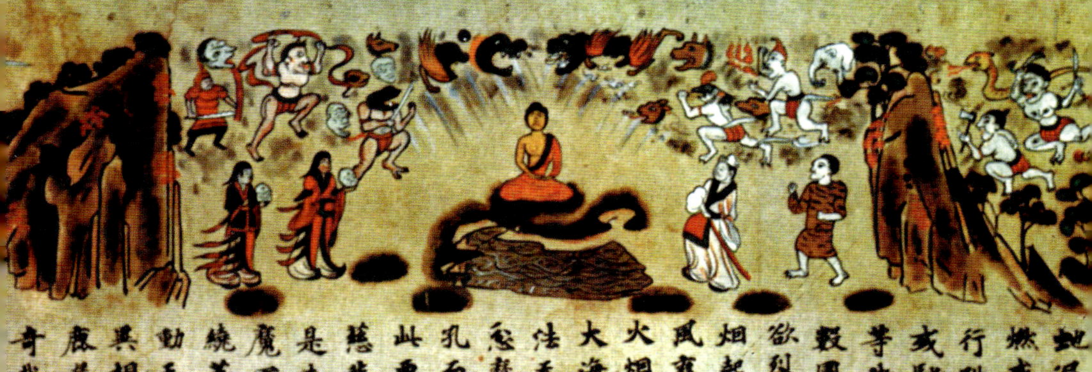
蚰遍經身或頭上大
燃或瞋目怒群或傍
行跳擲或空中掟轉
或馳走叫嘯有如是
等諸惡賴形不可稱
毀圉繞菩薩或復有
欲裂菩薩身或四方
烟起炎熖衝天或狂
風舊發震動山谷風
火熖塵暗九所見四
大海水一時涌沸諸
法天人諸龍鬼等悲
愍魔衆瞋恚增盛毛
孔而流淨居天衆見
此惡魔悩覗菩薩以
慈悲心而愍傷之於
是來下則塞虛空見
魔軍衆无量无邊圍
繞菩薩發大悲怦震
勤天地菩薩心定顏无
其相猶如師子衆於
麋羣中恋言嗚呼
奇我未曾有也菩薩

Dream of Maya

9th century CE **Borobudur Temple, Magelang, Java, Indonesia**

COMMISSIONED BY Sailendra dynasty **STYLE** Gupta Indian and native Indonesian **TOTAL OF RELIEF PANELS** 1,460

Chandi Borobudur is an impressive, tiered, stupa-like structure adorned with bas-relief narrative illustrations. On the lower terraces are illustrations of the Sanskrit *Lalitavistara* scripture, which relates the life of the Buddha. Later architects added upper levels to the building and these have representations of texts from the Mahayana school, a later development of Buddhism. Finally a top level was built and decorated with a series of bell-shaped stupas housing seated Buddhas; thus, the temple became a mandala in consonance with the arts of esoteric Buddhism. The monument's biographical depictions date to the earliest period when the life of the Buddha was the prime subject of the decor. The stories are read in a linear, chronological manner, indicating the scripture's important role in organizing the illustrations. Viewers relive the biography from birth to enlightenment as they walk around the tiers of the stupa. Here, reclining on her side, is the voluptuous semi-nude sleeping figure of Maya, the mother of the Buddha, during the conception. The smooth, curvaceous forms of her body contrast with the intricate details of her adornments – ornate necklaces, armlets, girdle and anklets. Both her facial expression and posture convey her dream state. The style of the figure's rendering recalls the 5th-century CE Indian Guptan era when corporeal beauty was believed to be a divine attribute; this led to sensuous depictions of the gods. The composition accords with the oldest representations. Figures placed around the reclining figure include beautiful harem women; one holds Maya's hand and fans her to keep her cool.

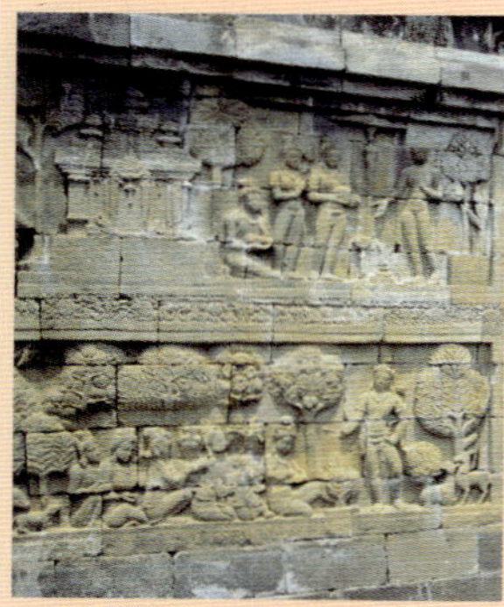

Narrative Ascent

Worshippers began their circumambulation at the foot of the monument and would slowly walk around the building until they had climbed to the upper terraces. In this way they ascended from the earthly realms, where the Buddha was born, to higher states of spiritual consciousness. Javanese artists deeply undercut the figures to make them project from the background and create shadows, making them easier to see.

'[Maya] was the most eminent of goddesses to the whole world.'

THE LIFE OF THE BUDDHA,
ASVAGHOSA

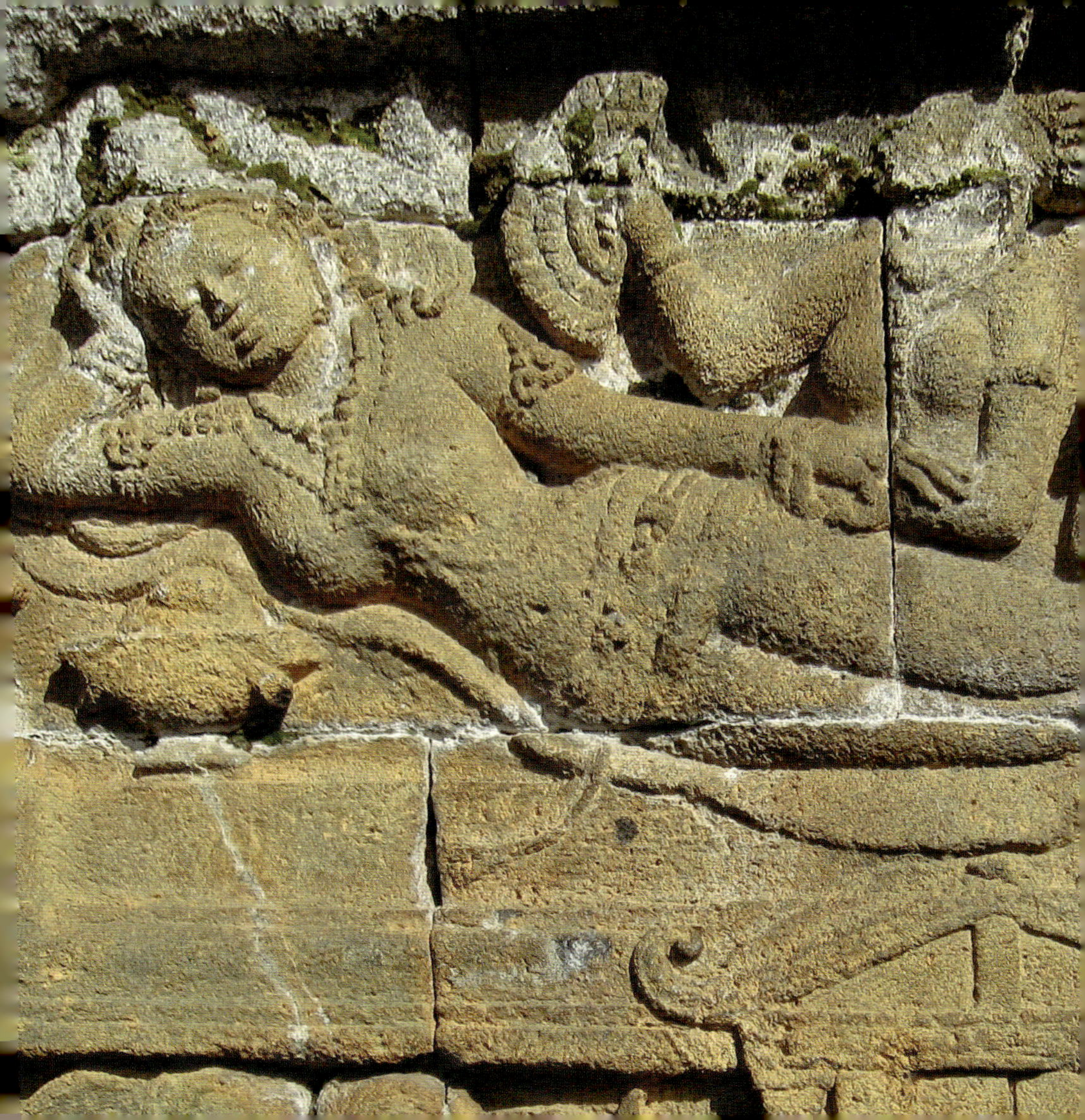

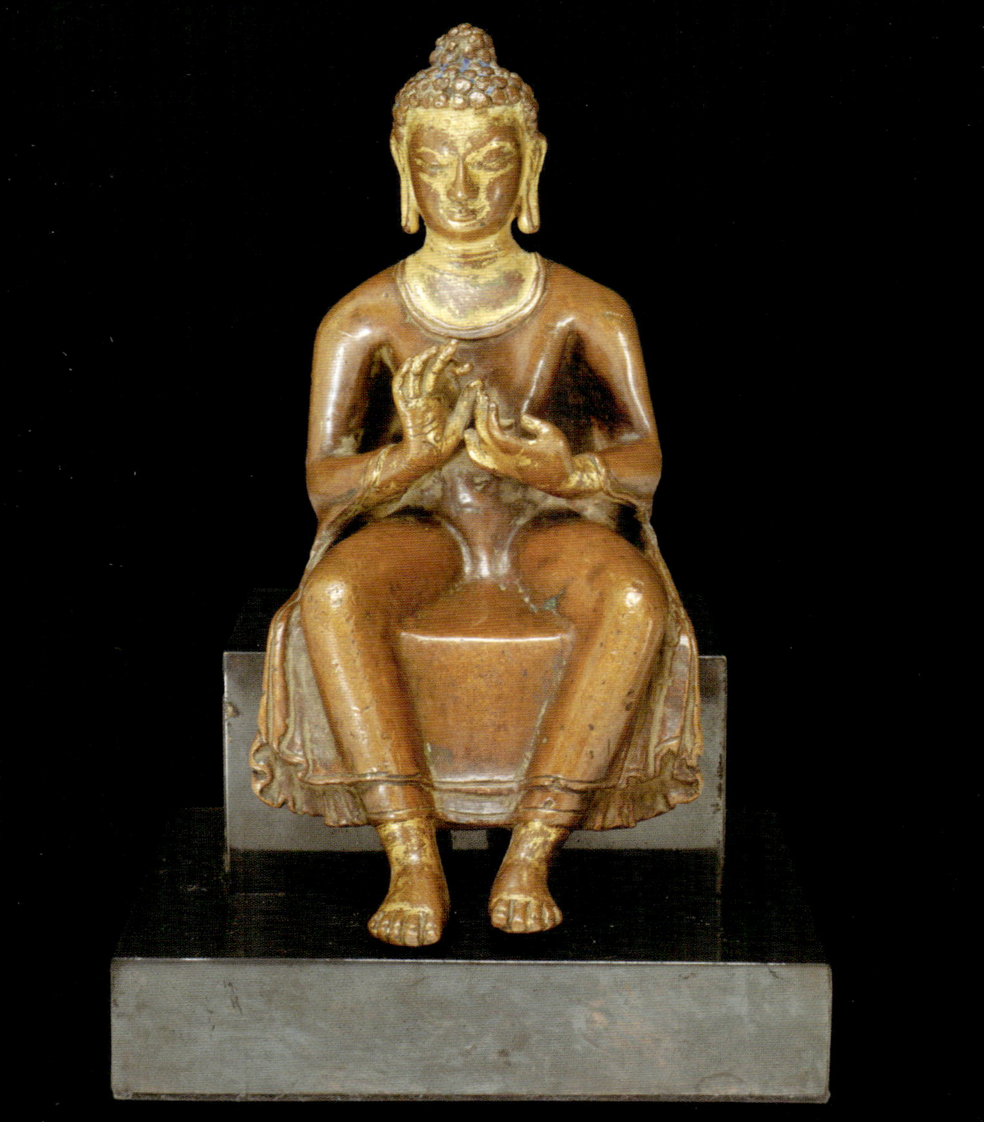

Seated Buddha of the Future

10th–11th century CE **Victoria & Albert Museum, London, UK**

ORIGIN Nepal **STYLE** Bihari **MATERIAL** Copper, with gilding and traces of paint **HEIGHT** 14 cm/5 ½ in.

Nepal, the birthplace of the Buddha, was an important place of pilgrimage and worship for Buddhists. There is evidence of several stupas erected by Emperor Ashoka (3rd century BCE), plus a building that replicated the temple of Bodh Gaya, which marked the place of the Buddha's enlightenment in India. Nepal is located near the centre of Buddhist practice at Nalanda University in Bihar, India, and was influenced by its style of art and iconography until Muslim invasions destroyed that site. In this seated Buddha from Nepal, Bihari style is evident in how the clinging monastic robe reveals the smoothly articulated body, its presence visible only at the neckline and wrists, and in the fringe of the skirt that falls in a delicate linear pattern. This Buddha is particularly Nepalese in character in its slim body; tall, narrow face; slender, elongated earlobes and nimble fingers. The bronze figure once had a gilt covering, an indication of the illumination of the Buddha. The pendant-legged posture identifies the icon as Maitreya Buddha, whose worship began a thousand years prior. In difficult times, Buddhists looked to a new golden age, which would be marked by the descent of this Buddha of the Future. Two ways of showing the figure were common: as a bodhisattva in the Tushita Heavens waiting his time to descend, or as a Buddha having come to earth. The teaching gesture of this Nepalese image indicates that in the future he will live a life similar to Siddhartha, by achieving enlightenment and preaching a First Sermon.

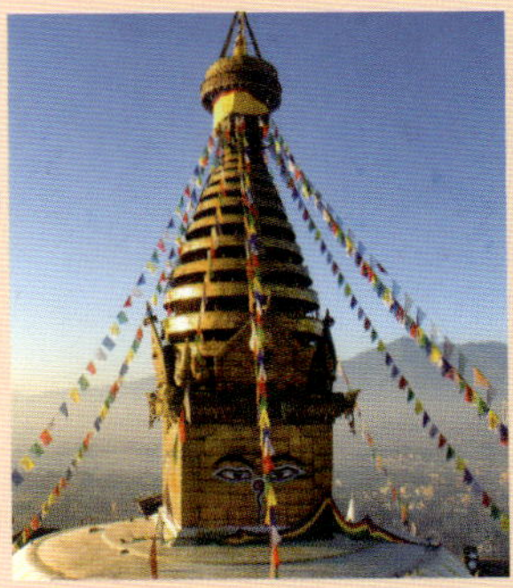

Swayambhunath Stupa

Nepal is famous for its great stupa at Swayambhu, Kathmandu, located on a high hill in the Kathmandu Valley. Though ancient in its origins, the stupa was first recorded as the focus of worship in the 5th century CE. The stupa has a huge white dome and a tall spire resting on a square base, on which pairs of painted eyes look out in four directions.

'The big debate has been about when the Buddha lived and now we have a shrine structure pointing to the 6th century BCE.'

ARCHAEOLOGIST ROBIN CONINGHAM, ANNOUNCING FINDS AT LUMBINI, NEPAL, 2013

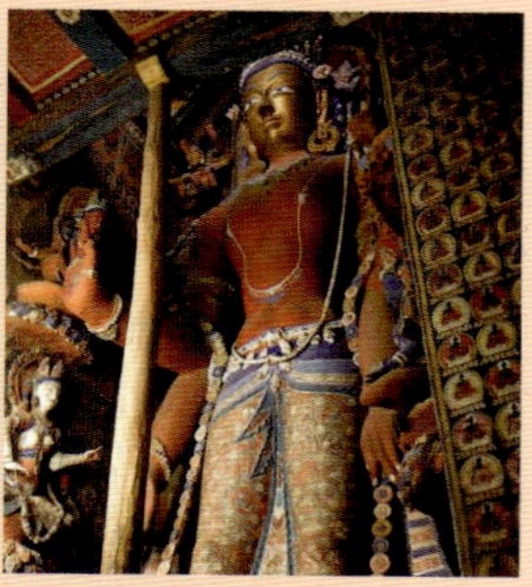

Alchi Bodhissattvas

The Sumtsek Temple at Alchi contains three colossal four-armed sculptures of Bodhisattvas: Maitreya (above), Chenrezig and Manjushri. All wear richly decorated dhotis – Chenrezig's with sacred places of Kashmir and Manjushri's with eighty-four Mahasiddha portraits.

'Thereupon the people hung a curtain about her, and retired. So her delivery [of the Buddha] took place while she was standing up, and keeping fast hold of the sal-tree branch.'

INTRODUCTION, *JATAKAS*

Birth of the Buddha

Late 11th–13th centuries CE   Alchi Monastery, Ladakh, India

STYLE Tantrayana   **MATERIALS** Clay, inks and paints
HEIGHT OF MAITREYA STATUE *c.* 4 m/13 ft

The life of the Buddha persisted as an important part of Buddhist iconographical programmes, no matter which sect. Within the Sumtsek Temple of Alchi Monastery, a huge clay statue of Maitreya, the Bodhisattva of the Future, stands flat-footed, his four arms making fear-not and charity gestures; multiple jewels and scarves adorn his body (see left). His dhoti garment, seen here, is painted with forty-eight scenes of the Buddha's life. The scenes are theologically consistent with the belief that the Buddha of the Future will have the same life as Shakyamuni. The scene of the Buddha's birth features his mother Maya, large and centrally placed, rendered in Indian fashion as a voluptuous, dark-skinned Yakshi or tree spirit, her hand grasping the bough of a tree. To the right her sister Mahaprajapati catches the child as he emerges from her right flank. Both the conception and birth of the Buddha are termed 'virgin' in that Siddhartha self-willed his birth, chose his respective parents and never came into direct contact with his mother's flesh (he was contained in a special sack, variously interpreted as being made of silk, diamond or glass). Seven days after the birth, Maya died and her sister raised the child as her own. Beneath the birth scene is the First Bath of the Siddhartha, where celestials pour rainwater from jugs over his body. The attendants and celebrating flying celestials flanking Maya are smaller in scale, and their native dress is less naturalistic and reflects the styles of the region. Overall, the biographical narratives are contained in large roundels that contrast with geometric forms filled with colourful, natural-world motifs.

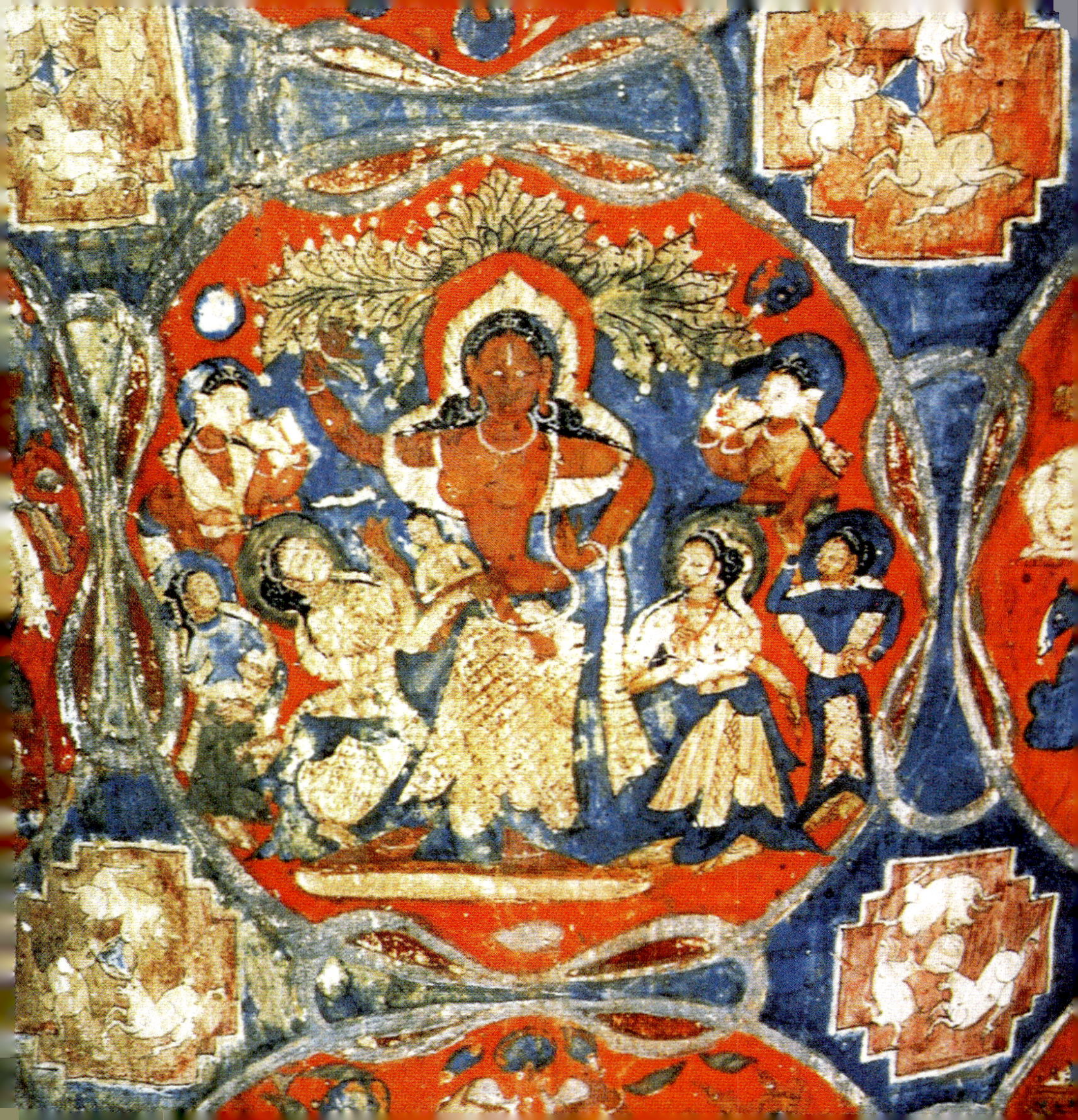

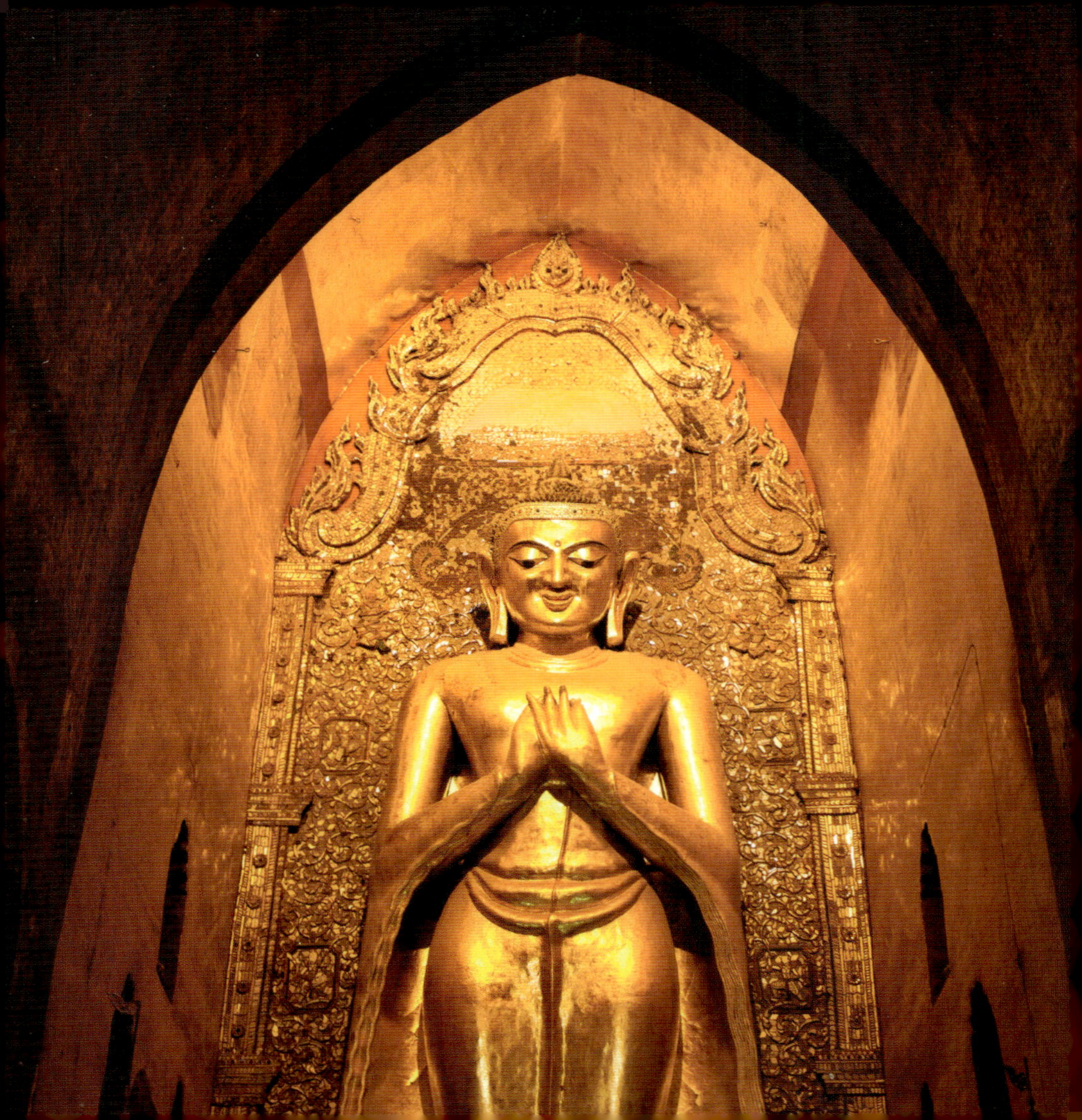

Standing Kassapa Buddha

1105 CE Ananda Temple, Bagan, Myanmar (Burma)

STYLE Theravad school **MATERIAL** Teak, gilded
HEIGHT Kassapa Buddha statue: 9.5 m/31 ft; base: 2.4 m/8 ft

King Kyanzittha (1030–1112) of the Pagan dynasty of Myanmar was a strong ruler who espoused Thervad Buddhism, the early school of teachings. Among the temples he had built in his capital, then called Pagan, the Ananda Temple is the most famous. Its ground plan is in the form of an equilateral cross: four directional halls face each of the cardinal directions from a central base, and each hall houses a standing gilded teak image of the Buddha. The four Buddhas belong to the set of twenty-eight Buddhas of the past described in Chapter 27 of the *Buddhavamsa* of the Pali tradition: Kassapa faces south, Kakusandha faces north, Konagamana faces east, and Gautama, the historic Buddha, faces west. Numerical sets of Buddhas are not only common in the Theravad tradition; in the Mahayana school there are the Buddhas of the Four Directions, and the Buddhas of the Present, Past and Future; the Vajrayana school has more complicated sets still. The four statues differ only slightly in their *mudras*, and the manner in which the drapery falls. The Buddhas in the north and south are original but those in the east and west are modern replacements; viewed in their narrow chambers, all are awesome in their size and splendour. Near the figure of Gautama are two life-sized seated figures made of lacquer that have been tentatively identified as King Kyanzittha, the donor, and Shin Arahan, the Theravada monk who was his spiritual advisor. The lower levels had nearly a thousand glazed clay plaques illustrating events in the life of the Buddha and his previous existences. The corridors encircling the base have over sixty sandstone reliefs with scenes from the life of the Buddha.

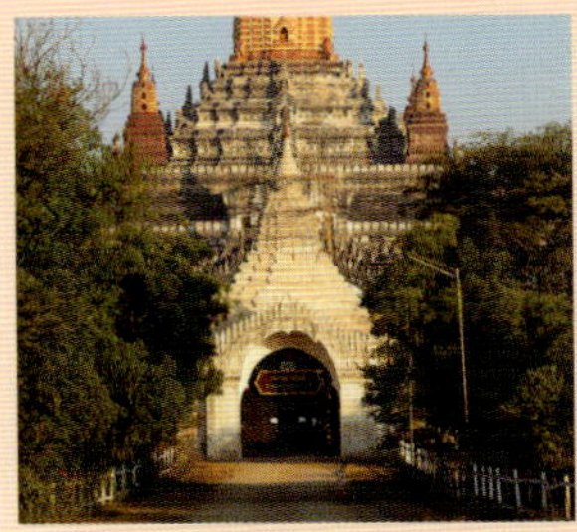

Ananda Temple

The Ananda Temple building at Bagan is seated on a main plinth with four receding courses, making a pyramid-shaped pagoda complete with an umbrella spire, or *hti*. The overall height is 51 metres (167 ft). The building's central floor is square, 53 square metres (570 sq ft) in area, while the gabled porches are 17 metres (178 ft) from the central hall. Each porch has an ornate entrance with a stupa at the top of the arch. A small stupa is also placed at each corner of the second main level.

'Those who take good care of my work of merit shall get equal share of merit with me.'

BUILDER'S INSCRIPTION AT A BAGAN MONUMENT

Buddha Seated on Naga

c. 12th century CE **Guimet National Museum of Asian Art, Paris, France**

ORIGIN Preah Khan Temple, Angkor, Cambodia
MATERIAL Bronze **HEIGHT** 111 cm/44 in.

Tradition asserts that after enlightenment, when the Buddha remained in meditation, a *naga*, or snake god, arched his seven cobra hoods over his head to protect him from inclement weather. From ancient times, *nagas* had a beneficial and fearsome identity in Asia. They were protectors, superior to men, who inhabited river and lakes, where they guarded the treasures of the aquatic realms. *Nagas* figure prominently in the life of the Buddha: they offer the First Bath, predict his enlightenment and afterwards offer homage. In this way, older gods were absorbed into Buddhist practice. The scene, rarely portrayed in India, was extremely popular in Southeast Asia. This figure has the Buddha seated in meditative position with his eyes closed. The planes of the body are smooth with little anatomical detail. There is a tall crown on his head and jewellery on his body, and later schools of Buddhism used these adornments in representations of the Cosmic Buddha. The sculpture comes from the Buddhist temple city of Preah Khan, built by the Khmer Jayavarman VII (c. 1120/25–c. 1220). The city has been reclaimed from the jungle, although some trees remain entwined with the buildings to preserve their integrity. After his victory against the Cham, the king built a capital at Angor Thom and commissioned many temples, including the great temple of Bayon and the Buddhist temple, monastery and school of Preah Khan, which was established in 1191. A stele discovered in the foundation of the latter temple records its construction and states that its main image was one of Avalokiteshvara, the Bodhisattva of Compassion, dedicated to, and made to resemble, Jayavarman VII's father.

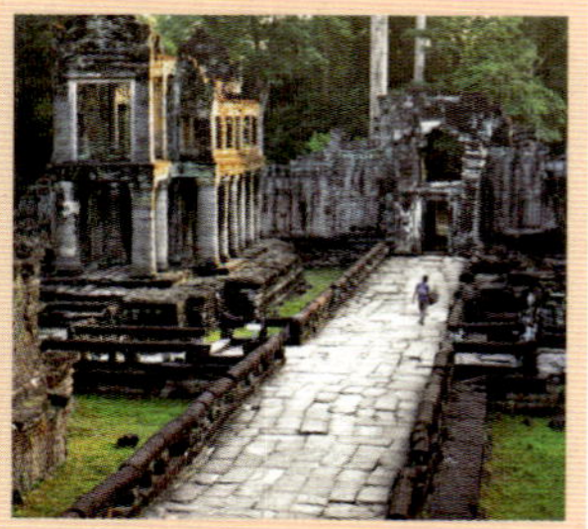

Preah Khan

Preah Khan in Angkor, near Siem Reap, in Cambodia is a temple city encircled by a great wall and moat. The sacred city, occupying 56 hectares (138 acres), is divided into four enclosures, the outermost of which was for locals who worked to meet the needs of the community.

'And the Naga king Mucalinda came out of his abode, and seven times encircled the body of the Blessed One with his windings, and kept extending his large hood over the Blessed One's head.'

MAHAVAGGA, THE BOOK OF THE DISCIPLINE

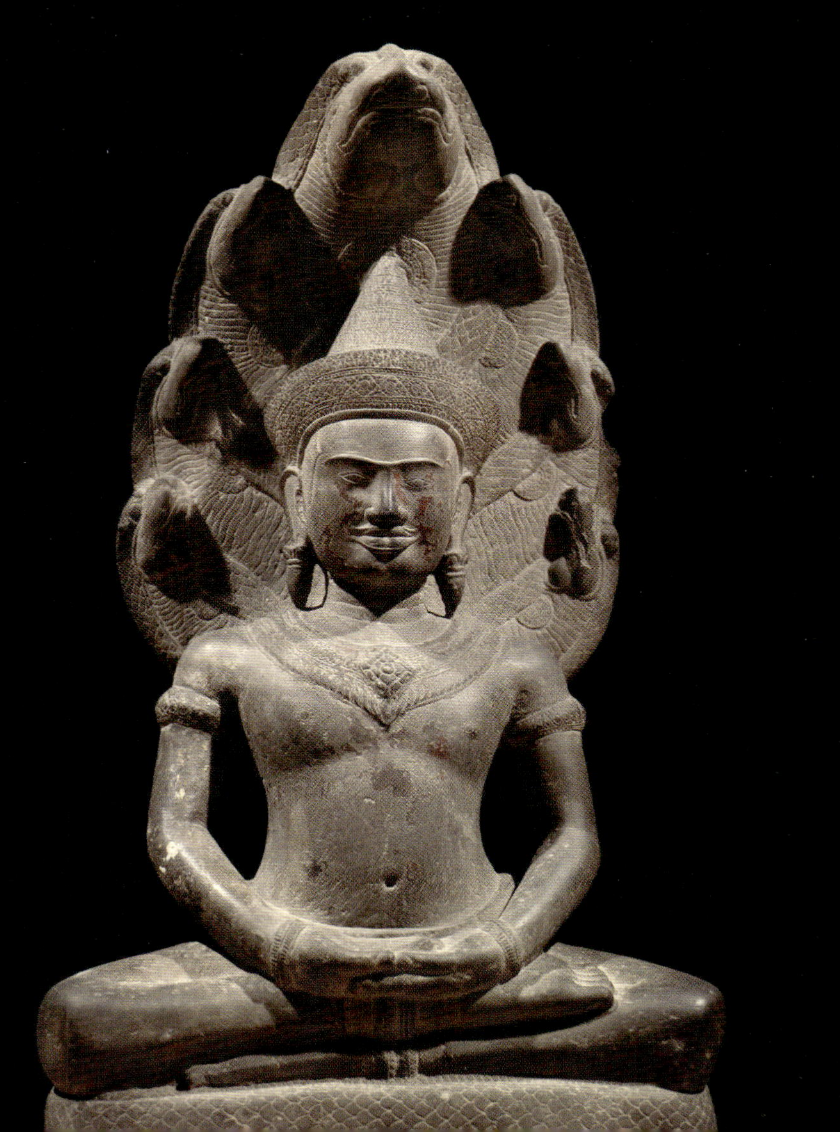

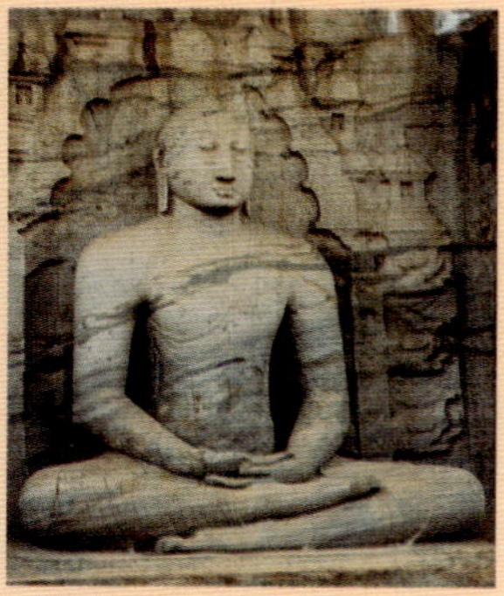

Buddhist Capital

Polonnaruwa was first declared the national capital city by King Vijayabahu I after he defeated the Chola invaders in 1070. He was succeeded in the 12th century by King Parakramabahu I, who commissioned large-scale Buddhist projects including a hundred temples and the Gal Vihara rock temple with its reclining Buddha and this 4.6-m (15-ft) high seated Buddha.

'For I have put away this painful vessel, I have stemmed the flowing sea of birth and death, free for ever now from pain!'

ASVAGHOSA, *BUDDHACARITA*

Colossal Parinirvana

12th century CE Gal Vihara, Polonnaruwa, Sri Lanka

COMMISSIONED BY King Parakramabahu (1153–86)   **STYLE** Sinhalese
LENGTH OF BUDDHA 24 m/79 ft   **HEIGHT OF ANANDA** 7 m/23 ft

In ancient Buddhist art, the *parinirvana*, or nirvana-after-death, of the Buddha was represented by the stupa, or domed funeral monument. When the Buddha image was invented in around the 2nd century CE, it was the reclining figure of the teacher that came to signal the *parinirvana*. In 2nd–4th-century bas-relief depictions from Gandhara, India, the reclining Buddha is shown considerably larger than the figures around him. The size of the Buddha increased gradually until figures grew to monumental proportions. The immense sculpture of the reclining Buddha at Gal Vihara, Polonnaruwa, is the largest in the Buddhist world. None of the usual narrative details are rendered, except for the presence of Ananda, the youngest disciple of the Buddha and his personal attendant, who stands, also in large scale, in his traditional position at the head of the bed, his arms folded in front of his chest. The Buddha is rendered in canonical fashion as described in the scriptures: he lies on his right side, his feet are placed one on top of the other, and he rests his head on his right hand, which is supported by a pillow. The Sinhalese style of depicting the Buddha, developing out of South Indian styles, shows him as a wide-shouldered, slender figure, and the parts of his body are harmoniously and gracefully articulated. His head is ovoid in shape and his features are abstractly rendered. Both the Buddha and Ananda are three-dimensional sculptures. Also at the site is a large seated Buddha, 4.6 metres (15 ft) tall, and a smaller one, 1.4 metres (4½ ft) tall. The figures once had architectural coverings, as ruined brick constructions nearby attest.

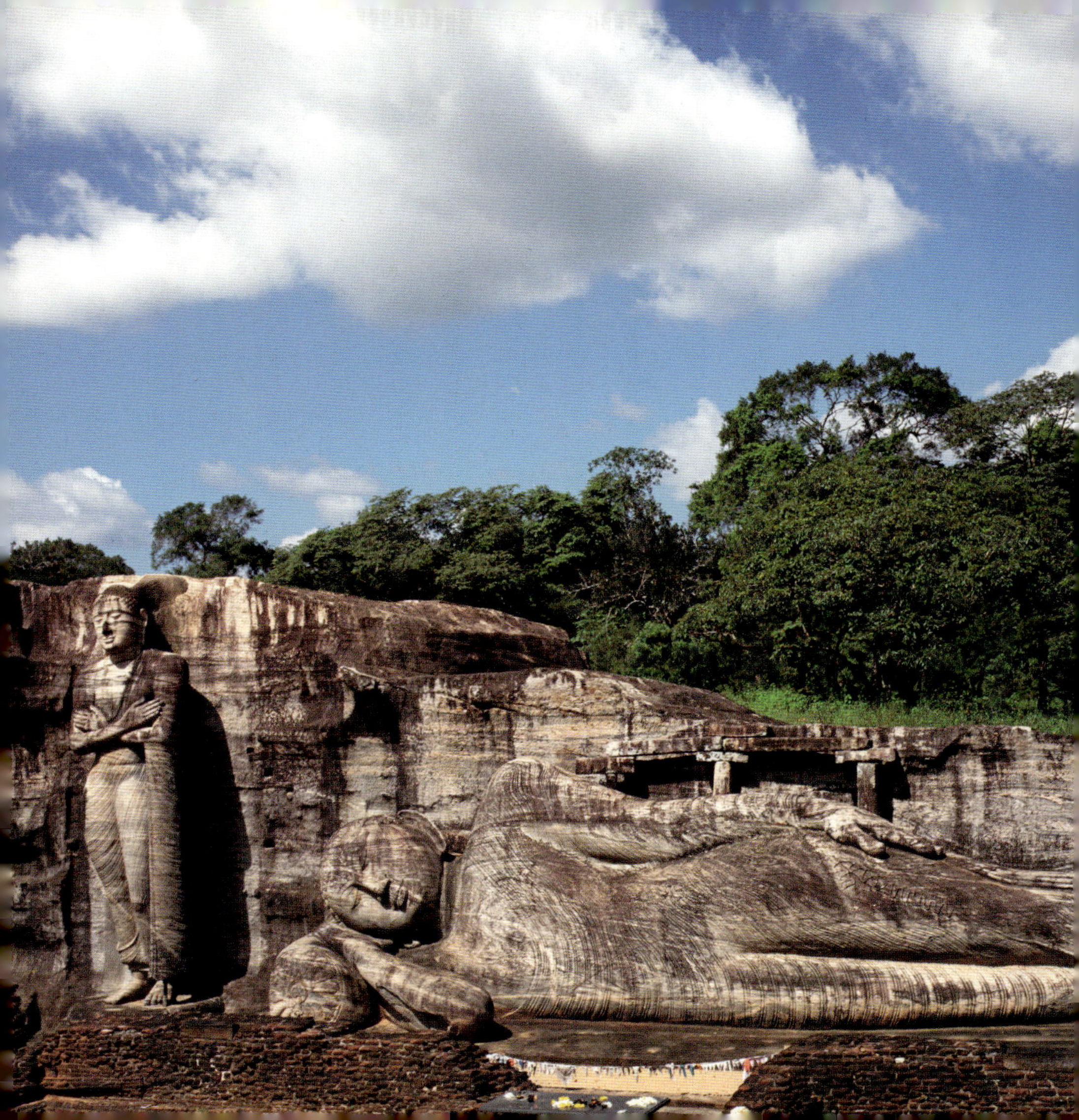

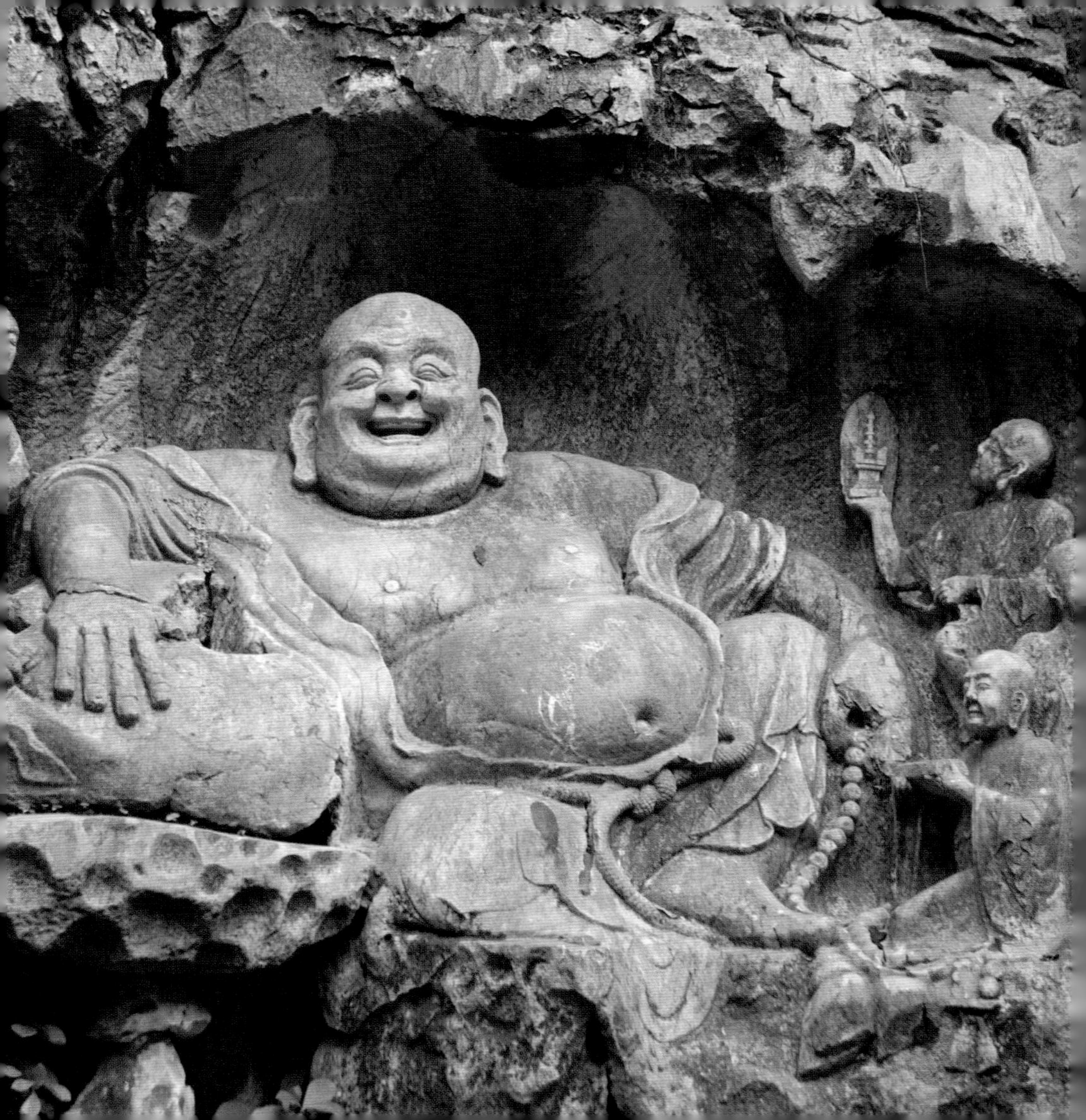

Laughing Buddha

12th–13th century CE **Feilai Peak, Hangzhou, China**

HEIGHT OF PEAK 209 m/685 ft   **NUMBER OF SCULPTURES** 330
MATERIAL Limestone   **STYLE** Vajrayana school

Traditionally, the Buddha of the Future is represented as a bodhisattva awaiting his time in Tushita Heaven, or as a Buddha descended to earth. But in the 10th century in southern China a new form of depiction arose, developing out of iconoclastic Chan (Zen in Japanese) teachings stressing that the path to enlightenment was possible without the aid of scriptures, icons and temples. Instead, the believer need only look inwards and meditate to discover the nature of Buddha present in all of humanity. The exact origins of the fat, nearly naked, laughing Buddha are not entirely clear, but it is posited that Qieci, a Chan practitioner, wrote a poem that identified a homeless man, spotted asleep under a bridge with all his belongings in a large sack, as the Buddha of the Future; thus, we must rely on meditation, not false hope in the intervention of gods. The laughing Buddha became an iconic image and popular motif for Chan painters. At the cliffs of Hangzhou in southern China, sculptors created dozens of niches containing large-scale images, in a seemingly random fashion. This fat laughing Buddha of the Future appears in the upper area of the escarpment. Seated in a relaxed posture, with one leg bent and the other hanging down, a posture of royal ease, he holds a rosary for meditation in his left hand. He has a capacious belly, triple chin and bald head. In much smaller scale are his attendants, the *luohans* or enlightened ones, whom the historic Buddha enjoined not to pass away but to await the descent of the Buddha of the Future. Although they are depicted as a variety of personalities and physical types, they are all bald headed and wear monastic robes.

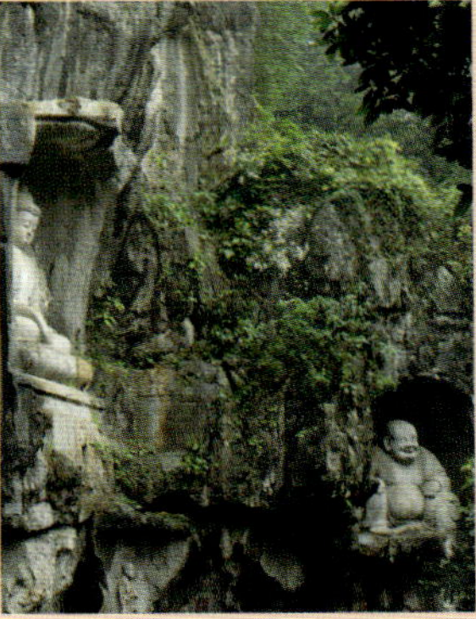

Feilai Peak

The name of the site derives from a legend that an Indian monk named Huili, arriving in the valley, noticed an unusual limestone formation among the sandstone cliffs. He thought it must have come from India and called it Fenglai Feng, meaning 'cliffs that fly from afar'.

'Reborn innumerable times / From time to time manifested to men / The men of the age do not recognize you.'

BY QIECI, A CHAN MONK; POSSIBLE INSPIRATION OF THE LAUGHING BUDDHA

Walking Buddha

13th–14th century CE **Wat Mahathat, Sukhothai, Thailand**

STYLE Theravad
MATERIAL Sandstone

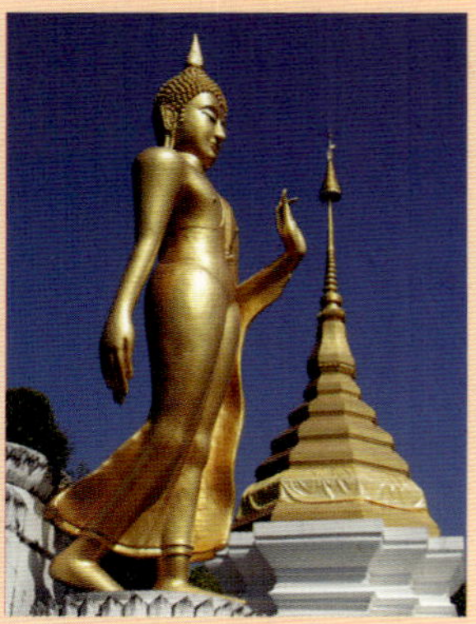

Wat Salaeng

The walking Buddha is particularly characteristic Thai iconography. This free-standing gilded bronze example, at Wat Salaeng, exhibits typical attenuated limbs and long, tapering hands. The left hand is raised in the *abhaya mudra*, meaning 'do not fear'.

'The walking pose had been used especially to denote two scenes in the Buddha's life: the taming of a wild elephant and his return from Tavistimsa Heaven ...'

BETTY GOSLING, *SUKOTHAI*

The southern Buddhist trade routes connecting South India to Sri Lanka and Thailand saw the evolution of a distinct style of Buddha icon. The works have the native body type of a supple-limbed yogi, rather than a Western athletic hero. Their drapery, rather than clinging to the body in the style of wet cloth, is rendered without folds and is apparent only across the chest and at the hem. In this Thai example at Wat Mahathat, the pieces of cloth wound around the body fall in a series of narrow folds on the right side of the chest. The Thai style is also unique in the body type, characterized by broad shoulders, a willowy elongated torso and sinuous limbs. The fingers of the hand are slender, tapered and supple. Set on a slender neck, the round face has highly arched brows, upturned, almond-shaped eyes, a slender aquiline nose and fleshy lips. The hair and cranial protrusion are treated as a cap of snail-shell curls. The three-quarter view has the Buddha walking with his garments swaying rhythmically. This Buddha is but one of many found at the vast complex of Sukhothai, which was active from the 13th to the 14th centuries CE. With his downward gaze, sweet smile and walking gait, the Sukhothai-style Buddha is more approachable than its austere northern counterpart. In the 14th century, with India made inaccessible by Muslim conquest, the Thais turned to Sri Lanka, which followed the Theravad teachings, for their Buddhist education. In this school, there are no celestial intermediaries to appeal to; the focus is entirely on the Buddha. Thus, at Sukhothai Park, huge sculptures of the Buddha are housed in pillared halls, narrow cells or set in the open air.

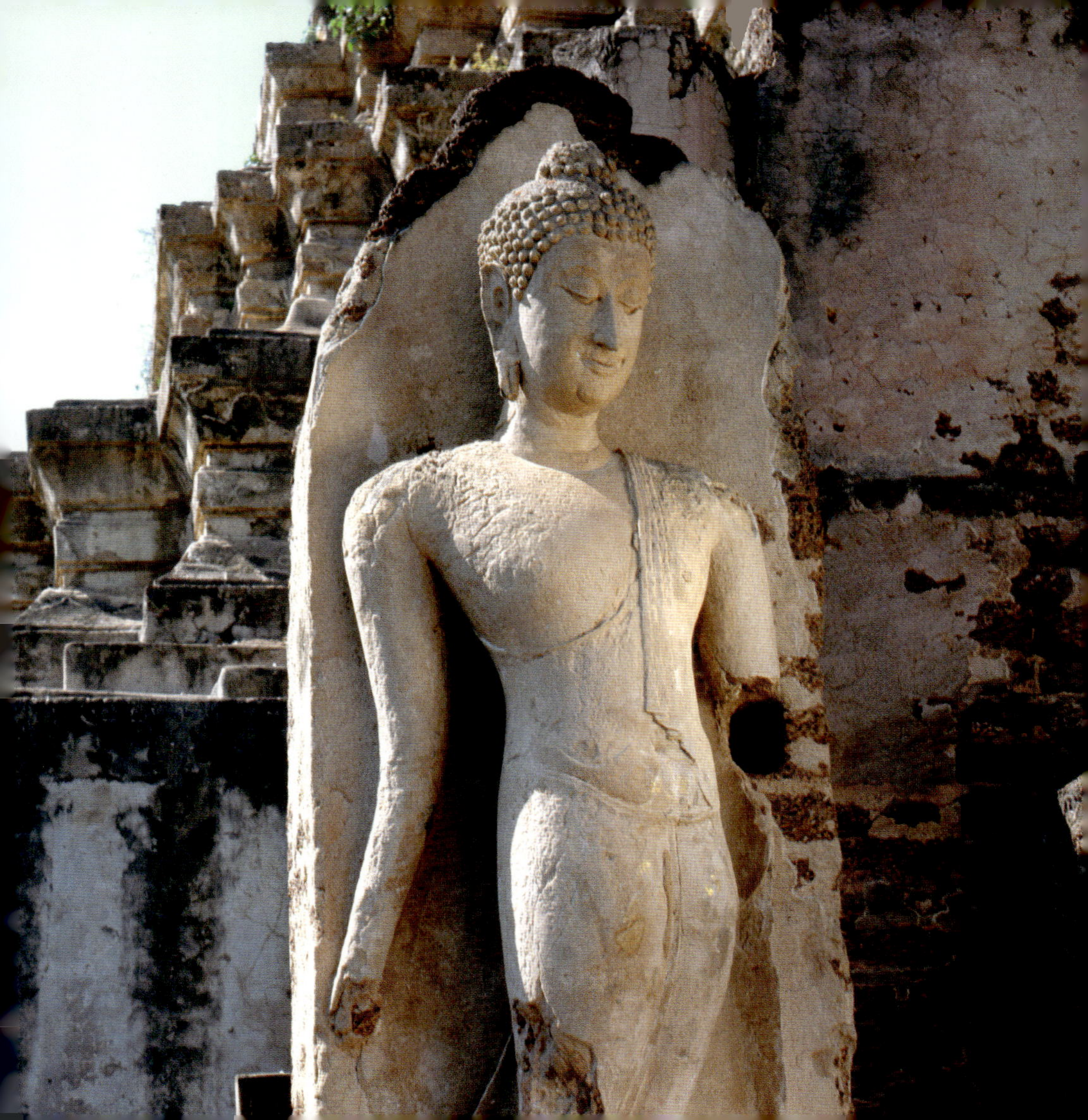

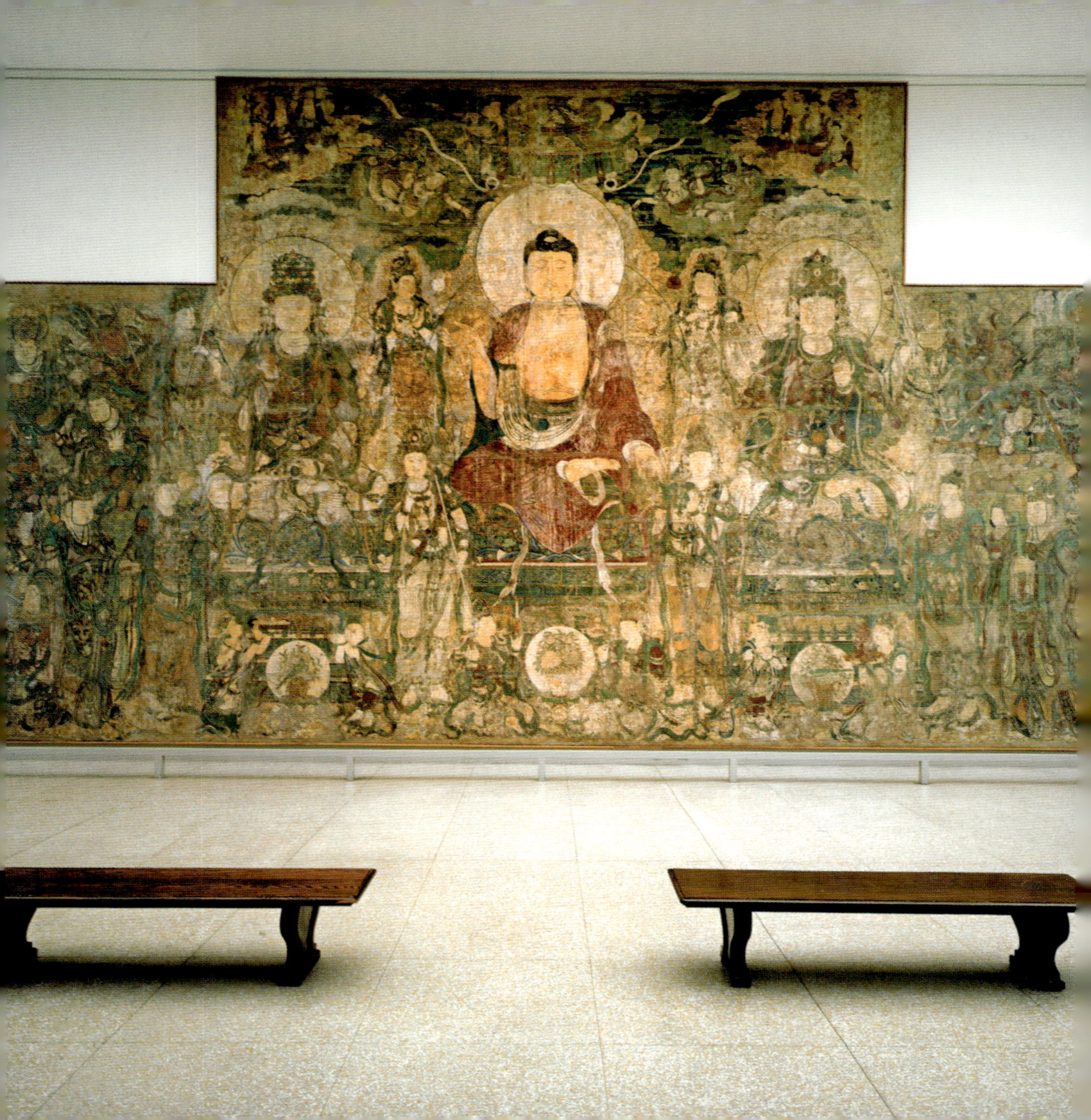

Healing Buddha, the Pure Land of Bhaishajyaguru

C. 1319 CE **Metropolitan Museum of Art, New York, USA**

MATERIALS Water-based pigment over a foundation of clay mixed with straw **DIMENSIONS** 7.52 x 15.11 m / 24 ¾ x 49 ½ in.

This mural is one of the Four Buddhas of the Cardinal Directions that once adorned the walls of the Main Hall of the Guangsheng Lower Monastery in Southern Shanxi. The Healing Buddha, Yaoshi (Bhaishajyaguru in Sanskrit), is seen seated at the centre and holding a medicine jar in his left hand. He is attended by four bodhisattvas: two on either side of him hold up the the sun and the moon, and two in the lower area hold the monk's staff (*khakkhara*) and bowl (*pdtra*) of the Buddha. Minor bodhisattvas are in attendance, and others in the foreground make offerings along with six miniature Buddhas. Descending from the sky are two angels, and above them are two groups of celestials seated on clouds. In the background are twelve figures, some of them in martial attire and horrific in aspect: these represent vows Yaoshi made to save the sick and suffering. In China, special painters had been trained in executing religious subjects since the 8th century. The tradition survived into the 14th century, when artists like Zhu Haogu, working in Shanxi, made paintings for both Daoist and Buddhist temples, utilizing the same formats and formulas for the figures and compositions but altering the necessary iconographical details. The complexity of the composition, with its many participants and the extravagant adornments of jewels, silk garments and scarves, attests to the late date of execution. In the early 20th century, monks at Guangsheng sold the murals to U.S. collections in exchange for funds to refurbish the monastery.

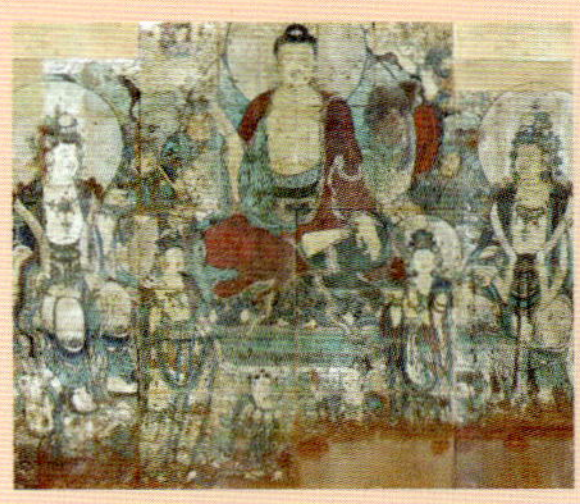

Companion Mural
This detail of another mural from Guangsheng, now at the Penn Museum, University of Pennsylvania, similarly depicts the Healing Buddha. The Bodhisattvas of the Moon and Sun, identified by the aureoles or circular lights around their heads, form a triad with the central Buddha.

'The Buddha then said to Ananda, "If sentient beings [beset by heavy karma] should hear the name of the Healing Buddha, single-mindedly recite and hold fast to it …, then it will be impossible for them to sink into the Evil Realms."'

SUTRA OF THE HEALING BUDDHA

Reclining Buddha

1357 CE **Wat Yai Chai Mongkhon, Ayutthaya Historical Park, Thailand**

COMMISSIONED BY King Ramathibodhi I **REMODELLED** 1965
MATERIALS Brick and stucco **LENGTH** 15 m/49 ft 3 in.

This colossal reclining Buddha was made in Thailand but differs from its Sri Lankan prototypes in several ways. The Buddha appears not yet to have passed away, as he rests his head on his hand. Also, compared to the Sinhalese examples, the figure has a more elongated body with sinuously shaped limbs and long, graceful fingers. The face is distinctive, with an elongated aquiline nose and slender lips. His hair is modelled as snail-shell curls, and a stylized flame emerges from the top of his head. More abstractly rendered are the arches of his brows and his nearly closed eyes. True to Theravad, or the older school of Buddhism, the focus is on the historic Buddha Shakyamuni, rather than bodhisattvas, or saviour gods. The sculpture was remodelled in 1965 after the original was damaged, and further repairs are underway. Buddhism is, of course, still actively practised in Thailand, and an orange cloth, similar to that worn by Thai monks, is usually seen draped over the body of the Buddha. The statue is found in the second capital of Thailand, Ayutthaya, established in in 1350 by King U-Thong. In 1357 two young princes died of cholera and in the same year King Ramathibodhi I had Wat Yai Chai Mongkhon monastery built for the use of monks returning from study in Ceylon; the princes were buried at the site and an image of the Buddha was installed. At the end of the 16th century, during the reign of King Naresuan, the Vihara (monastic quarters) of the Reclining Buddha was constructed on the site. Then, in 1592, King Naresuan had a great stupa built on the site to celebrate his victory over the Burmese crown prince in a duel on elephants.

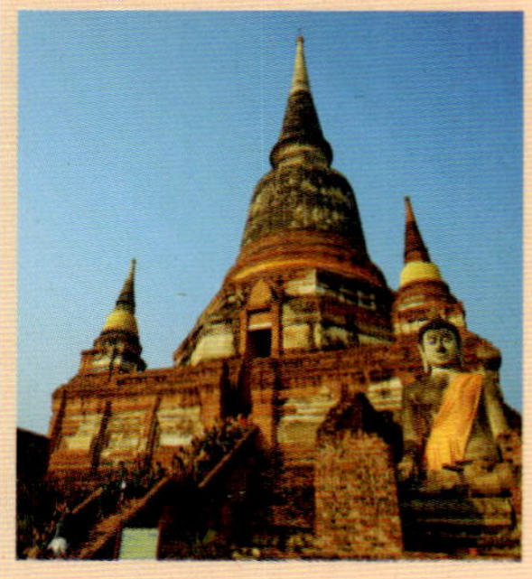

Ayutthaya

Ayutthaya was ideally located on an island surrounded by three rivers. The sacred park was once the site of over a thousand temples and over four thousand golden images of Buddha. Today much has been destroyed, but the many stupas, monasteries and image halls that remain, including Wat Yai Chai Mongkhon (above), are the focus of religious activity of monks and local residents.

'Behold now, brethren I exhort you, saying, "Decay is inherent in all component things! Work out your salvation with diligence!"'

MAHAPARINIBBANA SUTRA

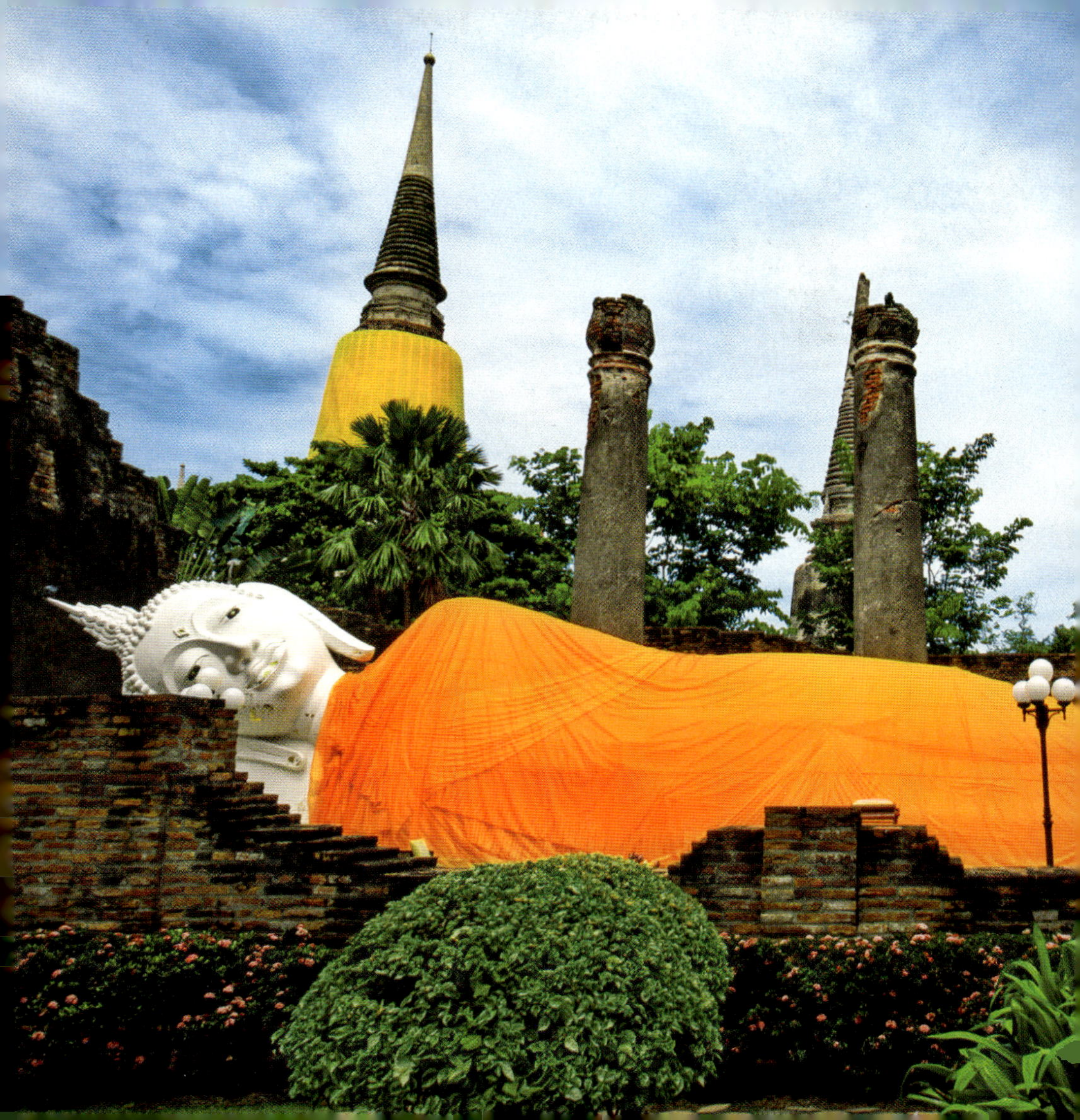

Buddha's First Sermon in the Deer Park

Late 18th century CE **British Library, London, UK**

ORIGIN Myanmar (Burma)   **FORMAT** Concertina-folded sheet
MATERIALS Ink and colours on paper

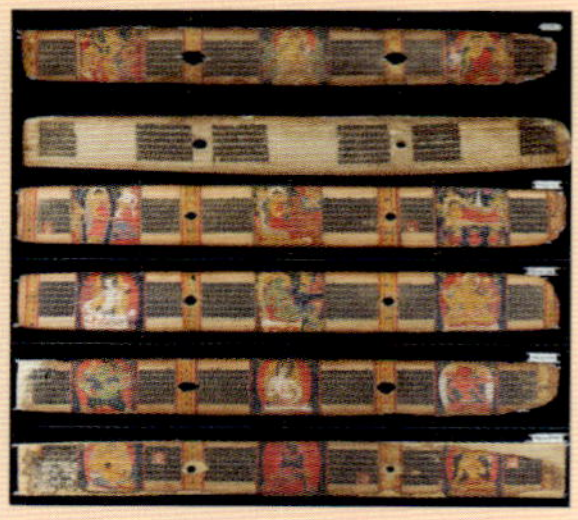

Nepalese Illustrated Manuscript

The Nepalese scroll above is perhaps the most remarkable of among eighty or so manuscripts collected by a British administrator and resident of Kathmandu, Brian Houghton Hodgson, and donated to the Royal Asiatic Society in 1835 and 1836. The scroll is a copy of the *Astasahasrika prajnaparamita,* or 'The Perfection of Wisdom in 8,000 Lines', and is thought to date from the 12th century CE. Produced on palm leaf, the scroll is celebrated for the vibrant illustrations that appear at regular intervals within the text.

'Buddhas ... turned the Wheel of the Law ... in Varanasi's Deer Park.'

SUTRA OF CAUSE AND EFFECT

Throughout Asia, followers learnt the details of the events in the life of the Buddha from artistic representations. The illustrations were one of the primary ways in which Buddhist principles, inherent in the pictorial hagiography, were disseminated. The scenes are always recognizable, despite the process of assimilation by which local styles and details replaced foreign ones. It helped understanding that the major figures were usually treated in a more orthodox manner. This Burmese manuscript is a case in point. A golden-skinned Buddha sits on a lotus; he extends his right hand to the earth, and the Bodhi tree blooms behind him. Seated in the left foreground are the five monks; on the right are a group of crowned figures, perhaps divinities, and three deer indicate the park in which the First Sermon was given. The house and princely figure on the right belong to another scene. Some of the ancient temples from the old Burmese capital at Pagan have murals depicting scenes of the life of the Buddha, but no manuscripts before the 18th century seem to have survived. At first, reading the life story was limited to monks and scholars who were literate in the Pali language, the religious lingua franca of South-east Asia. This situation changed when a Burmese monk, Dutiya Medi Hsayadaw (1747–1834), translated the detailed narrative into the local language. Brief descriptions in the vernacular, probably drawn from the monk's translation, accompany the illustrations at the bottom of the page.

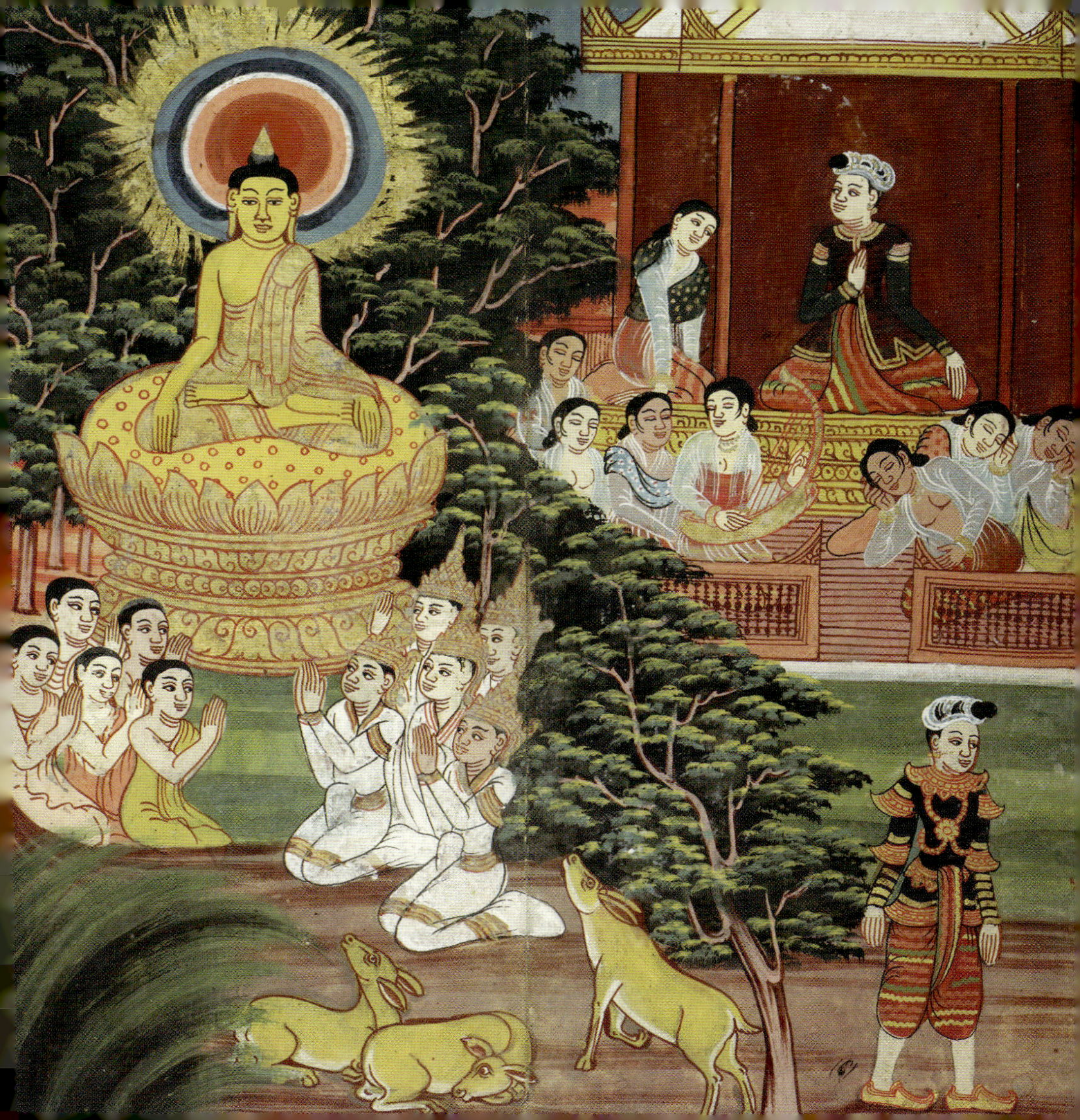

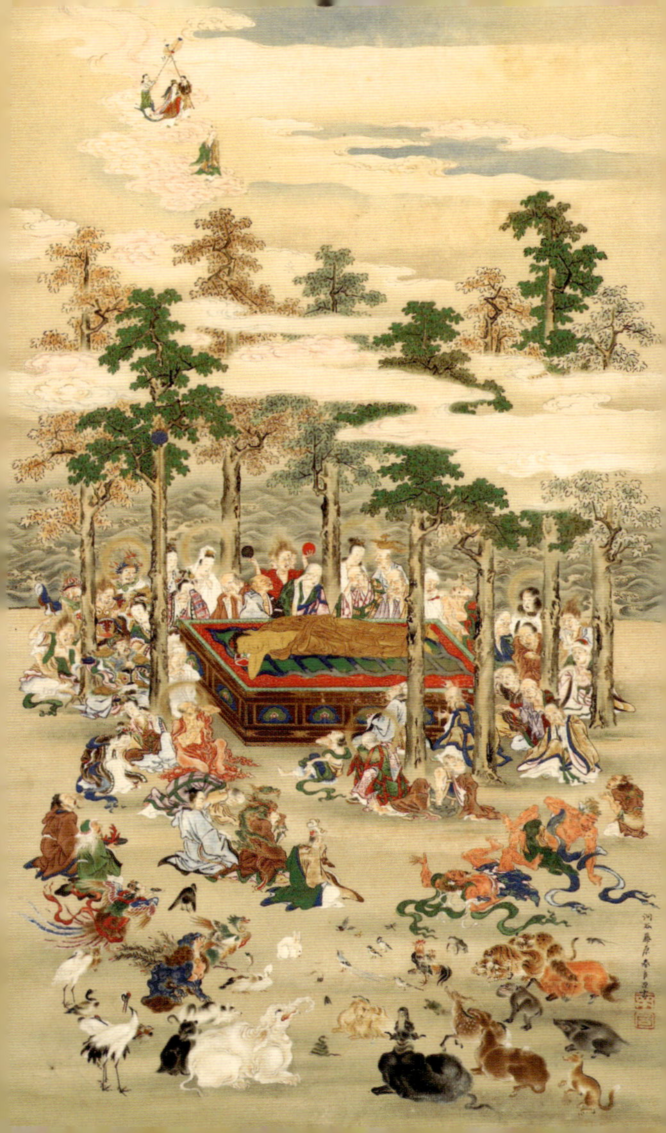

Death of the Buddha

1800–80 CE **British Museum, London, UK**

FORMAT Painted hanging scroll **MATERIALS** Ink and colours on silk
DIMENSIONS 93 × 40.2 cm/36 ½ × 15 ¾ in.

This portable hanging silk scroll, when not on display, can be rolled up for storage. It shows that, in contrast to decorous Southeast Asian Theravada depictions of the Buddha's death scene, Japanese, Mahayanist portrayals of the *Mahaparinirvana* (death of the Buddha) include a huge congregation of mourning figures to attest the universality of the event. The mother of the Buddha, Maya, who predeceased him and for her merit was awarded rebirth as a god in the highest heaven, appears in this scene in her earlier guise as an aristocratic figure accompanied by several attendants, descending from the sky to bid him farewell. A variety of deities are present, like the red-robed Asura, who stands behind the bed holding the orbs of the sun and moon in his hands. To the right is a haloed Japanese Shinto goddess. Court nobles in gorgeous robes are also in attendance, and monks in patchwork robes surround the Buddha. Two semi-naked divine guardians thrash about in front of the bed, and closest to the viewer is a large assortment of grieving animals, both natural and divine: a lion, sheep, goat, chicken, snake, birds, deer, water buffalo, dog, monkey, rat, phoenix, elephant and more. The tall trees of the Sala grove encircle the bed, but, somewhat inexplicably, the scene is set by the sea, with swelling waves delineated in a fine linear fashion. In Japan the death of the Buddha was annually celebrated on 15 February, when all temples displayed their illustrations of the final nirvana. Many such paintings still exist and art historians are able to trace the gradual development of how the scene was depicted, from simple compositions to more complex ones.

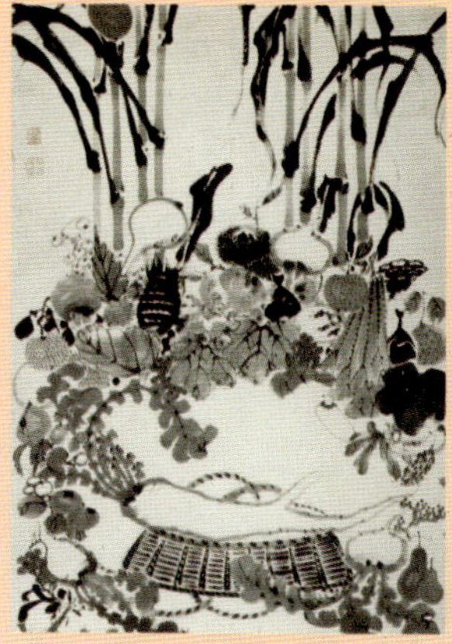

Ito Jakuchu

In a witty expression of the Zen doctrine that everything is the Buddha, Zen practitioner and professional artist Ito Jakuchu (1716–1800) rendered the Buddha's death scene with ink on paper as a monochrome still life of vegetables. He transformed the participants from the human, divine and animal realm to the vegetal one, and the dying Buddha into a giant radish.

'Everything has to die and has just so long to live.'

MUJU, *SHASEKI-SHU* (COLLECTION OF STONE AND SAND)

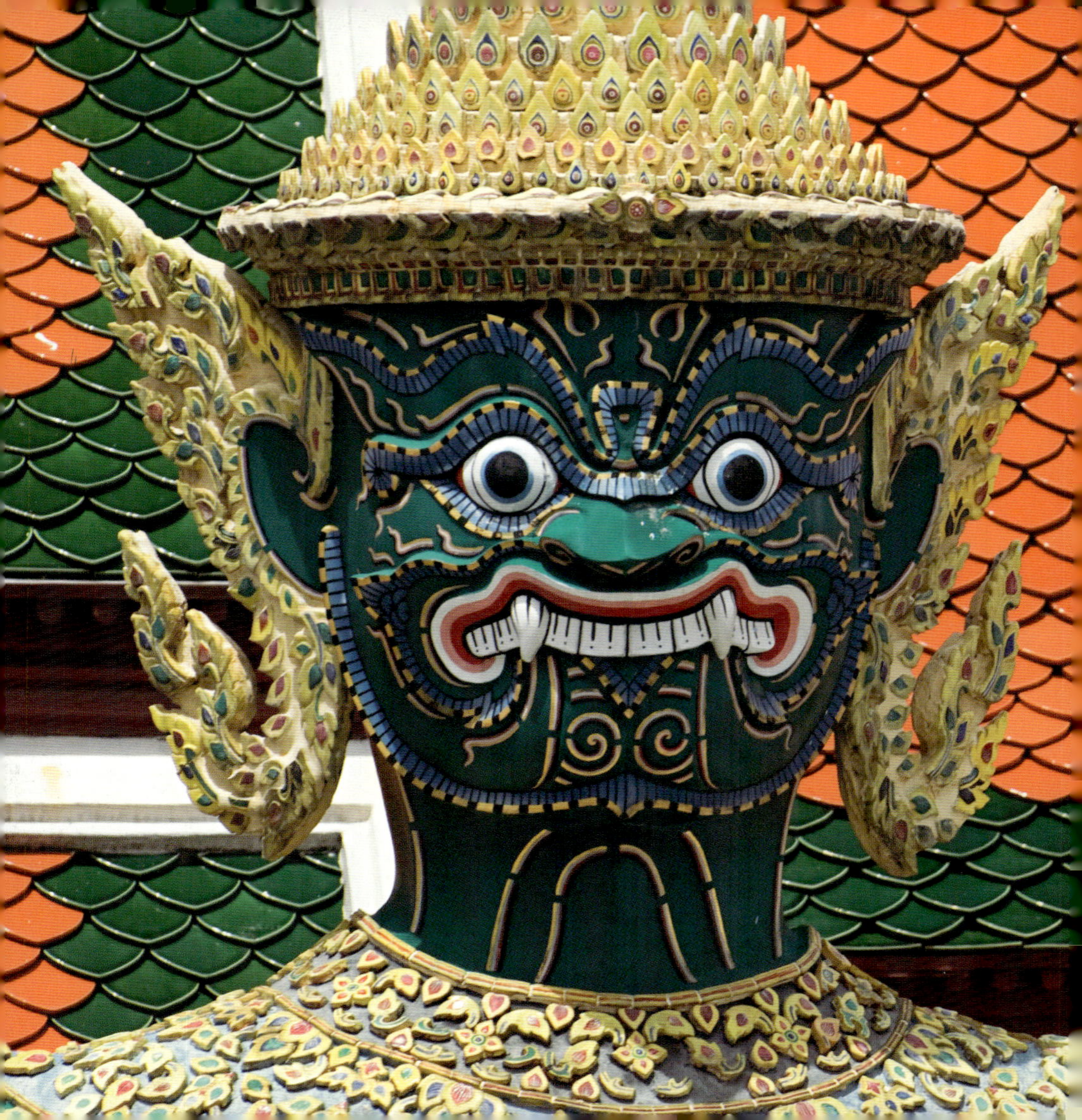

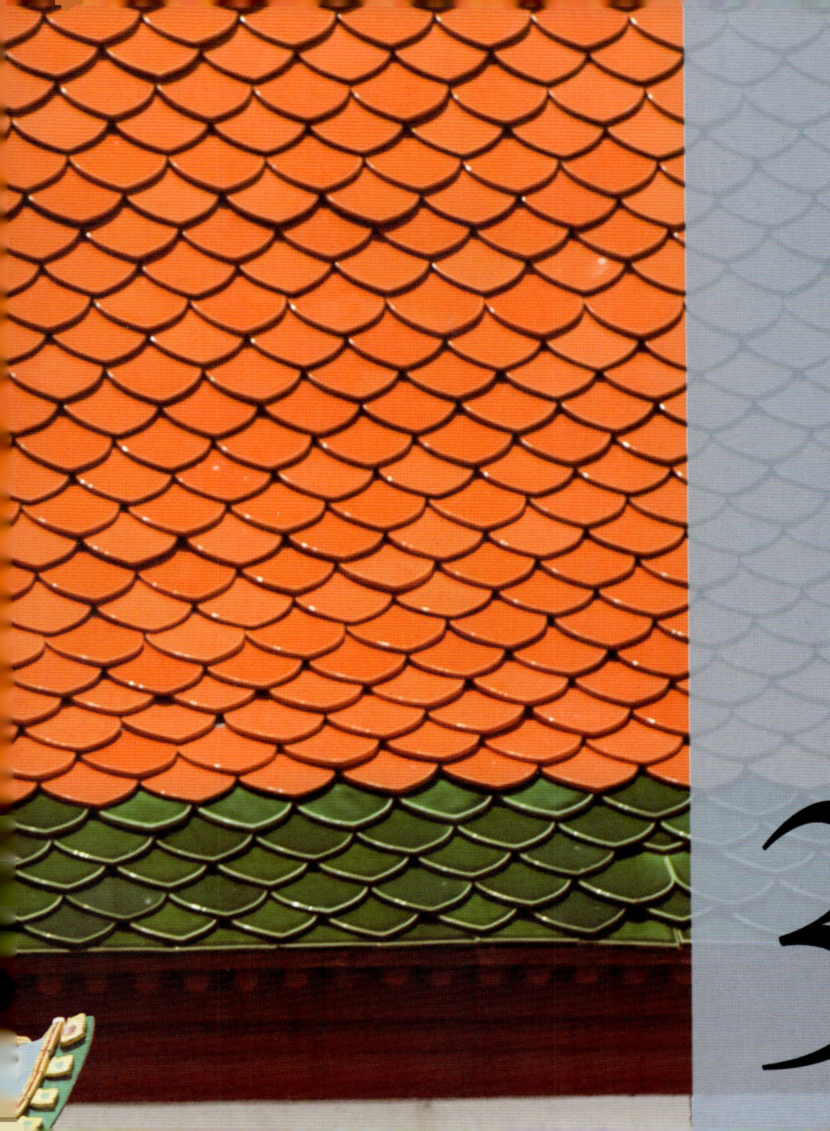

3 Buddhist Divinities

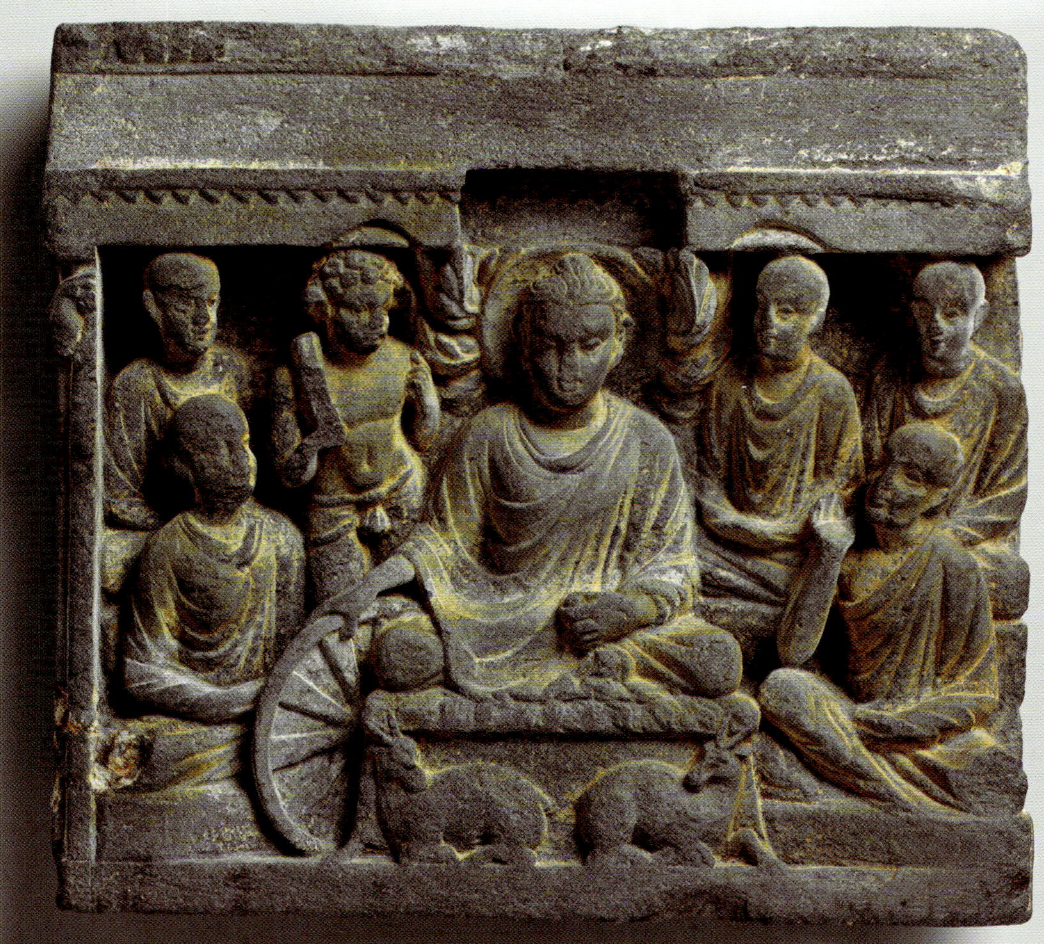

Monks at the Buddha's First Sermon in Sarnath

c. 2nd century CE **Metropolitan Museum of Art, New York, USA**

FORMAT Bas-relief **MATERIAL** Grey schist
DIMENSIONS 28.6 x 32.4 cm / 11¼ x 12¾ in.

It was not until five hundred years after the death of the Buddha that the first anthropomorphic icons were created. Why they came to be allowed at this time is not agreed, since earlier teachings had held them to be inappropriate because the Buddha ceased to be only a man. Other dramatic changes took place around this time, too. The Kushans from central Asia would come to dominate northern India from around the 2nd to the 4th centuries, weakening native prohibitions. As the Kushans responded to various influences, both artistic and religious, carried along the Silk Road, Buddhist practices began to change. The Buddha's disciples also came to be represented anthropomorphically. The first opportunity to represent them occurred in renderings of the First Sermon, when the Sangha (monastic community) was formed. One of the three jewels of Buddhism, along with the Dharma and the Buddha, the Sangha assured the perpetuity of the teachings before the written transmission of the Dharma. In this 2nd-century bas-relief from Gandhara, Pakistan, the monks are readily recognizable by their shaven pates and monastic garments, worn either with both shoulders covered or one shoulder bare. Here they are not distinguished as individuals, but in time their personalities emerge and they become identifiable characters, such as the youthful and faithful Ananda and the elder and wise monk Kasyapa. Soon the disciples would become a regular feature in the Buddha's retinue, along with bodhisattvas and guardians.

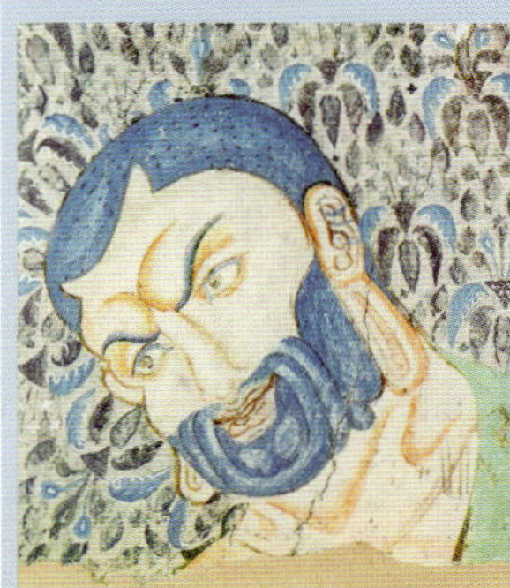

Head of Kasyapa

This fragment portraying Kasyapa, the eldest and most brilliant of the Buddha's disciples, comes from a mural of the Death of the Buddha which was a primary theme among the caves at Kizil in Xinjiang, China. At this Sarvastivada Buddhist site, monks and the historic Buddha were of primary importance. The naturalistic style of Indian art has here absorbed Chinese artistic preferences, resulting in harsher modelling of his features.

'The monk...will not accept gold or silver, raw grain or raw meat. He will not accept women or girls.'

THE BUDDHIST TRADITION

Winged Cupids Holding Wreath over Buddha

4th century CE   **Musée Guimet, Paris, France**

ORIGIN Monastery of Tapa-Kalan, Hadda, Afghanistan
DIMENSIONS 56 x 49 x 32 cm/22 x 19⅓ x 12⅗ in.   **MATERIAL** Stucco

The original doctrine of the Buddha eschewed supernatural creatures, gods and the like because they were irrelevant to the pursuit of enlightenment. In the following centuries, however, Buddhism was transformed from a disciplinary path of meditation and self-detachment to a formal religion with a full pantheon of deities to whom the faithful could appeal. In Afghanistan, many of these deities were appropriated from Classical art found in cities such as Begram. Ancient tombs in Tillya Tepe, Afghanistan, dating back to the 1st century CE, were excavated and yielded a wealth of Western art objects and ornaments, including figures of Hercules, Silenus, Venus and Eros, and these influenced local artists making Buddhist art for Kushan patrons. The adoption of the cherub, in particular, into Buddhist art was also facilitated by Buddhist texts that emphasized the supernatural nature of moments in the Buddha's life by describing how divinities in the sky joyfully threw flowers and played musical instruments. Thus, at the Birth, First Sermon and other events, celestials were said to have appeared in the sky. Buddhist artists adopted Western winged, cupid-like figures and transformed them into images of flying divinities. In this example, Western prototypes are readily evident in the skilful line drawing of the childlike body, the pinwheel pose of the legs to suggest rapid flight and the Western features of the faces. Moreover, the cupids hold a wreath, a Western emblem of victory, over the preaching Buddha's head.

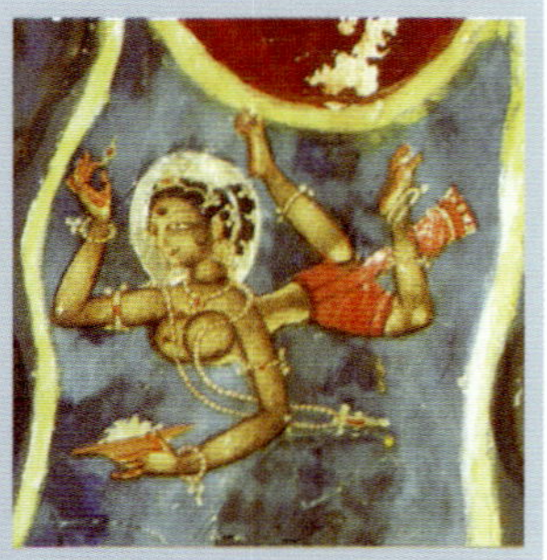

Flying Celestial

This flying celestial, a detail on the skirt of a statue of Avalokiteshvara at Sumtsek Temple, Alchi, India, is unusual in being a voluptuous semi-naked female, a transformation of the standard male putti figure. Her posture, with her legs raised high in the air behind her, is as described in Mahayanist literature and suggests a supernatural event.

'Meanwhile Devas [celestials] in space, seizing their jewelled canopies, attending, raised in responsive harmony their heavenly songs to encourage him.'

ASVAGHOSA, *BUDDHACARITA*

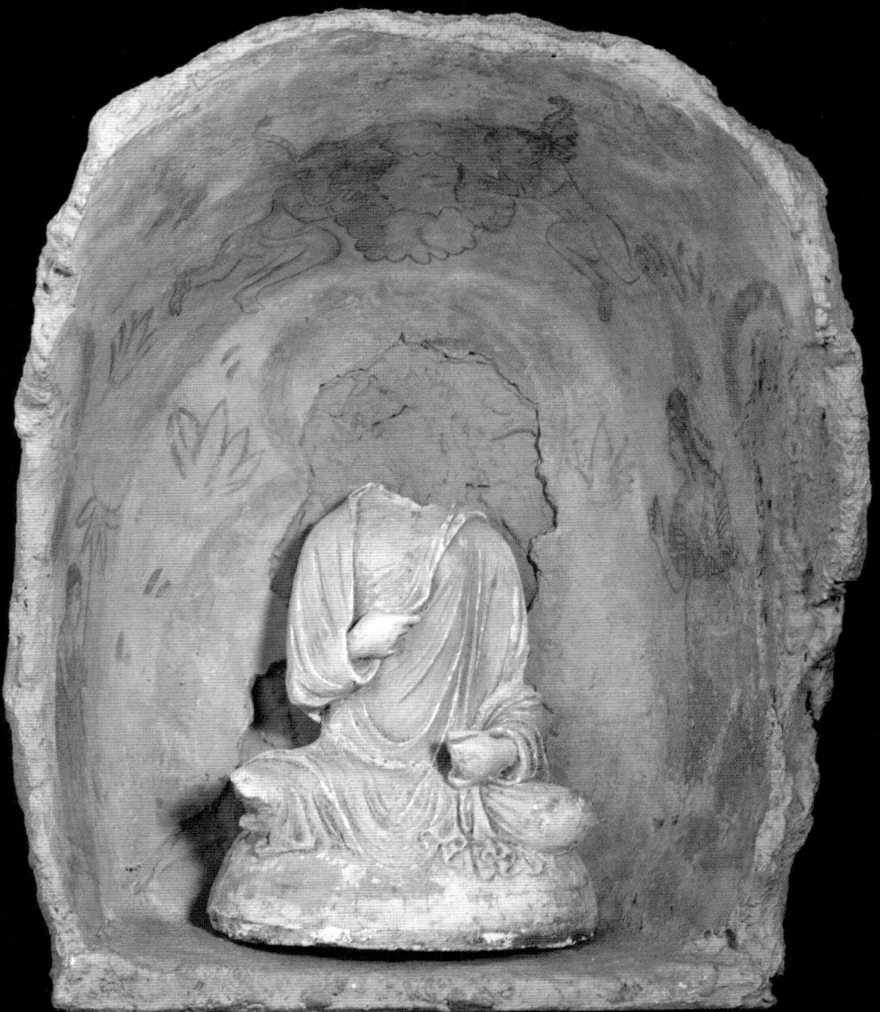

Bodhisattva Avalokiteshvara

Late 5th century CE **Cave 1, Ajanta, Aurangabad, Maharashtra, India**

STYLE Gujarati with Western influences
MATERIALS Paints on a prepared surface

New deities began to appear in India after its peoples made contact with Persian religions via the Silk Road. In one of the most important texts of the Mahayana, or Greater Teachings, the 1st-century CE *Lotus Sutra* introduces the deities as bodhisattvas dedicated to the salvation of humankind. Chapter 25 of the scripture describes the most important of them, Avalokiteshvara, the Bodhisattva of Compassion, along with manifestations that he will assume to aid the faithful, and the nine dangers he will save them from: shipwreck, fire, brigands, jail, hell, wild animals, the land of ogresses, ghosts and execution. To the rear of Cave 1 at the Ajanta complex at Aurangabad, a mural of two bodhisattvas flanks a small recessed room containing an oversized sculpture of the Buddha. Before this mural was painted, the walls were covered with thatch, mud and layers of plaster to create a smooth surface. Using red paint, the artists drew the composition, later filling in the colours and details. Afterwards, they burnished the walls to strengthen the adhesion of the pigment. The highlighting and shading of the anatomy and facial features show Western influences, and as yet the deity's attributes are not fully codified. The bodhisattva appears as a long-haired prince offering a lotus, a classic symbol of purity. He wears a dhoti, scarves, a tall, golden, jewel-encrusted conical crown and regal jewels – a necklace, armlet and girdle. The figure sways his hips as if dancing, turns his head slightly to the right and his eyes are cast downwards.

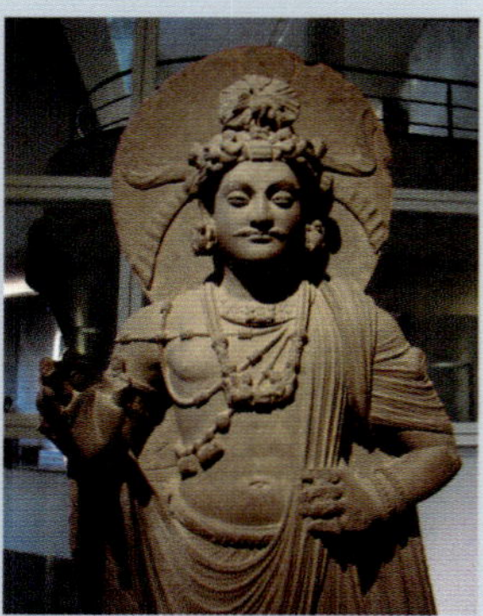

Standing Bodhisattva

All bodhisattvas, like Buddhas, look the same; their specific identities come from their attributes and poses. This Gandharan bodhisattva looks Roman, with an athletic body, long hanks of hair, a classic face and a halo. His intricate adornments are carefully carved.

'The Bodhisattva ... looks on all beings as though victims going to slaughter. And immense compassion grips him.'

ASTASAHASRIKA PRAJNAPARAMITA SUTRA

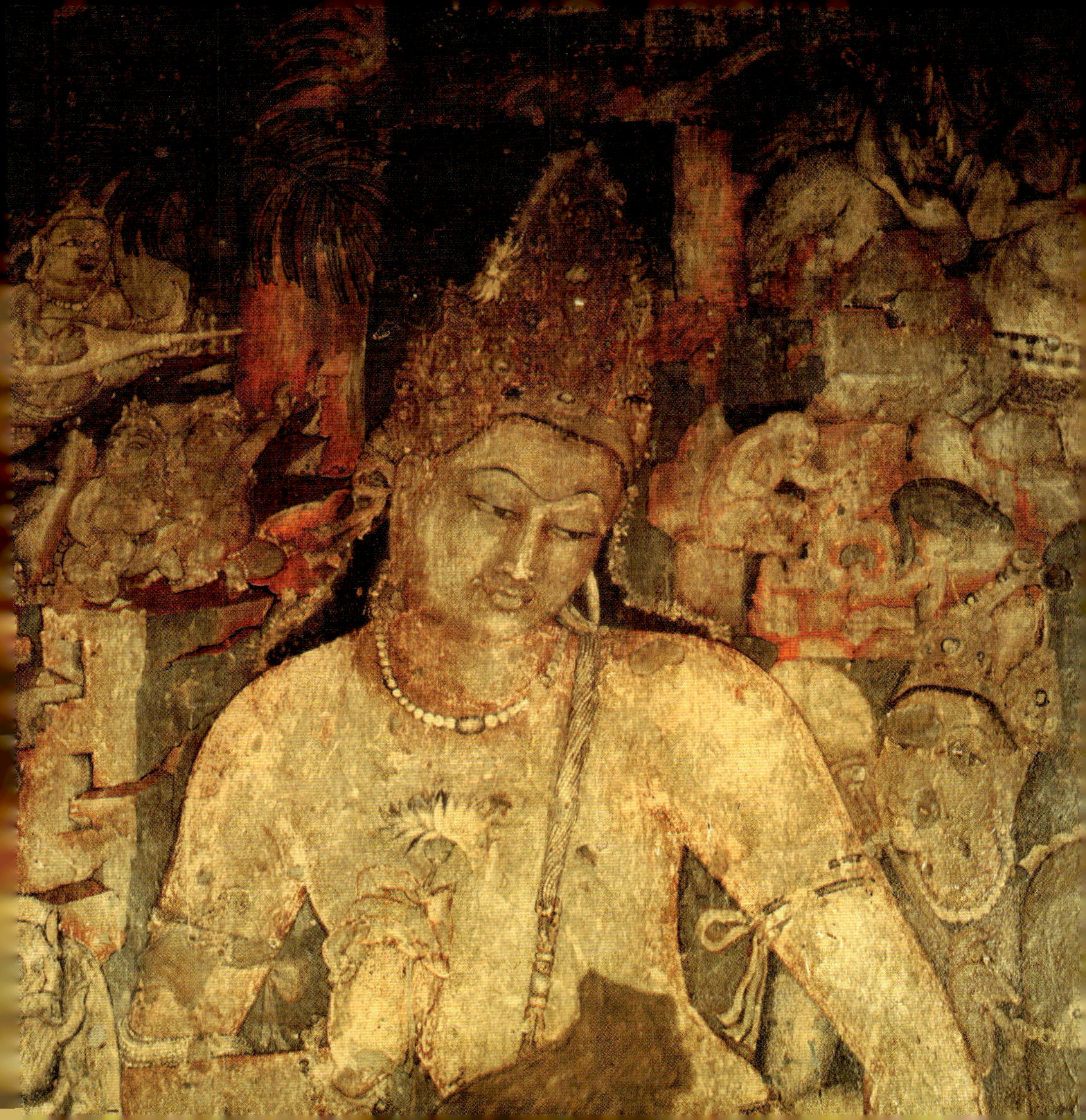

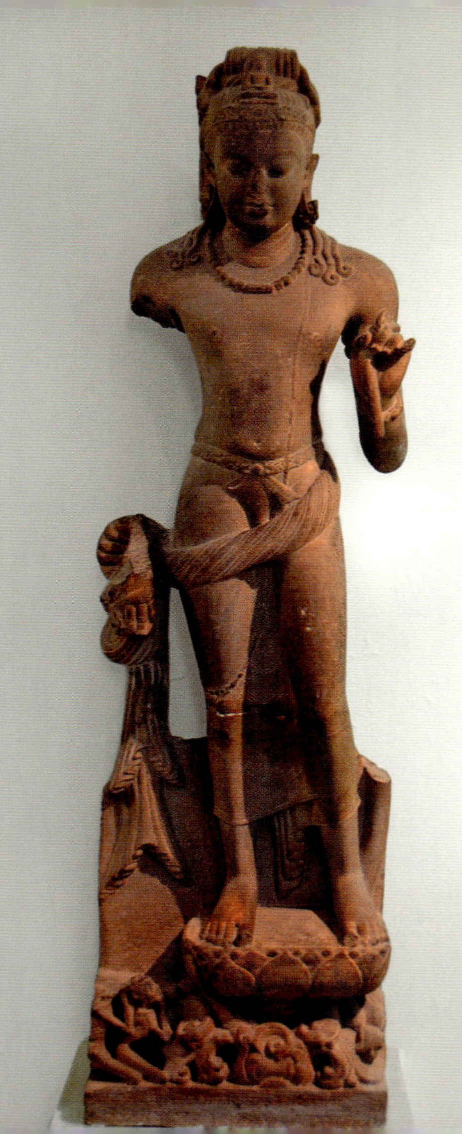

Bodhisattva Avalokiteshvara

Late 5th century CE **National Museum of New Delhi, India**

ORIGIN Sarnath, Varanasi, Uttar Pradesh, India
STYLE Guptan **MATERIAL** Sandstone **HEIGHT** 136 cm/53 ½ in.

This sandstone sculpture of the Bodhisattva of Compassion, found at Sarnath in Uttar Pradesh, India, is relatively complete in its representation of the bodhisattva's iconographical attributes. In the figure's crown, a small, seated figure of the Buddha of the Western Paradise attests to their filial relationship: Avalokiteshvara is an attendant bodhisattva in the Pure Land. The sculpture's missing right arm would have been extended in a gesture of compassion; he is offering sustenance to the hungry ghosts (Preta in Sanskrit) seen kneeling on the base. Preta live in a realm characterized by perpetual hunger; having throats the width of a slim needle, they cannot swallow food, and liquids turn to molten bronze. Thus, they can only tolerate sanctified offerings. In his left hand, Avalokiteshvara holds a long-stemmed lotus flower, a reference to one of his names, Padmapani, or 'bearer of the lotus flower', and a symbol of his purity. Characteristically, Avalokiteshvara's head is lowered slightly as he looks down with concern at the worshipper. The slender body has smooth planes of flesh offset by intricately detailed jewellery. The face has highly arched eyebrows, an aquiline nose and sensuous, pursed lips with a suggestion of a slight smile. This graceful, slightly swaying icon of Avalokiteshvara is an example of idealized representations of beauty that were formulated in Sarnath in the Guptan era. Thanks to India's successful trade along various sea and land routes, the Guptan style spread throughout the Buddhist world.

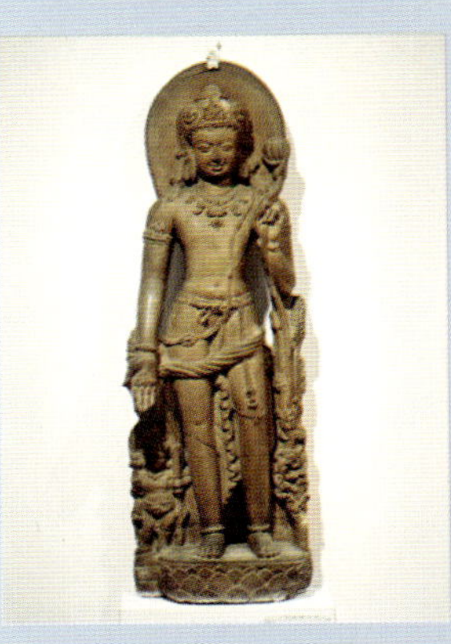

The Pure Lotus

Buddhist deities stand or sit on lotus flowers to convey their celestial status, as in this statue of Avalokiteshvara from Nalanda. The lotus symbolizes purity because it grows in dirty water yet produces pristine flowers.

'The hundred thousands [of creatures] who in this world are suffering troubles will, if they hear the name of the Bodhisattva … be released from that mass of troubles.'

LOTUS SUTRA

The Western Paradise

550–570 CE **Freer Gallery, Smithsonian Museum, Washington DC, USA**

FOCUS Amitofu (Amitabha in Sanskrit) **MATERIALS** Limestone and pigments (traces) **DIMENSIONS** 159.3 x 334.5 cm/62 ¾ x 131 ¾ in.

This bas-relief, from Cave-chapel 2, Xiangtangshan Caves, Hebei, is the earliest surviving illustration of the Western Paradise in China. Amitofu, the Buddha of the Western Paradise, sits at the centre, flanked by his attendant bodhisattvas and worshippers. Two angels riding clouds and the jewelled canopy over his head convey that this is a celestial setting. In the foreground is the lotus pond where newcomers wait to be released from their lotus buds. In addition, multiple Buddhas appear at the top of the vision, seated on lotus flowers. The perfection of paradise is represented by the strict symmetry of the placement of the flanking pavilions and the multiple divine characters. This kind of iconography arose because traffic along the Silk Road brought India into contact with the Persian Zoroastrian religion. This teaches that good and evil, light and dark, are in a constant and intense struggle, one that will only cease at the end of time with the triumph of good and the arrival of the brilliant, good and everlasting kingdom of light. Zoroastrians worship the god of the sun and perform fire rituals, but during the first millennium the land of infinite life and light became identified in India with Amitofu. Like Zoroastrian texts, the *Lotus Sutra* describes the kingdom as flat, with ample water, flowering gardens, pleasant breezes, temperate weather and brilliant light. Worshippers need only recite the name of the Buddha of Infinite Light devoutly to be reborn in his paradise, but they must wait in the calyx of a lotus bud until their karma (bad behaviour) is expiated before being fully reborn. People of perfect virtue, however, are immediately received in the immortal realm.

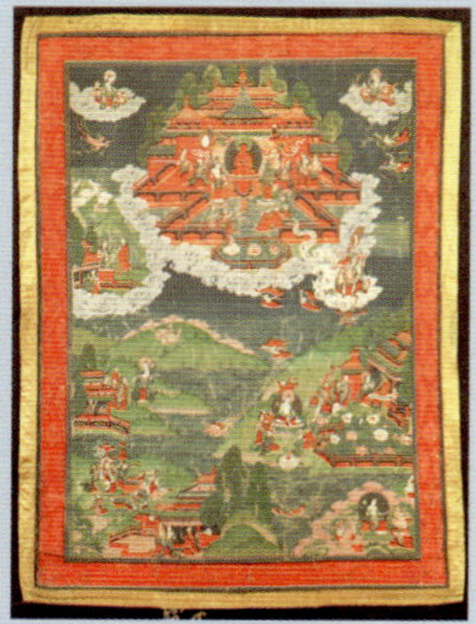

Material World

While the Theravada school of Buddhism emphasized faith and self-sacrifice, the Mahayana school promised believers everlasting life in paradise, exemplified by this colourful Tibetan thangka of the Paradise of Amitabha.

'After the believer ... experiences the pleasures of the first opening of the lotus, his joy becomes a hundred times greater than before.'

ESSENTIALS OF SALVATION, GENSHIN (942–1017 CE)

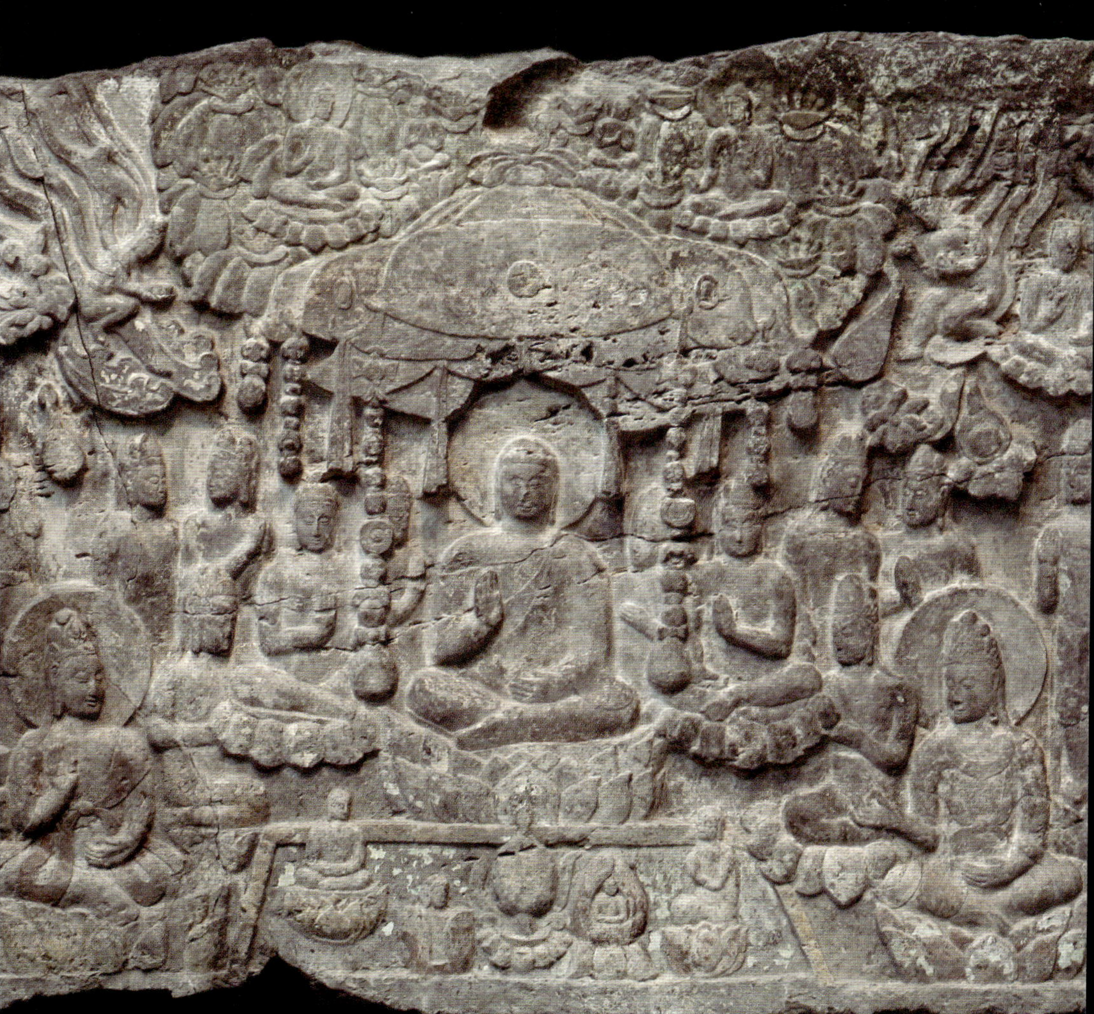

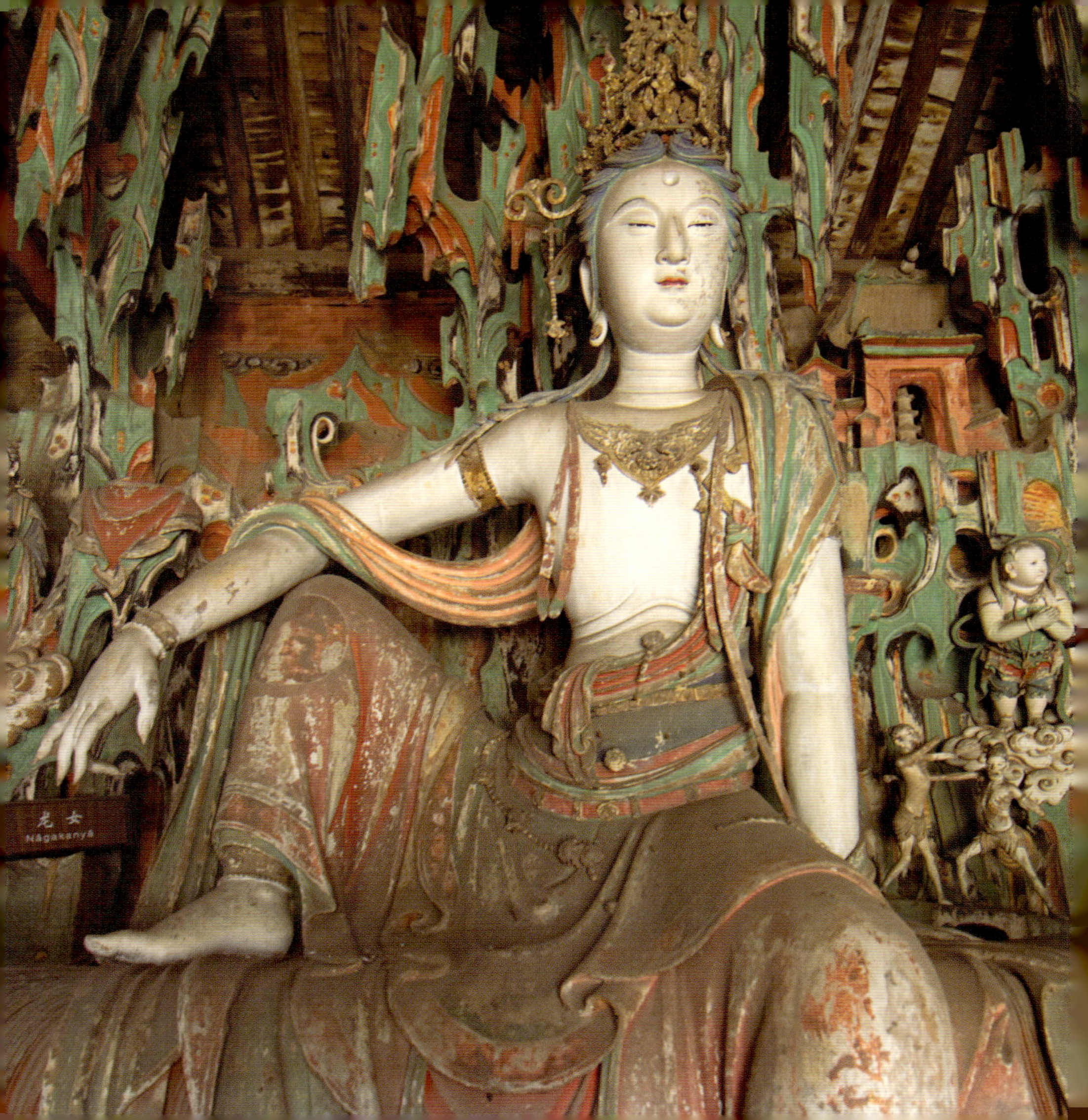

龙女
Nāgakanyā

Guanyin in Potolaka

c. 7th–9th century CE **Shuanglin Temple, near Pingyao, Shanxi, China**

SUBJECT Guanyin, Bodhisattva of Compassion (Avalokiteshvara in Sanskrit)
MATERIALS Stucco and pigments

According to Chapter 32 of the *Avatamsaka Sutra*, the Bodhisattva of Compassion, known in China as Guanyin, when he is not engaged in helping people, rests in the remote and magical island of Potolaka. By the time of the Tang dynasty, Potolaka's location was identified as Mount Putuo, an island in the East China Sea, which became both a setting for miraculous events and a focus of pilgrimage and worship. The island became renowned for a large statue of Guanyin, which faced the sea. At the height of its popularity as a holy place and pilgrimage centre, Mount Putuo, had three main temples, eighty-eight monasteries, and more than four thousand monks. The island was the target of pirate attacks in the 15th century, and it suffered destructive attacks again in the modern era. Rebuilt in the 1980s, the monasteries and temples are much visited, and a colossal statue of the god once again stands in the harbour. So important was the idea of Guanyin in Potolaka that since the Song dynasty it became the subject of a sculptural tableau that commonly occupied the rear face of the altar of the first hall of many Buddhist temple compounds. In this stucco example, at Shuanglin Temple, near Pingyao in Shanxi province, Guanyin is seated in the posture of royal ease, with his right knee raised and left leg pendant. The beautiful white-skinned deity displays a torso swathed in multiple scarves and delicate jewels. He and his attendants, the Jade Maiden and Golden Boy, along with guardian figures and *arhats* or enlightened monks, are set in a polychrome clay landscape with mountains, forests, caves and billowing waves, all populated by a variety of creatures.

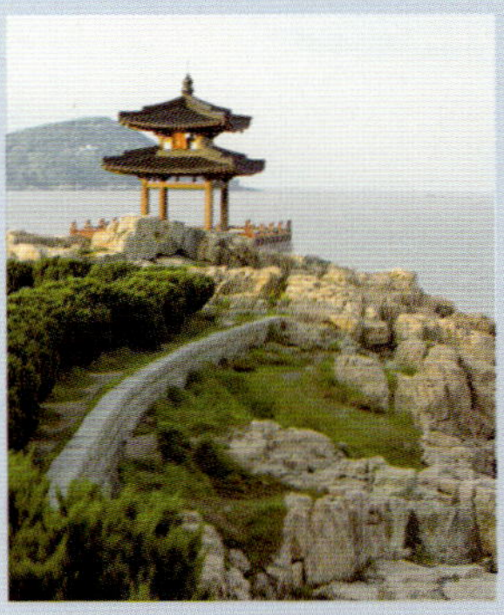

Mount Putuo
Ancient myth asserts that the Mount Putuo pilgrimage site was established when a Japanese monk was bringing a statue back from Mount Tiantai to Japan. Finding himself unable to leave the site, he installed it there.

'If sentient beings encounter … difficulties and disasters and their sufferings are unlimited, they will be delivered right away when they hear the name of *Kuang-shih-yin* [*sutra*] and be freed from all pain.'

LOTUS SUTRA

Mural of Guanyin

705–781 CE **Cave 45, Dunhuang, Gansu, China**

SUBJECT Guanyin, Bodhisattva of Compassion (Avalokiteshvara in Sanskrit)
MATERIALS Pigments on a prepared surface

Occupying the entire left wall of Cave 45 at the Dunhuang cave complex in Gansu province is a mural that illustrates Chapter 25 of the *Lotus Sutra*, which was compiled around the 1st century CE and is the most important of the Mahayana scriptures. At the centre and in large scale stands Guanyin, the Bodhisattva of Compassion, light skinned, a little portly and rather effeminate. A network of delicate jewels covers his figure, and over his head is a lavishly jewelled canopy. In the foreground on either side of the figure are depictions of ills from which believers will be protected if they call upon the Bodhisattva – the perils of hell, the island of ogresses, shipwreck, jail, bandits, goblins and more. On the right, for example, a ship with a striped sail is encircled by predatory fish. Further right and slightly higher on the wall is a jail. Flanking the upper part of the figure are illustrations of the thirty-three incarnations – guardian king, goblin, nobleman – that the Bodhisattva is able to assume when helping believers, along with depictions of persons whose prayers he answered. Each is accompanied by a small cartouche identifying the manifestation; larger cartouches include passages of scripture. This is the earliest known illustration of the manifestations and it is important to note that some of them are female. This is of significance because, once the Bodhisattva began to be pictured as a female, the garments changed and clothes covered the previously naked torso. In contrast, Avalokiteshvara in India came to acquire two female attendants, or Shakti: Tara, who materialized from a tear Avalokiteshvara shed for the suffering of mankind, and Bhrkuti.

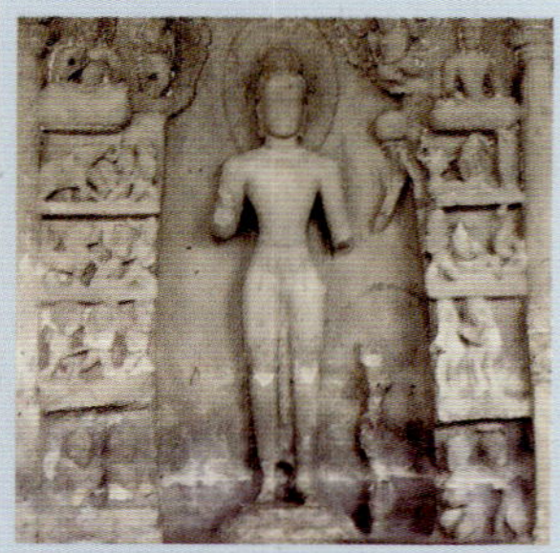

The Litany of Avalokiteshvara

This large, 5th-century bas-relief sculpture stands outside Cave 4 at the Ajanta cave complex in Maharashtra, India. The so-called litany or exposition of the perils from which the Bodhisattva Avalokiteshvara will save the faithful is set out in vertical zones flanking the central figure. In China, the format was adopted at Cave 45, Dunhuang, and elsewhere.

'In some worlds, young man of good family, [Avalokiteshvara] preaches the law to creatures in the shape of a Buddha; in others he does so in the shape of a Bodhisattva.'

LOTUS SUTRA

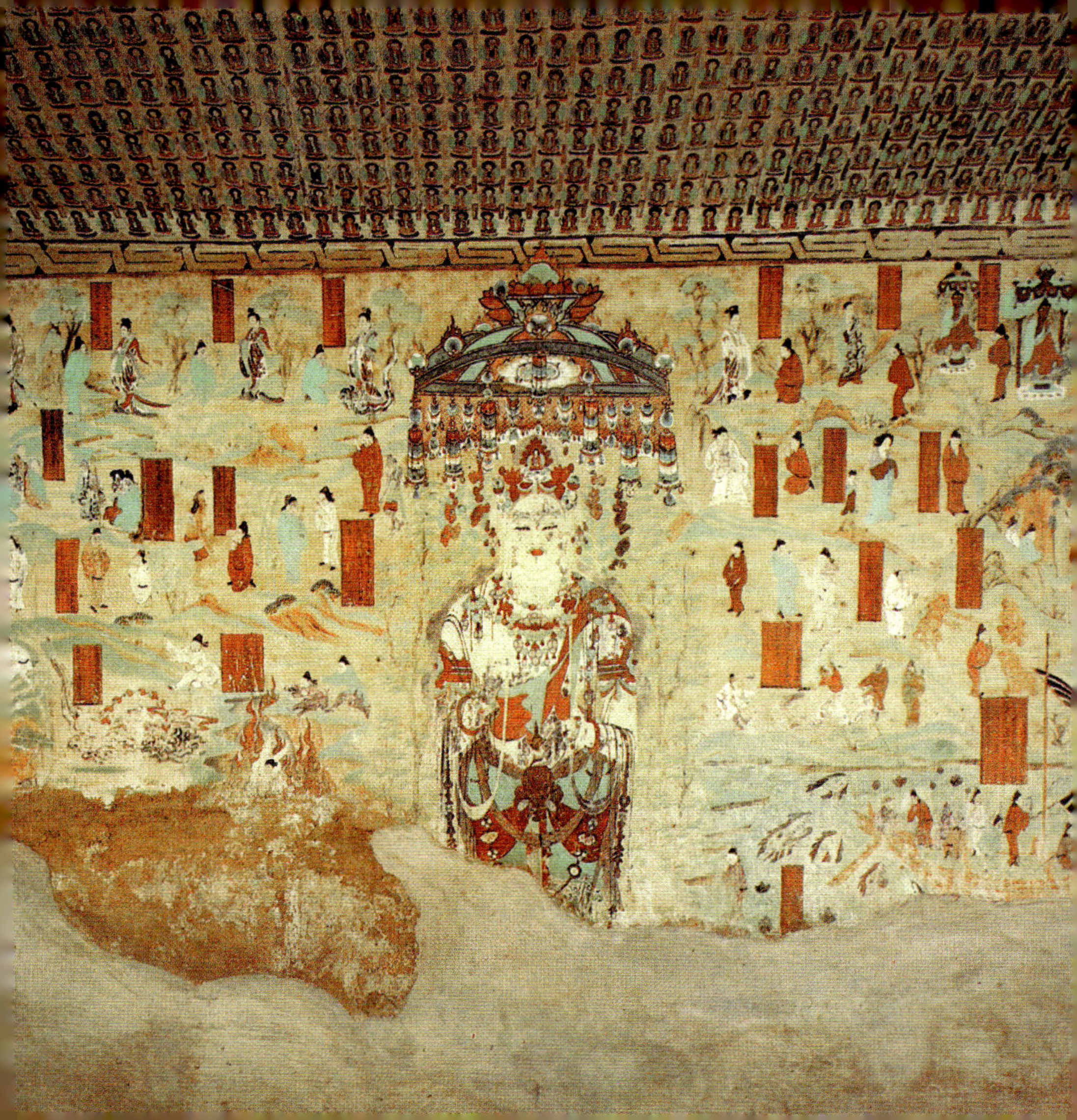

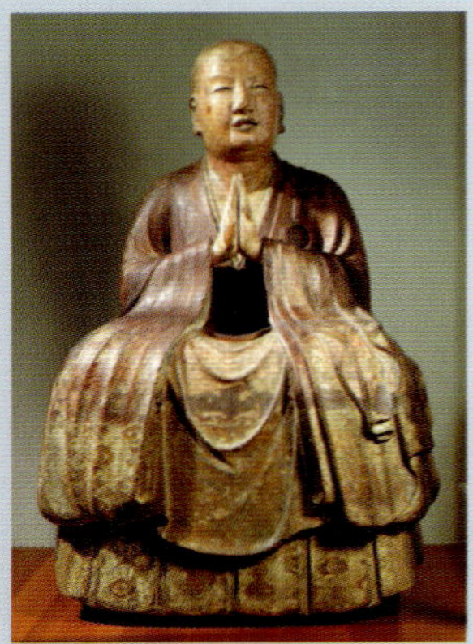

Shan-tao

The eminent priest Shan-tao (613–681 CE), here represented by a 14th-century Japanese wooden statue, espoused the painting of visions of paradise as an aid for the faithful, and he himself created hundreds of scenes.

'The melody of the wheel of the wonderful Law, as it turns, flows throughout this land of jewelled sound. ... Palaces, halls, forests and ponds shine and glitter everywhere ...'

ESSENTIALS OF SALVATION

The Western Paradise of Amitofu

c. 750 CE Cave 217, Dunhuang cave complex, Gansu, China

MATERIALS Pigments on plaster
DIMENSIONS 3.1 x 4.86 m / 10 x 16 ft

By the 8th century CE, worship of the Pure Land was dominant in China. Buddhist sites like Dunhuang, remotely situated in the Gobi Desert, include dozens of cave murals portraying the Western Paradise. Buddhists ritually perform meditative visualizations in which they, guided by scriptures or works of art, envision features of the immortal land. This representation of the Paradise of Amitofu (Amitahba in Sanskrit), painted on the north wall of Cave 217 at Dunhuang, is a Chinese interpretation of an imported vision, that of a garden paradise. The Chinese re-imagined the Pure Land as a great palatial complex because they saw royal life as a metaphor for the divine. Here, a central hall and smaller, symmetrically placed halls and pavilions are rendered in brilliant colours. Influences from the Silk Road have resulted in the Buddha being rendered as dark-skinned. He is flanked by many deities arranged in hieratic order, and celestials descend on clouds from the heavens. Before the Buddha is the lotus pond from which newborn faithful emerge from calyx containers; others are still encased in buds. In the immediate foreground, dozens of musicians make celestial music, and two angels dance at the centre, their scarves streaming. In Cave 217, to the left and right of the composition, are pictorial aids to help in visualization and scenes from the *Lotus Sutra*, respectively. Tang Buddhist art is extremely naturalistic, and here Western-style highlighting and shading are used throughout to suggest three-dimensional forms.

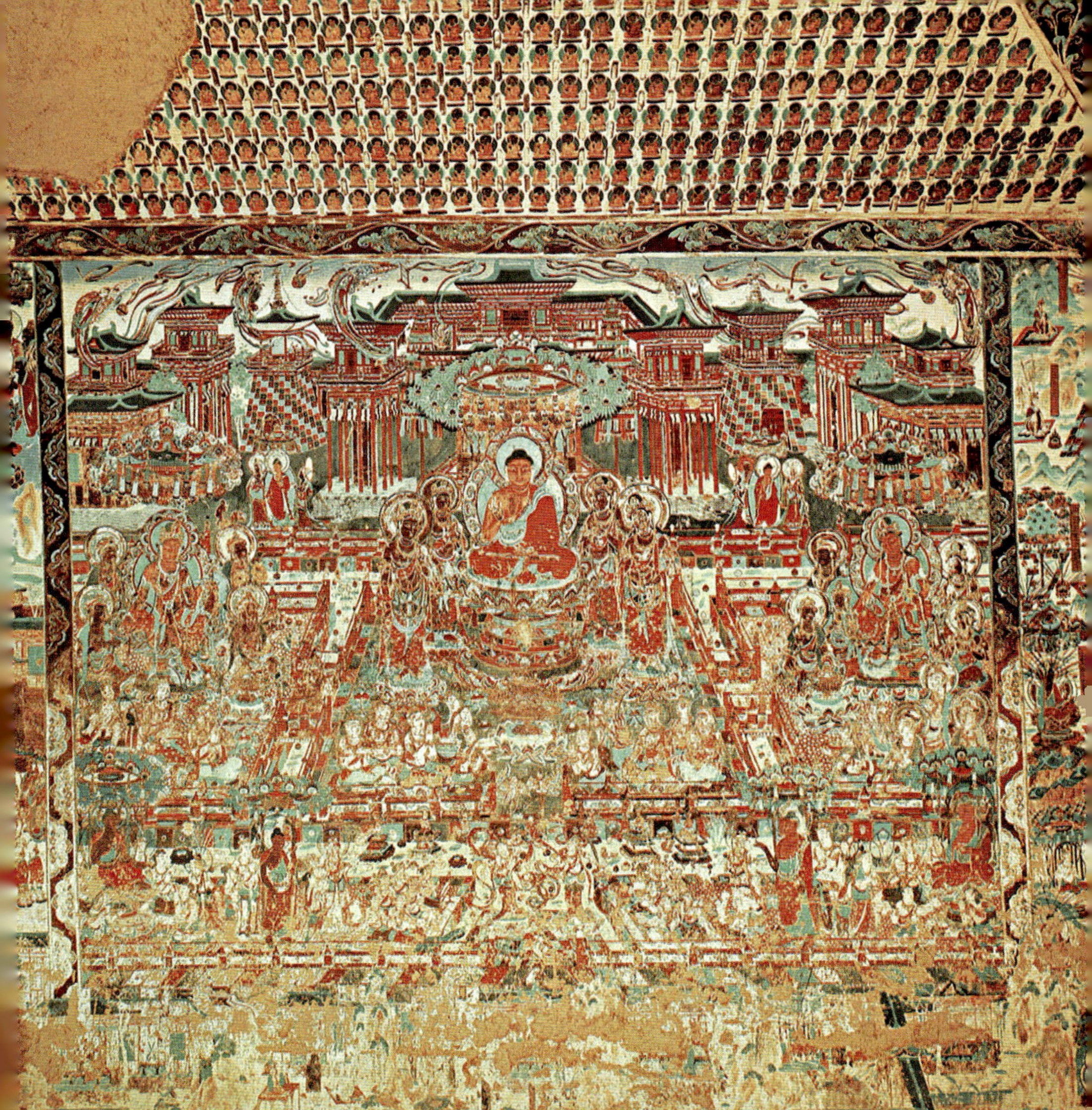

Borobudur Hell Scenes

c. 8th century CE **Borobudur, Magelang, Java, Indonesia**

COMMISSIONED BY Shailendra dynasty   **NUMBER OF BASE PANELS DEPICTING KARMA LAW** 160   **MATERIAL** Sandstone

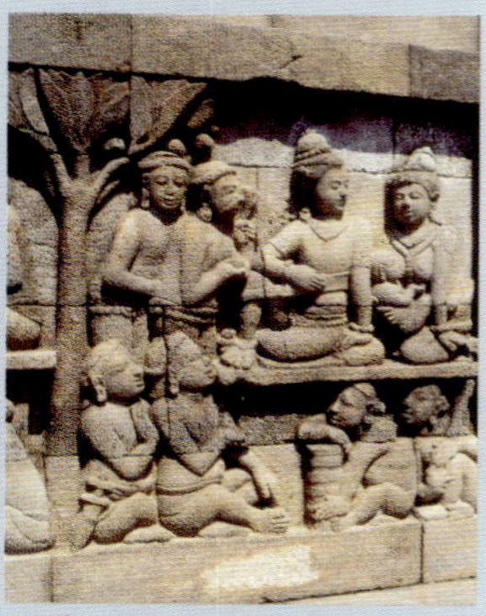

Virtue Rewarded

The recently uncovered base panels are not all concerned with hell, nor is the text on which they are apparently based. The *Maha Karmavibhanga*'s main theme is the effects of karma, both good and evil. The detail above portrays good behaviour being rewarded by future happiness.

'All sufferings are merely the result of one's own karma and represent its reward. The places of hell are painted by the brush of the painter's desire.'

D. AND A. MATSUNAGA, *THE BUDDHIST CONCEPT OF HELL*

Borobudur, the largest Buddhist temple in existence, comprises nine levels, all featuring carved panels. Construction took place over three phases, and each addition not only altered the monument's appearance but also its religious messages. This carved hell scene was among panels at the base uncovered in the 1970s while repairs were being made to the temple; the architects of the final phase of construction in the 9th century had covered them with a broad terrace, balustrades and narrowed entrances. The scene depicts torments of the damned: being thrown in a flaming pit, submitting to a sword-yielding attendant of hell, and being crowded together in a great cauldron set atop a fire. Yet inscriptions dating from 778 CE to the first half of the 9th century provide evidence that Buddhist art and thought were evolving. Such hell scenes as this represent beliefs belonging to the early Theravada, or Way of the Elders, and are based on the *Maha Karmavibhanga*. That text briefly describes various crimes — theft, murder, rape, torture — and graphically depicts the torments suffered by perpetrators: being cut up with a saw, burnt, or kept in bondage with hot chains. Here sinners are left to their fate, while other panels show the damned dreading coming torture. Later Mahayanist hell scenes feature divine helpers of universal compassion mediating on their behalf. Clearly the panels were didactic in intention, urging the faithful to consider the consequences of their behaviour, but within a century this forbidding iconographical programme at Borobudur was replaced by a kinder one promoting higher levels of consciousness.

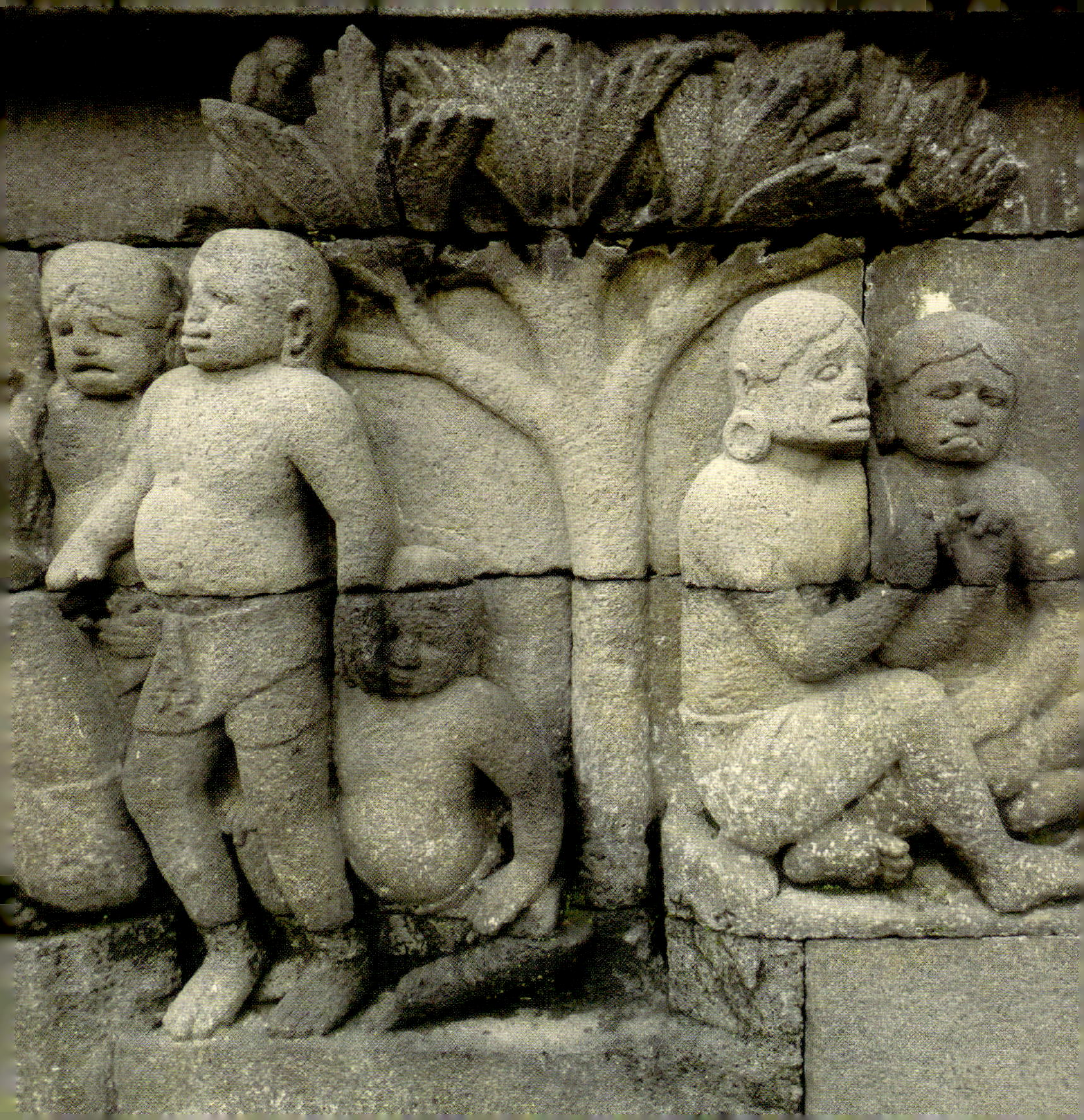

Seated Avalokiteshvara

8th–9th century CE **National Museum, Colombo, Sri Lanka**

ORIGIN Veragala Sirisangabo Vihara, Allavava, Anuradhapura, Sri Lanka
MATERIAL Solid-cast gilt bronze, jewels   **HEIGHT** 49.8 cm/19 ½ in.

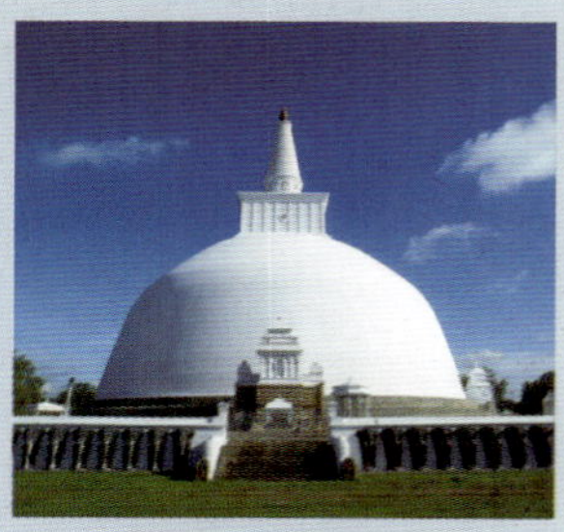

Anuradhapura

The ancient capital of Sri Lanka, established in the 4th century BCE, was the island's political and religious centre for 1,300 years. Although the city was deserted in the 10th century, its ancient Theravad and Mahayanist monuments have once again become the focus of worship.

'Just as all the previous Sugatas, the Buddhas / Generated the mind of enlightenment ... / So will I too, for the sake of all beings / Generate the mind of enlightenment / And accomplish all the stages / Of the Bodhisattva training.'

AVATAMSAKA SUTRA

Buddhism in Sri Lanka underwent several major periods of development after its introduction by Emperor Ashoka's son in the 3rd century BCE. By the 3rd century CE, Mahayana Buddhism had introduced its pantheon of saviours, of whom the Bodhisattva of Compassion gained significance through association with the Sri Lankan royal family. It became accepted during the Anuradhapura period that a righteous and powerful Buddhist king could become a bodhisattva. For example, King Buddhadasa (r. 337–365) took the bodhisattva vow and lived as a bodhisattva; King Dhatusena, (r. 455–475) was a fervent worshipper of the bodhisattva ideal and ordered an image of a bodhisattva be made. By the 7th century the Abhayagiri and Jethawana monastery complexes in the capital of Anuradhapura were centres of Mahayana practice. Royal associations are apparent in this gilt bronze, jewelled sculpture of the Bodhisattva Avalokiteshvara discovered in 1968 at the Veragala Sirisangabo Vihara (monastery) at Allavava in Anuradhapura. The figure has inset eyes of crystal, and large jewels in his waistband and elaborately piled hair. Due to the lack of a seated Buddha in his crown, and other attributes, it is impossible to identify this bodhisattva with certainty, but the tilted head and princely posture are characteristic of Avalokiteshvara. According to Chinese monks who visited Sri Lanka and kept records of their experiences, both Mahayana and Theravada co-existed, and by the 9th century CE Vajrayana, or esoteric practice, was established too.

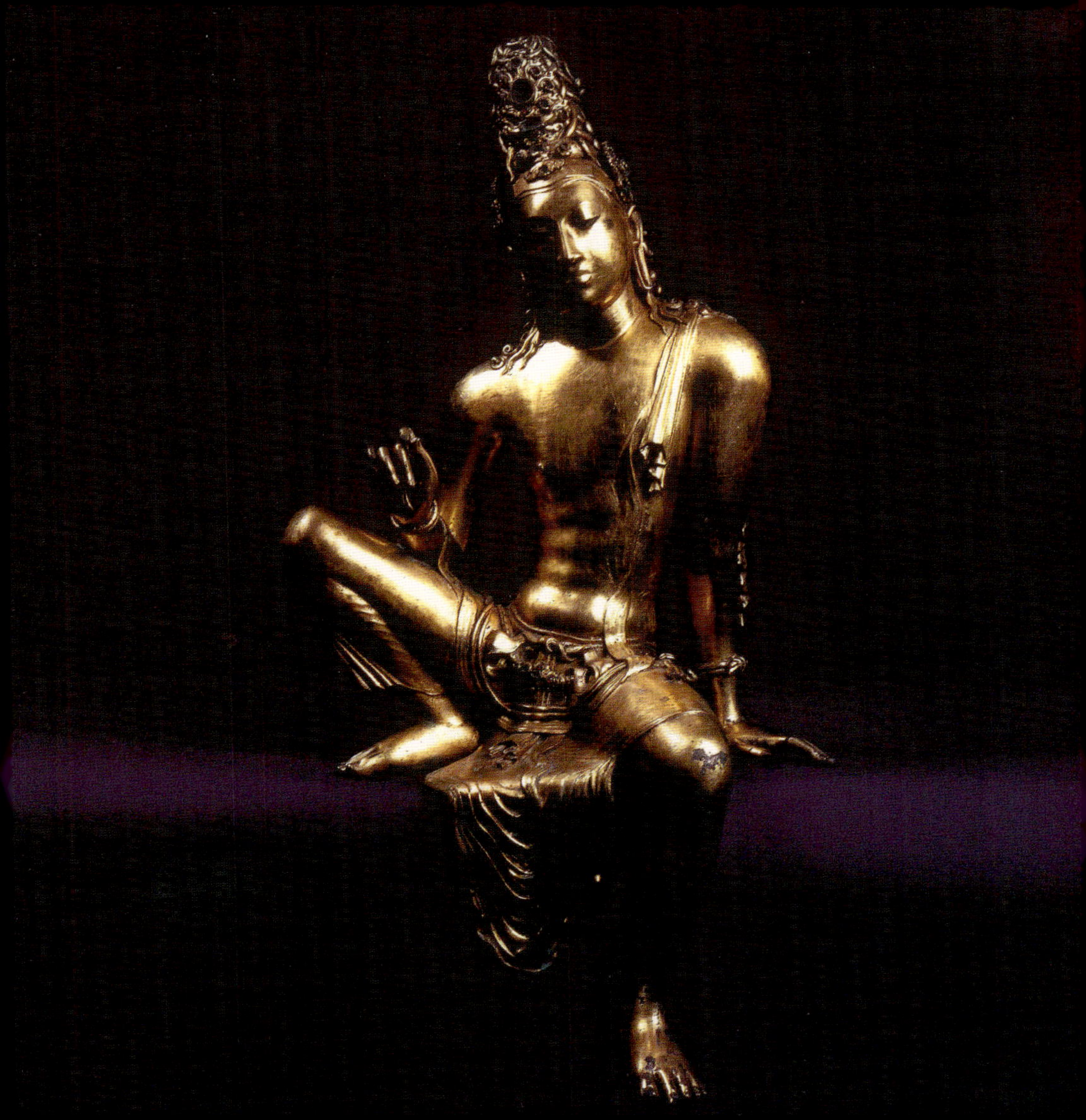

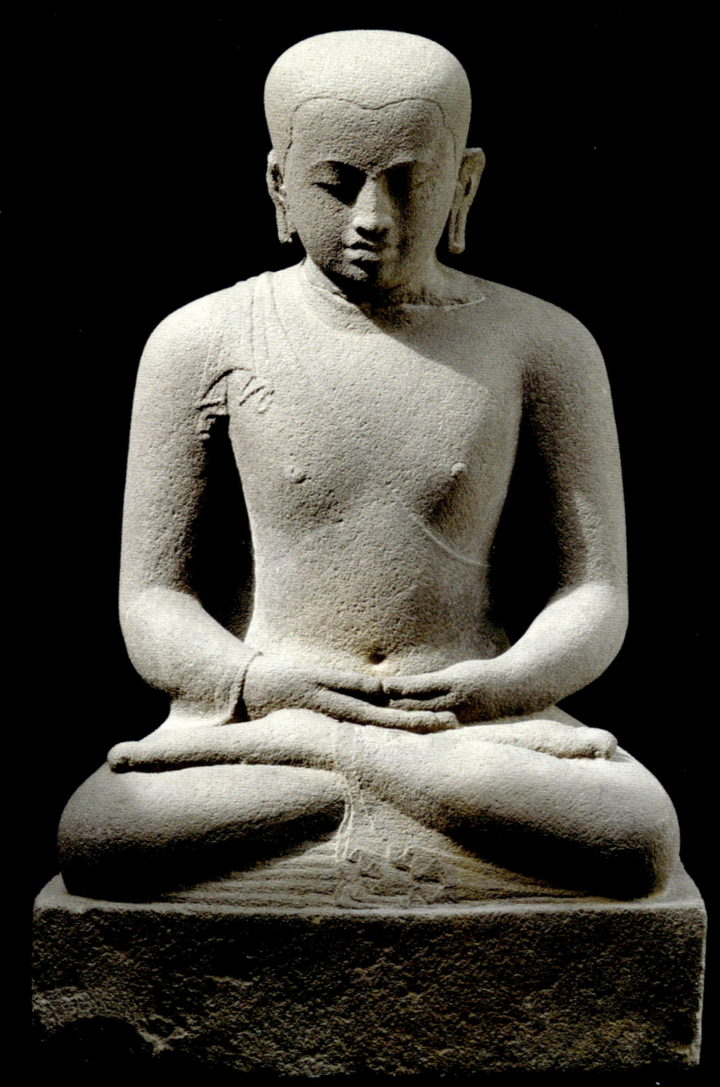

Meditating Monk

9th century CE Archaeological Institute, Prambanan, Java, Indonesia

COMMISSIONED BY King Rakai Pikantan **MATERIAL** Volcanic rock
HEIGHT 104 cm/41 in.

Buddhism entered Hindu Java through contact with the Srivijaya Kingdom, which ruled the Straits of Malacca from the 7th to the 11th century CE. The local Sailendra kings sponsored the building of the great temple at Borabudur and the monastic compound of Candi Plaosan, both in central Java, as well as other temples. Candi Plaosan is a unique complex that consists of two *viharas*, or monastic quarters, surrounded by 116 stupas and temples. Three storeys high, each building has three chambers at each level. Icons of Buddhas and bodhisattvas were placed at the rear and side areas of the lower floor, leaving a large open space for the congregation of monks. The second storey may have been a place for storing sacred objects and texts. Both Borabudur and Candi Plaosan, where this sculpture of a monk seated in meditation was found, are unique Javanese interpretations of traditional Buddhist forms. The portrait-like quality of the face suggests that the figure is not generic but a rendering of a particular individual, and the elongated ears indicate that the subject was a nobleman or prince who gave up the royal life to be a monk, as had Siddhartha. The figure is simply incised and modelled from roughly textured volcanic rock. Seemingly diaphanous robes reveal the nipples and navel. The monk leans forwards, his head is slightly lowered, and the shape of his head and the definition of his facial features are unlike idealized forms of the Buddha; also, there is no suggestion of the Buddha's slight smile. Several remarkably similar portrait sculptures, some of them fragmentary, were also found at Candi Plaosan, and they may all be sculptures of the same individual.

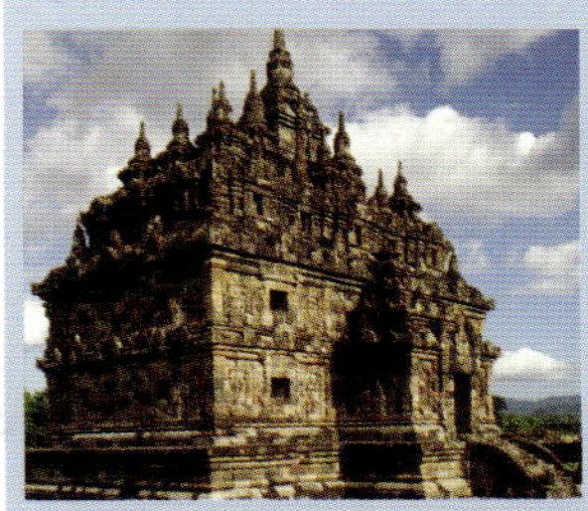

Candi Plaosan

About 50 kilometres (30 miles) south-west of Borobudur, the complex at Plaosan was built in the mid-9th century by Pramodhawardhani, queen consort of Rakai Pikatan of the Medang Kingdom. At the heart of the complex are twin *viharas*, or shrine buildings. Their collections of icons are all seated on lotus thrones on a raised altar. The wall relief carvings of one *vihara* are mostly of male deities; those of the other are mostly female ones.

'He recites the Sacred Texts ... truly knowing, with mind well freed, clinging to naught here and hereafter, he shares the fruits of the Holy Life.'

NARADA MAHA THERA, *THE BUDDHA AND HIS TEACHINGS*

Bodhisattva Maitreya

c. 9th–10th century CE **National Museum, Jakarta, Indonesia**

STYLE Pala, Srivijayan **ORIGIN** Komering, Palembang, southern Sumatra, Indonesia **MATERIAL** Bronze **HEIGHT** 24.5 cm/9 ¾ in.

Buddhists consider the appearance of a Buddha in the world as a cyclical occurrence. Hope in a Buddha of the Future is common to the three major schools of Buddhism and is attributed to historic contact with the Persian religion of Zoroaster, which holds that there will be a golden age of the Future. Etymological similarities attest to a relationship between the Christian Messiah, Buddhist Maitreya and Zoroastrian Ahura Mazda, as do eschatological teachings of a period of utter destruction prior to renewal of the cosmos. The earliest depictions of the Buddha of the Future, emerging in the early centuries of the first millennium, show him as a bodhisattva holding a water jar, or wearing a small stupa in his crown. Another composition presents him seated with crossed ankles under a trabeated arch – interpreted as a representation of the Tushita Heaven – where he waits his time to descend to earth. This is how Maitreya appears in this bronze sculpture from Komering in southern Sumatra, seat of the Srivijaya Kingdom. The Kingdom was an important study centre for monks travelling eastwards, being part of a network of ports on sea routes linking India, Sri Lanka, Thailand, Java and China. The monks brought with them the Pala style of art and iconography of north-east India, with its soft-fleshed figures wearing delicate, jewelled adornments, bringing it south and then to China. The notion of Maitreya was especially appealing to monks; along with other devotees, they prayed either to be reborn in the Tushita Heaven so that they could accompany the saviour when he descended to earth, or simply to be reborn at the time of his descent.

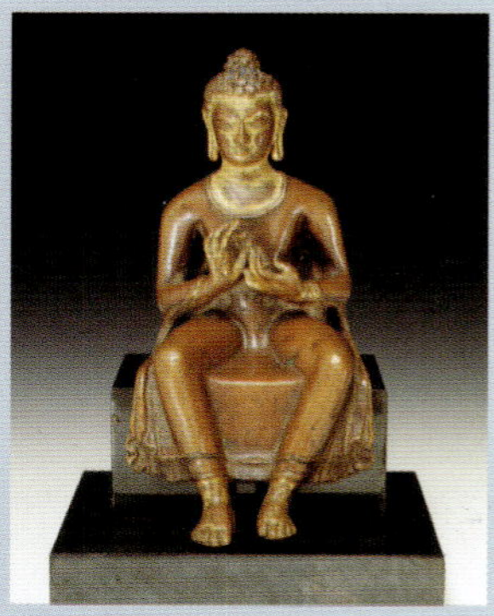

Nepalese Buddha

This copper sculpture of Maitreya from Nepal sits with legs pendant in the 'Western' posture often used to identify the Buddha of the Future, incarnate on earth. The hands' teaching gesture foretells that the Buddha of the Future's life will follow the events of the historic Buddha's life.

'[After death the believer in Maitreya] shall enter the company of Tushita-gods, where the Bodhisattva Mahasattva Maitreya is residing [and] preaching the law.'

LOTUS SUTRA

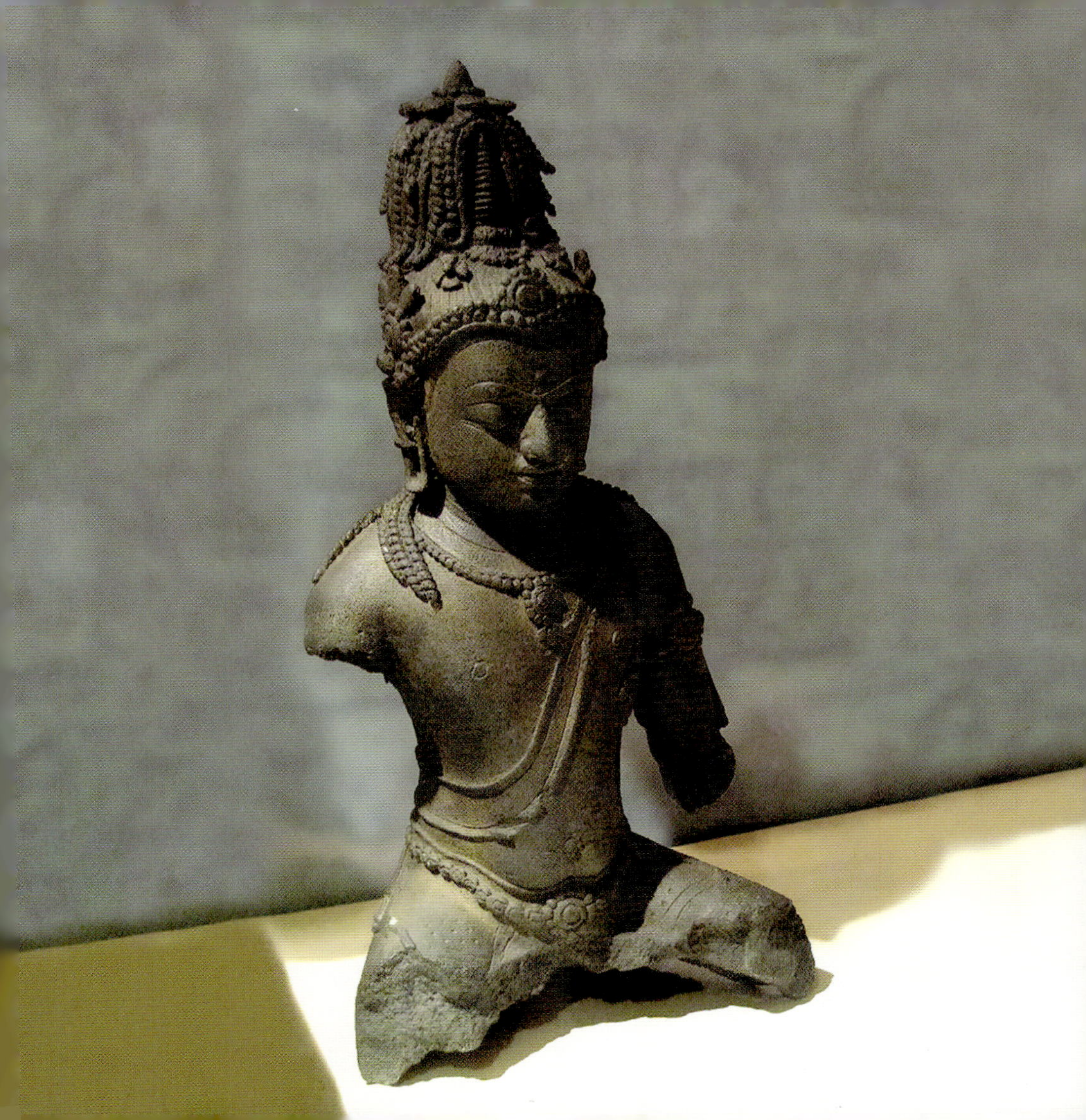

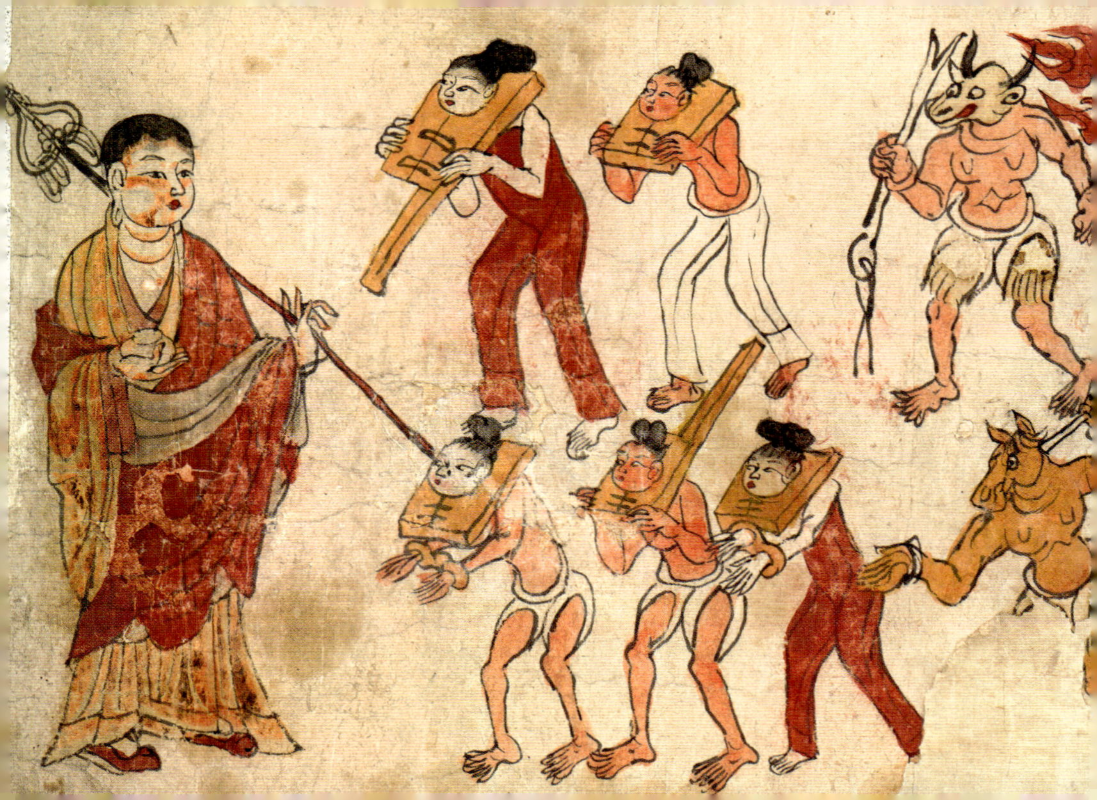

The Ten Kings of Hell

c. 10th century CE **British Museum, London, UK**

ORIGIN Library cave (Cave 17), Dunhuang, Gansu, China **MATERIALS** Ink and colours on paper scroll **DIMENSIONS** 50 x 29 cm/19 ½ x 11 ½ in.

Sir Marcus Aurelius Stein was on a series of expeditions in the early 1900s, tracing the 7th-century CE travels of the Chinese monk Xuanzang, when he discovered the Dunhuang Caves in the Gobi Desert. Tens of thousands of documents, secular and religious, lay in one cave, among them an illustrated scroll, the *Ten Kings of Hell*, based on an apocryphal sutra of 903 CE recounting the journey of the soul after death. There are ten hell scenes, each presided over by a judge seated at a desk with attendant scribes and demonic enforcers. This peculiarly Chinese concept of netherworld magistrates imitates worldly courts of justice, with magistrates making judgments and henchmen carrying out punishments. One of the kings of hell points out six possible paths of rebirth: celestial, divine, human, animal, hungry ghost and hell. In contrast to the tormented sinners, saved souls also appear, carrying scriptures and images. In the Theravada vision of hell transgressors are left to fend for themselves, but this scroll includes a large-scale representation of a bodhisattva, Dizang (Kshitigarbha in Sanskrit, see left), figured as a shaven-pated monk in monastic robes and carrying a monk's staff and wish-fulfilling jewel (*Cintamani*). The bodhisattva, who has the ability to intervene on behalf of the judged, has vowed not to enter Nirvana until all are saved. Herded by horse-headed and bull-headed demons and trapped in cangues (wooden yokes), the denizens of hell rush towards Dizang for help. The scripture of the ten kings explains that serving as a king in hell is a form of punishment, but also asserts that reincarnation is possible after transit of the hells.

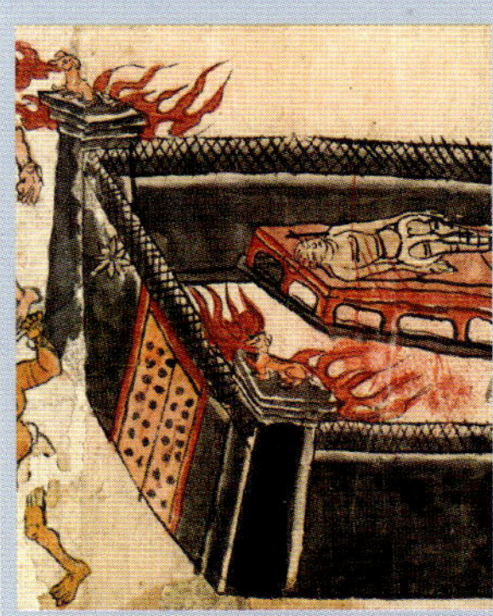

Torments of the Damned

To the right of the portrait of Dizang (see left), an infernal walled and gated city is shown. Dogs perch on its towers, and inside are flames and a soul being tortured. This is one of the stages of the afterlife that the damned must endure as they make their way through the ten hells.

'The ox heads who guide the way clasp cudgels at their shoulders,
The ghost soldiers who press people ahead raise pitchforks in their hands.'

S. T. TEISER, *THE SCRIPTURE ON THE TEN KINGS*

Lacquered Wooden Icon of Amida

1053 CE   Byodo-in Temple, Uji, Kyoto, Japan

COMMISSIONED BY Fujiwara Yorimichi
MATERIAL Wood, lacquered and gilded   **HEIGHT** 2.95 m/9 ft 8 in.

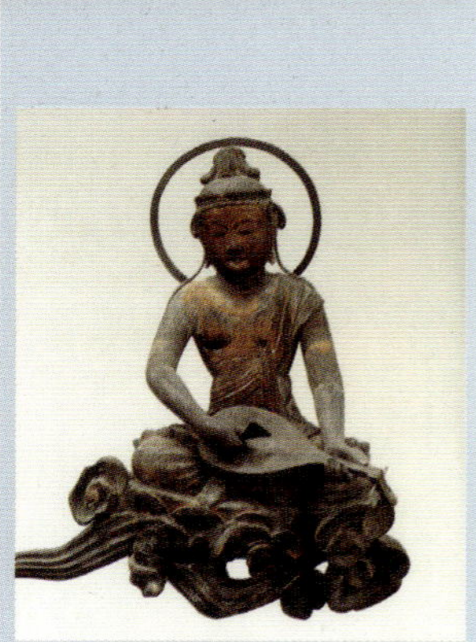

Wooden Angel

Surrounding the seated Buddha, Jocho placed fifty-two expertly carved sculptures of angels making music. Each has its own posture as it plays — standing, seated, kneeling — and is seen from a frontal, three-quarter-frontal or rear viewpoint. The clouds on which they rest convey an impression that they are descending from heaven.

'If you pray Namu-amida-butsu [Adoration for Amida Buddha], your life will be renewed in the Land of Happiness.'

HONIN (1133–1212), FOUNDER OF JODO AMIDA WORSHIP

Icons of Amida (Amitabha in Sanskrit) and his two attendant bodhisattvas were made in Japan from the 7th century CE, but by the 11th century a growing belief in *Mappo*, or latter days of the law, had greatly increased Amida's popularity. Buddhists assume that time is cyclical, and each epoch has a Buddha who lives and dies. Towards the end of the cycle, life becomes immoral, chaotic and perilous; *Mappo*, universal destruction, then occurs until the birth of a Buddha inaugurates a new cycle. In Japan *Mappo* was predicted for 1052, and faith in Amida grew as he offered the only means of salvation. Thus, Amida appears at the Byodo-in, a villa reworked by Fujiwara Yorimichi (992–1074) as a temple for the coming age of destruction. The sculptor Jocho (d. 1057) was in overall charge, and dominating the central hall is the icon he made of Amida, whose large size was made possible by Jocho's technique of *yosegi*, or joined wood. Jocho also introduced a notion of ideal beauty, based on mathematical proportions and harmonious geometric forms, that replaced the naturalism of earlier times. The visual impact of the Buddha figure, sitting in meditative posture, is enhanced by its verticality. A tall, hourglass-shaped pedestal supports an open-petalled lotus seat, from which a high wooden mandorla (almond-shaped shell) reaches up to an ornate giltwood canopy. Cut into the mandorla are intricate openwork carvings of floral and flame motifs, and the halo has rich rinceau (foliage) designs of branches, stems and leaves.

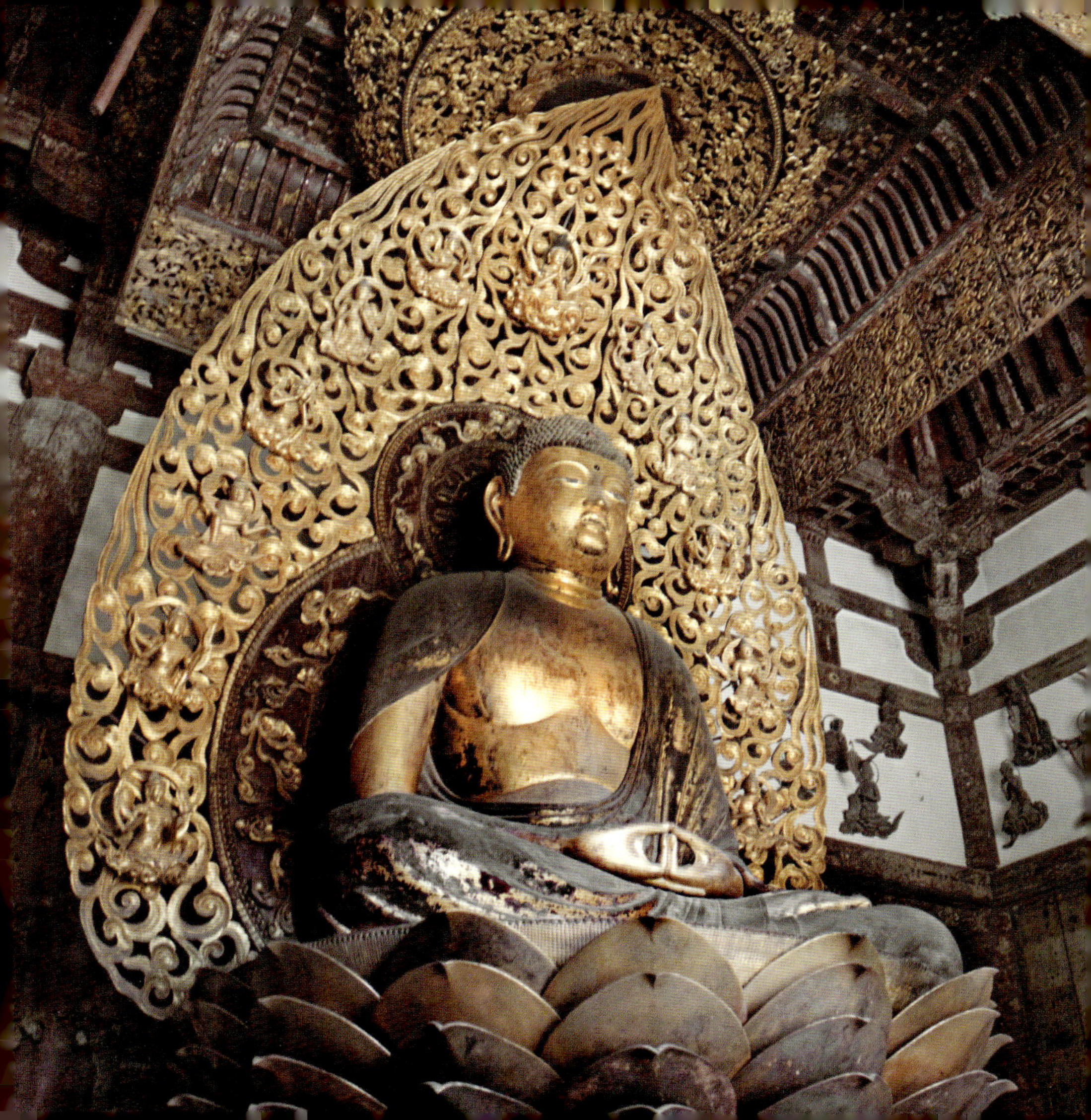

Luohans

c. 11th–12th centuries CE   **Lingyan Temple, Jinan, Shandong, China**

STYLE Song   **MATERIALS** Clay and polychrome paints
SIZE Life-sized, so figures vary

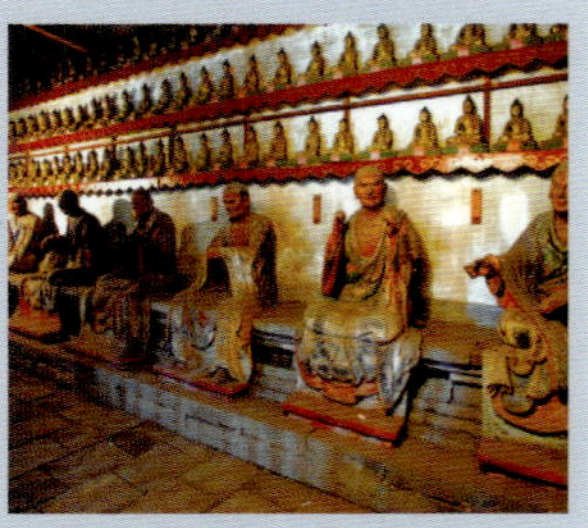

Lingyan Temple

At its height during the Song era, Lingyan Temple consisted of forty different wooden structures and a population of more than five hundred monks. The sculptures of the Thousand Buddha Hall are so lifelike that it seems possible that monks in residence may have been the models. Monks would have been inspired by seeing these highly evolved luohans.

'The Monk practises the way and substitutes that for pleasures of disporting himself in the world. He accumulates goodness and wisdom in exchange for the joys of wife and children.'

MOUZI, *THE DISPOSITION OF ERROR* (LIHOULUN)

Luohans (*arhats* in Sanskrit) are monks who, having achieved enlightenment, remain on earth teaching at the request of the Historical Buddha Shakyamuni, who instructed them to wait until the time of the Buddha of the Future before departing the world. A set of luohans usually numbers eighteen, but some temples have as many as five hundred in a group. Lingyan Temple, the Temple of the Spiritual Rocks, is located in a valley near the Taishan heavenly mountain range; it was established in the 4th century CE and underwent several periods of reconstruction. At this temple's Thousand Buddha Hall, forty individual life-sized clay and polychrome sculptures sit along a narrow bench that runs along the rear and side walls. Groups of life-sized sculptures of monks engage in lively discourse, showing a variety of postures and gestures. The range of body types, facial features, skin colours, garments and poses indicates that some of the monks come from far afield. The extremely naturalistic and individualized polychrome clay portraits have the hallmark of the Song dynasty (960–1279 CE). The faces are very life-like, with expressions that convey the monks' interior thoughts. In this example, the artist has well observed the shadows of the Luohan's shaven pate, the loose skin around his mouth and the furrow at his brow – clearly, this monk is no longer young. His hand gesture, narrowed eyes and look of concentration suggest that he has reached an important point of his argument. Care has been taken in the articulation of his strong neck and clavicle, and in reproducing the bright colours and delicate brocade patterns of his monastic robes.

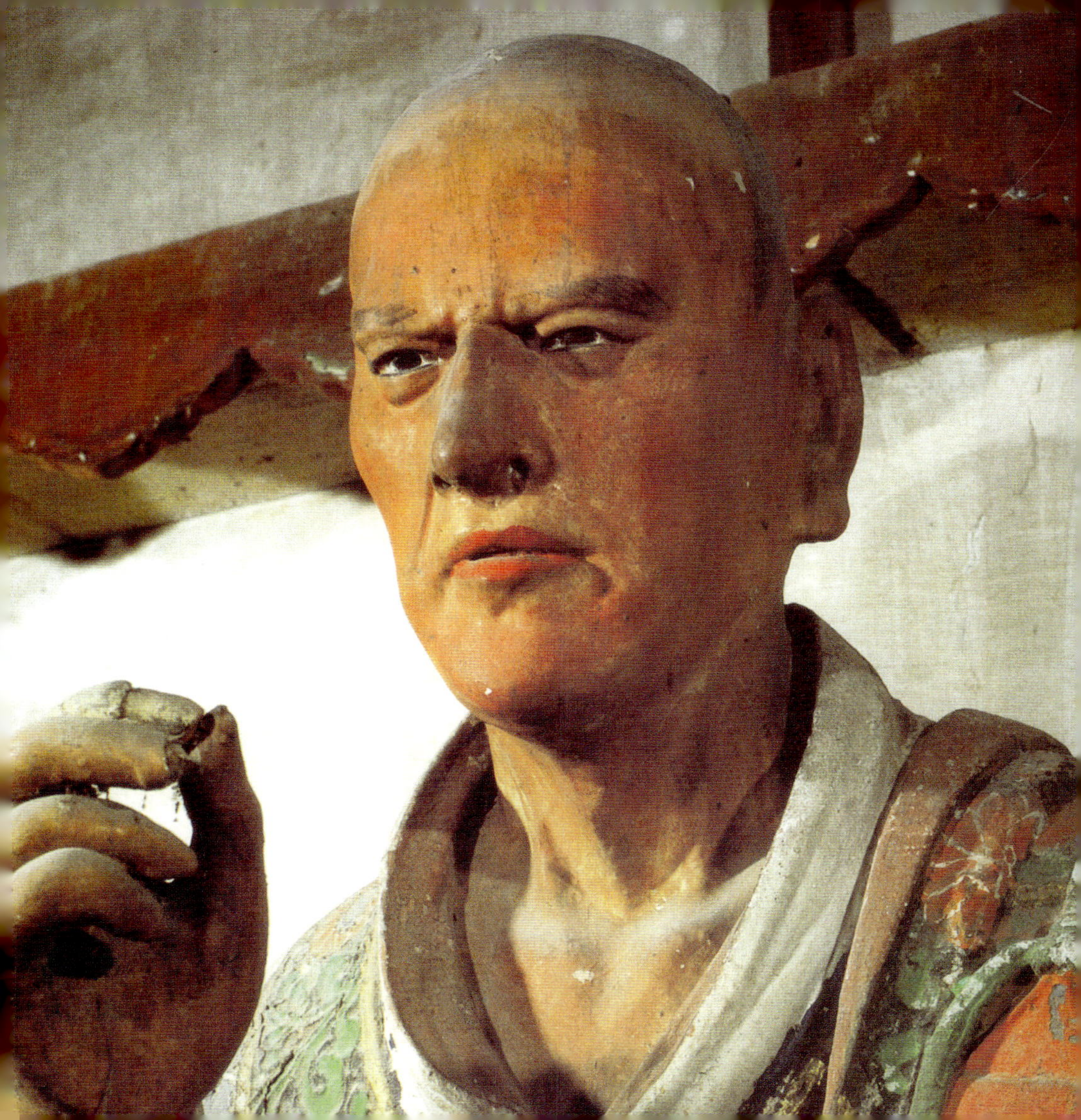

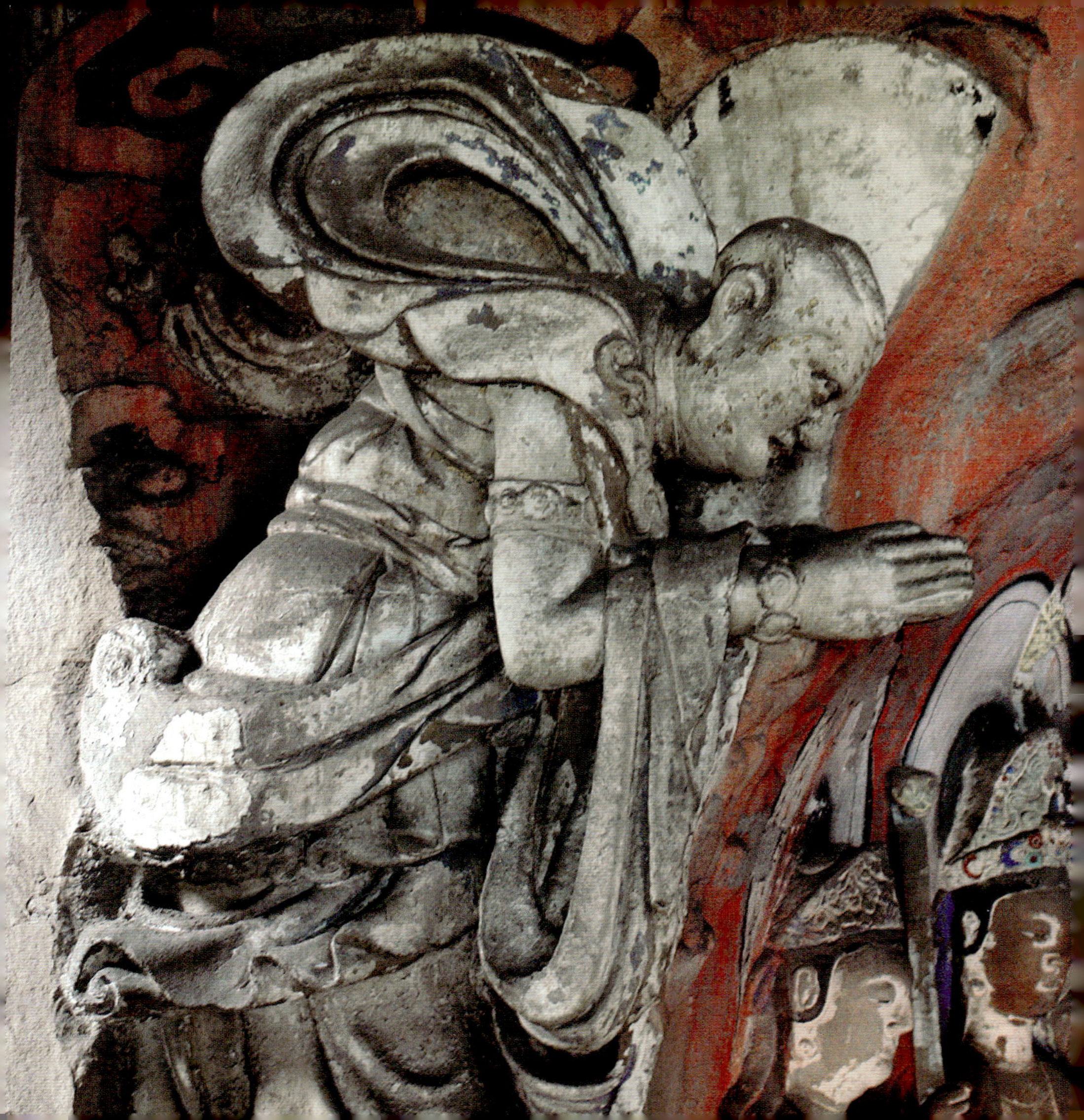

Adoring Angel

12th century CE **Erfo cave-temple, Laitan, Sichuan, China**

STYLE Zen
MATERIALS Stucco and polychrome paints

The northern Indian angel, based on the chubby flying putti of Western art, underwent several stages in its transformation from a Western theme into a Chinese Buddhist one. Early in the first stage of Buddhist art in China, the Western angel was adopted and included in all manner of cave décor at Yungang, Dunhuang and elsewhere. The angels became increasingly acrobatic as they flew in the sky, but soon the figures are dramatically altered, their aerial propulsion being suggested by billowing scarves rather than wings. Angels may have lost their wings because their hybrid nature – half-bird, half-human – disconcerted the Chinese, or perhaps it was thought that truly celestial angels would need no feathered appendages. By the time the Erfo cave-temple was created in Sichuan, further changes had taken place. This angel at Erfo looks distinctly corporeal rather than angelic. Indeed, it is only his placement high up in the arch of the cave that identifies him as a celestial. The portrait-like rendering of the face is unique, and his expression has an emotional intensity that contrasts with the detached demeanor more usual in angels. His body and garments have a weight and solidity that also seem earthbound. The skill demonstrated in rendering these realistic characteristics is consistent with the accomplishments of Song-dynasty artists, who excelled in naturalistic representation of figures. Perhaps the anomaly of representing a celestial with human features is in keeping with the fact that the Erfo cave-temples were dedicated to Zen Buddhism, in which the concept of celestial realms has no part. In Zen, only by meditating does one achieve enlightenment.

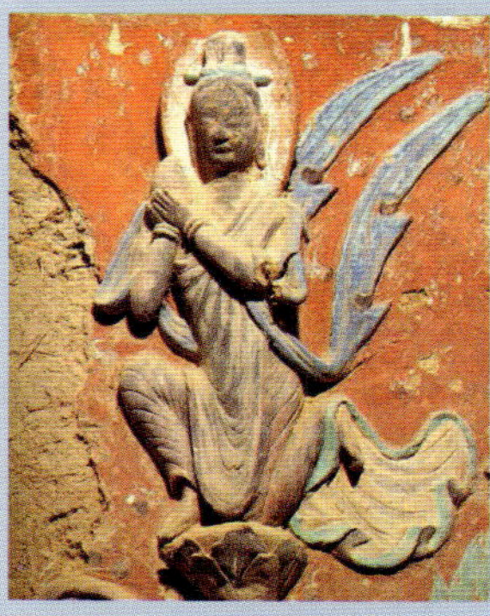

Dunhuang Angel

This angel, in Cave 248 at Dunhuang, dates from the Northern Zhou period (557–581 CE). It has billowing scarves rather than wings, and the body is robed rather than exposed to view. In China, angels or *feitian*, who lived in the celestial zone, were an important element of Buddhist iconography, but Western models were replaced by beings of more slender, elongated proportions.

'The devas (angels) and Naga spirits with one voice praised the Buddha's virtues; men ... were all rejoiced in turn.'

ASVAGHOSA, *BUDDHACARITA*

Hell of Measurements

12th century CE **Nara National Museum, Kansai, Japan**

COMMISSIONED BY Emperor Go Shirakawa **MATERIALS** Ink on paper
SCROLL DIMENSIONS 26.5 x 454.7 cm/10 ½ x 179 in.

Religions that offer salvation tend to be rich in representations of hell. The typical Christian church tympanum shows the saved on one side and the wretched damned on the other, and the threat of hell is equally well represented in Mahayana Buddhism. Now held at the Nara Museum, the *Illustrated Scroll of the Six Paths of Rebirth* is based on the *Scripture of the World Arising* (Kisekyo in Japanese), which had been translated into Chinese by Jnanagupta (d. 600). The sutra describes the six paths of rebirth with depictions of seven of the sixteen lesser hells: the Hell of Excrement, Hell of Measurements, Hell of the Iron Mortar, Hell of the Black Sand Cloud, Hell of Pus and Blood and Hell of Foxes and Wolves. The illustrated scroll, a long, horizontal composition, is unrolled bit by bit and read from the right to left; after reading, it is rolled up and put away. The scroll opens with passages of text that begin, 'There is yet another hell . . .', before relating that hell's particular sins and punishments. Shown here is the Hell of Measurements, a torment meted out to those who have cheated others in financial transactions: they are forced to hold burning bricks. The hell is depicted as a dark and bleak place. The damned, grimacing in their pain and horror, are nearly naked, while a grotesque, semi-naked ogress with fangs, three eyes, a bald head and pendent breasts oversees the administration of justice. In another example, the Hell of the Flaming Cock, a giant flaming rooster viciously pecks those who have harmed animals. The written text is unusual in that it is not executed in Chinese, the lingua franca of Buddhism, but in the newly formed Japanese phonetic script.

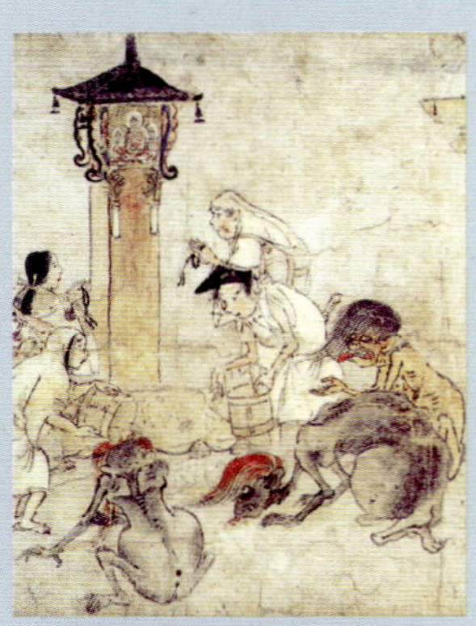

Hell of Hungry Ghosts

In Buddhist texts, illustrations of hungry ghosts, like hell scrolls, are depictions of punishments. Hungry ghosts can only eat decayed human flesh, excrement and consecrated water. They have skeletal bodies but bloated bellies. Here they wait to drink the sanctified water offered by nuns at a Buddhist pillar.

'The sinner here eats of the dung and all the assembled maggots swarm at once for food.'

GENSHIN (942–1017), ON THE HELL OF EXCREMENT, *THE ESSENTIALS OF SALVATION*

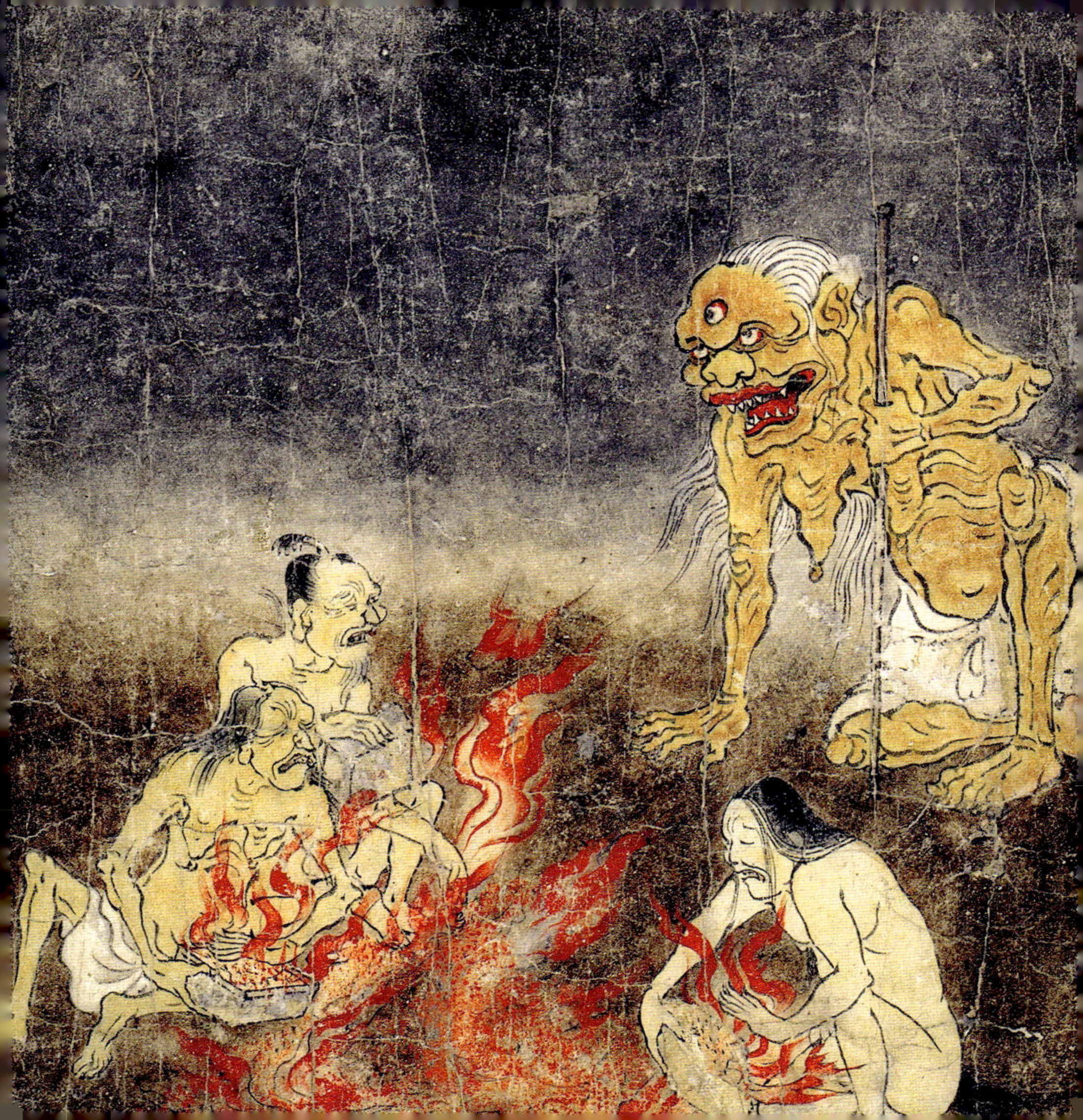

Naga Guardians

12th century CE **Vatadage, Polonnaruwa, Sri Lanka**

COMMISSIONED BY Nissanka Malla   **NAGA GUARDIANS** Total of eight
UPPER-LEVEL BUDDHAS Total of four   **MATERIAL** Sandstone

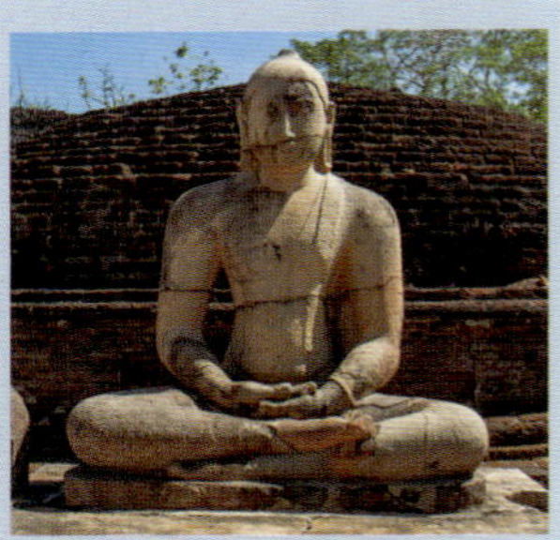

Vatadage Stupa

Vatadage is a 12th-century stupa that once contained a sacred tooth relic of the Buddha. The stupa is set on two high bases approached by steps and is surrounded by four seated Buddhas oriented to the centre and the four cardinal directions. In contrast, the guardians that protect the lower precinct represent the earthly realm.

'We Deva Kings … will protect that king and his people, give them peace and freedom from suffering, prolong their lives and fill them with glory. Most Revered One!'

THE BUDDHIST TRADITION IN INDIA, CHINA AND JAPAN

Protective guardians have appeared consistently in the decoration of Buddhist monuments. Perhaps the most ancient example, from the 1st century CE, may be seen at Sanchi Stupa in Bhopal, India, where a princely turbanned and jewelled figure armed with a spear stands at the base of a gateway pillar. But the guardians at either side of the staircase at the entrance to the Vatadage, in the ancient Sinhalese capital city of Polonnaruwa, are contained in separate free-standing arched frames and bear no weapons – only their vigilance suggests their defensive function. The bejewelled figures have nine-headed cobra hoods over their heads that identify them as *nagas*, or snake gods. An ancient Indian tradition asserts that the presence of fecundity and beauty, often manifested by either the glamorous female tree spirit Yakshi or the portly earth god Yaksha, also has an apotropaic (evil-averting) function; thus, these snake-god guards representing tutelary deities may be understood in this context as well. Standing in a slight hip-sway posture, wearing a headdress and multiple jewels, they each hold a round pot filled with flowers in one hand and a long-stemmed lotus flower in the other; both are symbols of prosperity and aquatic fertility. At the feet of each are two small dwarf-like figures, perhaps personifications of earthly riches. The deployment of guardian figures by the approach to a stupa is first seen in Sri Lanka at Ruwanweli Saya Stupa in Anuradhapura, which was built around 140 CE. That the guardians are found over a thousand years later at Polonnaruwa attests that such paired stele became a distinctive Sinhalese Buddhist architectural feature.

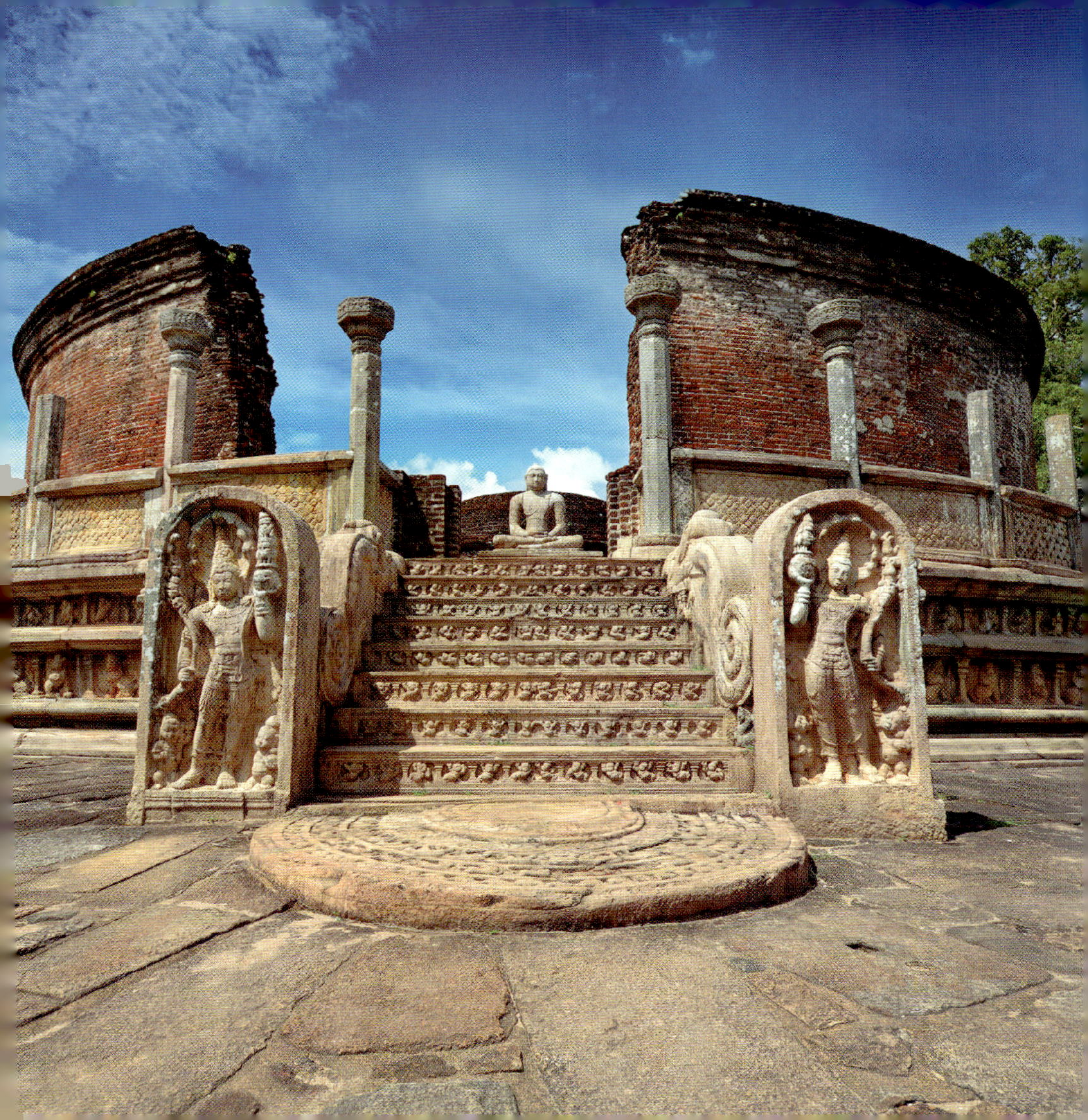

Guardian Kings

1203 CE **South Gate, Todai-ji, Nara, Kansai, Japan**

CARVED BY Unkei and Kaikei **FUNCTION** Protector of the faith
MATERIAL Wood, formerly painted **HEIGHT** 8.5 m/28 ft 10 in.

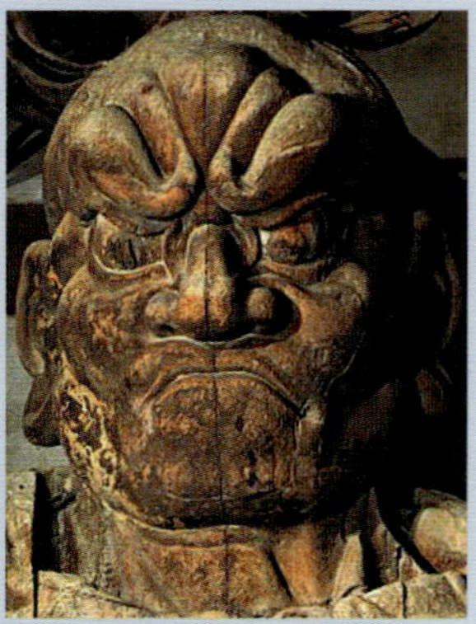

Fearsome Aspect

As this head, the pair of the figure at right, shows, Asian artists were not concerned with realist depiction. Disfigured by rage, the faces are rendered in a cartoon-like manner, with trapezoidal eye sockets housing round eyeballs under frown-contorted brows.

'Produced under the direction of Unkei and Kaikei, the statues ... were completed in the amazingly short time of two months.'

HISASHI MORI, *SCULPTURE OF THE KAMAKURA PERIOD*

Guardian figures, appearing early in Buddhist art, were to evolve repeatedly over the centuries. The first and earliest were guards placed on either side of entryways to Buddhist places of worship, such as the figures carved on the pillars of the Sanchi stupa in Bhopal, India. These ancient prototypes, princely in appearance, are naked to the waist, wear a turban and jewels and carry a lance. A second type, heavenly guardians of the four cardinal directions, stand at the four corners of Buddhist altars. Known as Tianwang or lokapalas, these have a specific set of attributes: they wear armour, jewels and crowns and stand on sub-human creatures, as though vanquishing threatening forces. Each holds an attribute associated with his identity and direction: the guardians of the east and south hold the sword of conquest, the west has a scripture representing the all-conquering Dharma and the north holds a reliquary representing the Buddha. In the later 7th century CE, at the Fengxiansi Caves in Longmen, China, a third type of guardian king appeared. There, a contrast is drawn between the contained martial strength of the heavenly king and the ferocious power of the guardian king. The latter are distinguished by their exaggerated muscular physiques and faces distorted in ugly grimaces. This guardian king (Nio in Japanese) is one of two installed five hundred years later at the entrance of the south gate of Todai-ji temple in Nara, Japan. Semi-naked, both assume dramatic active postures, as if coiling their energy for an assault. Their force is enough to cause their skirts, ribbons and scarves to fly around them, and it extends even to their flexed fingers.

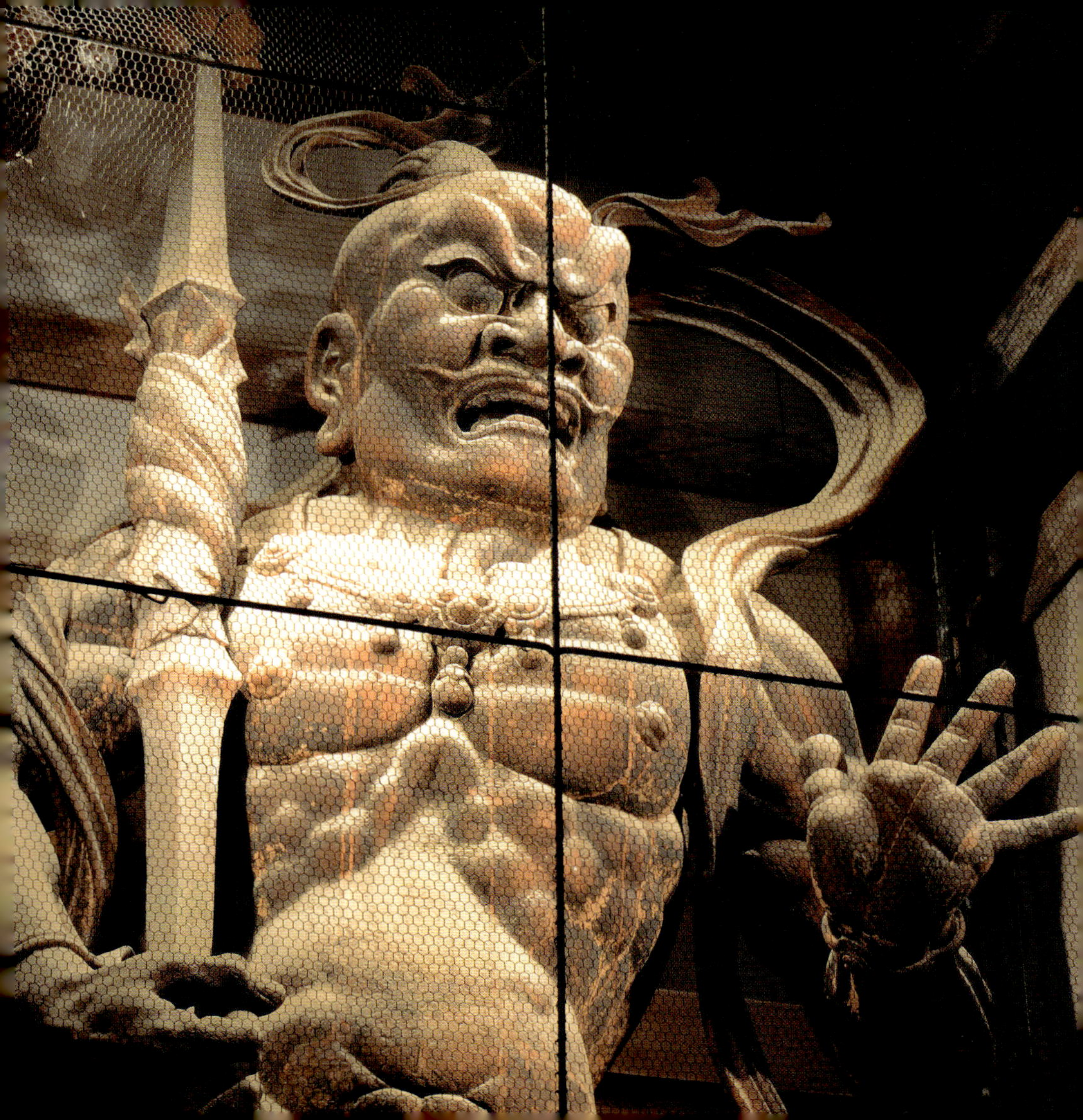

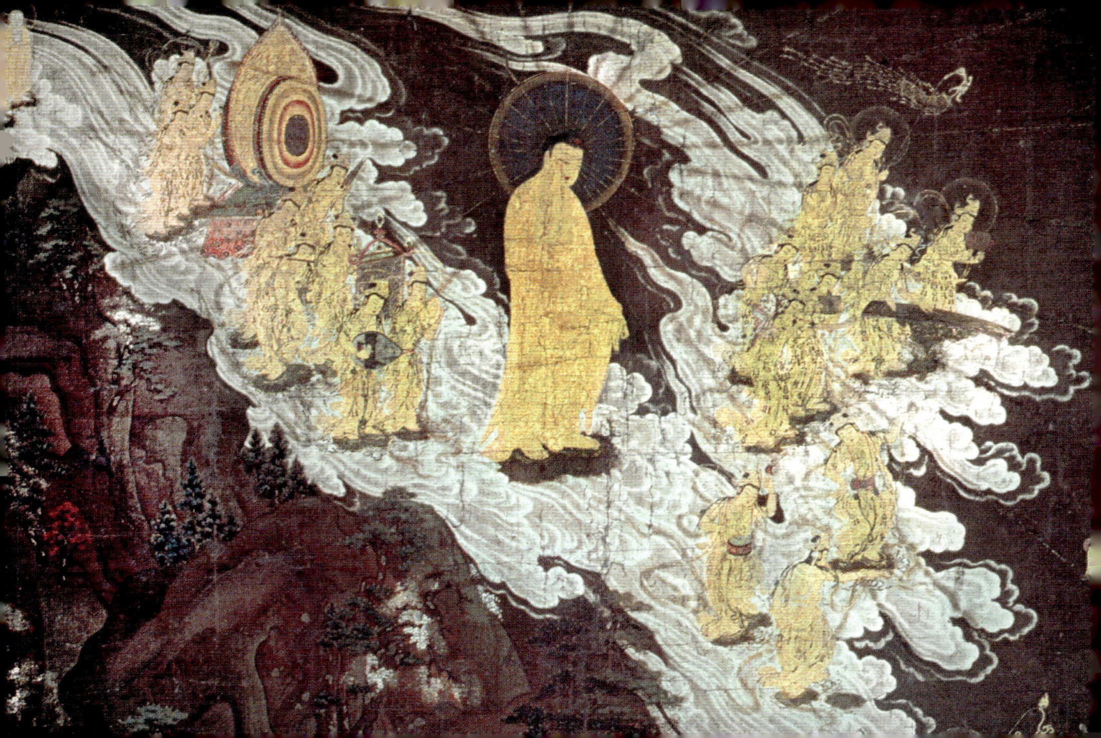

Descent of Amida and Twenty-five Attendants

13th–14th century CE **Kyoto National Museum, Japan**

FORMAT Hanging scroll **MATERIALS** Coloured and gold threads on silk
DIMENSIONS 145.1 x 154.5 cm/57 x 61 in.

Whereas the Chinese tended to imagine Amida dwelling in a remote palatial complex, the Japanese preferred to create images of his *haya raigo*, or rapid descent to earth. This silk painting, a detail of a large hanging scroll originally from Chion-in, Kyoto, depicts Amida descending on clouds towards a pious dying monk who is seated in prayer in his home (depicted further to the right of this detail). Amida, with a blue circular halo and his two feet resting on golden lotus flowers, stands in three-quarter frontal profile, looking down compassionately on the devout monk. Celestial attendants announce his arrival, playing music on drums, flutes and stringed instruments; others joyously dance. Their descending bank of purple clouds is touching plants and causing them to bloom out of season. A dozen tiny standing Buddhas float in the sky, and lotus petals flutter down. The background of lushly forested, low-rolling hills is painted in brilliant greens and browns. The artists have conveyed the great speed of the cloud's descent by placing the figures on a sharp diagonal, and by dispersing the secondary figures in small groups around the main ones. The fragmented cloud on which they stand appears to skip over some parts of the landscape and slide rapidly over others. In addition, the linear definition of the cloud swirls have a downward rhythm that is emphasized by the fluttering of the sleeves and scarves of the Buddha's retinue – all suggest irresistible downward motion.

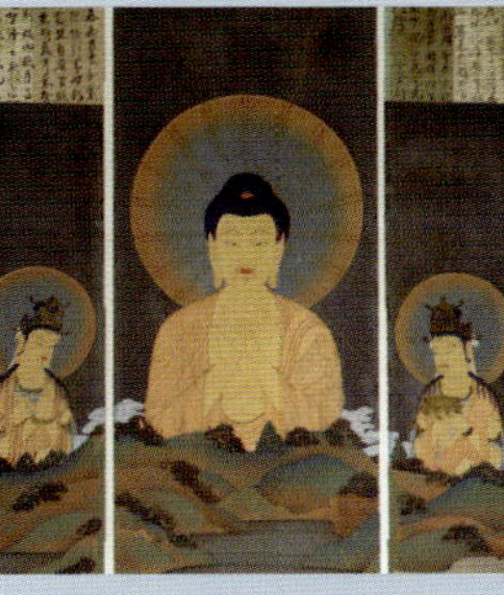

Amida as the Sun

The Japanese have represented Amida in different ways. One genre depicts him and his two main attendants as half figures behind low, rolling Japanese hills (see example above, from 1909). With his large halo, he resembles the setting sun, an allusion to the Buddha's Paradise in the West.

'When a pious person dies, the Buddha appears before him. The Lord of Compassion ... brings a lotus flower to carry the pious soul, and the Lord of Might reaches him welcoming hands ...'

ESHIN, *OJU YOSHU (BIRTH IN THE LAND OF PURITY)*

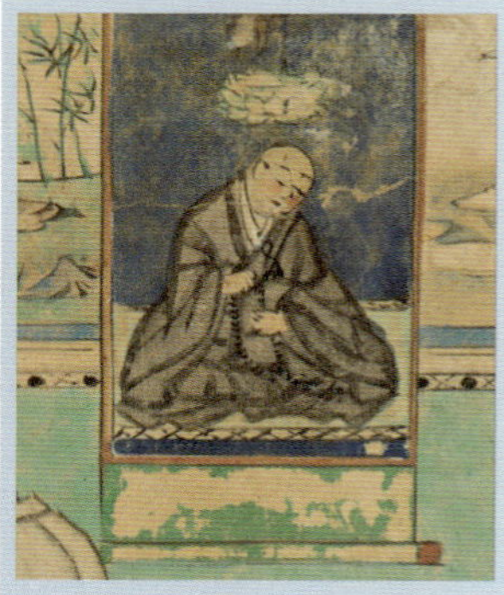

Biographical Scroll

Pictorial scrolls were often employed In Japan to illustrate the lives of important people, the histories of shrines and temples, major events and literary works. The detail above from the pictorial biography of Honen is a portrait of the patriarch on a vertical hanging scroll, which he inscribed for one of his students.

'He never fails
To reach the Lotus Land
of Bliss
Who calls
If only once,
The name of Amida.'

POEM BY KUYA,
PREDECESSOR OF HONEN

Biography of Honen

14th century CE Chion-in Temple, Kyoto, Kansai, Japan

FORMAT Total of forty-eight horizontal hand scrolls SOURCE OF DETAIL Scroll Thirty-four MATERIALS Colours and inks on paper

The evangelist Honen (1133–1212), founder of the Pure Land sect, advocated pure faith and established belief in Amida (Amitahba in Sanskrit) as a separate school of Buddhism. Dissatisfied with current practices, Honen had found inspiration in the words of the Chinese priest Shandao (613–81): 'Only repeat the name of the Amida with all your heart …. This is the practice which brings salvation without fail, for it is in accordance with the original vow of the Buddha.' Honen and his followers chanted the *nembutsu*, or name of the Buddha, calling on the deity for salvation up to 70,000 times a day. The temple of Chion-in holds a set of horizontal scrolls that illustrate events in Honin's life, including his tonsure, studies in the temple, travels through the Japanese countryside, conversions of high and low to the Pure Land sect and his death-bed farewell. In a meticulous and observant way, using brush, ink and pale colours on paper, the artists detailed not only the biography but also daily life in medieval Japan. In this scene they render the architecture – the wooden house, its doors opening to reveal interior sliding blue doors and walls and green *tatami* (grass) mats – and monks seated in varied poses listening to their master recite the scriptures. Outside the house, devotees gather from all walks of life to listen to Honen. There are monks with their shaven pates and white or black gauze robes, nuns in white garb, travelling pilgrims with great straw hats, soldiers and aristocrats wearing tall, conical silk caps and holding fans. The illustrations are a rich source of information about the life of the famous patriarch and the world he inhabited.

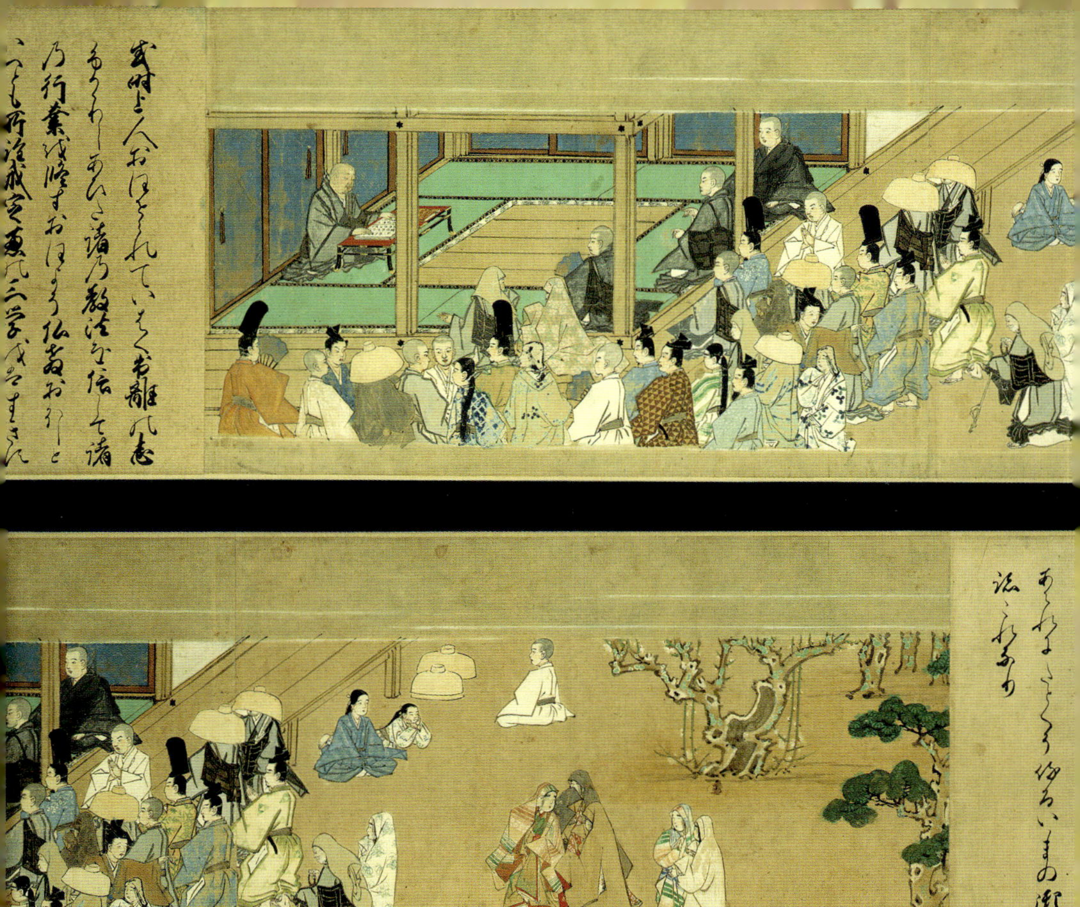

武府上人おほせられていをく苦離凡惡
あうれ／＼あひき諸乃敬法を伝して諸
乃行業戒修すおほうう佛あおおりと
こし所治戒定恵氏三学戒乃つまん

あまさこう御あいまの御敬あ況
況、欲なう

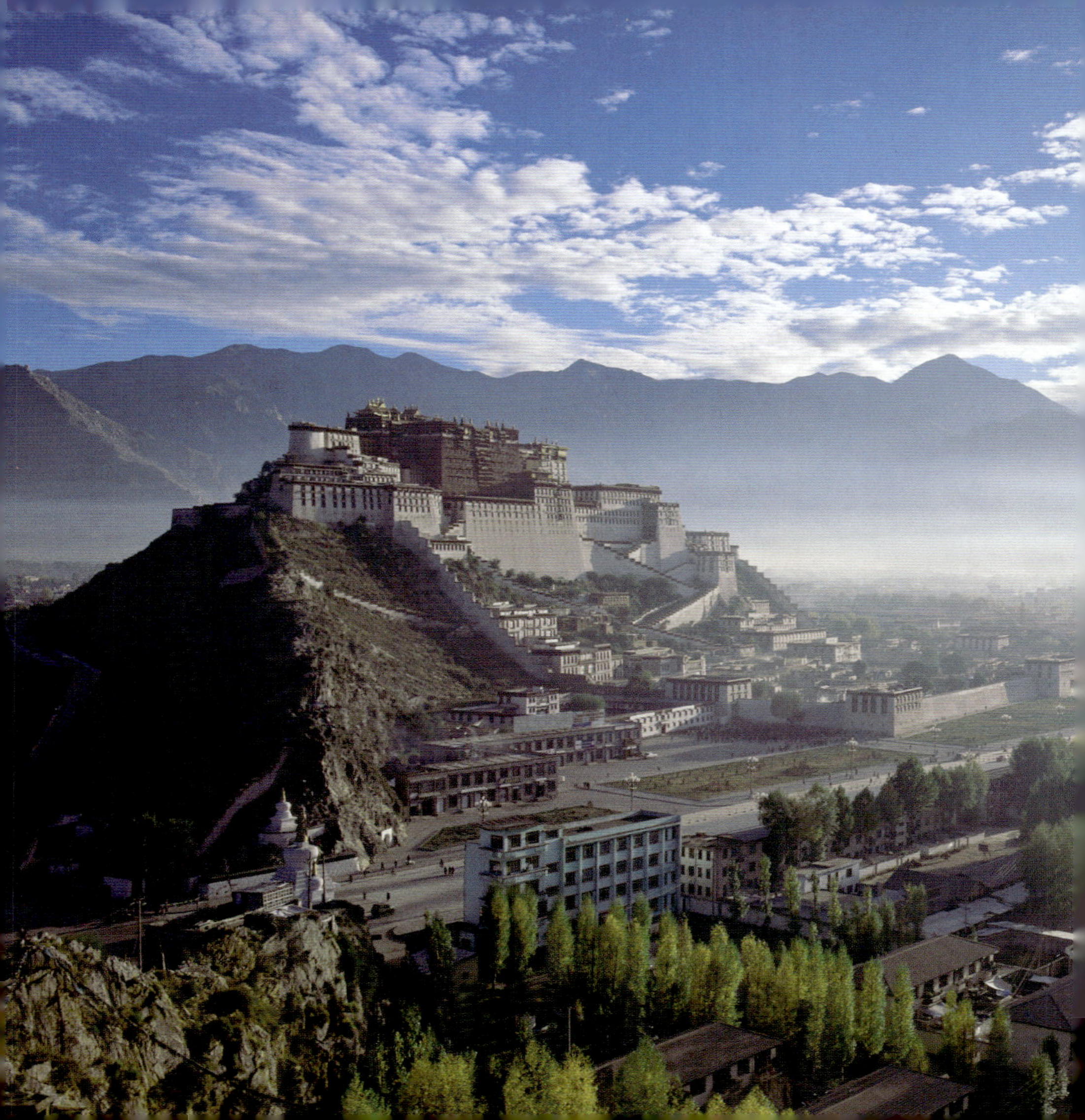

Potala Palace

1645 CE **Lhasa, Tibet Autonomous Region, China**

AREA OF BUILDING 400 x 350 m/1,312 x 1,148 ft **STOREYS** Thirteen
ROOMS 1,000 **HEIGHT OF BUILDING** 117 m/384 ft

Tibetan Buddhism holds that the Dalai Lama, or Great Teacher, is a manifestation of Avalokiteshvara. It is believed that when the Dalai Lama dies, he chooses to be reincarnated so that he might continue to serve the community rather than simply pursue his own salvation. In Tibetan tradition, three years after the death, a search is inaugurated among the local boys for the new incarnation. Many sets of ritual objects are shown to the children, and the one who prefers those dear to the past Dalai Lama is identified as the present incarnation; he is brought to the Potala Palace in Llasa where his education as a spiritual leader commences. The Potala Palace is named after Mount Potalaka, the abode of the Bodhisattva Avalokiteshvara, and is a recreation of the deity's mountain home. The Fifth Dalai Lama started its construction in 1645 on the 300-metre (985-ft) 'Red Hill'. Today it contains 10,000 shrines and about 200,000 statues. The heart of the palace, the administrative and spiritual centre, is painted red; the ancillary buildings are white, like the snow-capped mountains of the Himalayas. The whole appears as a mystical abode hovering above the city. Tibetan Buddhism, a form of esoteric teaching, requires a number of ritual objects and works of art to help the *lamas* (teachers) instruct the faithful in their spiritual journey. Thus the palace is also a vast museum, with tens of thousands of icons, bells, candleholders, incense burners, and more, fashioned in gold, gilt bronze and other precious materials. There are also polychrome murals and mandalas (portable paintings of the Buddhist cosmos) and portraits of teachers of the past.

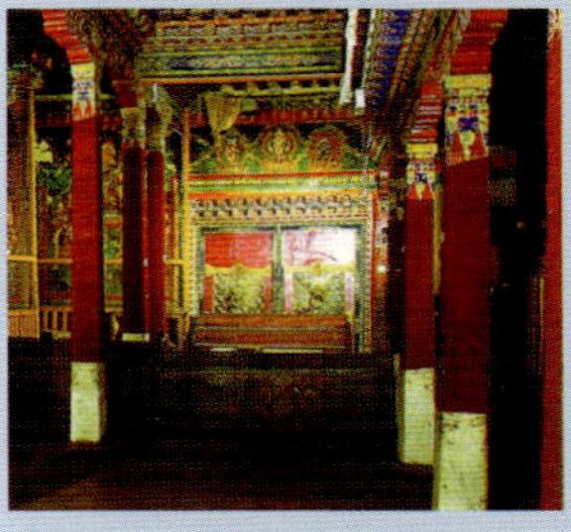

Palace Interior

Inside the Potala Palace, which functions as the home of the incarnated Bodhisattva Avalokiteshvara, the rooms are ornately decorated. Red is an auspicious colour and used liberally. In this interior view, the columns are painted red in the middle with white bases; the white tops have geometric and floral designs. At the rear of the hall is a small throne covered in red for use by the Dalai Lama.

'Never have any doubt ye sages, for I [Avalokiteshvara] shall strengthen you, I am the leader who speaketh infallible truth, and my knowledge is unlimited.'

LOTUS SUTRA

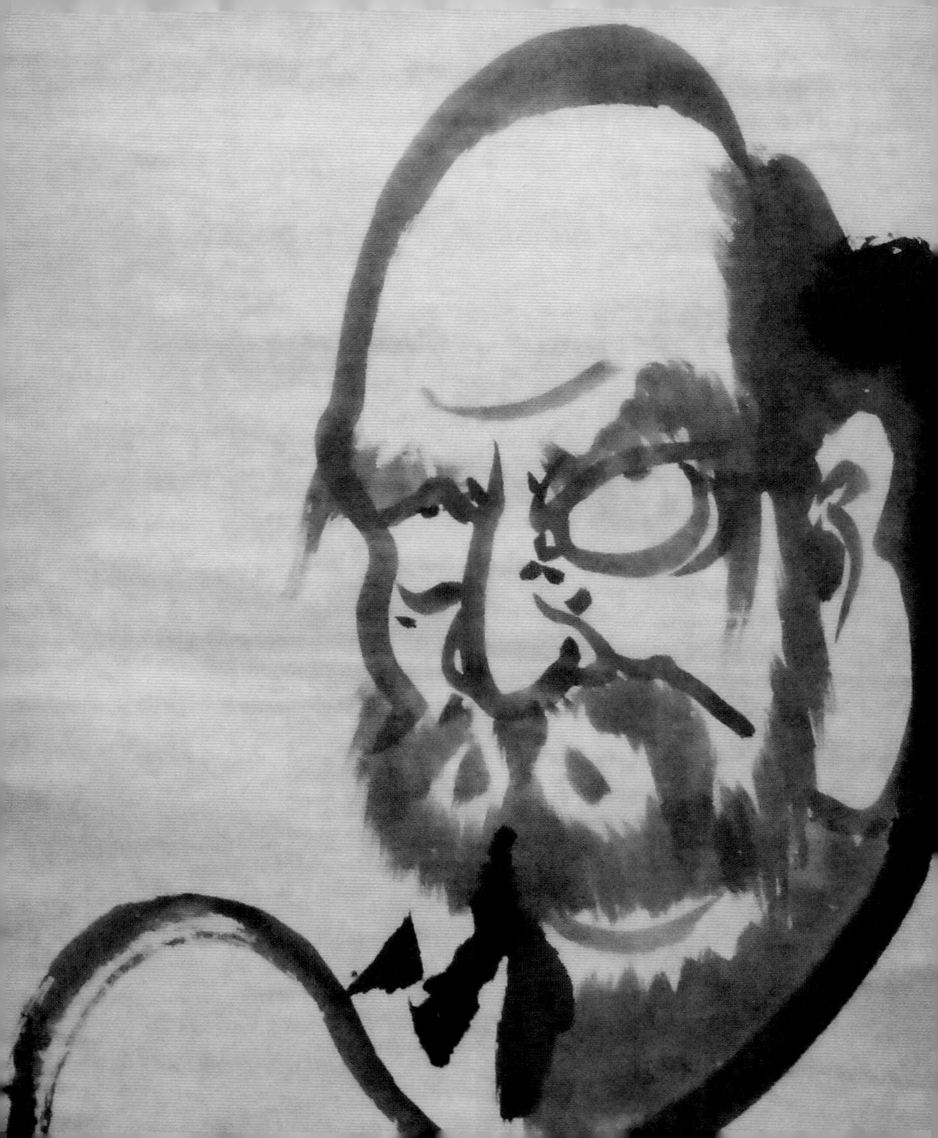

Bodhidharma

1751 CE **Indianapolis Museum of Art, Indiana, USA**

STYLE Zen **FORMAT** Hanging scroll **MATERIALS** Ink on paper
DIMENSIONS 224.8 x 136.4 cm/88½ x 53¾ in.

Hakuin Ekaku (1686–1768) became a monk at the age of fifteen and spent the early part of his career studying Buddhism. In his later years he sought to reform the Zen Rinzai sect. His teachings are set forth in voluminous writings that appropriate poetry, prose and exposition, some illustrated by ink paintings. He began to paint at the age of sixty and continued until his death at age eighty-four, leaving over a thousand paintings. Infused with mystical simplicity and wry humour, his works vary widely in content: traditional iconoclastic Zen themes; the homeless vagrant Hotei, the Buddha of the Future; Kannon, the Bodhisattva of Compassion, demons and animal caricatures. This example is a portrayal of Bodhidharma (Daruma), the monk who brought Zen teachings from India to China and founded the Zen Rinzai sect. It was, like all Zen paintings, executed as an act of meditation; the artist begins with a clear mind, empty of thought, then performs the brush strokes rapidly and without hesitation. To look at such a painting is regarded as an act of meditation also, because doing so leads beyond words and images to an insight or realization of the Buddha's mind that is beyond perception and thought. Hakuin created his works rapidly using a calligraphic brush, occasionally adding delicately coloured highlights. A dedicated teacher, he lived among villagers in small monasteries in the countryside, but he also gave lectures to high-ranking individuals. Hakuin is best known for his mastery of the Zen *koan*, a question or phrase that has no logical answer. He illustrated his most famous *koan*, 'What is the sound of one hand clapping?', in many ink paintings.

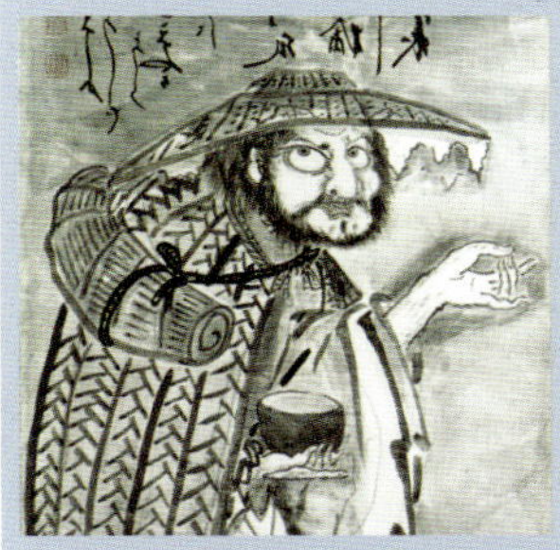

Master Portraitist

As a reformer of the Zen Rinzai sect, Hakuin had a great respect for the historic Japanese priests who first established Buddhism in Japan, and he produced many paintings of them. The example (above) is a depiction of the monk Shuho Myocho, also known as Daito Kokkushi (meaning 'National Teacher of the Great Lamp'), who founded the Daitoku-ji temple complex in Kita-ku, Kyoto, in the early 14th century. The painting is now in the National Museum, Tokyo.

'All you clever people
No matter what you say,
If you don't hear the
sound of one hand,
Everything else is rubbish.'
HAKUIN EKAKU

Demon Guardian

18th century CE **Temple of the Emerald Buddha, Bangkok, Thailand**

MATERIAL Wood, painted and gilded   **HEIGHT** 5 m/16 ft
TOTAL OF DEMON GUARDIANS Twelve

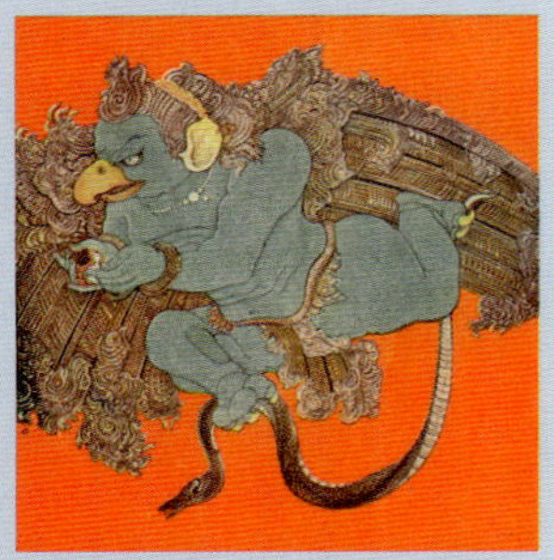

Protective Garudas

Garudas are among the many supernatural creatures placed as guardians at Buddhist monuments. Half man, half bird, the Garuda became an emblem of protection that was appropriated by the Thai kings as an emblem of their royalty. Garudas are often shown vanquishing their enemy the *nagas* (snake deities).

'[We, the Four Guardian Kings] with the twenty-eight great generals of the Yakshas, and with numerous hundreds of thousands of Yakshas, will ... protect the whole of Jambuvipa [earth].'

SUTRA OF THE GOLDEN LIGHT

Giant, supernatural guardian figures flank the entrance to the Wat Phra Kaew, or Temple of the Emerald Buddha, in Bangkok. Although their postures and weapons are similar to Indian prototypes, these are Thai figures. They are dressed in elaborate, jewelled armour, with long-sleeved tunics, trousers and slippers rendered in exquisite, jewel-like colours and intricately decorated with a variety of textured patterns in gold. They wear golden caps with tall crests, and tufts of hair emerge at the sides of their heads. With antecedents that are over two thousand years old, these supernatural door guards demonstrate the highly conservative nature of Buddhist imagery. At the same time, native preferences for the imaging of the otherworldly dominate. The guards have demonic faces, strange facial features with fangs, and unnatural skin colours. Their grand costumes reflect their status, as this is the most important temple in Thailand. The Temple of the Emerald Buddha is named after its jade carving of a seated Buddha, 66 centimetres (26 in.) tall and clothed in golden garments. The icon has a complicated, 1,500-year long history. Originating in India, it was carried to Sri Lanka, Cambodia and Laos; it was captured and enshrined in Thailand in 1552, and later, in 1782, King Rama I (1782–1809) had the Wat Phra Kaew built in the grounds of his Grand Palace to house it. This national treasure is so revered today that no one but the king himself is allowed to touch it; he changes its clothes three times a year to ensure good fortune for Thailand. Copies of the Emerald Buddha may be found in temples in Myanmar (Burma), Cambodia, China and elsewhere.

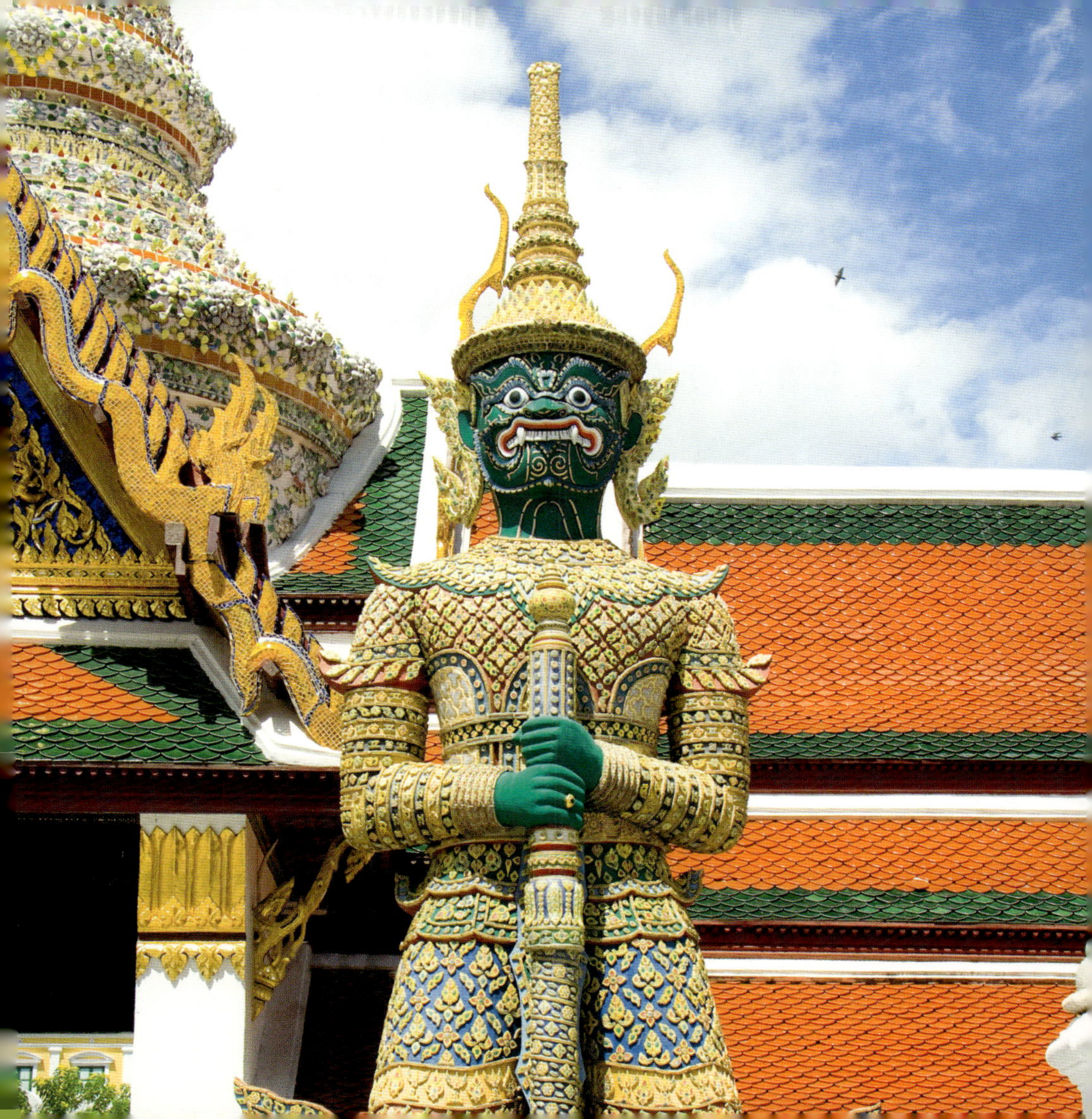

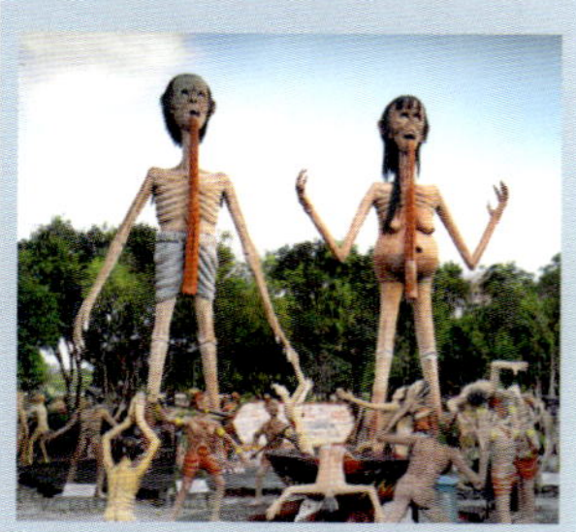

Centrepiece of Horror

Dominating the Hell Garden are two gigantic demons, tall and emaciated with long tongues reaching the length of their torsos. Also present are twenty-one kinds of animal-headed incarnations. Each one is the punishment for a particular crime; corruption results in a pig's head, selling drugs in a cow's head, stealing rice in a bird's head. Hungry ghosts await sanctified water offered by the faithful.

'Breaking the fast, damaging the precepts, slaughtering chickens and pigs /Are reflected clearly in the mirror of actions — retribution is never void.'

SCRIPTURE OF THE TEN KINGS

Theravadin Hell Garden

20th century CE **Wang Saen Suk Hell Garden, Saen Suk, Thailand**

MATERIALS Cement, plaster and paints **TOTAL OF DIORAMAS** 150
TOTAL OF STATUES 1,000 **HEIGHT** Mostly life-sized

Wang Saen Suk Hell Garden is a form of theme park containing surreal scenes in diorama form of the Narakas, or Ten Buddhist Hells. It is the largest of around a dozen such underworld theme parks in Thailand. It represents a Theravad Buddhist inferno that offers the damned no chance of immediate redemption, nor deities to offer salvation. Rather, the gruesome scenes portrayed are intended to convince beholders that they must avoid sinful behaviour. Parks such as this have become favoured destinations for parents who take advantage of the dioramas of both reward and punishment to give moral instruction to their children. A large-scale Buddha greets the visitor, followed by scenes of a pleasant and peaceful existence. But at the centre of the park is the 'death king', Phya Yom. His attendant, a clerk holding a golden ledger, records good and bad behaviour and the king pronounces reward or punishment for the deceased. A sign at the entrance warns: 'If you meet the Devil in this life, don't postpone merit-making which will help you to defeat him in the next life.' Further signs at the dioramas specify which sin merited the punishment shown — for example, to be stabbed in the heart with a spear might be a punishment for lying or deception. Visitors learn that the Hell Garden was created 'for the good progress and spiritual benefits of the venerable monks'. Buddhist parks are not unique to Thailand. Contemporary religious theme parks have been built in India, including the Maitreya Project, in Kushinagar, Uttar Pradesh, which opened in 1990 to provide entertainment and religious education.

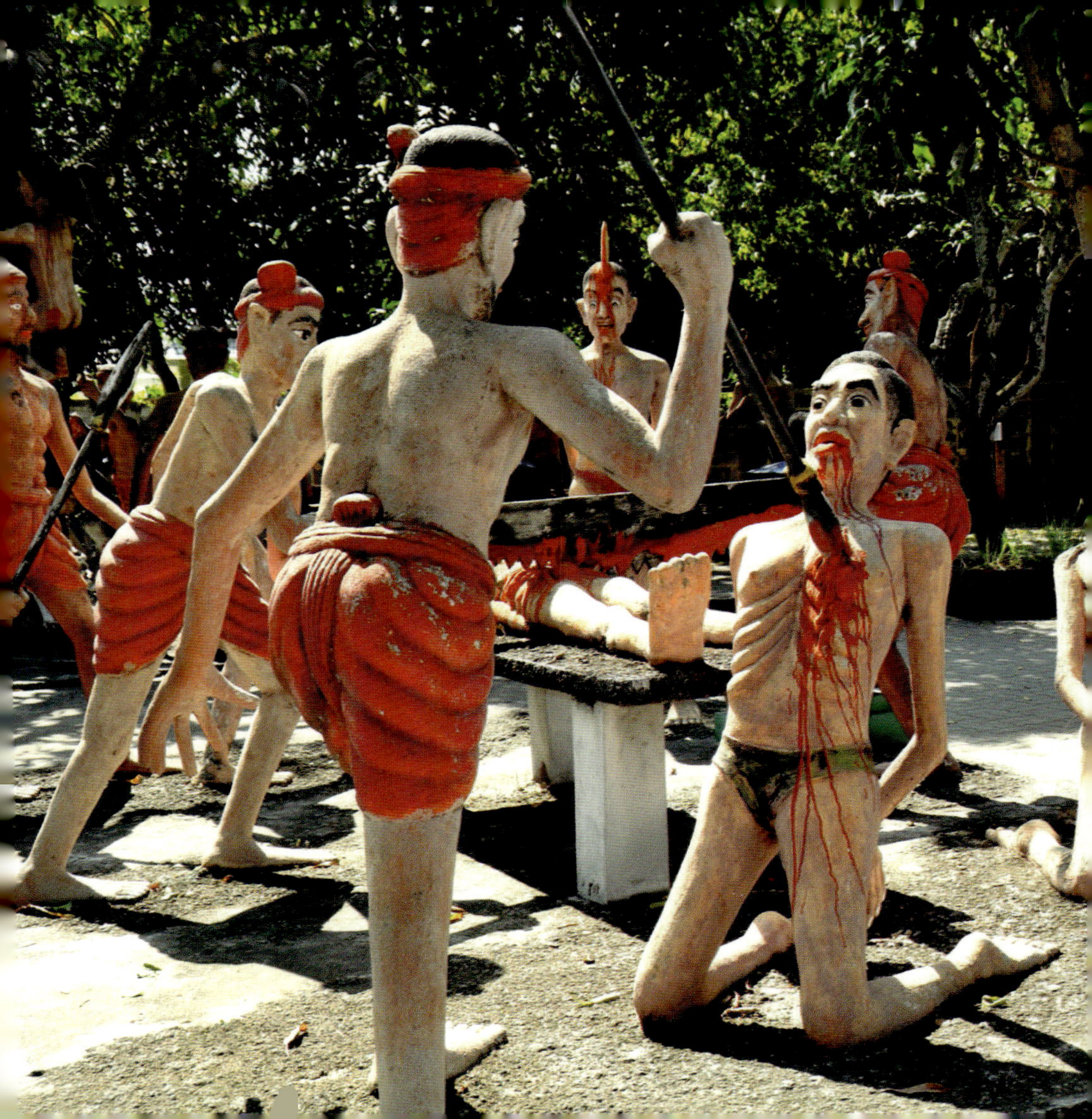

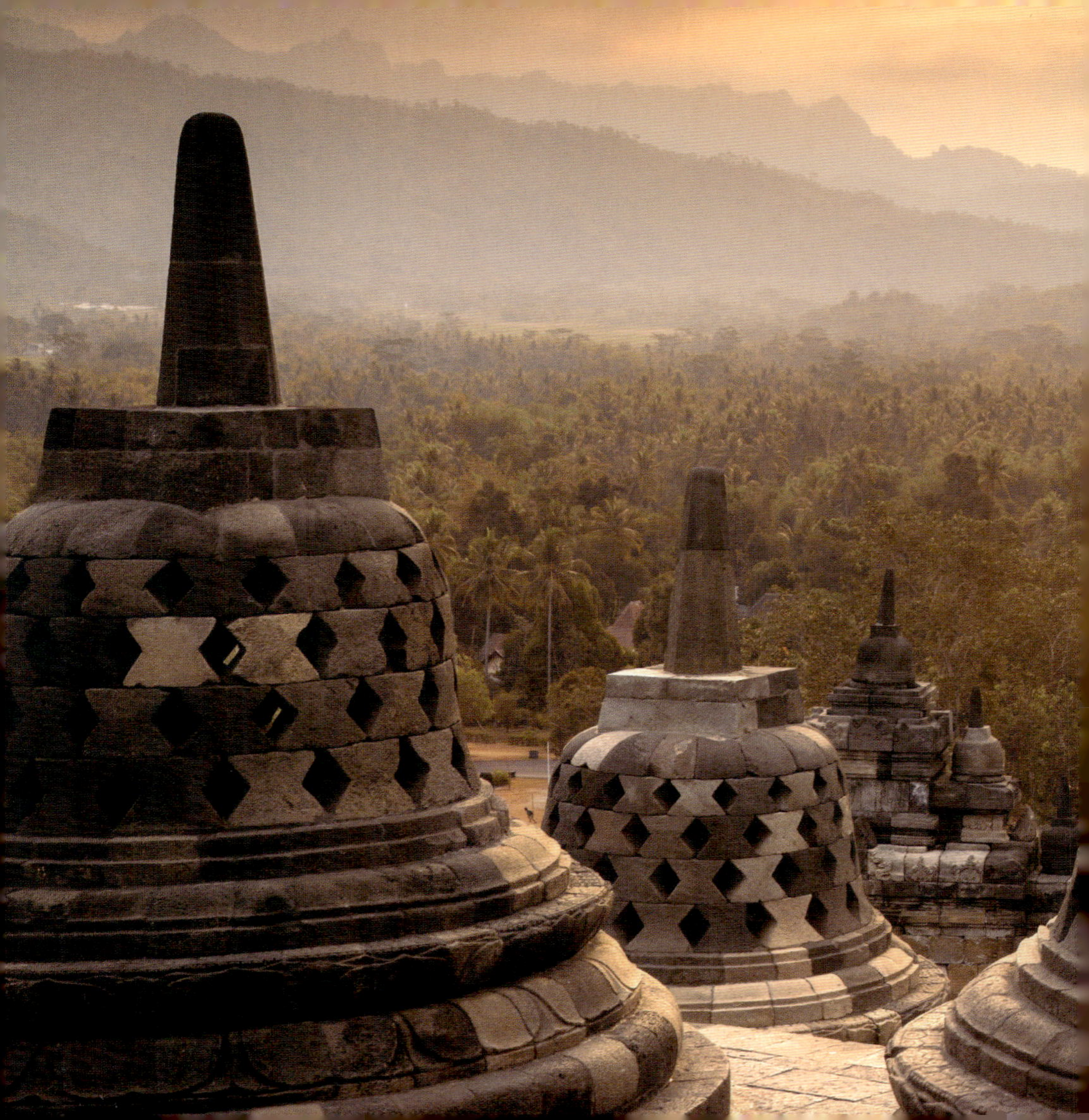

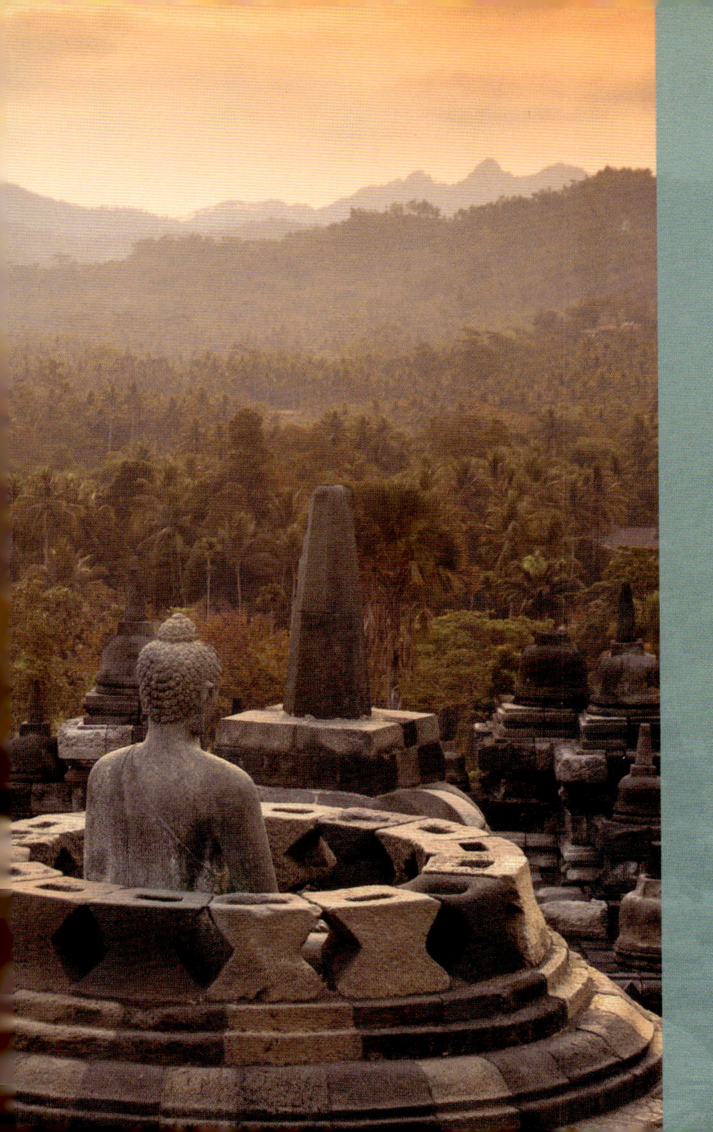

4

Esoteric Buddhism

Eleven-headed Guanyin

Early 8th century CE **Beilin Museum, Xi'an, Shaanxi, China**

STYLE Late Tang **ORIGIN** Leshan Nunnery, Xi'an, Shaanxi, China
MATERIAL Marble **HEIGHT** 3.75 cm/1½ in.

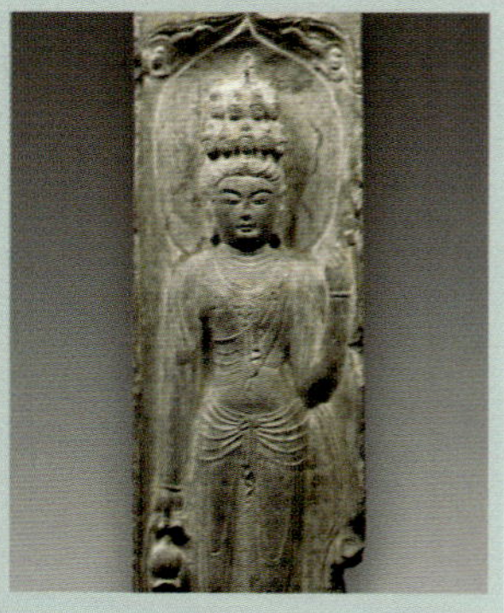

Early Prototype

This standing image of Guanyin, which dates to the 7th century CE, is one of the earliest examples. Its ten extra heads are piled up in conical fashion; they are not clearly individuated. The figure stands stiffly, holding the water bottle and lotus flower, traditional symbols of Guanyin.

'This dharani of mine [Avalokiteshvara] is impregnated with magnificent power. A single recitation will ... release all the sinners in the five eternal hells.'

THE HEART DHARANI SUTRA

The esoteric school of Buddhism introduced new deities and reinvigorated ancient ones by providing them with new guises to symbolize their awesome divine powers. The eleven-headed Guanyin, the earliest in the esoteric transformations of the Bodhisattva, was a form heralded in a scripture translated in the 6th century CE. The deity Guanyin was given ten extra heads, so it is hypothesized, to provide him with many more sensory organs with which to see the distress of those in need and hear their cries, the better to be able to assist them. An alternative explanation of the supernumerary heads suggests that the Bodhisattva felt such chagrin when he realized how many people remained to be saved, despite his efforts, that his head split into ten fragments. This 8th-century example was originally found at the Leshan Nunnery in Xi'an, the ancient capital of the Tang dynasty. An inscription on another, 7th-century image explains that such images were created for the protection of the state. Here, Guanyin's ten additional heads appear as a tall crown on his main head. In the front of the 'crown' of small heads, a standing image of Amitofu (Amitabha in Sanskrit) symbolizes Guanyin's paternal relationship with the Buddha of the Western Paradise, for whom he acts as soul catcher. Most of the ten heads look benign, but three in the rear are horrific, with fangs and snarling expressions. It is speculated that certain heads express sympathy with sufferers, others anger with evil, and others joy about goodness. In typical late Tang fashion, Amitofu's face is fleshy with mature features, and rings of fat lie beneath the chin.

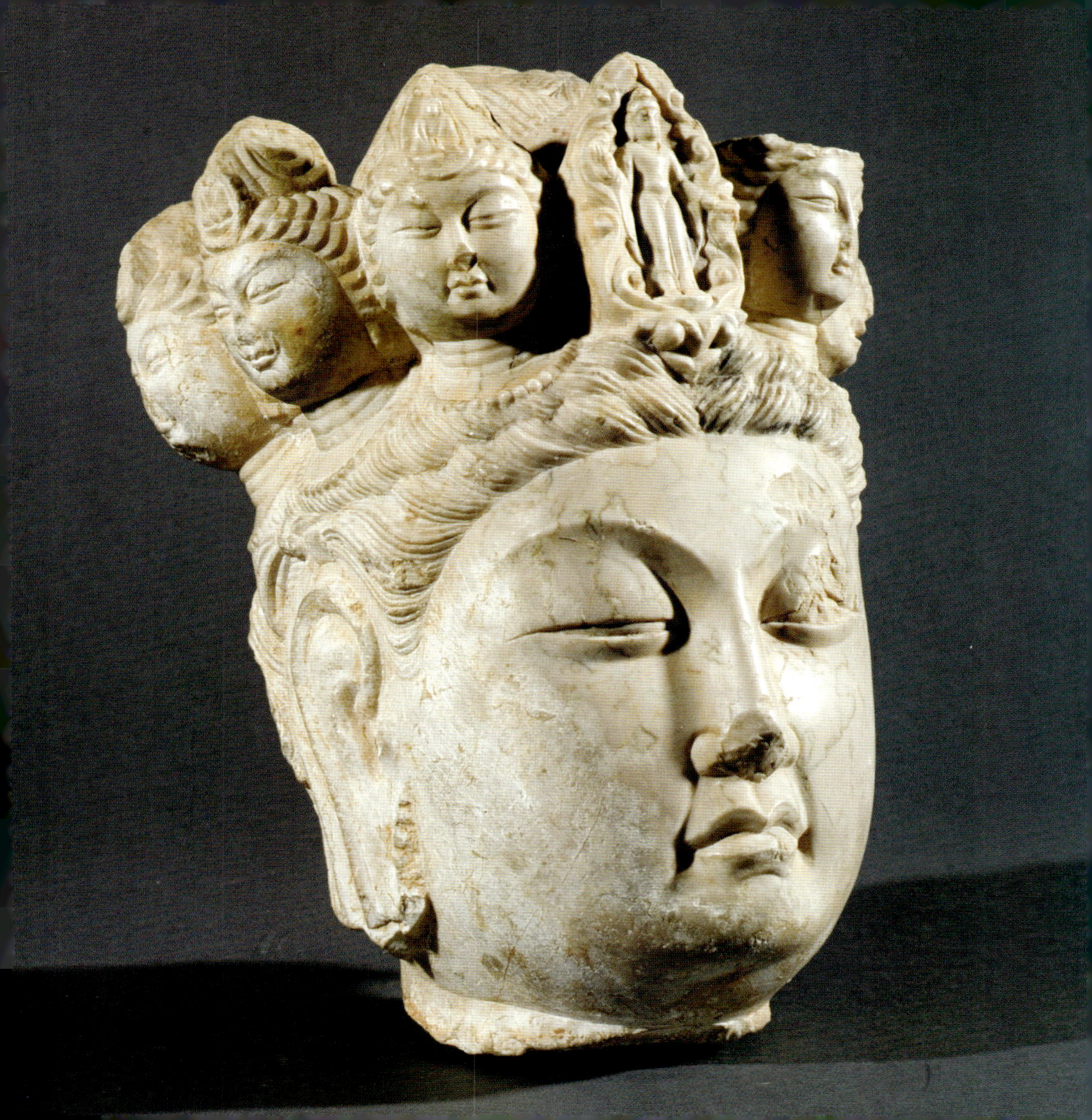

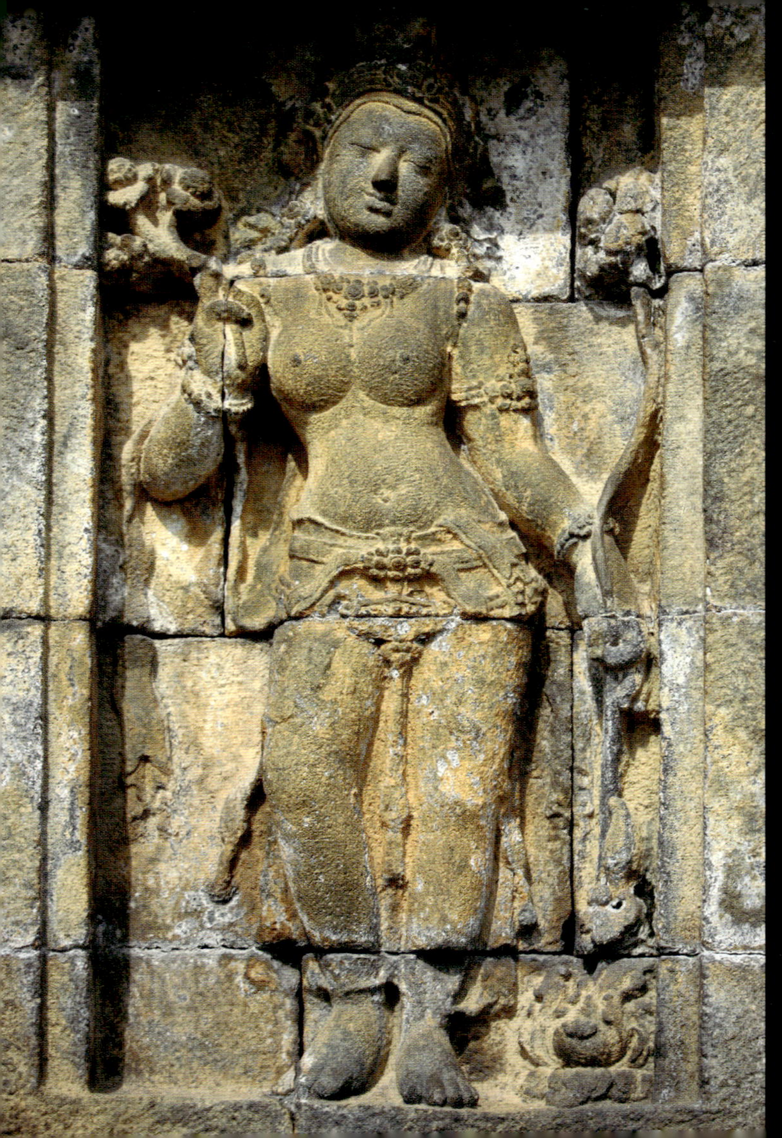

Bas-relief of Tara, Mother of Liberation

8th century CE **Borobudur, Magelang, central Java, Indonesia**

MATERIAL Sandstone **LOCATION** Lower outer wall of Borobudur temple

The name of the female Bodhisattva Tara means 'star'. At first she was worshipped for guiding seamen to safety, but later she came to represent liberation and safe passage for travellers. With the advent of Tantrayana in India, Tara entered the Buddhist pantheon as a female embodiment of Avalokiteshvara, the Bodhisattva of Compassion. Tantric belief affirms the duality of the universe, often cast as the opposition of the male and female principles, the resolution of which results in nirvana. One expression of this duality is the principle of Shakti; male deities acquire female counterparts, and Tara was born of a tear that Avalokiteshvara shed for mankind. As the embodiment of maternal compassion and spiritual wayfaring, Tara is portrayed as a beautiful young woman. In this bas-relief at Borobudur, she raises her right foot as if to take a step and exit the narrow rectangular frame in which she is contained. Naked to the waist, she is decorously bejewelled in the manner of a princess, with crown, earrings, necklaces, armlets, bracelets and belt. In her left hand she holds a long lotus flower, the attribute of Avalokiteshvara as the lotus bearer Padmapani; in her right hand she has a bunch of flowers. Tara inclines her head with a dreamy expression and sweet smile. An inscription dated 778 CE at the Candi Sari temple, also in central Java, records that the Sailendra dynasty dedicated both the temple and a nearby monastery to Tara. Several images at the temple show her carrying flowers, as she does in this sculpture at Borobudur.

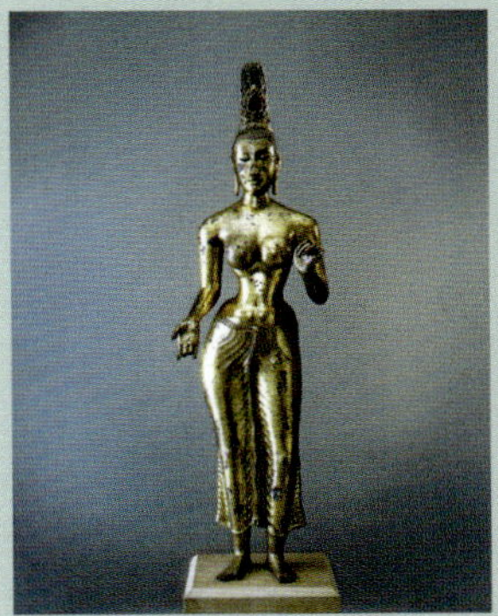

Tara in Sri Lanka

The worship of Tara quickly became important in Sri Lanka, too, after Tantric Buddhism was introduced there. This bronze figure (700–775 CE) is similar to the semi-naked and bejewelled example of the same period from Borobudur, but for the piled-up hair on the top of her head.

'[Tara's] blazing light is embraced by a hundred thousand suns / Shining upon a piled heap of ... emeralds / [Her] smiling face is the giver of the highest gift ...'

FIFTH DALAI LAMA

Eight-Arm Deity Mandala

Late 8th century CE **Shijian Brickyard, Luoyang, Henan, China**

TECHNIQUE Woodblock printing **MATERIALS** Ink on paper made from silk and hemp **DIMENSIONS** 38 x 29.5 cm / 15 x 11 ½ in.

The mandala, a complex diagram of the organization of the spiritual forces of the universe, is an essential object of worship in tantric Buddhism. This rare example of a Tang-dynasty mandala, unearthed at Shijian Brickyard at Luoyang, exemplifies the early use in China of the woodblock technique and paper — both Chinese inventions — and it also provides evidence that Buddhists adopted printing to propagate the scriptures. As is often the case, the mandala has its most important deity placed at the centre: an eight-armed Guanyin, each arm holding a different attribute: sword, wheel of the law, rosary, trident, and symbolic hand positions, or mudras. Sanskrit text surrounds the deity, in both the inner circle and the outer square; flying angels fill the inner corners. At the corners of the outer border are four guardian figures holding weapons, and midway along each side is a seated Buddha. Between these figures are circles, inside which lotus flowers support Sanskrit syllables that stand for sacred incantations or mantras. These alternate with the repeated symbol of the double-headed trident, or *vajra*, which represents the power of lightning. On the left border, an inscription in Chinese establishes that the mandala was made in the late Tang (618–907) and assures protection to those who wear it. Mandalas, inscribed with deities and incantations, were used as magic charms or talismans, either worn on the body or placed in tombs. In ancient times, lay worshippers paid monks to recite a scripture; with the advent of writing, they had copies transcribed; the woodblock technique then enabled multiple copies to be printed quickly and cheaply.

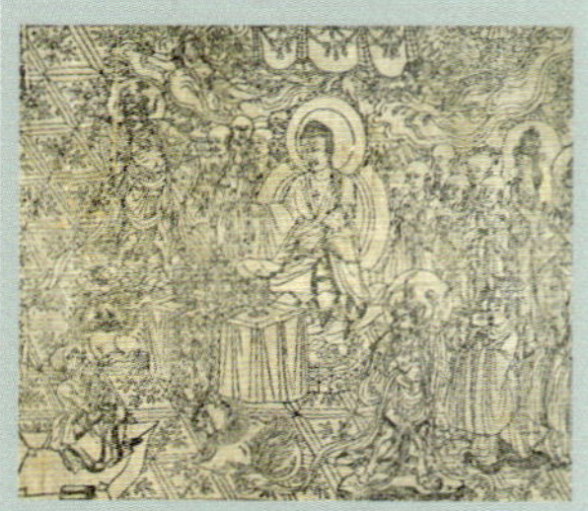

Woodblock Buddha

This image is the frontispiece of a long, woodblock-printed scroll of the *Diamond Sutra,* found at Dunhuang Library Cave 17, in Gansu, China. The woodcut print shows a complex assembly of worshippers and monks listening to the seated, preaching Buddha. A colophon at the end of the scroll reads: 'Reverently made for universal free distribution by Wang Jie on behalf of his two parents on the fifteenth of the fourth moon of the ninth year of Xiantong [11 May 868].'

'As many beings as there are in this world of beings … with name or without name … all these must be delivered by me in the perfect world of Nirvana.'

THE DIAMOND SUTRA

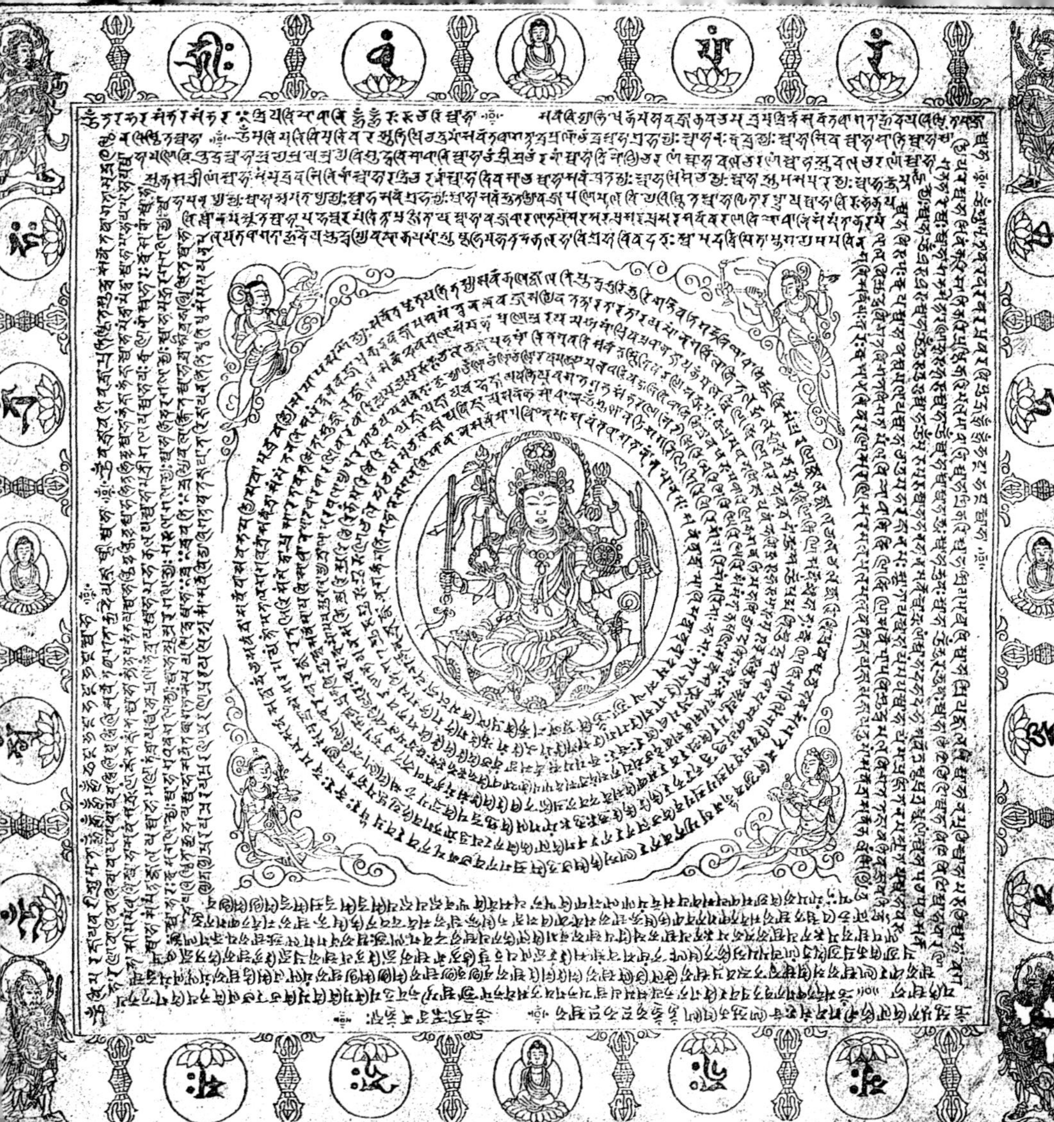

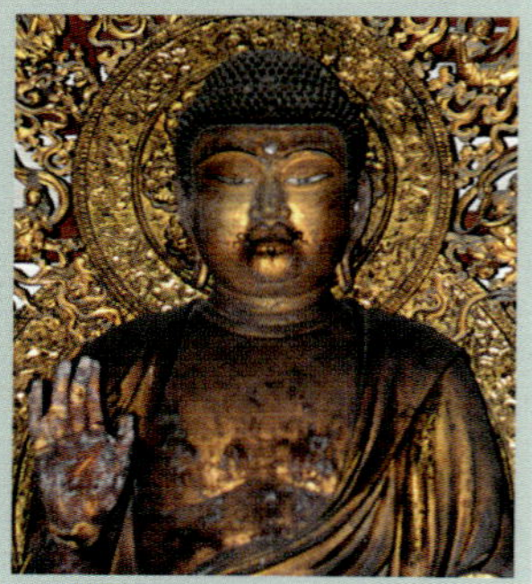

Stern Buddha

At Toshodai-ji, this image of the Buddha is flanked by Kannon (right) and the Healing Buddha. It represents Vairochana, the Cosmic Buddha, and as an esoteric image it is deliberately forbidding of countenance, unlike the warmly smiling Mahayana Buddhas of a century before.

'I can appear with two, four, six, eight, ten, twelve, fourteen, sixteen, eighteen, twenty, twenty-four and up to 108, 1,000, 10,000 and 84,000 arms making various gestures ...'

SURANGAMA SUTRA

Thousand-armed, Eleven-headed Kannon

Late 8th century CE Kondo, Toshodai-ji, Nara, Kansai, Japan

COMMISSIONED BY Ganjin   **MATERIAL** Wood, with gold leaf over dry lacquer   **HEIGHT** 5.36 m/17 ft 7 in.

Heralded in scriptures first translated in China in the 7th century CE, the eleven-headed icon was described in numerous texts by eminent clerics such as Vajrabodhi (in 731–736) and Amoghvajra (in 732); icons with multiple arms, often eight in number, evolved only slightly later. A Tang dynasty thousand-arm form was carved at Longmen, Henan province, but is now badly damaged. Esoteric Buddhism entered Japan soon after its introduction to China, and a number of Japanese eleven-headed Kannon (Avalokiteshvara in Sanskrit) date from the 7th century onwards. Of the thousand-armed, eleven-headed icons in Japan, the most extraordinary example is at the Toshodai-ji *kondo* in Nara. It was commissioned by the Chinese monk Ganjin, who established the Chinese-style Toshodai-ji temple for Emperor Shomu (701–756). Here, Kannon's head has a third eye, the eye of spiritual vision, and his nine extra heads form a kind of diadem; a tenth head is set on the top of these. At the front of the crown is a standing figure of the Buddha of the West, surrounded by a body mandorla. Kannon has twenty large hands, and each holds a precious attribute that identifies one of his various capacities: the sun, moon, wheel of the law, rosary, scriptures, a wish-fulfilling jewel (*cintamani*), lotus flowers, fly whisk, water jar, rosary, reliquary, monk's staff and weapons – a noose, sword and others. The remaining 980 arms were individually crafted out of wood; 967 have survived. This sculpture is one of the few that articulated all one thousand arms.

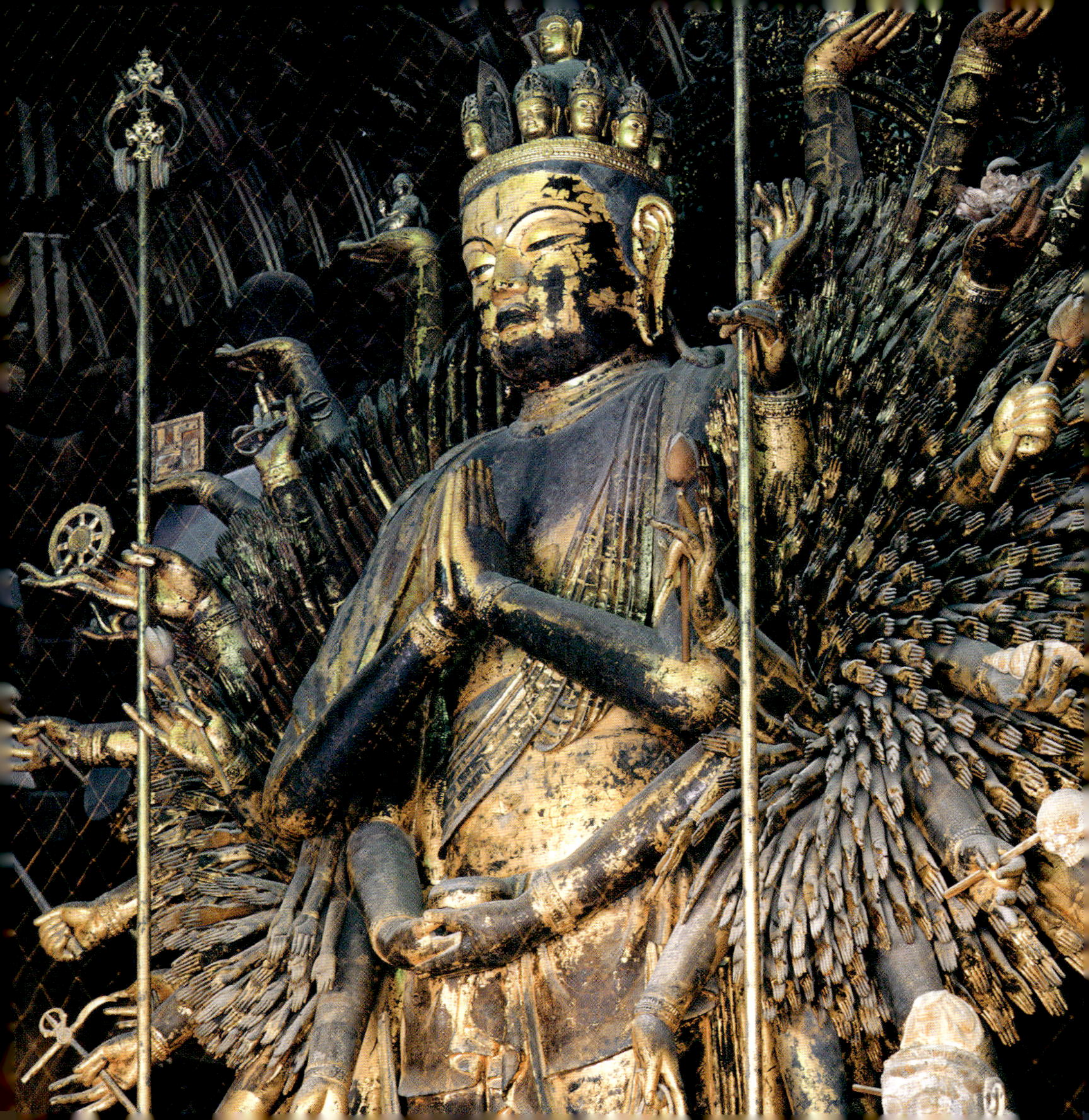

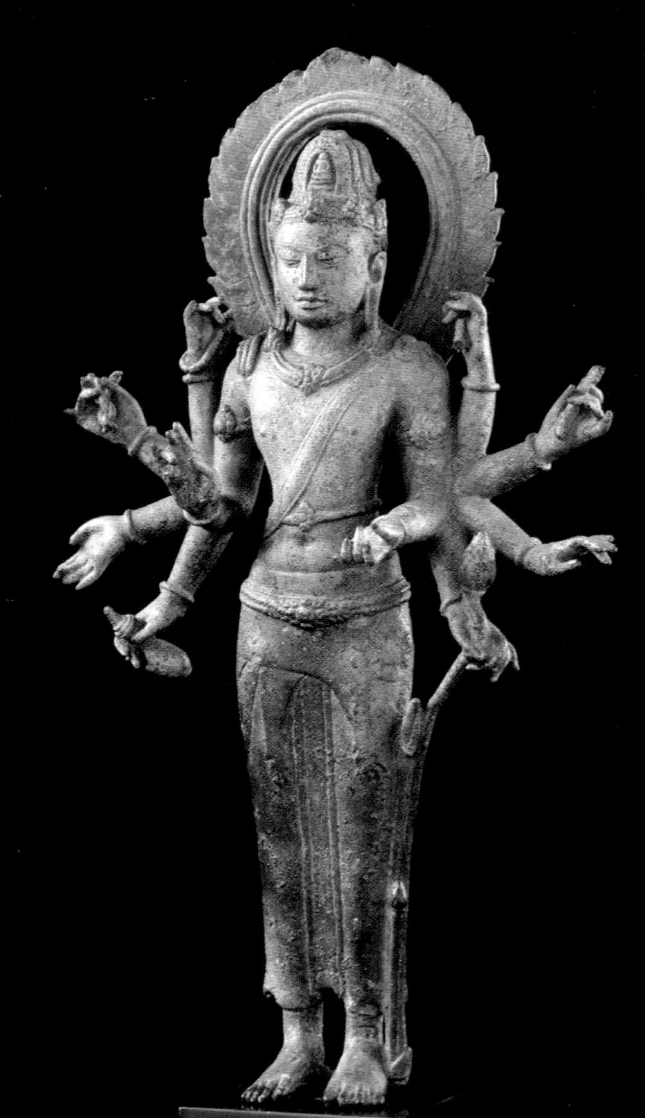

Standing Ten-armed Avalokiteshvara

c. 8th–9th century CE **Musée Guimet, Paris, France**

PROCESS Investment (lost-wax) casting **MATERIAL** Bronze
DIMENSIONS 34 x 20 x 8 cm / 13 ½ x 7 ¾ x 3 ¼ in.

Esoteric Buddhist images are characterized by their increasing number of physical attributes, which were intended to express the growth of their spiritual powers. This image of Avalokiteshvara, from central Java, Indonesia, has ten arms, some of which appear to emerge just from the elbow. The hands either hold an attribute – a water jar, rosary, scripture, lotus flower – or assume a symbolic gesture. The figure, much more slender than Indian examples, has an attenuated body and simplified jewels, but in all its iconographical aspects it is correct. By the time this cast bronze icon was made, esoteric Buddhism was spreading along trade routes, in this case the sea route from south-east India via Sri Lanka and Thailand to Java, and it was the Saliendra dynasty in Java that, in the 9th century CE, was promoting Buddhism with its enormous monuments. Buddhism was being propelled through the world by waves of proselytizing monks and merchants, and the traffic between east and west became an important medium of cultural exchange. From the earliest times, Buddhism appealed to merchants travelling the Silk Road that linked the various oasis cities of the Gobi Desert and those sailing the south Asian sea routes. Such merchants spread the doctrine just as they established the prosperity of Buddhist sites on the trade routes. For them, possessing a many-armed image, such as this one of Avalokiteshvara, promised powerful protection from shipwreck and dangers such as being stranded on islands of ogresses.

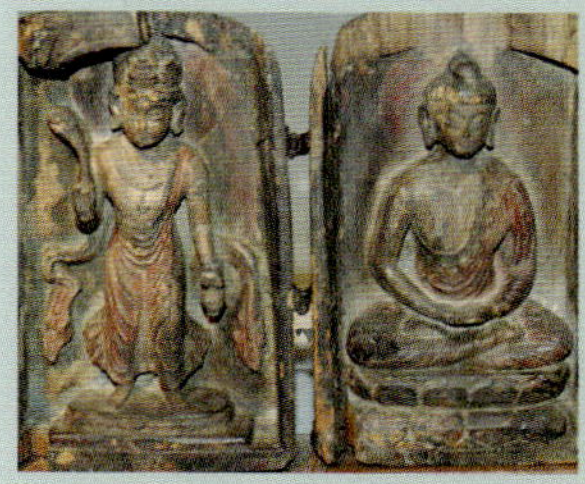

Travelling Shrines

Pilgrims would carry travelling shrines, such as this one, discovered in Dunhuang, a Buddhist cave site on the Silk Route, in Gansu province, China. The polychrome wooden shrine may have belonged to a monk or merchant. Chinese monks like Fa Xian, who travelled around Asia in the 5th century, particularly favoured Avalokiteshvara as their protective deity – in time he was the most popular god of both the Mahayana and Vajrayana schools.

'These auspicious perfumes, divine substances / Pure and born from purity, I present with devotion / Having enjoyed them, make me joyful.'

KRIYA TANTRA

Borobudur Mandala

9th century CE **Magelang, central Java, Indonesia**

COMMISSIONED BY Sailandra dynasty **MATERIAL** Sandstone
ABANDONED Some time between 928 and 1006 **HEIGHT** 35 m/115 ft

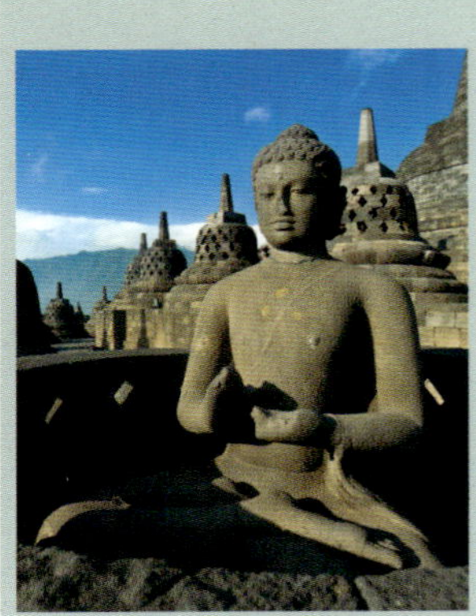

Seated Buddha

This Buddha at Borobudur has lost its enclosing stupa and is open to view. All of the Buddhas face away from the site. Buddhas also appear on the lower levels of the upper terraces, but without the architectural shells that are in keeping with the secret, esoteric nature of Vajrayana Buddhism.

'The appearance in this World of all Buddhas, past, present and future, is solely for the purpose of preaching the Law and helping all [to] cross over to the shore of Liberation.'

MUSO KOKUSHI (D. 1351)

The funerary monument of Borobudur is designed as a giant, three-dimensional mandala, with six square terraces topped by three circular platforms (see right). Its decoration includes 2,672 relief panels and 504 icons of the Buddha. Though unique in the Buddhist world, it has precedents for its parts and symbolic meanings in early Indian prototypes. On the circular upper levels are seventy-two bell-shaped stupas, each housing a seated Buddha. The topmost level supports a massive stupa that is now empty; it is not clear if that was the original intention. Each square platform is bisected by a staircase that enables ascent to the topmost level. The monument represents Mount Sumeru, the cosmological structure at the centre of the universe that links earth and heaven. It also replicates the spiritual progress of Buddhist doctrine, ascending from the lower level of Kamadhatu (the world of desire), to Rupadhatu (the world of forms) and finally Arupadhatu (the world of formlessness). The world of desire is represented by narrative bas-relief illustrations of *jatakas*, or stories of the previous lives of the Buddha, and illustrations of the life of the Buddha based on the *Lalitavistara* scripture. Higher up the monument are depictions based on a Mahayana Buddhist scripture, the *Gandavyuha Sutra*, a part of the *Avatamsaka Sutra*. Construction of the monument took place in stages from the late 8th to the mid-9th century CE, and each stage seems to represent a different school of Buddhism. The first period belonged to the early teaching of the Buddha; the subsequent period represented Mahayana Buddhism; and in its final form the upper storeys symbolized Vajrayana Buddhism.

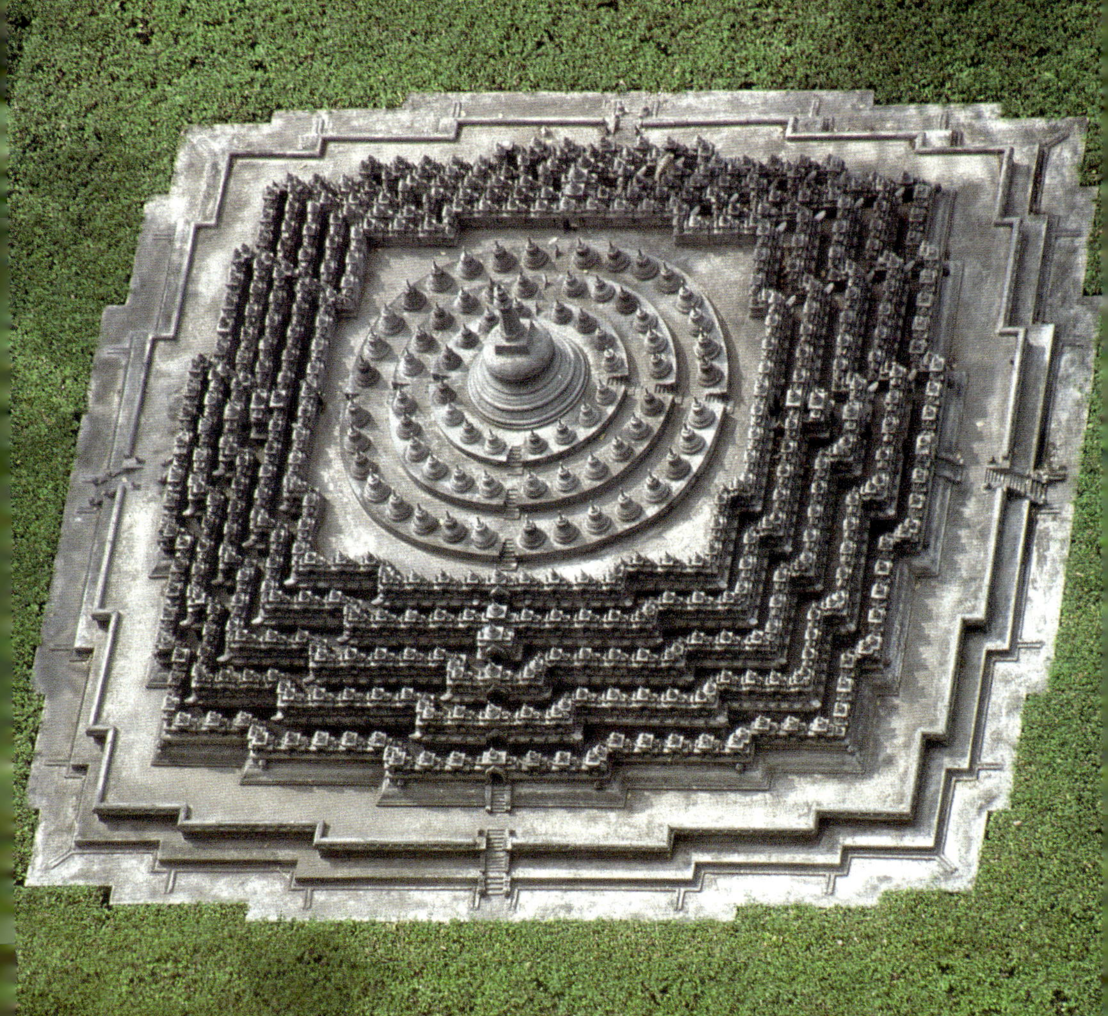

Mandala of the Two Realms

9th century CE   To-ji Temple, Kyoto, Kansai, Japan

FORMAT Hanging scrolls (two)   **MATERIALS** Colours on silk
DIMENSIONS 185.1 x 164.3 cm/73 x 65 in.

The mandala as a geometric diagram of the relationship of the deities of the esoteric pantheon is one of the essential implements of Vajrayana Buddhist practice. Separate mandalas express the dual aspects of Buddhist reality, the eternal and the transitory, but they are often referred to in conjunction. The eternal or adamantine, unchanging aspect of reality is illustrated by the Diamond World (Kongokai) mandala; the Womb World (Taizokai) mandala represents the ever-changing, transient aspect of nature. The Diamond mandala comprises nine major squares, which are subdivided into a number of subsidiary circles, each containing a deity. In this example, from the To-ji Temple in Kyoto, the most powerful deities appear in the top row; the most important of them, Vairochana, the Cosmic Buddha, is shown as a bodhisattva and his hand gesture symbolizes his role as source of the cosmos. The Womb World mandala with which it is paired at To-ji is shown at left. Both Diamond and Womb World mandalas were used in initiation ceremonies. The two mandalas would be hung on a wall and the acolyte would throw a lotus flower at each of them in turn. The deity struck by the flower would become the initiate's chosen divine guide, first for the adamantine aspect of the universe and then for the transient aspect. Mandalas take many forms other than painted representations in both Buddhist and Hindu art and architecture. The stupa in particular is seen as a mandala, a diagram in three dimensions of the comic forces, as are plans of Buddhist temples, but mandalas may also take the form of sculptures, portable paintings or sand installations.

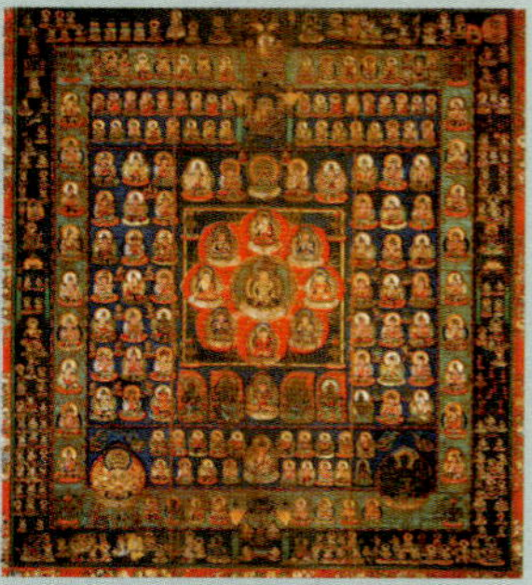

Taizokai Mandala

This Womb World mandala, the pair of the Diamond one from To-ji, has a central lotus plant occupied, again, by the Cosmic Buddha making his 'source of the cosmos' hand gesture. Lesser gods occupy the spaces around him.

'The secrets of all the sutras and commentaries can be depicted in art, and all the essential truths of the esoteric teaching are all set forth therein. Neither teachers nor students can dispense with it. Art is what reveals to us the state of perfection.'

KUKAI (9TH CENTURY)

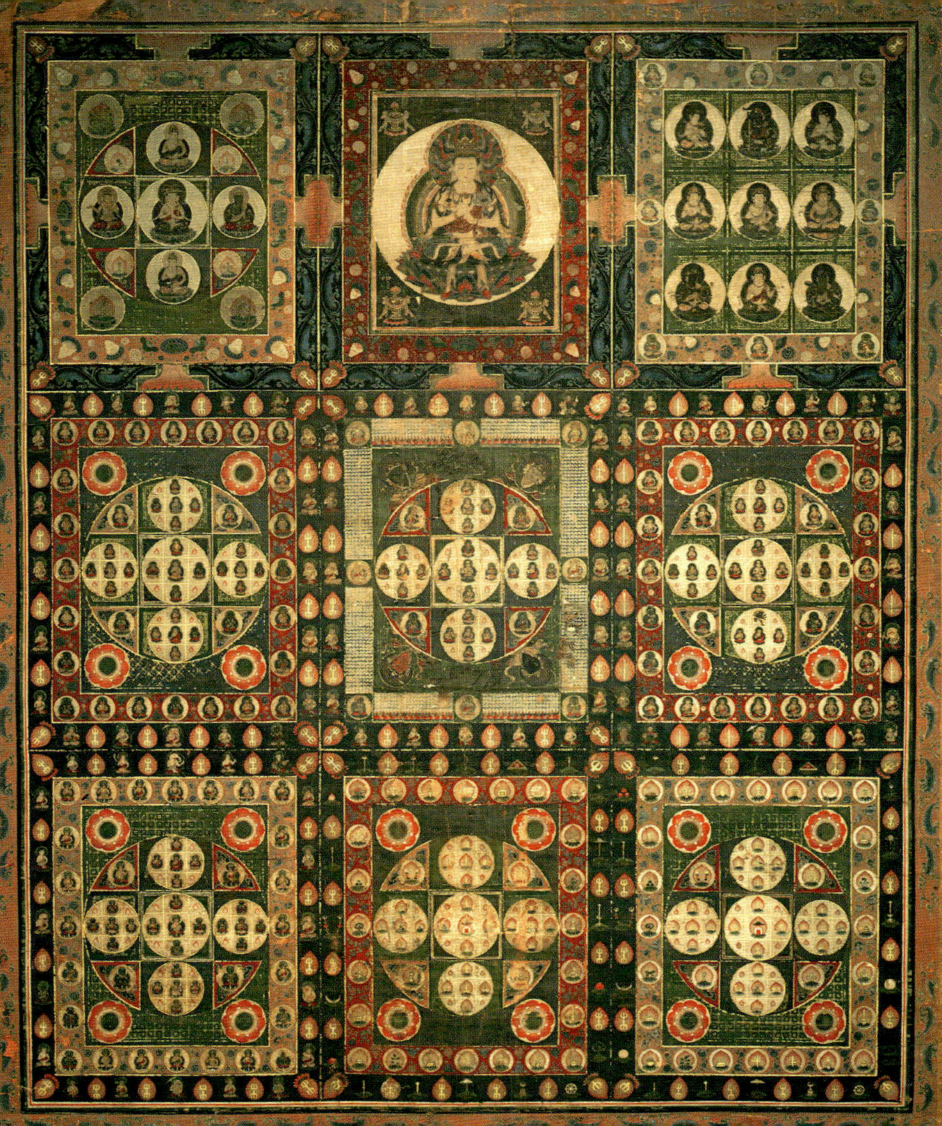

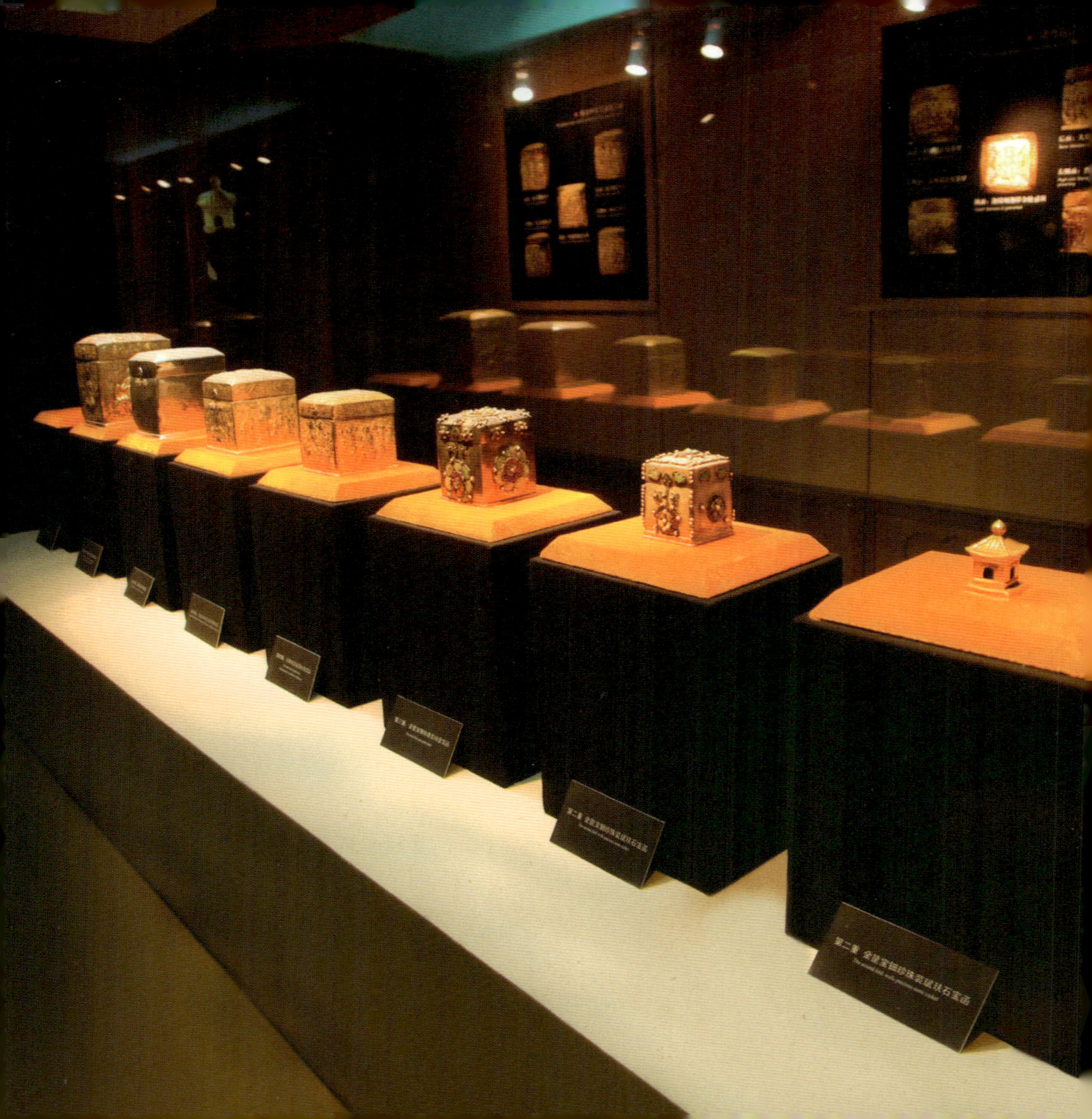

Reliquary of a Sacred Finger Bone of the Buddha

9th century CE **Famen Temple, Xi'an, Shaanxi, China**

MATERIALS Sandalwood, jade, and precious metals **DIMENSIONS** Series is 166 cm/65 in. long in total **HEIGHT** Largest shown: 17 cm/6¾ in.

Famen Temple, near Xi'an in Shaanxi, China, has been known since the medieval period for possessing a sacred finger-bone relic of the Buddha. In 1980 its pagoda was destroyed in an earthquake. During the restoration, workers found evidence of several periods of construction, three subterranean rooms and a hidden chamber filled with precious ritual objects from the 9th century CE. One chamber was organized like a mandala, with a boxed sacred relic at the centre, surrounded by four protective guardian kings in defensive postures. It is unknown why the treasures were hidden underground. The archaeologists found a total of four sets of nested boxes, executed out of luxurious materials and each containing a bone relic. One relic, found in a miniature jade coffer encased in crystal in a secret square pit beneath the rooms, is, some argue, the only genuine one. Another set of eight nested relic boxes (see left) was found in the rear chamber. It is made from a number of precious materials: the outermost box was sandalwood, now broken (not shown); the others are gilt silver, silver, gilt silver, gold, jade and gold and jade inlaid with pearls; a small solid gold pagoda contains the bone. Set one inside the other, these boxes comprise a mandala, and the decoration on the four sides of three of the boxes portrays divine assemblies. In the lower rooms, monks would prepare the relic chamber with prayer, chant mantras, and perform symbolic hand gestures (mudras) while offering incense paste, flower garlands, food and drink.

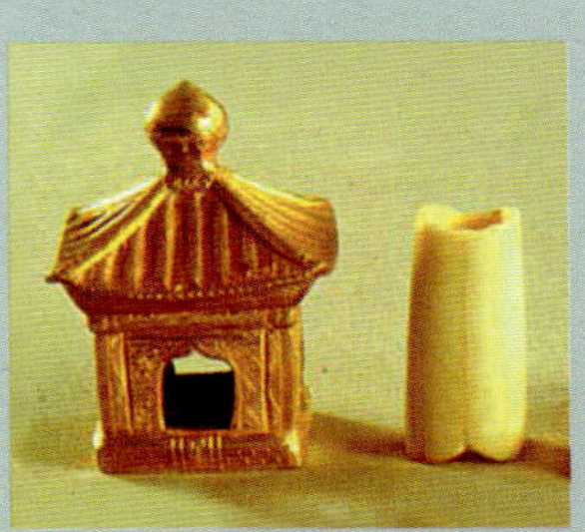

Precious Artefact

The solid gold pagoda finger-bone reliquary (above) is just one of the incomparable treasures of Famen. Fashioned variously out of solid gold, gilt silver, bronze, glass and porcelain, they include incense burners, lamps, plates, cups, vases, candle holders, braziers and tea-ceremony implements, such as hand-blown glass cups and their saucers. Also notable are a solid gold begging bowl and gold-embroidered vestments.

'The Dharma, incomparably profound and exquisite, is rarely met with, even in hundreds of thousands of millions of kalapas.'

EDWARD COWELL, *BUDDHIST SCRIPTURES*

Six-armed Avalokiteshvara

10th century CE   **Indian Museum, Kolkata, West Bengal, India**

STYLE Pala   **ORIGIN** Nalanda University, Bihar, northern India
MATERIAL Stone

Believers in Vajrayana or tantric Buddhism hold that the duality of the universe is resolved by enlightenment. This state of bliss can be achieved in a lifetime, but only with the aid of teachers who can explain the difficult, esoteric doctrine using diagrams of the deities in the cosmos (mandalas), sacred Sanskrit syllables (mantras) and secret hand gestures (mudras). By the 8th century CE India was largely ruled by Hindu kings, but in the Buddhist heartland of Bengal and Bihar, in places such as Bihar's Nalanda University, the teachings of Esoteric Buddhism continued to develop. Indeed, some see this later stage of Buddhism as an adaptation to Hinduism: each perceives a cosmic being in both a mote of dust and the greatest expansion of the universe, and both have gods with extra heads and appendages that express their ineffable divinity. Three hands of this six-armed representation of Avalokiteshvara, originally from Nalanda, hold symbolic attributes: a lotus flower (one of the oldest emblems of the bodhisattva), rosary beads for meditation and a jar filled with the water of immortality. Two of the remaining hands assume the gestures of fear-not (palm forward, fingers pointing up) and charity (palm forward, fingers down). Identifiable by the seated figure of Amida Buddha in his crown, Avalokiteshvara sits on a high-backed throne in the princely pose (*lalita sana*), his left leg is bent at the knee, the other pendant. Beneath him are two female spirits: Tara, and Bhrkuti, the abundantly full-minded or enlightened one. They are two of his feminine embodiments, an esoteric development. A worshipper completes the trio on the base.

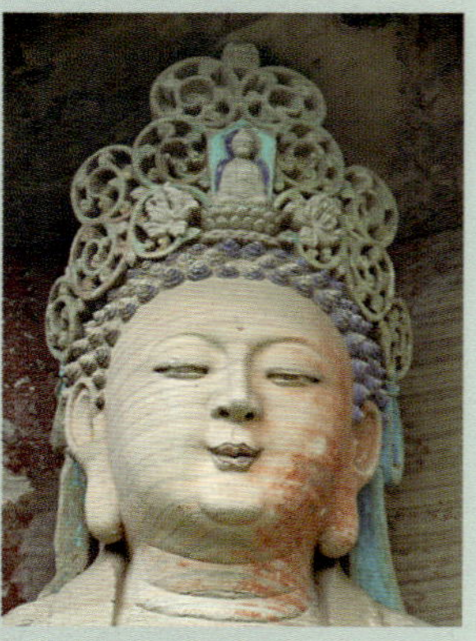

From God to Goddess

In India the Bodhisattva of Compassion never took on a feminine persona but, by the the time of the Song dynasty (960–1127 CE), Guanyin – his equivalent in China – is shown as a female figure, as this vividly coloured example from the Anyue Caves in Sichuan illustrates.

'I salute him , the ever merciful one / Called by the name Avalokita / Who is praised by all Buddhas / And has accumulated holy Merits.

KRIYA TANTRA SUTRA

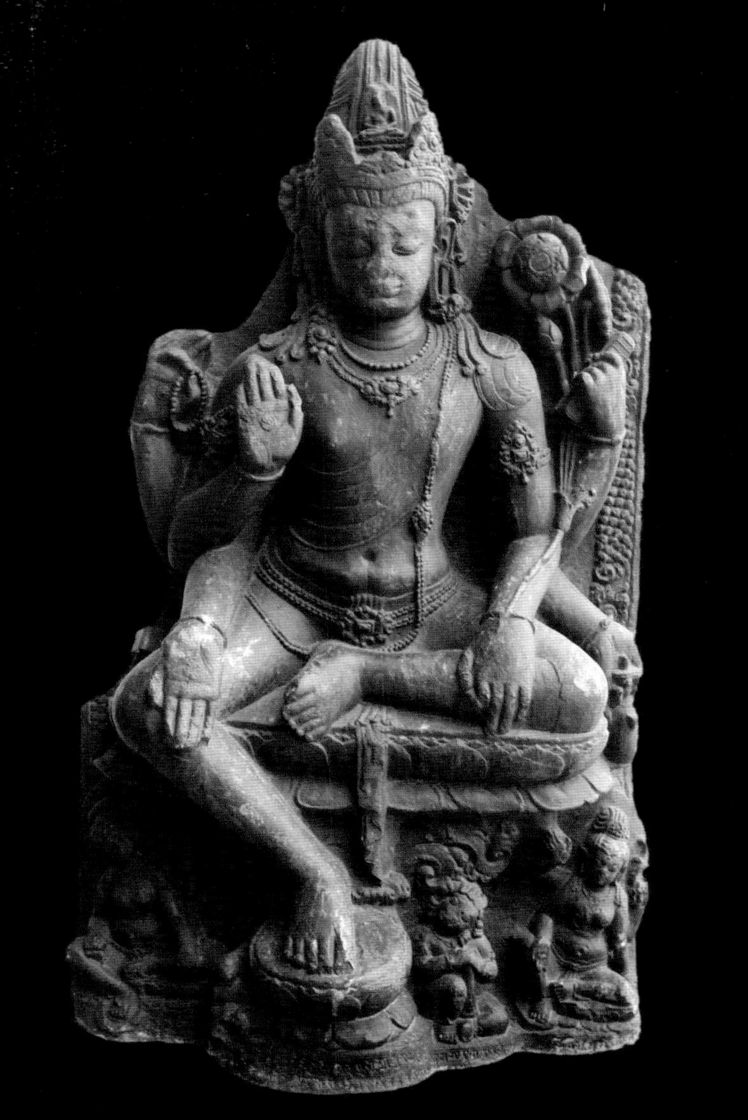

Standing Avalokiteshvara

c. 10th century CE   **Indian Museum, Kolkata, West Bengal, India**

STYLE Vajrayana   **ORIGIN** Lalitagiri, Odisha, India
MATERIAL Sandstone

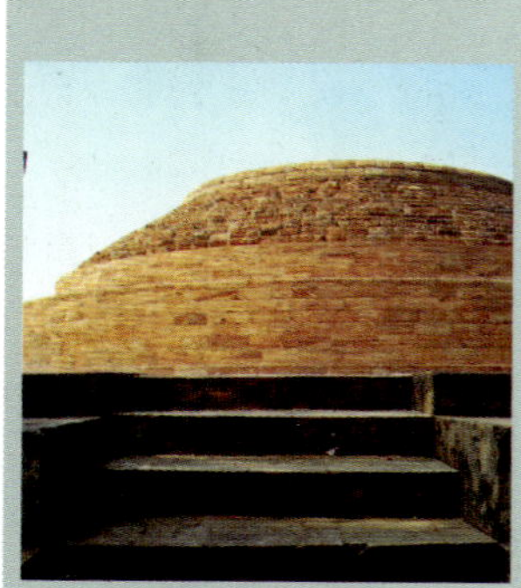

Lalitagiri Stupa

The stupa at Lalitagiri (2nd century BCE) sits atop a tall hill and is approached by a flight of forty-five steps. Only the solid brick structure remains. The Archaeological Survey of India, excavating it in from 1985 to 1992, found three relic caskets with small pieces of bone inside. Hundreds of small votive stupas surround the ancient building.

'Someone is called a Bodhisattva if he is certain to become a Buddha, a "Buddha" being a man who has first enlightened himself and will ... enlighten others.'

ARYASURA, *JATAKAMALA*

This oversized standing portrayal of Avalokiteshvara was found in the monastic compound of Lalitagiri, which was one point of the so-called Diamond Triangle of Buddhist settlements (the others were Ratnagiri and Udaigiri) near the coast of Orissa (now Odisha), south-east India. The three famed monasteries were on the itinerary of foreign monks – the Chinese pilgrim Xuanzang visited Orissa in 639 CE and found Buddhism flourishing there. Lalitagiri was the oldest site, having been in continuous use since the 2nd century BCE; excavations reveal that Vajrayana, or esoteric Buddhism, was the dominant practice. Images of Avalokiteshvara and Tara, his female manifestation, are common at Vajrayana monastic sites, and some are at least 3 metres (10 ft) tall. In this example, Avalokiteshvara appears as Padmapani; his left hand (now lost) held a lotus flower, and his right hand is in the palm-forward charity mudra. Two flowers emerging from his lotus base support his *shakti*, Tara and Bhrkuti, representing female spiritual energy. Tantric deities embody dual personalities of opposing but complementary forces, and worshippers aim to reconcile the distinctions using spiritual insight. At the top of his mandorla, two angels carry garlands. In relatively late examples of tantric art such as this, the naturalistic ideal of the Guptan era, which continued into the later era of the Pala dynasty, gave way to a stiffer and more formal style. Artists relied on a canon of figure types, proportions and attributes to make sure that images were properly made, believing that if an error occurred while an icon was created, the deity would not inhabit it and it would be useless.

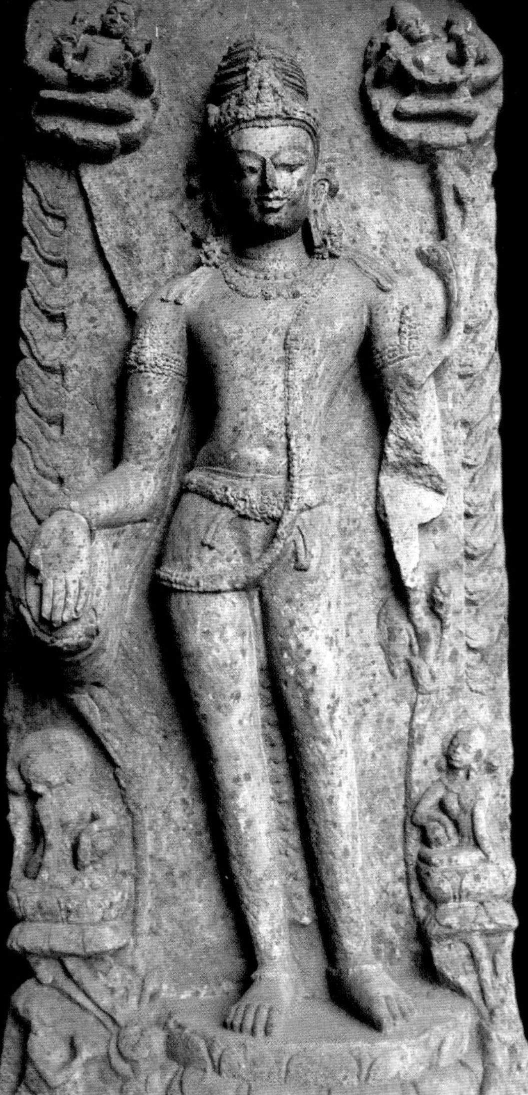

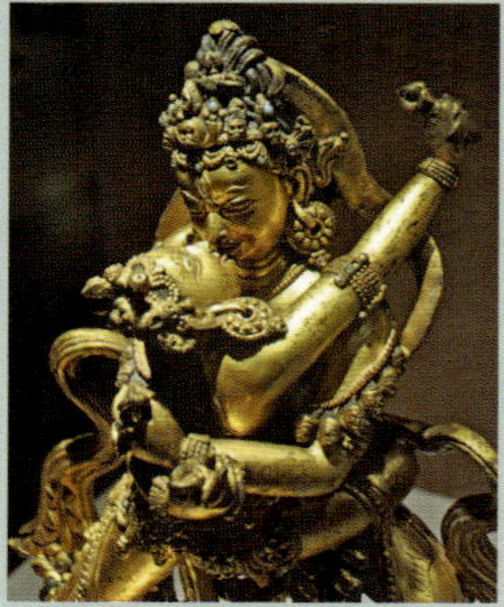

Yab-yum Coupling

In Buddhist tantric art, such as this Ming bronze figurine of Samvara and a Shakti, *yab-yum* coupling represents resolution of irreconcilable aspects of life and death, and liberation from the wheel of causation. In contrast, Hindus see the sensual aspect of human relations as a metaphor for the yearning of the soul to merge with the divine.

'Eternal truth (*tathata*) transcends form, but only by means of form can it be understood.'

KUKAI, *MEMORIAL ON THE PRESENTATION OF THE LIST OF NEWLY IMPORTED SUTRAS*

Chakrasamvara Mandala

C. 1000 CE Metropolitan Museum, New York, USA

MATERIALS Distemper on cloth
DIMENSIONS 67.3 x 50.2 cm/26 ½ x 19 ¾ in.

The meaning of a mandala is not always easily accessible and a teacher is often needed to make it clear. Chakrasamvara (Wheel of Perfect Bliss, or Wheel of Union) is a tantric meditational deity. At the centre of this Chakrasamvara mandala from Nepal is Samvara with his Shakti, Vajravarahi. Samvara, one of the principal esoteric deities and an emanation of the Buddha Aksobhya, is presented here in his terrible aspect, with a blue-coloured body, four faces and twelve arms. Standing on a corpse, he wears a crown encircled by skulls, he has a necklace of severed heads hanging from his neck, and he holds a weapon in each hand. He is locked in a procreative embrace with his female Shakti. The divine coupling of Samvara, often called *yab-yum*, is a metaphor for the union of opposites such as male and female, knowledge and compassion, bliss and emptiness. In the mandala, the divine couple are at the centre of a red, six-petalled lotus flower, and each petal has a different manifestation of the horrible aspects of the deity. The architecture of the mandala is clear: an inner circle within a square, within a circle, within a square. The square surrounding the central circle has four gates orienting the design to the four directions. Just beyond the gates are four palatial cities. Outside the sacred circle are eight cremation grounds, where ascetics practise meditation and ordinary life takes place and ends. Here all kinds of entertaining vignettes are drawn: there are ecstatic dancers, lovers, preaching lamas, ascetics in meditation or performing austerities, and deities. At the bottom of the mandala are the five forms of the compassionate goddess Tara.

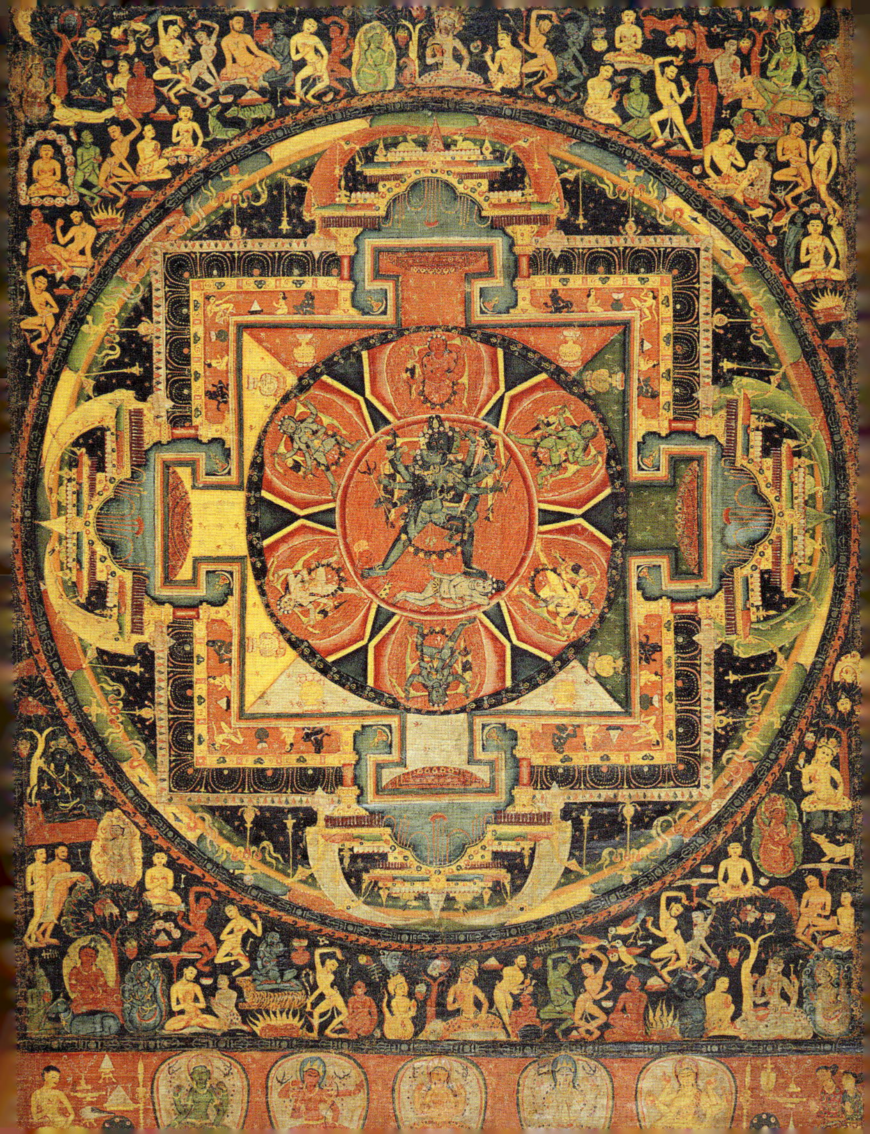

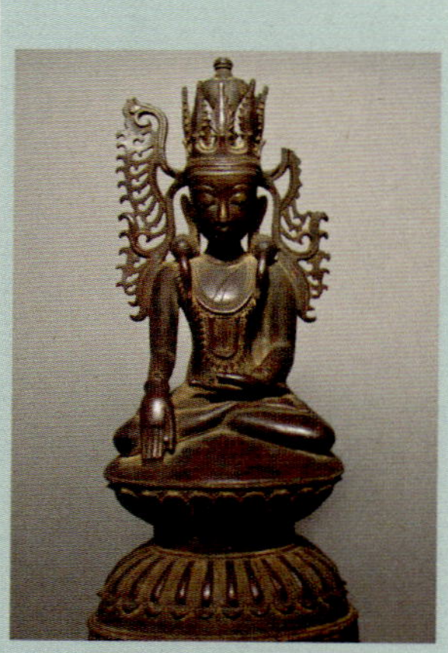

Jambupati Buddha

This 17th-century Burmese sculpture derives from Indian prototypes, called Jambupati Buddhas, that placed the crowned and bejewelled Buddha on a double lotus base – resplendent enough to convert a king.

Crowned Buddha

c. 10th–11th century CE **Metropolitan Museum of Art, New York, USA**

STYLE Kurkihar **MATERIALS** Bronze inlaid with silver, lapis lazuli and rock crystal **HEIGHT** 32.1 cm/12 ¾ in.

Artists devised several ways of expressing the teachings of the Vajrayana doctrine. This crowned, bejewelled and enthroned Buddha image from Bihar, India, is intended as a representation of the Cosmic Buddha, for his royal features clearly distinguish him from Shakyamuni, the ascetic Buddha who stayed in the woods to achieve enlightenment. Shakyamuni is important to all schools of Buddhism, and icons of him and references to his life are frequently found in Vajrayana art. Here, though, the Buddha is crowned and bejewelled. He wears the monastic robe, and his hand is in the *Bhumisparasa mudra*, which signifies the attainment of enlightenment; he sits under the limbs of a stylized Bodhi tree, to be seen at the top of his halo. Moreover, this icon is made of bronze and silver, and its crown, necklaces, hourglass-shaped base and halo are studded with semi-precious stones and rock crystal; the image is a veritable treasure. The royal symbolism manifest in such exquisite treasures was appropriated by Buddhist, Christian and other religious traditions as a metaphor to convey the spirituality of the divine. Expensive materials also came to be used in the making of the treasured ritual objects of esoteric teachings; utilitarian plates, cups, ritual bells, incense burners and *vajra* (symbolic thunderbolts) were transformed into ornate vessels inhabited by spirits. Monks from central Asia, China, Japan, Tibet and South-east Asia came to study at the universities of Nalanda in Bihar and Vikramashila in Bengal, where images such as this one were made. Returning, they carried scriptures, ritual implements and small, portable images that were closely copied at home.

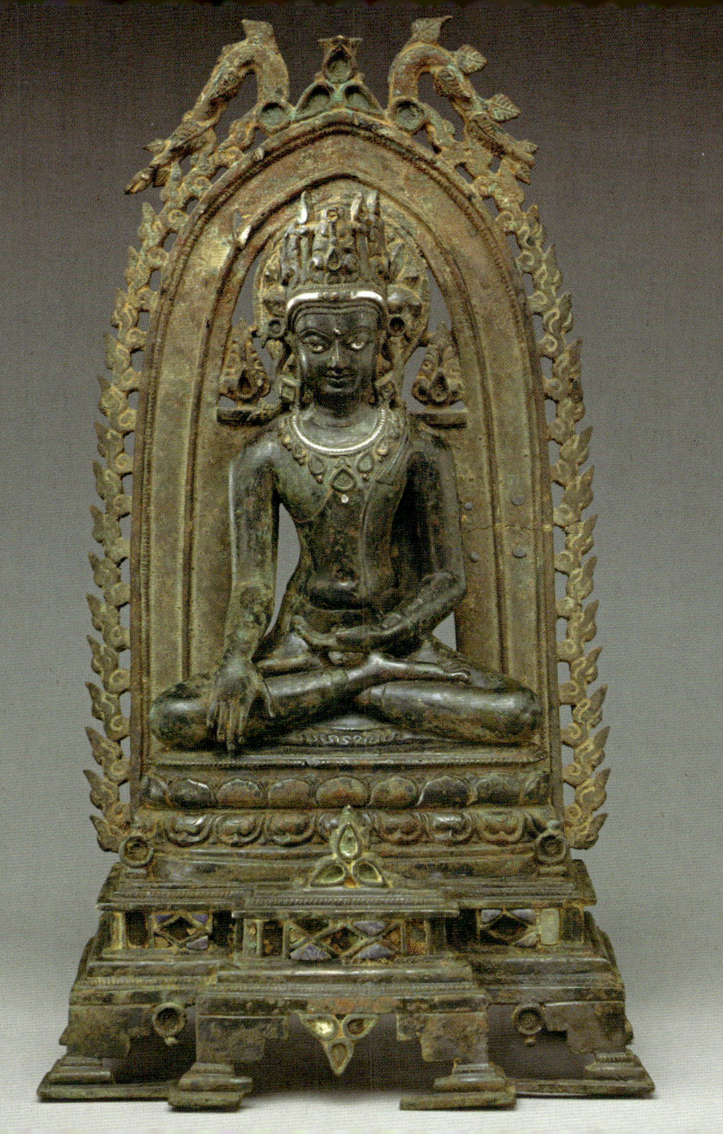

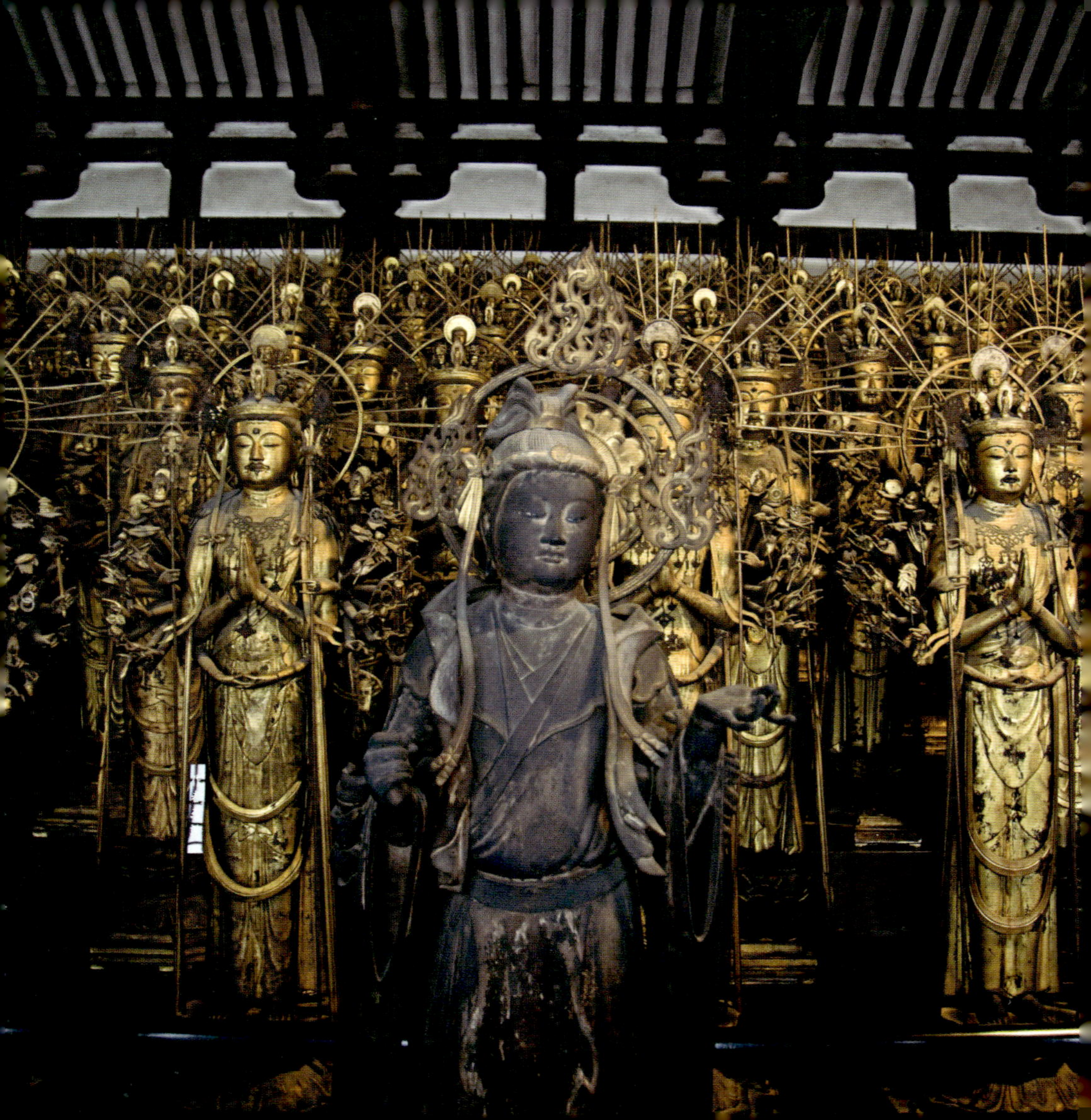

1,001 Thousand-armed Kannon Statues

1164 CE Rengeo-in Temple, Kyoto, Kansai, Japan

COMMISSIONED BY Emperor Go Shirakawa **SCULPTED BY** Tankei
MATERIAL Cypress wood, gilded **HEIGHT** 1,000 are life sized

At the Rengeo-in Temple in Kyoto there is a hall, the Sanjusangen-do, which, at 120 metres (394 ft), is the longest building in Japan. Inside the hall are 1,000 standing statues of the eleven-headed, thousand-armed deity Kannon (Sahasrabhuja-arya-avalokiteshvara in Sanskrit), executed in cypress wood. They flank a much larger, central, thousand-armed Kannon icon (see right) made by the master sculptor Tankei, making 1,001 sculptures in all. Tankei was part of an atelier of master sculptors who were leading artists of their time; the Kei School specialized in Buddhist icons and fostered a style of naturalism in rendering not only portraits of the Buddhist patriarch but also these extraordinary visions of deities. The life-sized standing statues are set in ten rows and fifty columns. A fire in 1249 left only 124 of the originals without damage, but the destroyed ones were all replaced in the 13th century. Also present are twenty-eight statues of guardian deities, and celestial musicians stand in front. The name of the long hall means 'thirty-three sections', and refers to the canonical number of manifestations Kannon will assume to help those who call upon him, as stipulated in the *Lotus Sutra*; in sum the statues represent 33,033 manifestations. The figures stand somewhat stiffly and are rather ethereal, being slender-bodied, pillar-like forms with two sets of arms and twenty smaller ones with hands holding various attributes. The delicate circles of the figures' haloes are intersected by five thin bars representing rays of divine light.

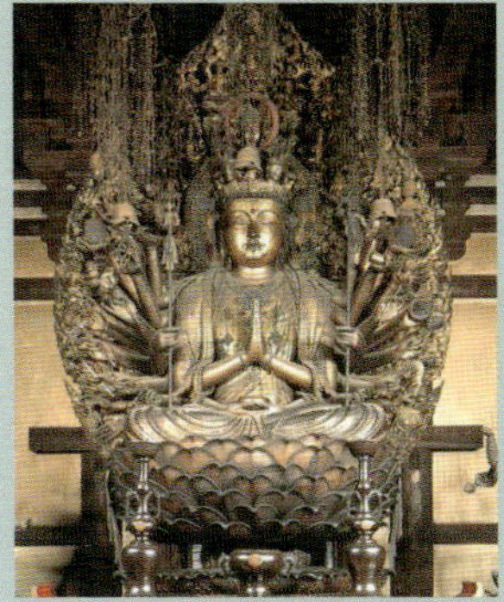

Kannon by Tankei

Tankei's 3.4-metre (11-ft) Kannon has 1,000 arms radiating outwards. Two arms are in Anjali (palms clasped together), and two hold a begging bowl in his lap. Forty-two major arms carry various attributes, and the rest radiate around the figure, echoing the shape of the body mandorla.

'If I will be able to give benefit and happiness to all living beings in the future, let me have one thousand hands and one thousand eyes immediately.'

DHARANI SUTRA

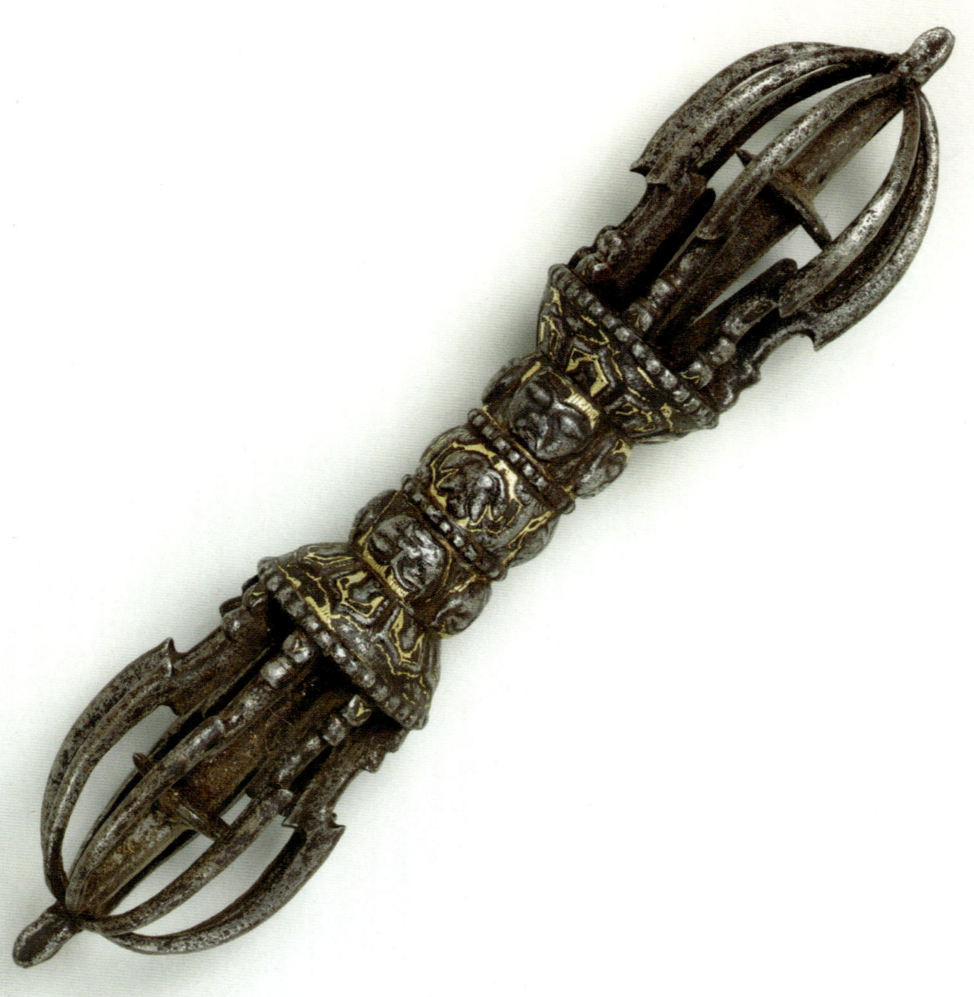

Vajra, or Symbol of the Sacred Thunderbolt

12th century CE **Victoria & Albert Museum, London, UK**

MATERIALS Steel and gold **NUMBER OF PRONGS PER HEAD** Nine
LENGTH 18 cm/7 in.

The *vajra*, or sacred thunderbolt, is the single most important symbol of Vajrayana, the tantric school of Buddhism, after which it is named. Used as a weapon by the Indian sky god Indra, the vajra is understood to be an instrument of destruction that cannot itself be destroyed. It represents the indestructible force or adamantine nature of truth. The symbol has Buddhist associations, especially in Tibet, but it is also important in the Indian religious traditions of the Vedas: Hinduism and Jainism. The vajra is sometimes imaged as a staff with three prongs, in which case it can signify the union of the two worlds, or the highest enlightenment. Often it has a trident-like head at both ends, as does this example. Different types of vajra have different meanings and much effort has gone into cataloguing them. For example, a vajra with open prongs is interpreted as peaceful; if the prong ends come together, it is wrathful. A vajra may have three, five or nine closed prongs at each end, and each form has a different ritual use. The nine-pronged form, for example, connotes the nine *yanas* (modes) of the Tibetan Nyingma tradition. Often the vajra is used in rituals with the bell, whose purpose may be to summon a deity. At these times, the vajra and bell assume diametrically opposed values, such as male and female, and compassion and wisdom, respectively. Deities are often depicted holding the vajra in the left hand and bell in the right. The vajra shape is commonly seen in bell handles, sword hilts and parts of other ritual objects.

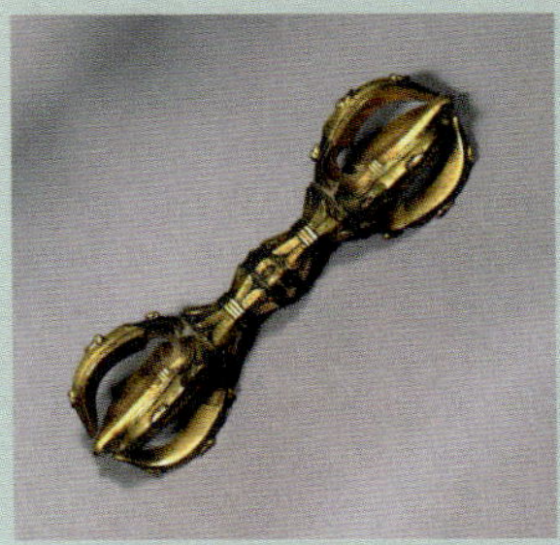

Japanese Vajra

Esoteric Buddhist art is ruled by a strict canon of attributes and procedures for manufacture. This five-pronged vajra, made in Japan in the late Kamakura period (14th century) is very similar to the one made in Tibet, even though they are separated by two hundred years and thousands of miles. The vajra is made of gilt bronze and is 19.1 centimetres (7½ in.) long.

'All the elements of the thunderbolts of body, of speech and of mind, of all the Tathagatas of the ten directions entered to direct his view into the five-pronged, white thunderbolt of his heart.'

THE FOURTH ABHISAMBODHI

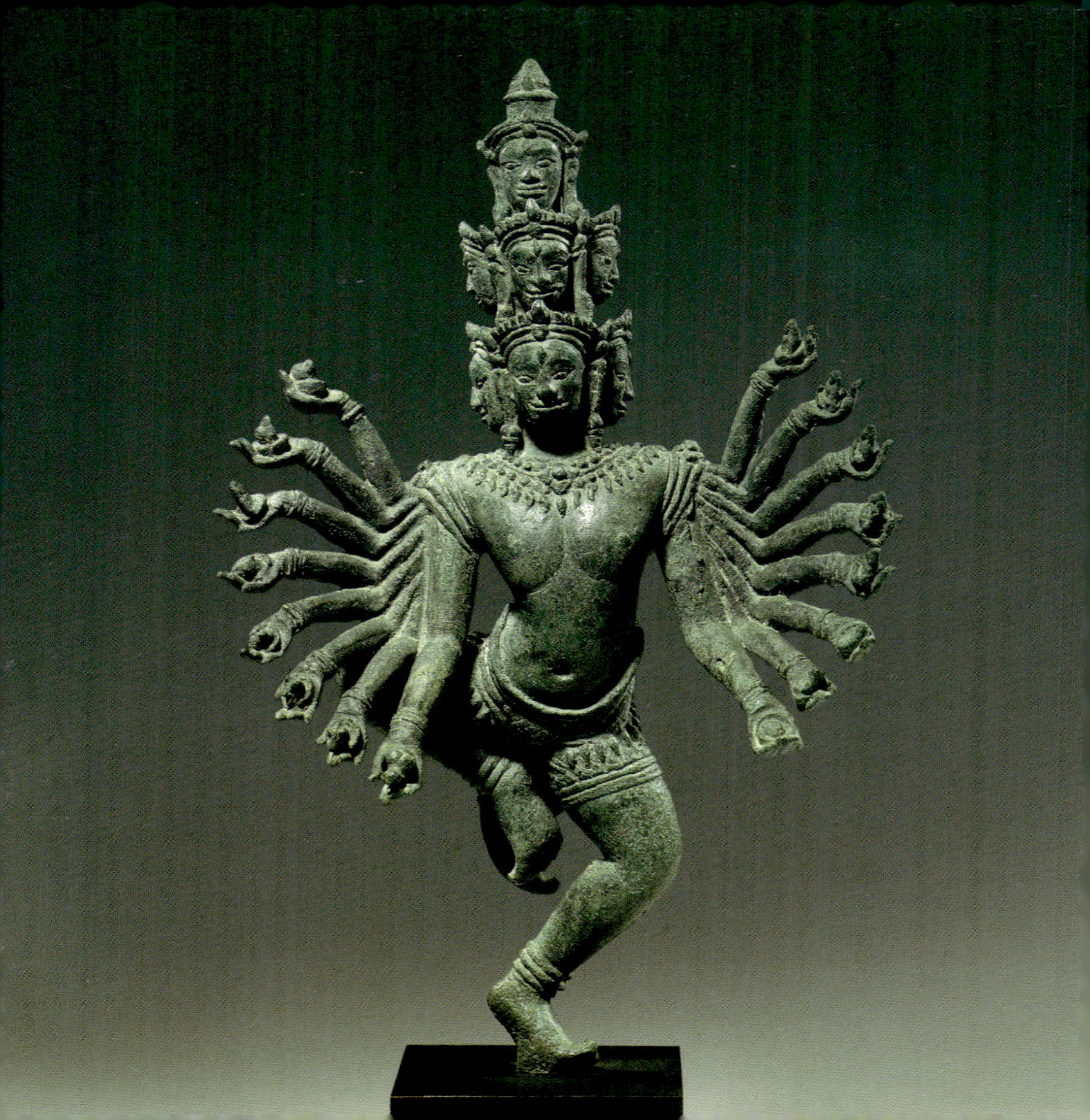

Hevajra

12th–13th century CE **Museum of Asian Art, Berlin, Germany**

STYLE Khmer **MATERIAL** Bronze
HEIGHT 31 cm/12 in.

Hevajra is a protective and militant deity associated in particular with victory over the enemy. Buddhists worship him for his material success, wealth, power and enlightenment. This bronze sculpture of the deity is thought to be from the era of Jayavarman VII (r. c. 1181–1218), King of Cambodia. The combative aspect of Hevajra's identity is usually made obvious by the fact that he is dancing on a corpse, but here the body is missing. Adopting a difficult dance position, he lifts his right leg and balances on the toes of his left. Sixteen arms fan out from his arm sockets, and eight heads, arranged in a tall, conical fashion and each wearing a crown, sit on top of his main head. The dynamic dance posture is balanced by the verticality of the heads and the swathe of cloth that descends from his belt. His eight left hands hold eight divinities; the right ones hold seven animals and a monk. Dance was clearly important in the mid-12th–early 13th centuries in Cambodia, evidenced not only by this small bronze figurine, but also the number of portrayals of dancing *apsara*, or angels, singly or in pairs, carved on the square columns of King Jayavarman VII's temple of Banteay Kdei, or Citadel of Chambers. This monastery in the Angkor complex had a vast rectangular hall that may have served as a space for ritual dance. Dance was considered the highest form of art in India too, and deities such as Siva, lord of creation and destruction, were sometimes portrayed dancing ecstatically. A bronze sculpture like this one is a relatively rare find at Angkor because most have been melted down over the centuries by non-believers for the value of their metal.

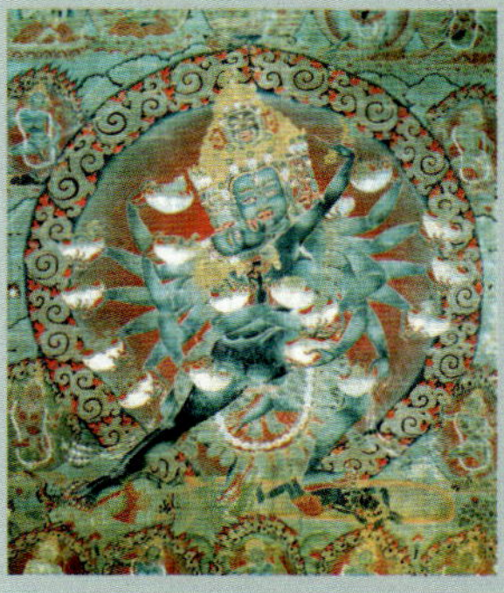

Tutelary God

In this painting on silk, produced by the Tibetan Civilization in the 17th century, Hevajra is represented as a tutelary (guardian) deity. Holding the female deity Nairatmya in a ritual embrace, his eyes are red from compassion; his body is black to indicate his friendly disposition.

'... persons who were full of the holy truth concealed for the benefit of future disciples many instructions concerning the most excellent spiritual potency ...'

EVA M. DARGYAY, *THE RISE OF ESOTERIC BUDDHISM*

Vairochana Mandala

12th–13th century CE   **Michigan University Museum of Anth. Archaeology**

ORIGIN Tabo Monastery, Spiti Valley, Himachal Pradesh, India
MATERIALS Gouache on cloth   **DIMENSIONS** 65 x 56 cm / 25½ x 22 in.

As a diagram of the cosmos, the mandala recreates the universal pillar that links heaven to earth within the four cardinal directions, encircled by a wall. With the rise of esoteric practice, mandalas became more varied and complex, and more essential to initiation, meditation and prayer. This mandala, probably from the Tabo Monastery in Spiti Valley, Himachal Pradesh, northern India, is laid out like a grid, and at the centre is the Cosmic Buddha Vairochana, the all-knowing, radiant one, flanked by two bodhisattvas. The Buddhas ranged around him are his emanations. Vairochana is identifiable by his white skin colour, symbolizing purity, and by the *Bodhyagri mudra*, signifying the highest enlightenment, which is the unity of all opposites. He sits in an Indian high-backed throne and is flanked by mythical creatures of land and sea in rampant poses – a symbolic depiction of his dominion over the world. Here Vairochana in his simple monastic robe resembles Shakyamuni Buddha, but the imagery of the *thangka* (painting), including the deities in the lowest range, attests to his cosmic identity. All but a few of the seated images are Buddhas in *Bhumisparsa mudra*, attaining enlightenment, but in the bottom rows are bodhisattvas and spirit guardian kings. This type of mandala would be used by a teacher to waken the spirit of Vairochana in an acolyte. Seated in meditation before it, the acolyte would observe it minutely, visualizing it with his spiritual sight, then transform the image into the true Cosmic Buddha. Using magical incantations (mantras) and hand gestures (mudras), he would draw the Buddha within himself and mystically identify with him.

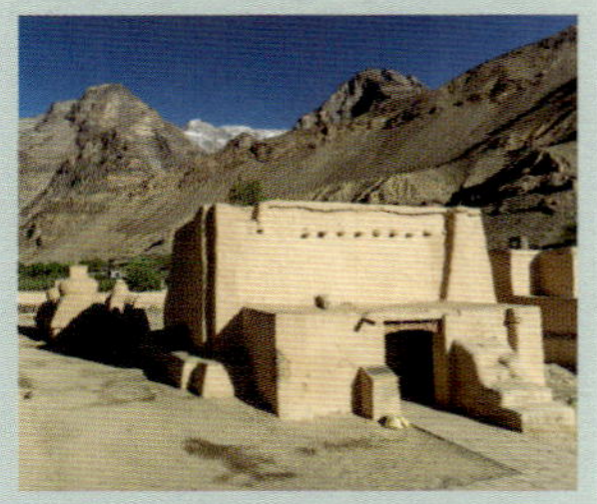

Tabo Monastery

The famous Buddhist teacher Atisa Dipamkara Srijnana (982–1054 CE) from Bengal wrote his treatise *A Lamp for the Path to Enlightenment* at Tabo and later carried his teachings to Tibet. Today much of the temple has been restored but painted mandalas are still extant on the surrounding walls. More than a thousand years old, Tabo is considered to be one of the holiest Buddhist monasteries.

'In each dust mote of these worlds are countless worlds and Buddhas / From the tip of each hair of Buddha's body / Are revealed the indescribable Pure Lands.'

AVATAMSAKA SUTRA

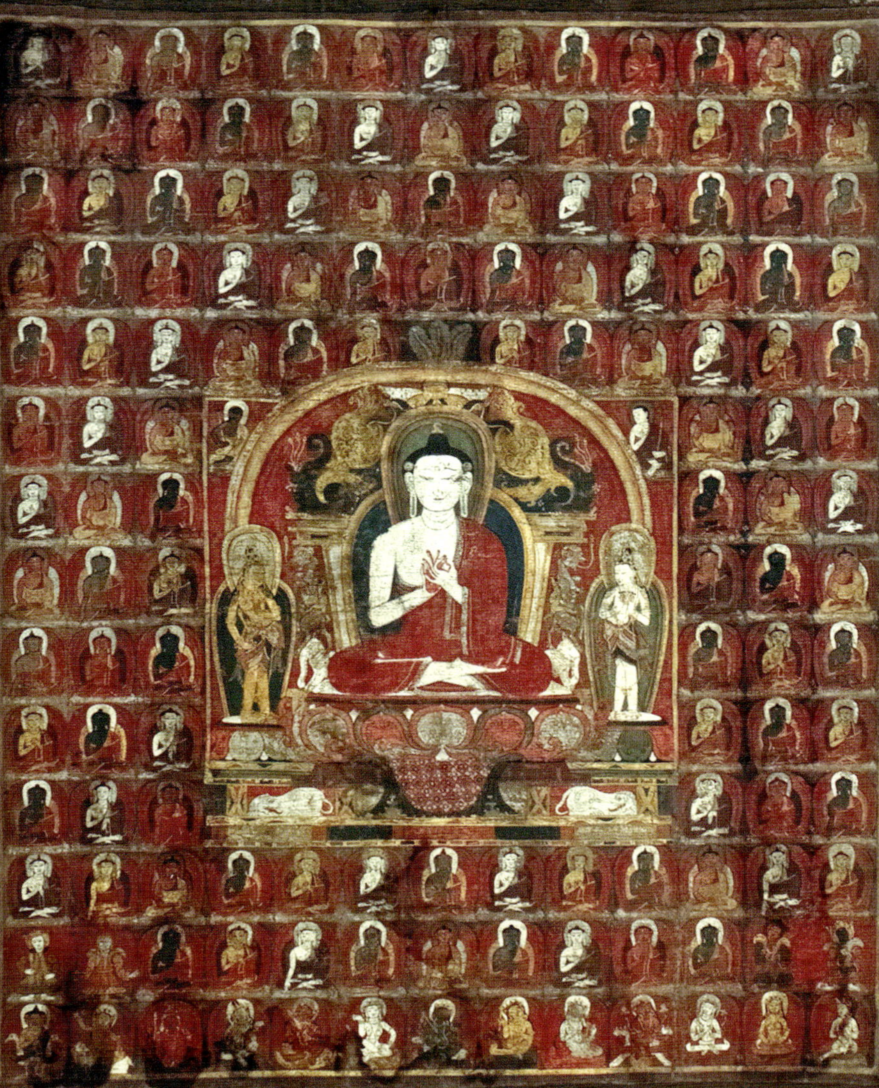

Seated Fudo Myoo

1203 CE **Daigo-ji Temple, Kyoto, Kansai, Japan**

SCULPTOR Kaikei (1185–1223) **STYLE** Kamakura
MATERIALS Wood, polychrome paints **HEIGHT** 53.3 cm/21 in.

The deity Fudo Myoo (Acala in Sanskrit), or the Immovable, embodies a wrathful form of divine compassion and uses his powers to conquer evil. As such he is a warrior god, armed and aggressive. In this Japanese icon of the 13th century, Fudo sits corpulent and dark-skinned on a rocky base; flames of destruction and enlightenment emerge around him. In his left hand he holds a lasso; in the right, his sword's hilt is shaped as a *vajra* (a double trident form symbolizing the power of the thunderbolt). His hair is braided and he has two tusks, one pointed up and the other down. As a protector god, he has an angry face, biting down on his lower lip, with his eyes looking askance. Though seated, he conveys great power and an immovable spirit. Fudo first appeared at the foot of a mandala along with four companion wrathful deities: Gozanze (Tralokyavijaya in Sanskrit), or Subduer of the Three Worlds; Gundari (Kundali), or Treasure Producer; Daiitoku (Yamanataka), or Awe Inspiring Power and Kongo Yaksha (Vajrayaksha), or Diamond Demon. Fudo's role was to protect the faithful in their search for enlightenment by burning away all impediments and defilements, and in war-torn medieval Japan he was the deity most often worshipped as an individual. Buddhist mandalas include representation of evil because evil is acknowledged as part of the cosmic order. Most other world religions, in the mode of Zoroastrianism, pit light against dark, good against evil in a battle until light eventually banishes dark. In contrast, esoteric Buddhism sees a resolution between the opposing forces and retains evil as part of the cosmic scheme.

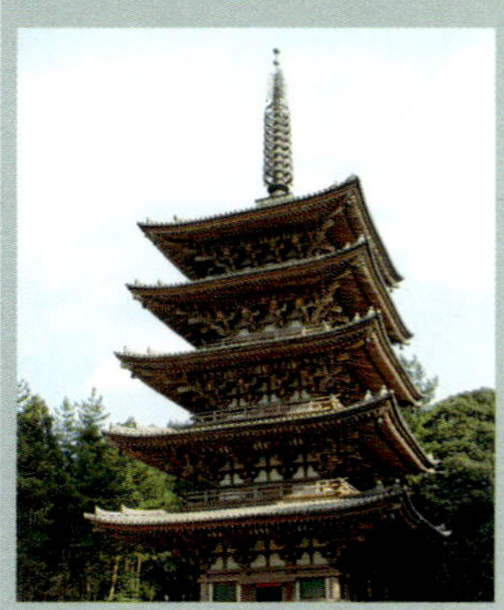

Daigo-ji Temple

Daigo-ji is a Shingon temple of the esoteric school introduced to Japan from China by Kukai Kobo-Daishi (774–835). In 874, Rigen-daishi (Shobo) founded the temple in homage to Kannon. It was sited on the slope of a mountain that was sacred to the local people. Thus esoteric Buddhism embraced native traditions, seeing them as manifestations of the Buddha.

'Our hearts ache and our sleeves are wet [with tears] until we see face to face the tender figure of the One.'

NICHIREN

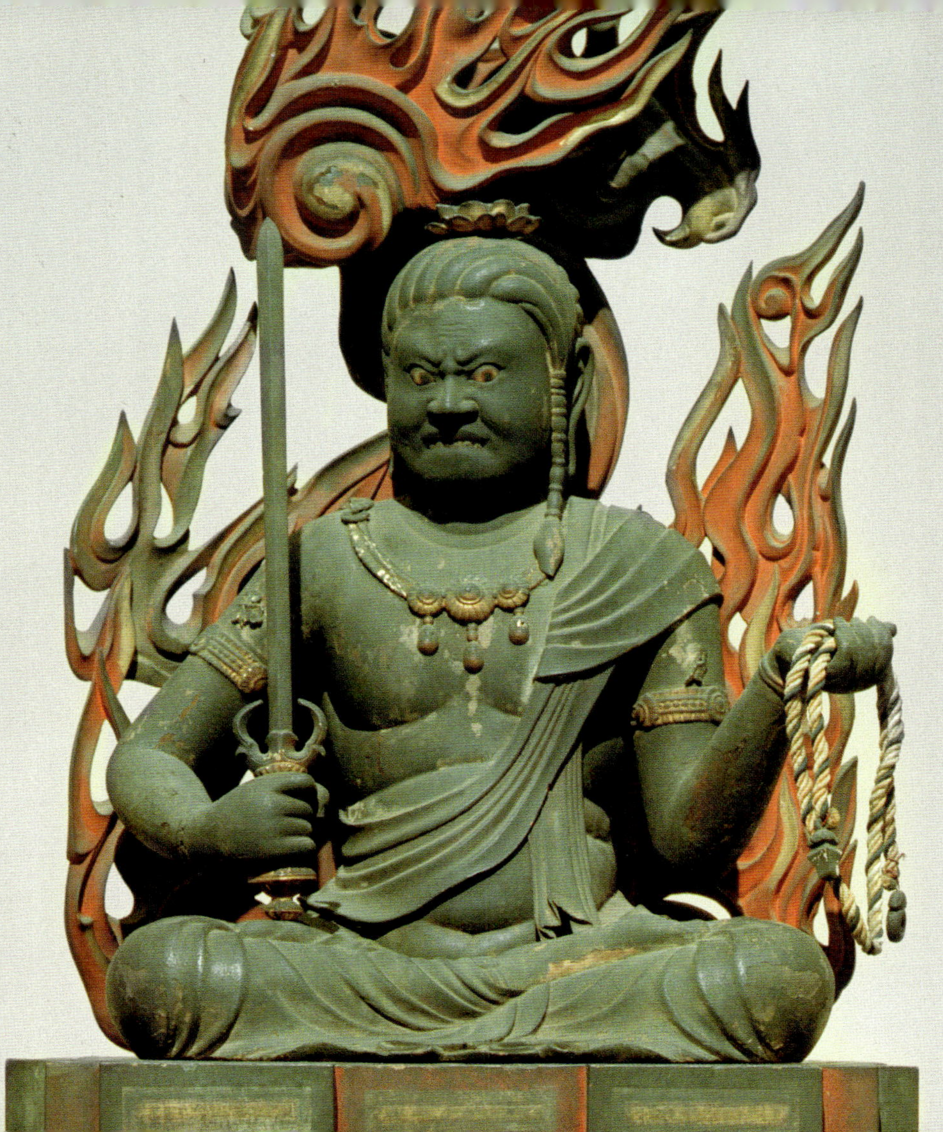

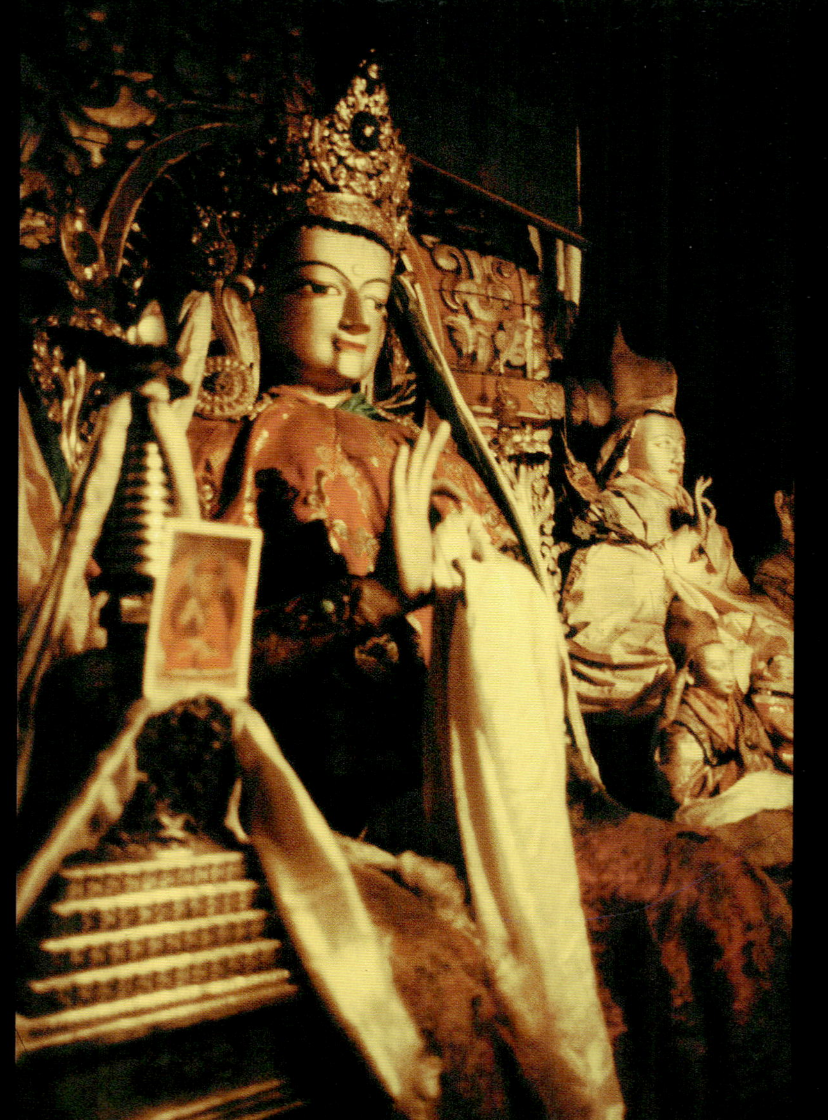

Crowned Bodhisattva and Multiple Deities

13th century CE **Potala Palace, Lhasa, Tibet Autonomous Region, China**

STYLE Esoteric Buddhist   **MATERIALS** Gilt bronze, with embroidered silk adornments

As the centre of esoteric Tibetan Buddhism, the Potala Palace in Llasa, Tibet, contains a multitude of icons, large and small, arranged in a way that appears haphazard to the uninitiated. In fact, the seemingly informal arrangement of deities is intended to conform to a mandala or diagram of the divine forces in the universe. Mapping the placement of the deities in such a scheme is the first step in understanding their relationships, and ultimately in controlling them and enlisting their help to achieve total awareness, or nirvana. Esoteric Buddhist icons, like the Hindu ones that inspired them, were manufactured according to a strict procedure that included prayer and meditation prior to their execution, the use of standard canons of proportion and a detailed encyclopaedia of attributes: skin colour, appendages, costume, jewellery, objects held in the hand, posture and others. As a part of worship, the deities are adorned in embroidered silk garments and jewelled crowns. This panoply of icons at Potala represents various paths to worshipping the Cosmic Buddha, who is at the centre of all being. Primary among the images is the bodhisattva, the incarnation of wisdom and compassion, who helps the faithful to attain their goals. Prominent among the icons on display are the lamas or great teachers of the past, who, as enlightened beings, eased the path for others with their translations of the scriptures, sermons, and art commissions. The icons are of various ages and represent different manifestations of individual deities.

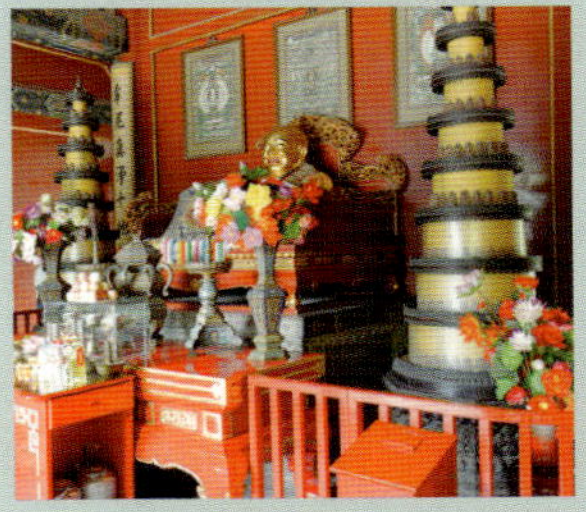

Lama Temple

This bodhisattva is worshipped at the Lama (Yonghe) Temple in Beijing. The temple was established by the emperors of the final Chinese dynasty, the Qing, who were followers of Tibetan Buddhism. The gilded deity is seated on a high throne and is covered by luxurious robes and silks. Before it are offerings from the faithful, such as flowers, candles, incense and fruits.

'Enlightenment is the highest quality of the mind…. As it is free from all [limiting] attributes of subjectivity, it is like unto space penetrating everywhere, as the unity of all.'

ASVAGHOSA, *BUDDHACARITA*

Kesi Green Tara

1300 CE Asian Art Museum of San Francisco, California, USA

TECHNIQUE Kesi tapestry   MATERIAL Silk
DIMENSIONS 23.2 x 19 cm / 9¼ x 7½ in. (inner image as shown)

Kesi is a technique of silk embroidery known for being extremely difficult and time-consuming, yet it results in exquisite images of great clarity and detail, and so meticulously done that the patterns may be viewed equally from the front and the back. There is evidence that kesi embroidery was practised in China during the Han dynasty (206 BCE–220 CE), and the art developed to reach a pinnacle of production during the Yuan dynasty (1271–1368). This example is attributed to the Xixia Tangut people, who lived in northern China, near Tibet. Buddhist images entered Xixia territory through the agency of Tibetan masters who, in the mid-12th to the mid-13th century, founded monasteries and brought works of art to be copied. Separately, a Nepalese artist, Anige (1245–1306), brought the kesi technique to the Mongol court, which set up official departments to oversee production of kesi imperial portraits and religious works, including this Green Tara. In Buddhist religious practice, Green Tara is a saviour goddess who helps her followers overcome fears, dangers and difficult situations. Green Tara is the personification of divine compassion and acts quickly to help those who call upon her. Here, though sitting in the posture of royal ease, she seems poised to act. She looks directly at the viewer with a concentrated expression. Her left hand makes the boon-granting gesture; her right hand is in the mudra (gesture) of granting refuge. She wears the rich jewels of a bodhisattva and sits on a lotus supported by an hourglass-shaped, jewel-encrusted throne. Her halo has a lush floral pattern and she has two full lotus flowers on either side.

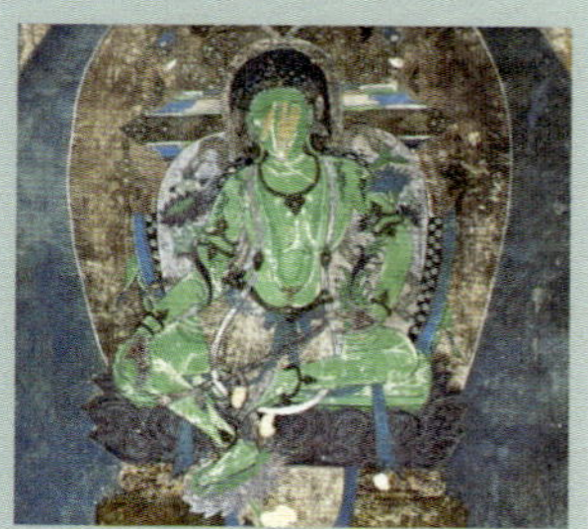

Yulin Cave Painting

The popularity of Green Tara as a Buddhist icon in the China of the Yuan dynasty (1271–1368) is further confirmed by this painting of her, located in Cave 4 of the Yulin Caves in Gansu province. The caves themselves are much older, dating back to the 7th century under the Tang dynasty.

‘On a lotus seat, standing for realization of voidness, [You are] the emerald-coloured, one-faced, two-armed Lady / In youth’s full bloom, right leg out, left drawn in, Showing the union of wisdom and art — homage to you!’

FIRST DALAI LAMA (1391–1474)

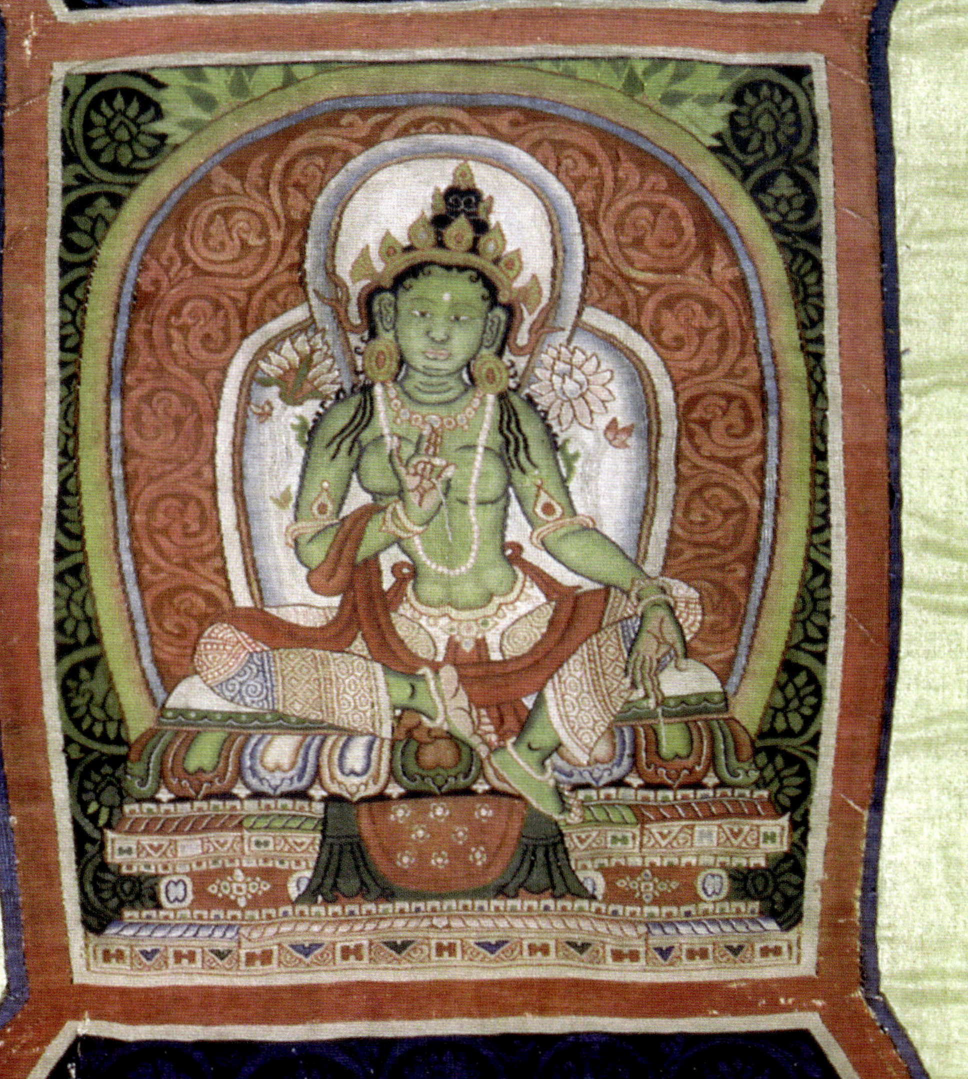

Thangka of Mahakala

C. 1500 CE **Metropolitan Museum of Art, New York, USA**

STYLE Nepali **MATERIALS** Gouache on cotton
DIMENSIONS 162.6 x 134.6 cm/64 x 53 in.

Mahakala, a fierce and powerful emanation of Avalokiteshvara, acts as the overcomer of obstacles. He is also a tutelary deity who protects the doctrine from hostile forces and corruption, and so the faithful call upon him to control their impure thoughts and actions and lead them from delusion. In tantric cosmology, Mahakala is one of the five emanations of the dhyani Buddhas, who are the five wisdoms or 'truth bodies', of enlightenment: Aksobhya, Amitabha, Amoghasiddhi, Ratnasambhava and Vairochana. These transcendent Buddhas are visualized in tantric meditation, and each represents a different aspect of enlightened consciousness and aids in spiritual transformation. Depicting Mahakala, this *thangka*, or Tibetan silk painting with embroidery, is portable but as large as a wall painting. The wrathful god is given a short, black, muscular body and is seen squatting, ready to jump. He stands on two trampled humans, a representation of his conquest of negativism. Among his horrific features are canine teeth, a crown with skulls and a necklace of severed heads. His weapons include a *karti* or chopper, a magic sword and a *vajra* (double-headed trident); he also holds a *kapala*, or skull full of blood. Here he has but one face and two arms, but in other manifestations he has more faces and from four to sixteen arms. Mahakala is dressed in all manner of jewels and fluttering green scarves; brilliant red flames emanate from his body, as do demon soldiers and wild dogs. Flanking the deity are two smaller manifestations of his persona, and around the periphery of the composition are portraits of lamas or teachers.

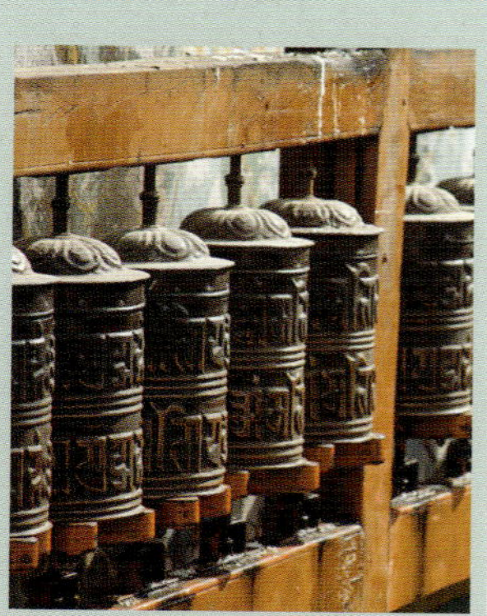

Prayer Wheels

A form of worship that evolved in Tibet was the rotation of prayer wheels (or bells), either small, hand-held ones or large ones worshippers would turn as they circumambulated stupas. Inside the wheels are scriptures, and believers gain spiritual credit by rotating the wheels.

'One left arm holds a skull cup of *amrita*, the intoxicating nectar of the gods, which is a means of pacifying. One right arm holds a hooked knife, a symbol of enriching.'

THE VIDYADHARA

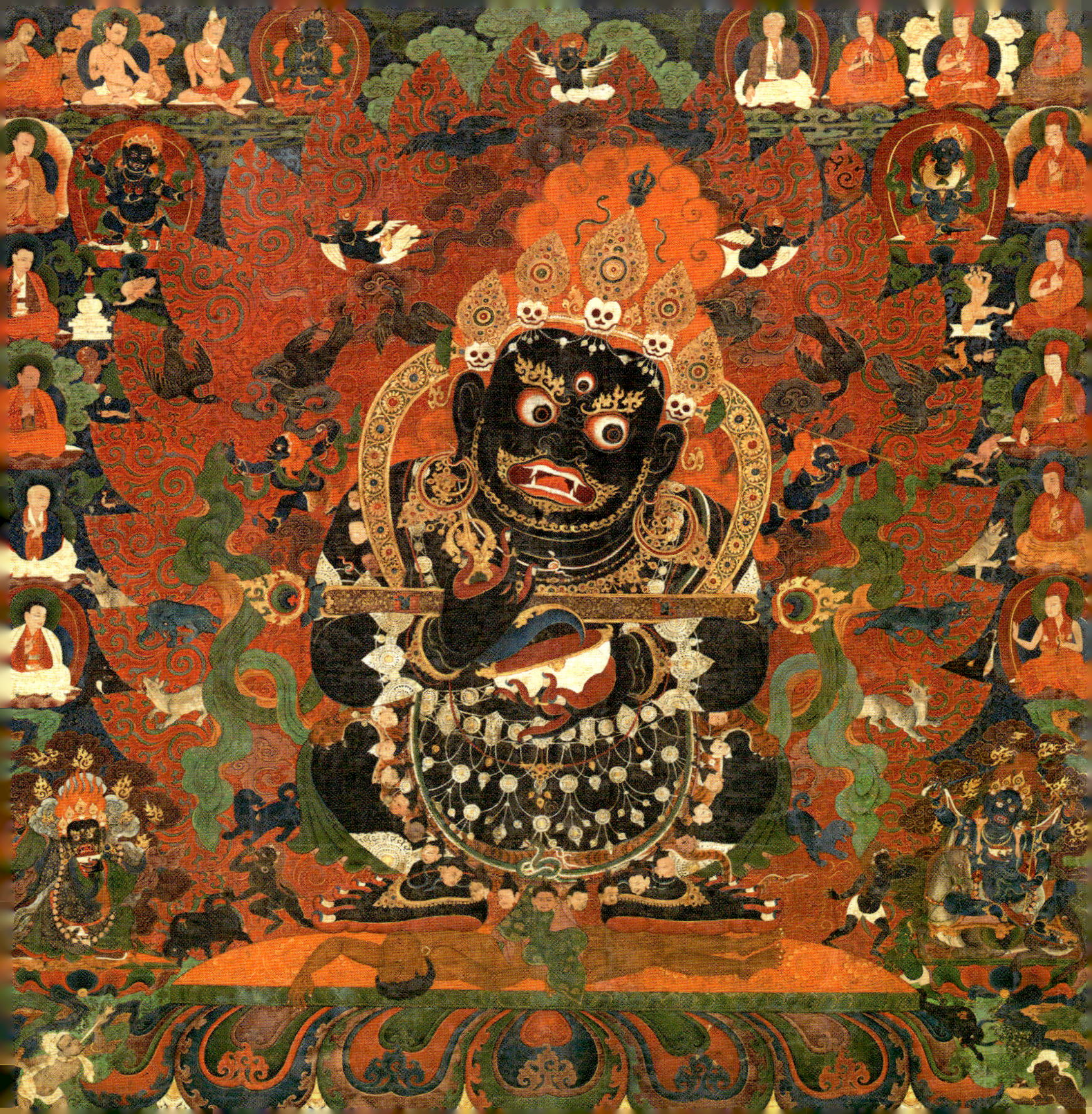

Jetsun Milarepa

MATERIALS Copper alloy, paint
DIMENSIONS 18 x 16 x 12 cm/7 x 6¼ x 4½ in.

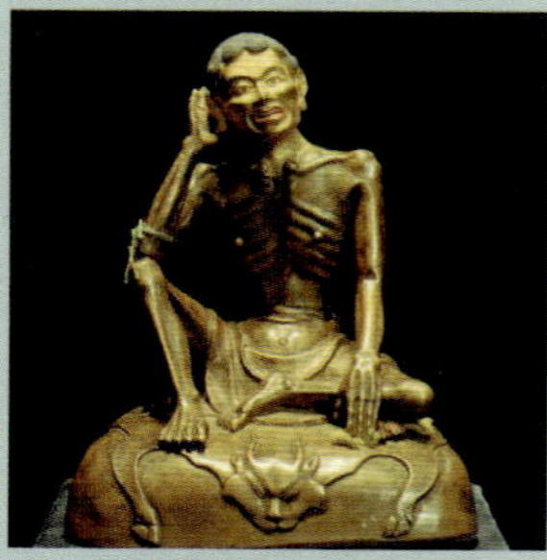

Listening Yogi

More than a hundred years separate this 18th-century Tibetan figure of Jetsun Milarepa, made from painted and gilded copper alloy, and the 16th-century one (see right). Yet it is remarkably similar in its listening gesture and the attitude of its limbs. Its ribs, made prominent by hunger, and animal pelt both refer to time spent in the wilderness.

'When you think of a delicious meal, Eat the food of Samadhi Ideal, Realize that all food is only delusion, Hold to the Dharmakaya's meditation.'

MILAREPA TO HIS
CHIEF DISCIPLE, GAMPOPA

In Tibet, transmission of the Dharma is linked to several specific patriarchs who founded sects. Such patriarchs play a fundamental role in tantric Buddhism because its abstruse and difficult teachings cannot be learned without their help. Jetsun Milarepa (1052–1135) was a student of Marpa Lotsawa (1012–97), who studied in India with the tantric master Naropa (1016–1100). He became a revered yogi and poet, a teacher of the Kagyu School of Tibetan Buddhism, and he wrote with mystical passion. Portraits made of patriarchs and teachers such as Milarepa were considered especially important in maintaining a sect's teachings and genealogy, and, like the Buddha, the teachers were honoured with representations that tried to convey their enlightened state. Large-scale *thangkas* or religious paintings show them in monastic garb, teaching in a landscape or surrounded by other lamas, Buddhas and bodhisattvas. Sometimes their footprints and handprints appear on either side of their portrait, rendered in gold. Sculptures, too, were crafted from precious materials. In this figure from central Tibet, Milarepa is shown as a yogi living in the wilderness, half-naked and barefoot, seemingly impervious to the cold. Seated in a relaxed position, one knee bent, he cups his right ear with his right hand in a singing or listening gesture. Resting in his lap, his left hand may hold a skull. Mountain creatures attend him, and here he gives audience to a kneeling devotee. An unconventional patriarch, Milarepa is not depicted as a dignified lama, but rather the saint known for his ecstatic revelations, beautiful singing voice and reclusive existence in a mountain cave.

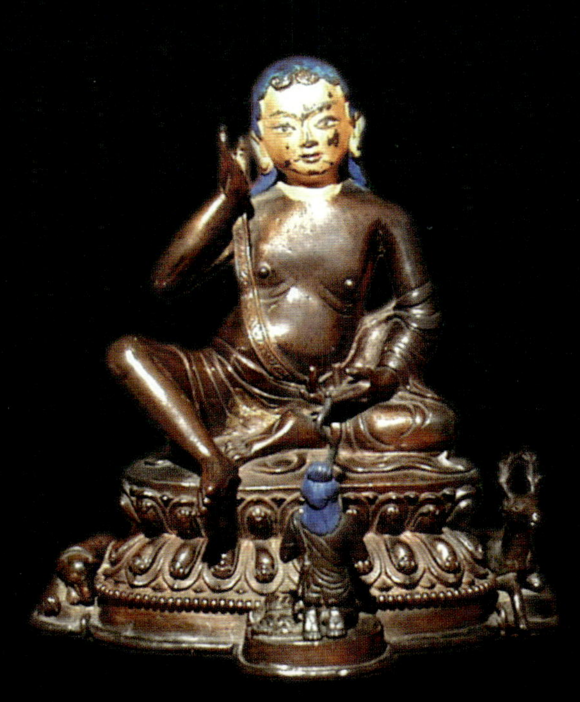

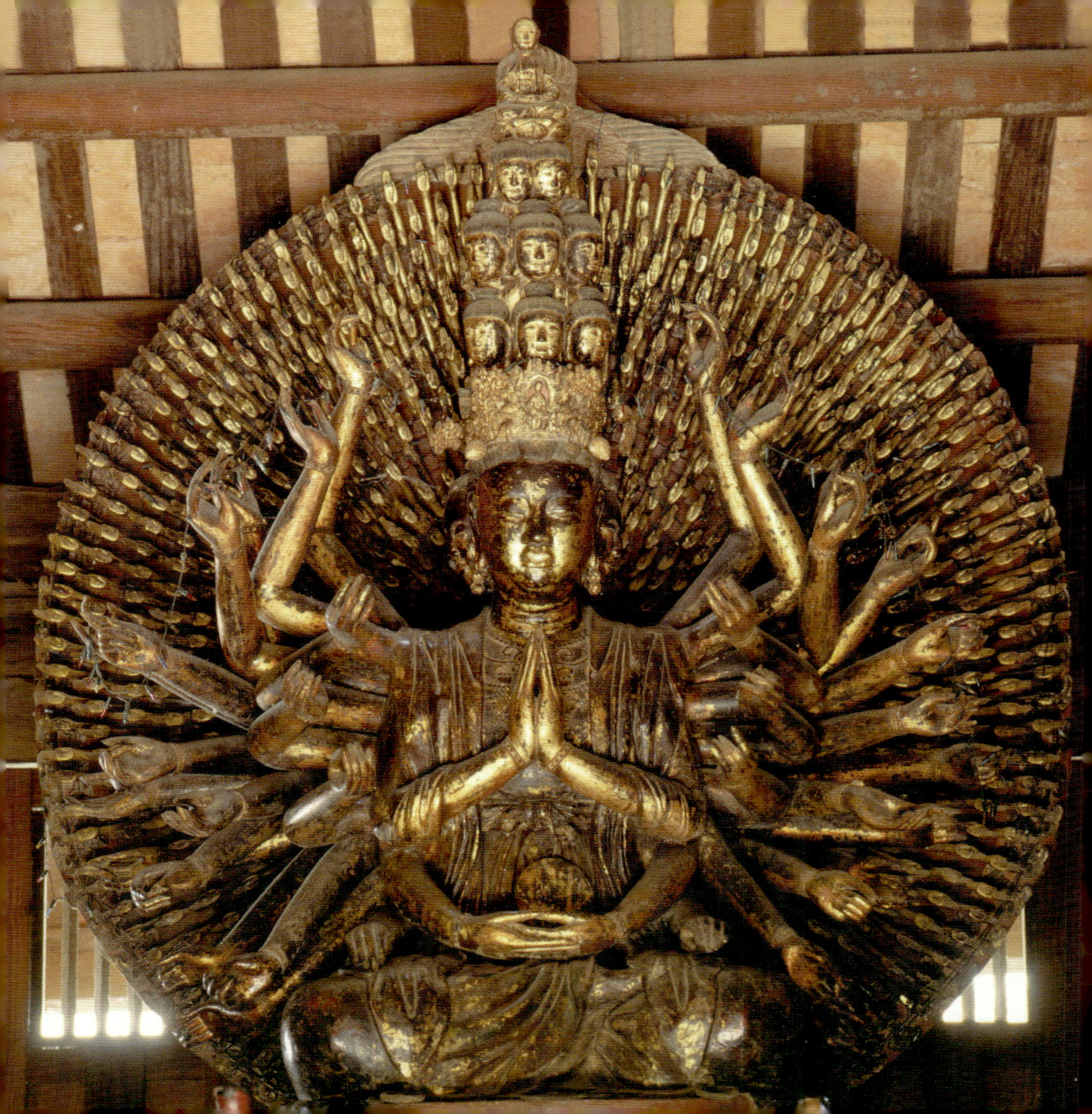

Thousand-armed, Eleven-headed Guanyin

1656 CE   **But Thap Temple, Bac Ninh, Vietnam**

MATERIAL Crimson-lacquered and gilded wood
HEIGHT 2.5 m/8 ft 2½ in., excluding pedestal and supporting dragons

But Thap Temple is famous for housing the world's biggest statue of Guanyin (Avalokiteshvara in Sanskrit) with a thousand eyes and a thousand arms. As is common, both normal-sized and tiny arms are present. Forty-two large arms emerge from the shoulders and torso; their hands assume various symbolic mudras (gestures). Each palm of a total of 789 smaller hands is incised with an eye. The arms form a halo 2.2 metres (7 ft 2½ in.) in diameter. Possessing eleven heads and hundreds of hands with eyes on the palms, the Bodhisattva has a greatly enhanced capacity to see the sufferings of sentient beings and remedy their problems. The icon was probably commissioned by the extraordinary Queen Trinh Thi Ngoc Truc, who first requested that the pagoda at But Thap be enlarged in 1646; the construction of the icon began ten years later. The queen, who was devoted to Buddhism, raised funds to refurbish temples and compiled Vietnam's first Chinese–Vietnamese dictionary. Such efforts at renewing Buddhist monuments came at a time of respite from a hundred years of civil war between north and south Vietnam, and the revival of Buddhism coincided with a period of rising economic and political success. The restored temples were an expression of gratitude, a celebration of peace and hope for the future. The Tibetan-Buddhist Qing dynasty, the last emperors of China, were commissioning many thousand-armed images, and Vietnamese architects took Chinese icons and monuments as their models.

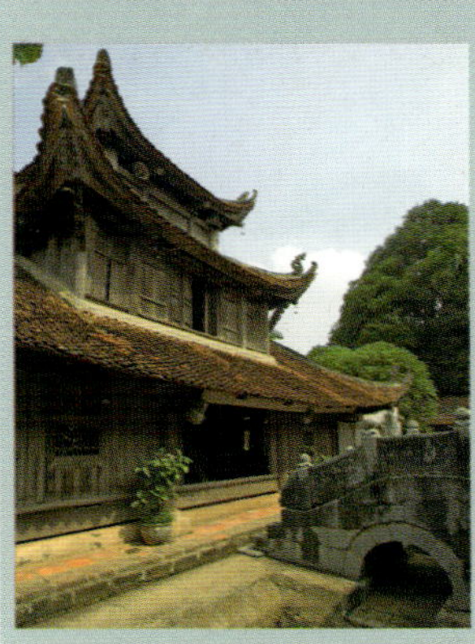

But Thap Temple

The architecture of But Thap Temple is essentially Chinese, but in local style its buildings include an Accumulated Good Deeds Sanctum, Middle Hall and Image Hall, made of wood and linked by a stone bridge. Two stupas in the rear of the temple contain the relics of two eminent priests.

'To the one who performs a leap of all fears … may I enter into the heart of the blue-necked one known as the noble, adorable Avalokiteshvara.'

DHARANI TO THE THOUSAND-ARMED DEITY

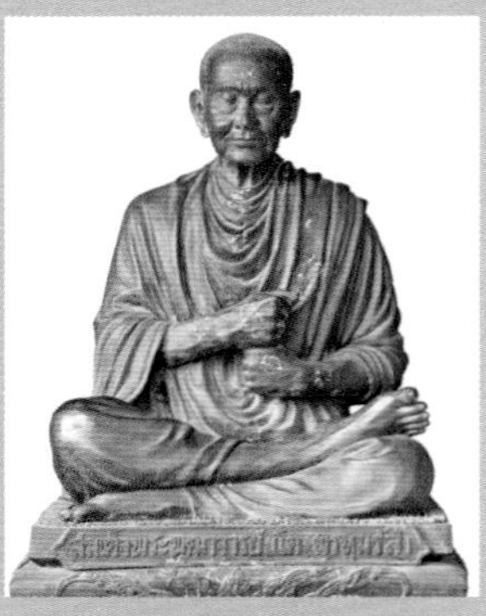

Ending Karma

In Buddhist thought, rebirth is understood as endless suffering. Even rebirth as a god in heaven is subject to karma and may be followed by rebirth in any of the realms. Buddhists meditate (above) to escape suffering and attain Enlightenment.

'At this juncture you will realize that you are dead…. Then there will shine on you the lights of the six places of rebirth … it is your own karmic disposition that determines your choice.'

TIBETAN BOOK OF THE DEAD

Thangka of the Bhavachakra Mandala

c. 1800 CE **Birmingham Museum of Art, Alabama, USA**

FORMAT Tibetan embroidered painting   **MATERIAL** Silk, appliquéed and embroidered   **DIMENSIONS** 283.2 x 203.2 cm / 111 ½ x 80 in.

The *bhavachakra* mandala, or wheel of causation, is a symbolic representation of how our karma (body of deeds and intentions) results in a cycle of death and rebirth. The Buddha's teaching is distinguished from other religions in India by its wish to end karma and escape rebirth. Seen here in the form of a *thangka* from eastern Tibet, the mandala has at its centre the causes of rebirth: a pig, snake and bird represent ignorance, anger and attachment. The second inner circle shows the effects of karma, as people rise or descend in their rebirths. In the third and largest section are the six realms of karma. At the top are the heavenly deities on Mount Sumeru, flanked to the left by the human realm and to the right by the heaven of the lower gods. At the bottom is hell, arranged in zones of punishment; the animal realm is to its left and the zone of hungry ghosts to its right. The fourth circle shows the twelve links of dependent origination – activities that hinder enlightenment. In the outer sky is the moon, which signifies liberation from the wheel of causation, and the Buddha, who is pointing to the wheel. The wheel itself is held by a large, black-skinned, demonic creature that represents impermanence. Traditionally, the wheel of causation was painted on the outside of monasteries for lay people to see, but this one functions as a hanging scroll. Over the centuries, learned teachers have expounded the simple and profound meanings of the *bhavachakra* mandala, making people aware of the forces that direct their lives.

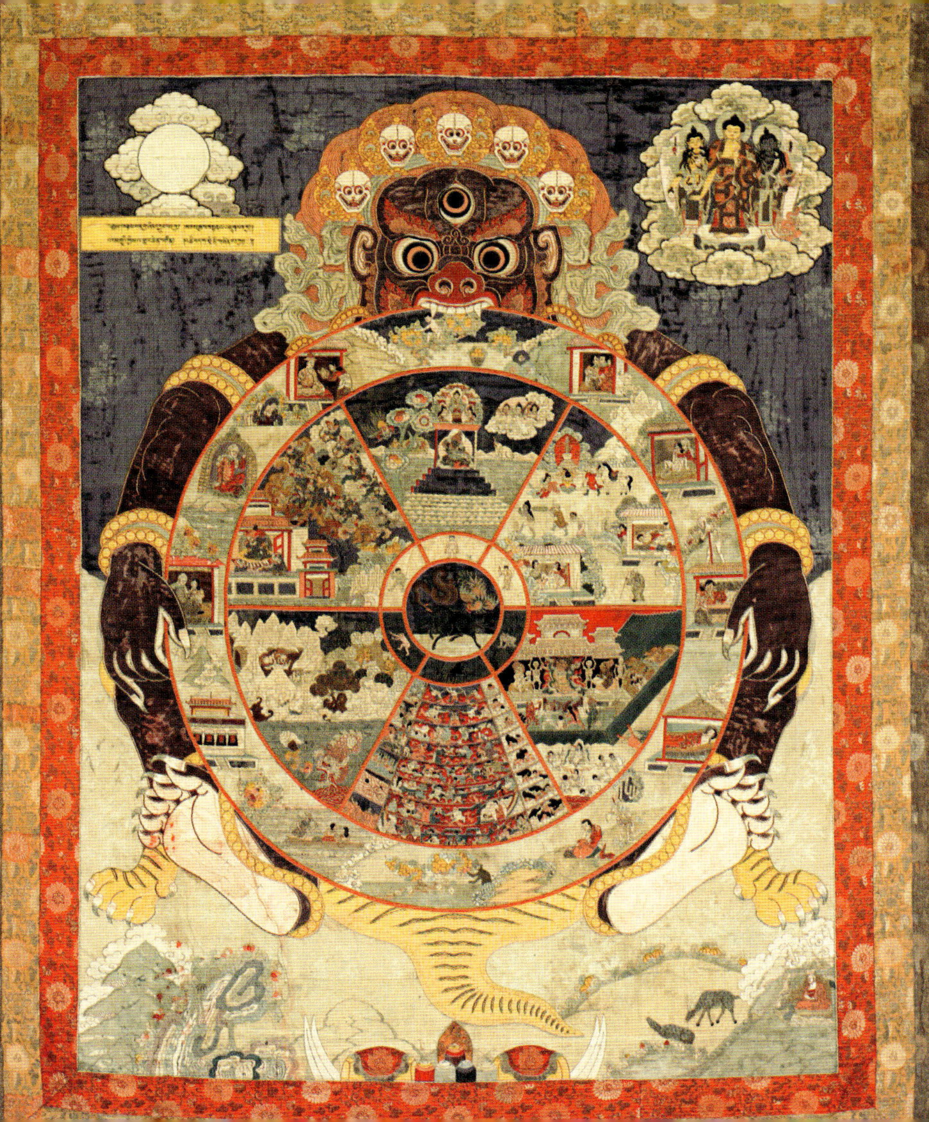

Tsa-tsa Shrine

19th century CE **British Museum, London, UK**

MATERIALS Wood frame and clay seals, painted and gilded
DIMENSIONS 43 x 62 cm/17 x 24½ in. (open)

Buddhism was transmitted from India throughout south-eastern
and eastern Asia by travellers, monks, merchants and missionaries.
At Buddhist sites in the oasis cities of central Asia, used as way
stations along the Silk Road, many of the objects they brought
with them on their travels have come to light. They include a
number of small, portable shrines; the owners would open these
to view the images of deities inside, but keep them closed to
protect the deities when they were travelling. The shrines were
used for devotional prayers in places far from home. Travellers also
brought back small architectural models of the places they visited,
or clay seals stamped with impressions of those monuments
and their resident deities. This Tibetan portable shrine opens to
display esoteric deities in all their complexity. Closed, the shrine
resembles the ogee-shape *chaitya* window of ancient Indian temple
facades. It opens rather as a temple door opens to reveal icons in a
worship hall. Inside are clay impressions, called *tsa-tsa* in Tibetan,
of twenty-nine Buddhist gods, painted gold and set in narrow
red frames. They are affixed to the back of the shrine in a loose
geometric fashion that suggests a mandala. The most prominent,
largest and most central figure is the bull-headed deity Yamantaka
Vajrabhairava, shown in his terrible aspect with multiple arms
and heads. Surrounding him are other many-armed deities, along
with Tara, the Mother of Liberation, on the left, and several lamas
(teachers) on the right. Painted on the side panels are offerings for
the gods, including bowls filled with fruits, vases of flowers, sea
shells, musical instruments and other auspicious objects.

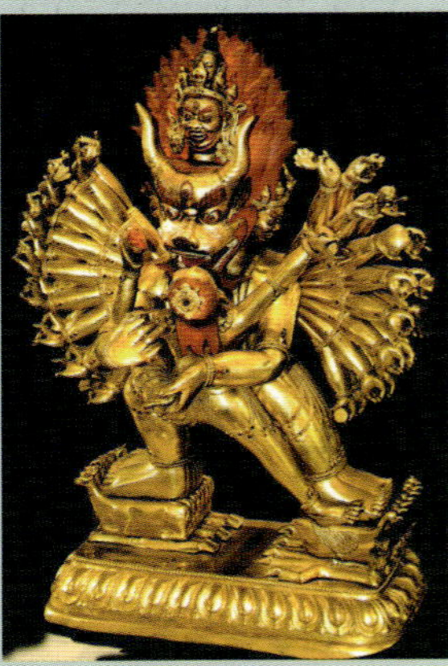

Bull-headed God

Yamantaka Vajrabhairava, here
as a 19th-century Tibetan statue,
is worshipped by the Buddhist
Gelug-pa school (known as the
Yellow Hats). The school, founded
by Je Tsongkhapa (1357–1419), was
the dominant sect in Tibet from
the end of the 16th century.

'Homage to thee, Perfect
Wisdom/Boundless, and
transcending thought!/
All thy limbs are without
blemish/Faultless those
who Thee discern.'

HYMN TO PERFECT WISDOM

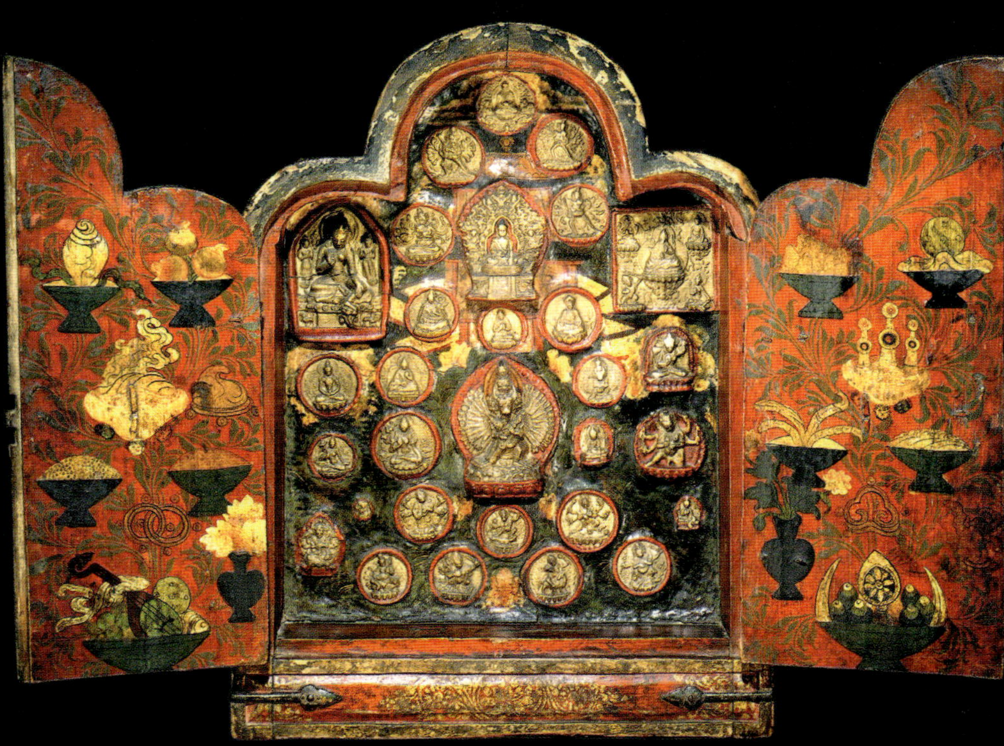

Tibetan Sand Mandala

2011 CE **Gallo Center for the Arts, Modesto, California, USA**

TECHNIQUE Infill and decoration of a line-drawn template
MATERIAL Coloured sands

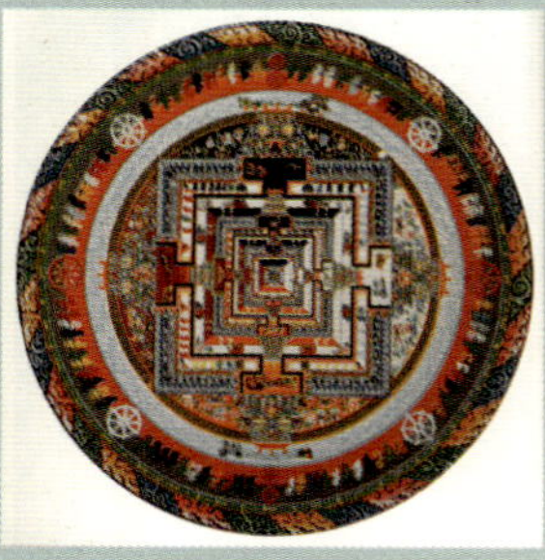

Kalachakra Mandala

Often reproduced with sands, the Kalachakra mandala is a very complicated design featuring 722 deities. The word *Kalachakra* means period of time. For Buddhists, time is manifested by change, and change is always associated with degeneration.

'... where one is going to draw, one places a drop of perfume and a small heap of flowers ... one must pitch a line at the outset so there will be no mistake regarding the placing of the divine marks of ... colour.'

TIBETAN TEXT ON MAKING SAND MANDALAS

Constructed entirely of coloured sands, Tibetan sand mandalas are destroyed upon completion to illustrate the impermanence of all things. As such, they are a clear and direct expression of an essential teaching of Buddhism. The ritual of creating a sand mandala is as exacting as the ritual to destroy it. Depending on the complexity of the design, the construction can take from days to weeks. From the assembling of the materials to execution and completion, the creation of the mandalas is subject to a strict protocol that includes prayer and meditation. The monks first consecrate the surface they will use for the design. Second, they draw the outlines of the mandala, usually a series of superimposed geometric shapes, mostly circles and squares. Then they pour coloured sand granules into designated areas, using traditional metal funnels called *chak-purs*. Tapping the funnels with a metal rod causes them to vibrate, facilitating the gentle flow of sand into the respective areas. The mandalas themselves have layers of meaning. Their outer appearance, with its representations of various deities, signifies the act of perception, but a deeper symbolic meaning is revealed by meditation of the images. Reading the mandala's symbols and figures in this focused manner offers a higher level of spiritual progress. Afterwards, in the deconstruction ceremony, the monks carefully sweep up the grains of sand and deposit them in an urn. The grains are then brought to a body of water and dispersed. It is believed that the dismantling of the mandala releases the spirits of the gods into the world, and so the mandala acts as an intermediary between the profane and sacred realms.

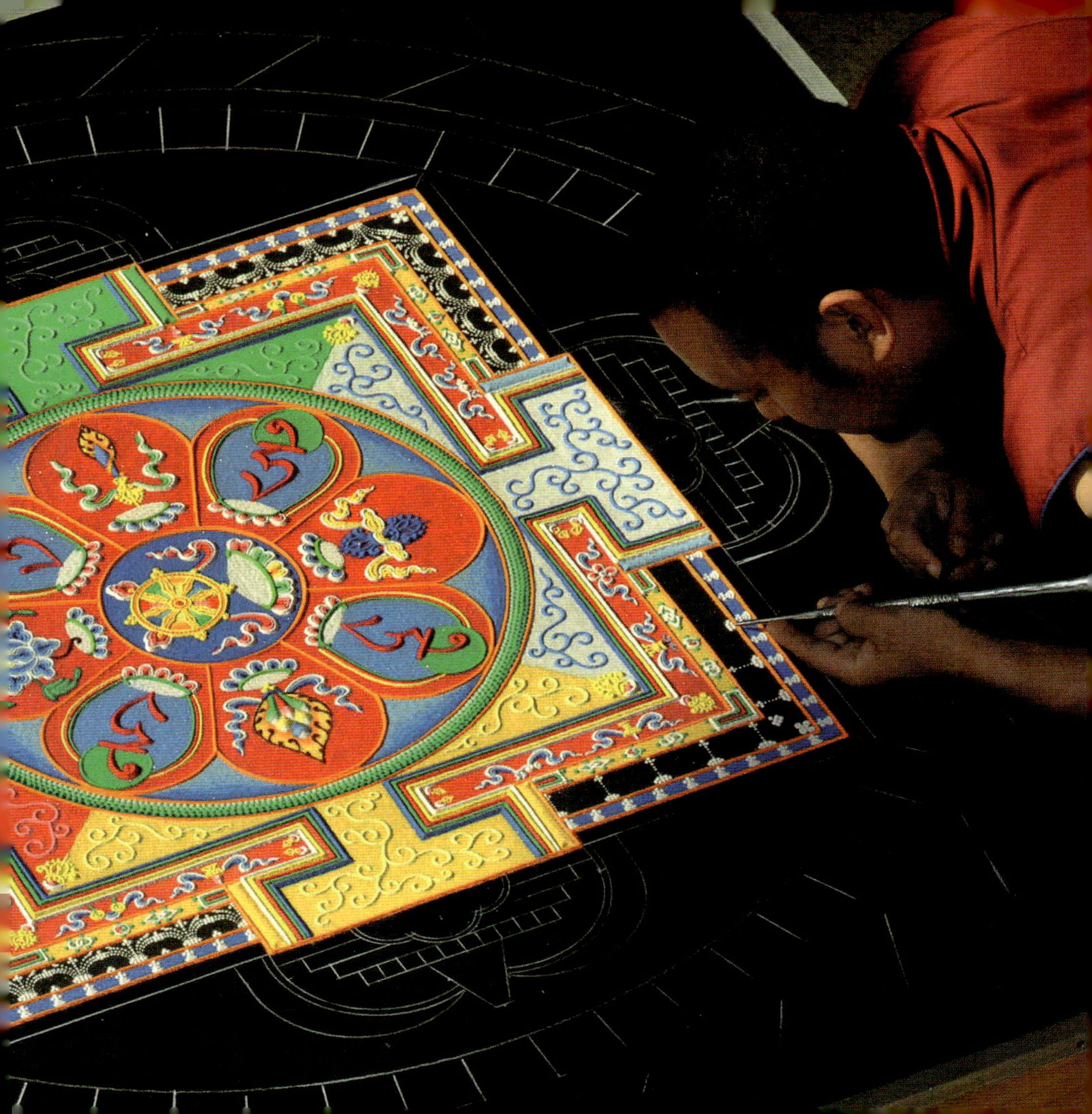

Glossary

Aksobhya Buddha
See *Dhyani Buddha*.

Amida, Amitofu
See *Amitabha*.

Amitabha
Primary deity in the Mahayanan pantheon and Buddha and ruler of the Western Paradise. Called Amida in Japanese and Amitofu in Chinese. The name translates as 'infinite light'.

Arhat
See *Luohan*.

Ashoka, Emperor
Ashoka Maurya (304–232 BCE), also known as Ashoka the Great, was an Indian emperor of the Maurya Dynasty who ruled almost all of the Indian subcontinent from c. 269 to 232 BCE. Converting to Buddhism c. 263 BCE, he established many monuments to mark sites that were significant in the life of Gautama Buddha.

Avalokiteshvara
The 'lord who looks down from above', or Bodhisattva of Compassion, the most represented bodhisattva in Buddhist art. This saviour figure is known as Guanyin in Chinese, Kannon in Japanese, and Lokeshvara in some South-east Asian countries.

Bhagavan
A Hindu name for God. In Buddhism, Bhagavan Buddha is a reference to Gautama Buddha as 'Lord Buddha'.

Bhavachakra
Wheel of causation, a diagram of the cycle of karma and rebirth.

Bhodi Tree
Sacred fig tree at Bodh Gaya, under which the Buddha meditated and attained Enlightenment.

Bodhisattva
Being in Mahayana Buddhism who has achieved enlightenment and who postpones accession to nirvana to help others to do so.

Bodhisattva of Compassion
See *Avalokiteshvara*.

Buddha of the Eastern Paradise
See *Healing Buddha*.

Buddha of the Future
See *Maitreya*.

Buddha of Infinite Light
See *Amitabha*.

Buddha of the Northern Paradise
See *Gautama Buddha*.

Buddha of the Southern Paradise
See *Maitreya*.

Buddha of the Western Paradise
See *Amitabha*.

Buddha of Wisdom
See *Manjusri*.

Buddha Shakyamuni
See *Gautama Buddha*. Shakyamuni was the name of the Buddha's tribe.

Buddhavamsa
Also known as the *Chronicle of Buddhas*: a Buddhist text about the life of Gautama Buddha and the twenty-four previous Buddhas who had prophesied his Buddhahood.

Chaitya
Buddhist shrine or prayer hall with a stupa at one end. The term *chaitya-griha* is often used to denote an assembly hall that houses a stupa.

Chedi
Thai name for stupa.

Cintamani
Wish-fulfilling jewel carried by some bodhisattvas, and also placed atop some buildings.

Cosmic Buddha
One of several Buddhas worshipped as incarnations of Buddhist cosmology, that is, philosophy of the origin, processes and structure of the universe. See also *Vairochana*.

Dagoba
Sinalhese for a Buddhist stupa.

Deva, devata
Respectively, a male or female deity.

Dharma

Cosmic law, represented by a wheel. The Dharmachakra, or 'Wheel of the Law', is said to have been set in motion when the Buddha delivered his First Sermon at Sarnath.

Dhyani Buddha

In Mahayana and Vajrayana Buddhism, any of five 'self-born' celestial buddhas who have always existed. They are Vairochana, Aksobhya, Ratnasambhava, Amitabha and Amoghasiddhi.

Fudo Myoo

Vajrayana Buddhist guardian deity revered in Japan, China and elsewhere. He is pre-eminent among the Five Wisdom Kings of the Womb Realm. The name, Acala in Sanskrit, means 'Immovable Wisdom King'.

Gandharan

Refers to the Kingdom of Gandhara that lasted from *c.* 1500 BCE to *c.* 1000 CE in what is now northern Pakistan and north-eastern Afghanistan. As a cultural centre it attained its height from the 1st to the 5th century CE under the Kushan kings.

Gautama Buddha

The sage, also known as Siddhartha Gautama, Shakyamuni or simply the Buddha, 'the Awakened One', whose teachings are the foundation of Buddhism. He is believed to have lived and taught mostly in eastern India some time between the 6th and 4th centuries BCE. Among many honorary titles he is known as the Buddha of the Northern Paradise.

Guanyin

See *Avalokiteshvara*.

Guptan

Refers to an Indian empire, founded by Maharaja Sri Gupta, that existed from *c.* 320 to 550 CE and covered much of the Indian subcontinent.

Healing Buddha

Bhaisajyaguru (Yakushi in Japanese), the Buddha of Healing in Mahayana Buddhism, and the Buddha of the Eastern Paradise. He is also referred to as the 'Medicine Buddha' because he uses the 'medicine' of his teachings to cure humanity's sufferings.

Hevajra

Prime deity in the Vajrayana Buddhist pantheon, usually represented with eight heads and sixteen arms.

Hungry Ghost

See *Preta*.

Jataka

Tales of previous lives of Gautama Buddha, intended as a guide to good morality and behaviour for the purpose of accumulating good karma.

Kannon

See *Avalokiteshvara*.

Karma

Accumulated good and bad acts in a person's life that determine whether their next rebirth will be favourable.

Koan

A Zen story, dialogue, question or statement used to provoke a monk or student's 'great doubt' and test their progress in Zen practice.

Kondo

Image hall of a Japanese temple. The name literally means 'golden hall'.

Laksana

The Buddha's thirty-two distinguishing marks, or marks of beauty.

Lokapala

Guardian kings (*shitenno* in Japanese) of the four cardinal directions.

Lokeshvara

See *Avalokiteshvara*.

Luohan

Chinese name for enlightened beings, portrayed as mystics or sages, often in groups of sixteen, eighteen or five hundred. *Arhat* in Sanskrit.

Mahakala

An emanation of Avalokiteshvara.

Mahayana

The second major school of Buddhism, known as the 'Great Path', which held that faith can secure salvation for an individual as long as the aid of the bodhisattvas is sought, rather than that of the Buddha alone.

Maitreya

Sanskrit name of a bodhisattva who is to appear on Earth, achieve complete enlightenment and teach the pure Dharma (law). Scriptures suggest that Maitreya will be a successor of Gautama Buddha. Also known as the Buddha of the Future and Buddha of the Southern Paradise.

Mandala

A diagram used as an aid to meditation, and also as a plan for Buddhist structures, usually temples.

Mandorla

Almond-shaped, elliptical or oval aureola or luminous cloud surrounding the whole body of the Buddha or other sacred person. A mandorla that encircles only the head is called a halo.

Manjusri

Bodhisattva of transcendent wisdom in Mahayana Buddhism. In Vajrayana Buddhism he is adopted as a meditational deity.

Mappo

The third and last of the Three Ages of Buddhism, known as the Latter Day of the Law, during which the Buddha is prophesied to lose all power of salvation; a new Buddha will then appear to save the people.

Mara

The god of karma and the demon of illusion. He attempted to seduce Gautama Buddha with beautiful women – some legends say his daughters – and personifies unwholesome impulses, distractions and negation of spiritual life.

Maya

Queen Maya of Sakya, birth mother of Gautama Buddha. In Buddhist tradition she died seven days after the birth but descended from heaven from time to time to offer her son advice.

Mudra

Significant hand gestures of the Buddha, indicating, for example, teaching, meditation, reassurance blessing, or the turning of the wheel of the Dharma (law). In particular, the art of esoteric Buddhism is rich in the variety of mudras it depicts.

Naga

Serpent guardian of subterranean regions and traditional enemy of the eagle-like, half man, half bird garuda.

Nirvana

Nothingness, or extinction of the cycle of death and rebirth.

Padamapani

A form of Avalokiteshvara known as 'the lotus carrier'. Padamapani, a popular god, is believed to have created the 'fourth world', the actual universe, including all animate things. He is the personification of the all-pitying one and the power of creation, of which the *padma* (lotus flower) is the symbol.

Pagoda

A tiered tower with a number of eaves, a blend of the architecture of Chinese towers and Chinese pavilions. An evolution of the stupa, the pagoda was used for the safe-keeping and veneration of sacred relics.

Parinirvana

The death of the Buddha. He is sometimes shown reclining with his head supported by one arm, rather than a pillow, with grieving disciples in attendance. Having attained Enlightenment, he has achieved nirvana, or freedom from physical existence and its sufferings.

Pradaksina

Circumambulation of a stupa or temple in a clockwise direction.

Prabhutaratna Buddha

The Buddha with whom Gautama Buddha is most closely associated.

Preta

Also known as a 'hungry ghost', a being that undergoes more than human suffering, particularly extreme hunger and thirst. As a punishment for wicked behaviour in a previous life, it is doomed to hunger insatiably for something repugnant or humiliating, such as faeces or human corpses.

Pure Land

Celestial realm or pure abode of a Buddha or Bodhisattva in Mahayana Buddhism.

Samvara

An emanation of the Buddha Aksobhya (see *Dhyani Buddha*).

Sangha

The monastic community of ordained Buddhist monks or nuns. The Sangha is the third of the Three Jewels in Buddhism.

Shakti

Spouse or female personification of a Brahmanistic god, which in Buddhism is an eternal perfect being, the highest state of being any person can achieve.

Shinto

Ancient religion of Japan, still practised in the modern world. Japanese Buddhist artists sometimes included Shinto figures alongside their own deities – an example of how Buddhism retained aspects of converted indigenous cultures.

Siddartha Gautama

See *Gautama Buddha*. The name 'Siddhartha' signifies 'he who has found meaning (of existence)' or 'he who has attained his goals'.

Stupa

Originally a dome-shaped burial ground. Buddhism adopted the stupa as a repository for relics of the Buddha.

Sutra

Buddhist scriptures based on the teachings of the Buddha.

Tara

Female bodhisattva in Mahayana Buddhism, and a female Buddha in Vajrayana Buddhism. She is known as the 'mother of liberation' and represents success and achievements.

Thangka

Also spelt tangka, thanka or tanka, a painting on cotton, or silk appliqué, usually depicting a Buddhist deity, scene or mandala.

Theravada

The 'Doctrine, or Way, of the Elders', the earliest form of Buddhism, based on the Pali Canon, a standard collection of scriptures preserved in the Pali language. The Canon originated in North India and was preserved by word of mouth until first written down by the Fourth Buddhist Council in Sri Lanka, in 29 BCE.

Tushita Heaven

Heaven where the Bodhisattva Svetaketu lived before being reborn on Earth as Gautama Buddha; also the home of the Bodhisattva Natha, who will be reborn as Maitreya, the next Buddha, or the Buddha of the Future.

Vairochana

Primary cosmic Buddha, often portrayed in heavenly surroundings and at the centre of a mandala. In Chinese, Korean and Japanese Buddhism, Vairochana also embodies the Buddhist concept of emptiness, or the true nature of things and events.

Vajra

Symbol of the thunderbolt, diamond or lightning, used in esoteric rites, hence Vajrayana.

Vajrayana

General term for esoteric or Tantric forms of northern Indian Mahayanan Buddhism, meaning 'Path of the Thunderbolt'.

Vihara

Residence hall for monks in a monastic complex, as opposed to the *chaitya*.

Yaksha, Yakshi

Respectively, male and female Indian fertility images dating from before the advent of Buddhism, but which adorn early Indian Buddhist stupas.

Yamantaka Vajrabhairva

Wrathful manifestation of Manjusri, bodhisattva of transcendent wisdom.

Yogi, Yogin

Devotee of ascetic meditation or yoga.

Zen

School of Mahayana Buddhism that developed in China, where it was called Chan, in the 6th century CE. From there it spread south to Vietnam, north-east to Korea and east to Japan. Practitioners of Zen attempt to attain enlightenment through meditation in a seated posture, transcending rational thought to discover the Buddha nature underlying all things.

Picture Credits

Every effort has been made to trace all copyright owners, but if any have been inadvertently overlooked, the publishers would be pleased to make the necessary corrections at the first opportunity.

Front cover Hugh Sitton/Corbis **Back cover** Bronek Kaminski/Corbis 2 Bridgeman Images 6 Reuters/Corbis 7 Trustees of the British Museum 8-9 Scott Stulberg/Corbis 10 Deborah Bowman 11 Ira Block/National Geographic Society/Corbis 12 Shutterstock 13 Andrey Khrobostov/Alamy 14 Shutterstock 15 Dinodia/Corbis 16 Atlantide Phototravel/Corbis 17 Lindsay Hebberd/Corbis 18 Paul Panayiotou/Corbis 19 Ken Wieland 20 IndiaPictures/UIG/Getty Images 21 Shutterstock 22 Green Light Images 23 Ian Trower/JAI/Corbis 24 Roman Soumar/CORBIS 25 amanaimages/Corbis 26 Xiaoyang Liu/Corbis 27 Shutterstock 28 Zoonar GmbH/Alamy 29 zheng huansong/Xinhua Press/Corbis 30 JTB MEDIA CREATION, Inc./Alamy 31 Bridgeman Images 32 National Museum of Japan, Kyoto 33 Yoshio Tomii/Getty Images 34 Museum of Fine Arts, Boston 35 2/Driendl Group/Ocean/Corbis 36 Michael Runkel/Robert Harding World Imagery/Corbis 37 Steven Vidler/Eurasia Press/Corbis 38 JTB MEDIA CREATION, Inc./Alamy 41 Martin Gray/Getty Images 43 norisons2005 44 The Asahi Shimbun/Getty Images 46 Phyo WP 47 Panoramic Images/Getty Images 48 BabelStone 49 Elias Nir/Reuters/Corbis 50 Shutterstock 51 Scott Stulberg/Corbis 52 Christophe Boisvieux/Corbis 53 Bruno Morandi/Corbis 54 Franck Guiziou/Hemis/Corbis 55 SuperStock/Corbis 56 B. Schmid/amanaimages/Corbis 57 Topic Photo Agency/Corbis 58 Sheldon Levis/Getty Images 59 Paul Thompson/Getty Images 60-61 Sheldan Collins/Corbis 62 Jean-Louis Nou/akg-images 63 DeAgostini/Getty Images 64 IndiaPictures/UIG/Getty Images 65 Andreas Praefcke 66 Shutterstock 67 akg-images 68 Victoria & Albert Museum 69 Stefano Baldini/Bridgeman Images 71 Trustees of the British Museum 72 Gerard Degeorge/akg-images 73 Gerard Degeorge/akg-images 74 Paul Almasy/Corbis 75 Peter Langer/Design Pics/Corbis 76 Christophe Boisvieux/Corbis 77 Luca Tettoni/Corbis 78 Keren Su/Corbis 79 Shutterstock 80 Trustees of the British Museum 81 Wolfgang Kaehler/Corbis 82 Luca Tettoni/Corbis 84 Roland and Sabrina Michaud/akg-images 85 IAM/akg-images 86 Nara National Museum, Japan 87 Courtesy of Patricia Karetzky 88 Edifice/Corbis 89 Anandajoti 90 Victoria & Albert Museum 91 Tuul/Hemis/Corbis 93 Courtesy of Patricia Karetzky 94 Kimberley Coole/Lonely Planet Images/Getty Images 95 Stuart Black/Robert Harding World Imagery/Corbis 96 Philippe Body/Hemis/Corbis 97 De Agostini Picture Library/G. Dagli Orti/Bridgeman Images 98 Images & Stories/Alamy 99 Stephanie Colasanti/Corbis 100 OTHK/Getty Images 101 Gaertner/Alamy 102 Bridgeman Images 103 Luca Tettoni/Corbis 104 The Metropolitan Museum of Art/Art Resource/Scala 105 University of Pennsylvania Museum of Archaeology and Anthropology 106 Tuul/Robert Harding World Imagery/Corbis 107 Ocean/Corbis 108 Bridgeman Images 109 The British Library 110 Trustees of the British Museum 111 Kyoto National Museum, Japan 112-113 Axiom Photographic/Design Pics/Corbis 114 The Metropolitan Museum of Art/Art Resource/Scala 115 Bridgeman Images 116 Courtesy of Patricia Karetzky 117 Jean Popovitch/Jacques L'Hoir/RMN-Grand Palais (musée Guimet, Paris) 118 Vassil 119 Luca Tettoni/Corbis 120 Courtesy of Patricia Karetzky 121 Hyougushi 122 Bridgeman Images 123 Freer Gallery of Art, Smithsonian Institution, Washington, D.C. 124 Martin Moos/Getty Images 125 Imagemore Co., Ltd./Corbis 126 Courtesy of Patricia Karetzky 127 Courtesy of Patricia Karetzky 128 De Agostini Picture Library/G. Dagli Orti/Bridgeman Images 129 Courtesy of Patricia Karetzky 130 Horst Wiegand/interfoto/akg-images 131 Courtesy of Patricia Karetzky 132 Dallas and John Heaton/Free Agents Limited/Corbis 133 Jean-Louis Nou/akg-images 134 Dirk Bakker/Bridgeman Images 135 Shutterstock 136 V&A Images/Alamy 137 Gunkarta 138 Trustees of the British Museum 139 Trustees of the British Museum 141 Steven Vidler/Eurasia Press/Corbis 143 Courtesy of Patricia Karetzky 144 Courtesy of Patricia Karetzky 145 Courtesy of Patricia Karetzky 147 Corbis 148 Shutterstock 149 Shutterstock 151 ThinkStock 152 Corbis 153 Christie's Images/Corbis 154 The Metropolitan Museum of Art/Art Resource/Scala 155 Kyoto National Museum, Japan 156 Rob Howard/Corbis 158 Daderot 159 INTERFOTO/Alamy 160 Stapleton Collection/Corbis 161 didi/amanaimages/Corbis 162 Amos Chapple/Getty Images 163 Lee Snider/Alamy 164-165 Jane Sweeney/JAI/Corbis 166 Museum of Fine Arts, Boston/Bridgeman Images 167 China Institute in America 168 Gunawan Kartapranata 169 Trustees of the British Museum 170 Earthsound 172 Hackenberg-Photo-Cologne/Alamy 173 Luca Tettoni/Corbis 174 St-Genès/Archives CDA/akg-images 175 Courtesy of Patricia Karetzky 176 Stéphane Lemaire/Hemis/Corbis 177 Charles & Josette Lenars/Corbis 178 Mandala Society 179 Brooklyn Museum of Art, New York/Bridgeman Images 181 Best View Stock/Alamy 182 Courtesy of Patricia Karetzky 183 Shutterstock 185 Indian Museum, Kolkata 186 Courtesy of Patricia Karetzky 187 The Metropolitan Museum of Art/Art Resource/Scala 188 The Art Institute of Chicago 189 The Metropolitan Museum of Art/Art Resource/Scala 190 Paulo Fridman/Corbis 191 Courtesy of Patricia Karetzky 192 Victoria & Albert Museum 193 The Brooklyn Museum 194 Bildagentur für Kunst, Kultur und Geschichte/Scala 195 G. Dagli Orti/De Agostini Picture Library/akg-images 196 Frank Bienewald/LightRocket/Getty Images 197 University of Michigan Museum of Anthropological Archaeology 199 akg-images 200 Erich Lessing/akg-images 201 Bruno Barbier/akg-images 202 Bridgeman Images 203 Asian Art Museum of San Francisco 204 Jonathan Irish/National Geographic Society/Corbis 205 The Metropolitan Museum of Art/Art Resource/Scala 206 akg-images 207 Los Angeles County Museum 208 Prisma Bildagentur AG/Alamy 209 Andrew Woodley/Alamy 210 Zoonar GmbH/Alamy 211 Birmingham Museum of Art, Alabama 212 Peter Horree/Alamy 213 Trustees of the British Museum 215 Debbie Noda/ZUMA Press/Corbis

About the author

Patricia Eichenbaum Karetzky has occupied the O. Munsterberg Chair of Asian Art at Bard College since 1988 and has been an Adjunct Professor of Art History at Lehman College, City University of New York since 1994. She served as the assistant editor, co-editor and editor of the *Journal of Chinese Religions* from 1991 to 1998. Her publications include *Chinese Religious Art* (2014); *Guanyin: Buddhist Deity of Compassion in China* (2004); *Chinese Buddhist Art* (2002); *Early Buddhist Narrative Art* (2000); *Court Art of the Tang* (1996); and *The Life of the Buddha: Pictorial and Scriptural Evidence in India* (1992).